THE TYPIKON DECODED

An Explanation of Byzantine Liturgical Practice

THE ORTHODOX LITURGY SERIES

The Orthodox Liturgy series provides an insightful, accessible, and lucid interpretation of the theology, meaning, and function of the liturgical life of the Orthodox Church.

Paul Meyendorff
Series Editor

BOOK 1
The Anointing of the Sick
by Paul Meyendorff

BOOK 2
Byzantine Liturgical Reform
by Thomas Pott

BOOK 3
The Typikon Decoded
by Archimandrite Job Getcha

BOOK 3 OF THE ORTHODOX LITURGY SERIES

The Typikon Decoded

An Explanation of Byzantine Liturgical Practice

Archimandrite Job Getcha

translated by
Paul Meyendorff

ST VLADIMIR'S SEMINARY PRESS
YONKERS, NEW YORK

Library of Congress Cataloging-in-Publication Data

Getcha, J. (Job).
  [Typikon décrypté. English]
  The Typikon decoded : an explanation of Byzantine liturgical practice / Archimandrite Job Getcha ; translated by Paul Meyendorff.
     p. cm. — (Orthodox liturgy series ; bk. 3)
  Includes bibliographical references.
  ISBN 978-0-88141-412-7
  1. Orthodox Eastern Church. Typikon. 2. Orthodox Eastern Church—Liturgy—Texts—History and criticism. I. Meyendorff, Paul. II. Title.

  BX350.G4813 2012
  264′.019—dc23

                    2012030822

Originally published as
Le Typikon décrypté: Manuel de liturgie byzantine
by Les Éditions du Cerf, Paris, 2009

This translation:
COPYRIGHT © 2012

ST VLADIMIR'S SEMINARY PRESS
575 Scarsdale Road, Yonkers, NY 10707
1-800-204-2665
www.svspress.com

ISBN 978-088141-412-7

Table of Contents

Preface

Then I saw a new heaven and a new earth ... And I saw the holy city, new Jerusalem, coming down out of heaven from God ... And I heard a loud voice from the throne saying: "'Behold, the dwelling of God is with men'" (Rev 21.1–3).

The vision of St John, which concludes his writing about the divine revelations, reveals the life of the Church, which stands to the right of the Lamb, bedecked, as with gold and silver thread, with its liturgical services and ceremonies, with its sacred architecture, with its icons, incense, lights, readings, blessings, and processions—with all these things which manifest the Kingdom of Heaven among us.

To live in the Church means to enter with all the saints into a dance company that unites earth to heaven, and which provides us with an experience of the glory of God, stripped of all subjectivism—as long as we have assimilated the rules which regulate this sacred dance and have learned the grammar of this polyphonic language of the liturgy, by means of which we are able to glorify the Holy Trinity in a proper way (*ortho-doxy*), and through which God comes to reveal himself to us.

The hymns, prayers, chants, and movement of the divine office, the succession of feasts and their arrangement through the year—all these are regulated in a choreographic manner by the Typikon, this "eye of the Church" which, far from being merely a collection of dry and legalistic rules, is in fact a summary of two millennia of the Church's experience. It is the Typikon which is the guarantee of the authenticity and objectivity of the transmission of this experience of the holy Fathers. It is living Tradition and the foundation of Orthodox spiritual life.

We can immediately sense the importance of an introduction to Orthodox liturgical life like the one Fr Job offers us here, and which is far more than just a course on rubrics. By placing each office in its proper historical context, he allows us to understand its meaning and organic function in the ensemble of the daily cursus. He thus prepares us to assimilate all the details of the celebration, so that everything can be done decently and in order (1 Cor 14.40), and especially in harmony and consonance with the experience of the saints who have preceded us and who have worshipped in this way.

For the older monks with whom we have lived and who have spent decades on the Holy Mountain, the Typikon became a way of existence, their very life. They identified so closely with the Church, with the feasts and the lives of the saints, that the Kingdom of Heaven was no longer for them just a hope, but a reality they lived daily, so that at the moment of their last breath, we have seen them make the sign of the cross and utter their last words, "Through the prayers of the holy Fathers . . . ," as they continued their doxology, in another form, among the great Assembly of the Saints.

It is in such a spirit that we urge the readers of this work to approach the services of the Church, so as to nourish their spiritual lives with this communion with the Church triumphant, a Pentecost which is only beginning.

Hieromonk Makarios of Simonos Petras
Mount Athos
August 15, 2007

Introduction

We knew not whether we were in heaven or on earth. For on earth there is no such splendor or such beauty, and we are at a loss how to describe it. We know only that God dwells there among men, and their service is fairer than the ceremonies of other nations. For we cannot forget that beauty.

This is how the Russian *Primary Chronicle* summarizes the impression of the legates of Prince Vladimir of Kiev, reporting on their participation in the liturgy of Hagia Sophia in Constantinople, which led decisively to the conversion of Kievan Rus' more than a thousand years ago. For Orthodox Christianity, doctrine remains to our own day inseparable from the glorification of God. In Greek, the word "doxa" means both doctrine and glorification. The term "Orthodoxy" can therefore designate both true doctrine and the proper glorification of God. No doubt for this reason, Fr Georges Florovsky calls Christianity a "liturgical religion." "The Church is," for him, "first of all a praying community. The liturgy comes first, then comes discipline."[1]

The Byzantine liturgy, because of its beauty, its richness, and its depth, never ceases to arouse interest, inspiration, and enthusiasm in countless Christians today. However, this ocean of mysteries at times remains incomprehensible and inaccessible. For many, this can be explained by the fact that there are few accessible works or manuals to enlighten the neophyte or the believer seeking to become more familiar with the sequence of offices in the Byzantine rite throughout the liturgical year. The Typikon, the liturgical book containing the ordo of the celebrations, and often called "the eye of the Church," because it guides the believers in their full adherence to the ecclesial community through its rules for liturgical prayer, is, at first glance, incomprehensible. Hence the need to decipher it, to decode it.

Such is the purpose of this work, which was not initially compiled as a manual. It began in 2005 as a series of courses at the St Sergius Orthodox Theological Institute in Paris, destined for theology students. It is they who encouraged me to publish it, saying that it was informative and that it would

---

[1]G. Florovsky, "The Elements of Liturgy in the Orthodox Catholic Church," *One Church* 13.1–2 (1959): 24.

make accessible in French an abundant bibliography that previously had been accessible only to those who knew Russian. For those who are interested, references can be found both in notes and in more technical bibliographies at the back of the book. I am also grateful to my students for their critiques of this present volume as it developed, which contributed greatly to its accuracy and clarity.

This manual describes the celebration of the offices of the Byzantine liturgical year: the divine office, the feasts, and the paschal cycle. We have deliberately omitted any commentary on the Divine Liturgy, preferring to address this in the context of other sacramental rites of the Byzantine *Euchologion*, to which we hope to devote a subsequent book. The reader will find here five chapters: the first will introduce the Byzantine liturgical books, and the second will describe the cycle of the hours. Chapter Three will focus on the office on weekdays, on Sunday, and on feast days. Chapters Four and Five will address the offices of Great Lent and the paschal season respectively. We will offer an analysis that is both historical and practical. We seek both to describe the order and content of the services, and to place them in the context of their historical development. Because the present work is not liturgical history as such, we have chosen not to trace the history of Byzantine liturgy, especially since there is a bibliography of works on this subject in accessible languages.[2]

For our description of the services, we generally follow the practice of the Russian Orthodox Church, as it is followed in the chapel of the St Sergius Institute in Paris, among other places. In our day, all the Orthodox churches in the world employ the same liturgical books and texts, even if they use different languages and musical styles. Thus, there are not major differences in the content of the services, even if there are occasionally minor variations in practice from one place to the next. This is precisely the origin of the Russian saying: "Do not go to another monastery with your own ordo." We should note, however, that the publication of a Greek "parish typikon" in 1838, widely used in the Greek-speaking world and in the Balkans, and about which we will speak later, has contributed greatly to the separation of "Greek" and "Slavic" usages. We have therefore tried, to the extent possible, to indicate in passing the divergences between these two major currents.

---

[2] Those interested can refer to: R. Taft, *The Byzantine Rite: A Short History* (Collegeville, MN: Liturgical Press, 1992); M. Arranz, "Les grandes étapes de la liturgie byzantine: Palestine-Byzance-Russie: Essai d'aperçu historique," in *Liturgie de l'église particulière, liturgie de l'église universelle*, Bibliotheca Ephemerides Liturgicae, Subsidia 7, (Rome, 1976), 43–72.

Here we must also thank Hieromonk Makarios of Simonos Petras, who, in addition to writing a preface to this work, carefully read it through and enriched it by offering his comments about Greek parochial usage as well as Athonite practice. We should note as well that the Holy Mountain remains to our day a point of reference in the Orthodox Church not only for spiritual life, but for liturgical practice as well.

At the back of the book, the reader will find a glossary of liturgical terms, together with their Greek and Slavic equivalents.

Our hope is that the publication of this work will contribute to the understanding and knowledge of the Byzantine liturgical offices and will allow us to progress in the knowledge of God, which is true theology.

Archimandrite Job Getcha
Paris, September 29, 2008
Feast of St Cyprian, Metropolitan of Kiev

List of Abbreviations

BELS = *Bibliotheca "Ephemerides Liturgicae,"* *Subsidia* (Rome, 1974–).

BT = *Bogoslovskie Trudy* (Moscow, 1960–).

DACL = F. Cabrol, H. Leclercq, H. Marrou, eds., *Dictionnaire d'archéologie chrétienne et de liturgie*, I–XV (Paris, 1907–1953).

Dmitrievskii, *Opisanie* = A.A. Dmitrievskii, *Opisanie liturgicheskikh rukopisei, khraniashchikhsia v bibliotekakh Pravoslavnogo Vostoka*, Vol. 1, Τυπικά, Pt. 1, *Pamiatniki patriarshikh ustavov i ktitorskie monastyrskie tipikony* (Kiev, 1901); vol. 3, Τυπικά, Pt. 2 (Petrograd, 1917).

DOP = *Dumbarton Oaks Papers* (Washington, DC, 1941–).

DS = E. Viller, et al., eds., *Dictionnaire de spiritualité, ascétique et mystique: doctrine et histoire*, I–XVII (Paris, 1931–1995).

Égérie, *Journal de Voyage* = Égérie, *Journal de Voyage* (SC 296), ed. and trans. P. Maraval (Paris, 2002).

Jean et Sophrone, *Narration* = A. Longo, "ll testo integrale della 'Narrazione degli Abati Giovanni e Sofronio' attraverso le 'ΕΡΜΗΝΕΙΑΙ' di Nicone," *Revista di study bizantini e neoellenici* 12–13 (1965–1966): 223–267.

Karabinov, *Postnaia Triod'* = I. Karabinov, *Postnaia Triod'. Istoricheskii obzor* (St Petersburg, 1910).

Lisitsyn, *Pervonachal'nyi Slaviano-Russkii Tipikon* = M. Lisitsyn, *Pervonachal'nyi Slaviano-Russkii Tipikon* (St Petersburg, 1911).

LO = *Lex Orandi* (Paris, 1944–1971).

Lossky, *Le Typikon byzantin* = A. Lossky, *Le Typikon byzantin: édition d'une version grecque partiellement inéditee; analyse de la partie liturgique*, 2 vols. (unpublished doctoral dissertation) (Paris: Institut Saint Serge, 1987).

Mansvetov, *Tserkovnyi ustav* = I. Mansvetov, *Tserkovnyi ustav (Tipik), ego obrazovanie i sud'ba v grecheskoi i russkoi Tserkvi* (Moscow, 1885).

Matéos, *Typicon*, I and II = J. Matéos, *Le typicon de la Grande Église*, I and II, OCA 165 and 166 (Rome, 1962–1963).

OCA = *Orientalia Christiana Analecta* (Rome, 1935–).

OCP = *Orientalia Christiana Periodica* (Rome, 1935–).

Pentkovskii, *Tipikon* = A. Pentkovskii, *Tipikon Aleksiia Studita* (Moscow, 2001).

PG = J.-P. Migne, *Patrologia cursus completus. Series graeca*, I–CLXI (Paris, 1857–1866).

PS = *Pravoslavnyi sobesednik* (Kazan, 1855–1916).

PTSO = *Pribavlenie k Tvoreniiam sviatykh Ottsov v russkom perevode* (Moscow, 1844–1891).

Renoux, I and II = A. Renoux, *Le Codex arménien Jérusalem 121*. I, PO XXXV, 1, No. 163 (Turnhout, 1969); II, PO XXXVI, 2, No. 168 (Turnhout, 1971).

RukSP = *Rukovodstvo dlia sel'skikh pastyrei* (Kiev, 1860–1917).

SC = Sources chrétiennes (Paris-Lyon, 1941–).

Skaballanovich, *Tolkovyi Tipikon*, vols. 1 and 2 = M. Skaballanovich, *Tolkovyi Tipikon*, vols. 1 and 2 (Kiev, 1910–1913).

SVTQ = *St Vladimir's Theological Quarterly* (Crestwood, NY, 1957–).

TDKA = *Trudy Kievskoi Dukhovnoi Akademii* (Kiev, 1860–1917).

TODRL = *Trudy Otdela Drevne-Russkoi Literatury* (St Petersburg, 1934–).

ZhMP = *Zhurnal Moskovskoi Patriarkhii* (Moscow, 1931–1935, 1943–).

CHAPTER ONE

The Liturgical Books

The celebration of the offices of the Orthodox Church requires a rather full library of liturgical books, which is a rather daunting reality for an amateur liturgist or a neophyte. Some of these are intended for those who preside and some are used by the choir. The latter are organized in connection with the different liturgical cycles. We will focus now on the fundamental liturgical books, without which the offices could not be carried out, namely: The Psalter, the Horologion, the Octoechos, the Menaia, the Triodion, the Pentecostarion, the Typikon, the Euchologion, the Epistle Book, and the Gospel Book.[1]

The Psalter

In the prayer of the early Church, the psalms appeared as "the mold of Christian prayer."[2] Thus the book of Psalms, the Psalter, became "the prayer book of the Church, par excellence."[3]

There were two ways to use the psalms in prayer. One could read the Psalter sequentially, from the first to the last, in numerical order. This form of continuous recitation was used for solitary prayer. But it is also employed within the context of the communal office, as is indicated in the rules governing psalmody in the office (see the tables on pp. 17–21). This continuous recitation of the psalms is rooted in Jewish tradition. Before becoming the prayer

[1]For the state of the question regarding the Byzantine liturgical books, we will refer to: E. Velkovska, "Byzantine Liturgical Books," in A.J. Chupungco, ed., *Handbook for Liturgical Studies*, vol. 1: *Introduction to the Liturgy* (Collegeville, MN, 1997), 225–40; E. Velkovska, "Sistema na vizantiiskite i slavianskite bogosluzhebni knigi na perioda na v"znikvaneto im," in V. Gruzelev and A. Miltenova, eds., *Medieval Christian Europe: East and West. Tradition, Values, Communications* (Sofia, 2002), 220–36.

[2]P. Deseille, "Les Psaumes: prières de l'Église, prières trinitaires," *Unité chrétienne* 144 (2001): 15.

[3]P. Deseille, "Introduction," *Les Psaumes, prières de l'Église* (Paris, 1979), 13. See also B. Fischer, "Les Psaumes, prière chrétienne. Témoignage du IIe siècle," in *La Prière des heures*, LO 35 (Paris, 1963), 85–99.

book for Christians, the Psalter was the prayer book of the Jewish people, who were aware that the psalms followed a very rigorous progression.

Another way to pray the psalms is to select them according to their appropriateness to the hour of the day or the liturgical feast. This is how the divine office came to be organized in the form of matins, vespers, and the different hours (prime, terce, sext, none, compline, midnight office). Psalms constitute the main part of these services, the skeleton, which the hymnographers subsequently embellished.

Yet another way to employ the psalms is to select individual verses or groups of verses with a very particular focus. We see this in the various daily offices in which, alongside entire psalms, we find isolated psalm verses serving as versicles (*stichoi*) or refrains (*prokeimena*).

For the continuous recitation of psalmody, the Church employs the liturgical book it calls the *Psalter*. For the liturgy of the hours, she uses the liturgical book entitled the *Horologion* (the Book of Hours).[4]

The Psalter used by the Orthodox Church is from the Septuagint, the ancient Greek translation of the Old Testament made in Alexandria during the period of the Ptolemies (3rd century BC). The Septuagint, considered to be an inspired translation, became the Bible of the apostolic Church and of the Fathers of the Church. The numbering of the psalms in the Septuagint differs from that in the Hebrew Bible (the Masoretic text), which is the source of most modern translations of the Old Testament, based on the Hebrew text. The liturgical books of the Orthodox Church thus still employ the Septuagint numbering.

Throughout history, there have been several ways to arrange these 150 psalms. Hilary of Poitiers (4th c.), for example, held to a division of the 150 psalms into three groups of fifty. Gregory of Nyssa (4th c.), however, held to an arrangement in five books.[5] Historians of the Byzantine liturgy distinguish the Constantinopolitan Psalter from the Palestinian Psalter.

The Constantinopolitan Psalter, used in the services following the Typikon (ordo) of the Great Church, was divided into seventy-four *antiphons*. Six of these antiphons were fixed, sung every day (generally, the first and last antiphons of each office), and the 68 others were distributed between vespers and matins following a two-week cycle. It consisted of 2,542 verses,

[4]On psalmody and its various uses, see the study of Matéos, reprinted in his book: J. Matéos, *La celebration de la parole dans la liturgie byzantine*, OCA 191, (Rome, 1971), 6–27.
[5]P. Deseille, "Introduction," *Les Psaumes, prières de l'Église*, 14.

and each psalm verse of these antiphons was followed by a *refrain*. Odd-numbered antiphons had the refrain "Alleluia," while even-numbered antiphons had as a refrain a short phrase, such as "Hear me, O Lord," or "To you, O God, is due a song." Several of these refrains have survived to the present in our liturgical services.[6]

The Palestinian Psalter is divided into twenty *kathismata* (from the Greek word κάθισμα, signifying that one can sit during this reading). It consists of 4,784 verses. At present, these verses are not intercalated with refrains. Each kathisma is in turn divided into three sections (στάσις) or "glories" (Sl: *slava*). Each of these contains an average of three psalms. Each section is followed by a doxology, during which we stand and say: Glory to the Father, and to the Son, and to the Holy Spirit, now and ever, and unto ages of ages. Amen. Lord, have mercy (three times). Glory to the Father, and to the Son, and to the Holy Spirit, now and ever, and unto ages of ages. Amen."

Arrangement of the Psalter into kathismata

Kathisma	Stasis 1	Stasis 2	Stasis 3
1	1–3	4–6	7–8
2	9–10	11–13	14–16
3	17	18–20	21–23
4	24–26	27–29	30–31
5	32–33	34–35	36
6	37–39	40–42	43–45
7	46–48	49–50	51–54
8	55–57	58–60	61–63
9	64–66	67	68–69
10	70–71	72–73	74–76
11	77	78–80	81–84
12	85–87	88	89–90
13	91–93	94–96	97–100
14	101–102	103	104
15	105	106	107–108
16	109–111	112–114	115–117
17	118:1–72	118:73–131	118:132–176
18	119–123	124–128	129–133
19	134–136	137–139	140–142
20	143–144	145–147	148–150

[6]On the number of verses, see M. Arranz, "L'office de l'Asmatikos Hesperinos," *OCP* 44 (1978): 400, note 85. On the Constantinopolitan Psalter, see M. Arranz, *Oko Tserkovnoe— Istoriia Tipikona* (Rome, 1998), 52–53. On the refrains in the Constantinopolitan Psalter,

It was the monks of Stoudion in Constantinople who were the first to adopt the Palestinian Psalter in the capital city. According to one of the most ancient known Studite typika, the Typikon of Alexios the Studite, one kathisma was read at matins during the summer, when the nights are short (from the Sunday after Pascha [Antipascha] until the Exaltation of the Cross). In winter, when the nights are longer, two kathismata were read (and in Lent, three kathismata were read). At vespers, kathisma 18 was always read, except on the eve of Sunday and of feasts, in which case kathisma 1 was sung—"Blessed is the man."[7] Beginning in the fourteenth century, however, when the Typikon of St Sabas became the norm, the number of kathismata at matins was increased, and the vesperal kathisma during the summer season varies according to the day of the week.

Comparison of the number of kathismata from the Psalter				
	Studite ordo Matins	Studite ordo Vespers	Sabaite ordo Matins	Sabaite ordo Vespers
Summer [Antipascha–Exaltation of the Cross]	1	1 [kathisma 18]	2	1
Winter [Exaltation of the Cross–Cheesefare Sunday]	2	1 [kathisma 18]	3	1 [kathisma 18]
Great Lent	3	1 [kathisma 18]	3	1 [kathisma 18]

Indeed, according to the Sabaite Typikon, there are customarily three kathismata at matins, and kathisma 18 is read at vespers. During the summer period, as well as during some festal periods of the year, only two kathismata are used at matins, and the third kathisma is transferred to vespers, replacing kathisma 18. Thus, during ordinary time, the Psalter is read in its entirety over one week. During Great Lent, however, the continuous reading of the Psalter is spread over matins, the hours, and vespers, so that the Psalter is read not just once, but twice in a week.

see O. Strunk, "The Byzantine Office at Hagia Sophia," *DOP* 9–10 (1955–1956): 185, 200–201.
    [7] See Pentkovskii, *Tipikon*, 403–04, 239, 282.

This is the practice that survives in the contemporary Byzantine rite. Either at the beginning or the end of liturgical Psalters, we find a table outlining the arrangement of kathismata in the divine office, thus regulating the continuous reading of the Psalter.[8] We should note, however, that in most Athonite monasteries today, even those that are most strict in following the Typikon, the summer arrangement is also followed in winter, and only during great Lent are three kathismata read at matins.

Arrangement of the kathismata from the Psalter in the divine office

1. From St Thomas Sunday to the close of the Exaltation of the cross (Sep 21); from the forefeast of the Nativity of Christ (Dec 20) to the close of Thephany (Jan 14); and during the weeks of Meatfare and Cheesefare:

	Matins	Vespers
Sunday	2, 3	—
Monday	4, 5	6
Tuesday	7, 8	9
Wednesday	10, 11	12
Thursday	13, 14	15
Friday	19, 20	18
Saturday	16, 17	1

2. From Sep 22 to Dec 19; from Jan 15 to the Saturday before the Sunday of the Prodigal Son:

	Matins	Vespers
Sunday	2, 3	—
Monday	4, 5, 6	18
Tuesday	7, 8, 9	18
Wednesday	10, 11, 12	18
Thursday	13, 14, 15	18
Friday	19, 20	18
Saturday	16, 17	1

[8]See the table in *Les Psaumes. Prières de l'Église. Le Psautier des Septante*, Archimandrite Placide Deseille, trans. (Paris, 1979), 281–82; J. Mateos, "La psalmodie variable dans l'office byzantin," in *Societas Academica Dacoromana, Acta philosophica et theologica*, vol. 2 (Rome, 1964), 328–29.

3. During Great Lent (except the 5th week):

	Matins	Prime	Terce	Sext	None	Vespers
Sunday	2, 3, 17	—	—	—	—	
Monday	4, 5, 6	—	7	8	9	18
Tuesday	10, 11, 12	13	14	15	16	18
Wednesday	19, 20, 1	2	3	4	5	18
Thursday	6, 7, 8	9	10	11	12	18
Friday	13, 14, 15	—	19	20	—	18
Saturday	16, 17	—	—	—	—	1

4. During the fifth week of Great Lent:

	Matins	Prime	Terce	Sext	None	Vespers
Sunday	2, 3, 17	—	—	—	—	—
Monday	4, 5, 6	—	7	8	9	10
Tuesday	11, 12, 13	14	15	16	18	19
Wednesday	20, 1, 23	4	5	6	7	
Thursday	8	—	9	10	11	12
Friday	13, 14, 15	—	19	20	—	18
Saturday	16, 17	—	—	—	—	1

5. When Annunciation falls on Thursday of the fifth week of Great Lent, and the Great Canon is sung on Tuesday:

	Matins	Prime	Terce	Sext	None	Vespers
Sunday	2, 3, 17	—	—	—	—	—
Monday	4, 5, 6	7	8	9	10	11
Tuesday	12	—	13	14	15	16
Wednesday	19, 20, 1	2	3	4	5	—
Thursday	6, 7, 8	9	10	11	12	—
Friday	13, 14, 15	—	19	20	—	18
Saturday	16, 17	—	—	—	—	1

6. During Holy Week:

	Matins	Prime	Terce	Sext	None	Vespers
Sunday	2, 3	—	—	—	—	—
Monday	4, 5, 6	—	7	8	—	18
Tuesday	9, 10, 11	—	12	13	—	18
Wednesday	14, 15, 16	—	19	20	—	18
Thursday	—	—	—	—	—	—
Friday	—	—	—	—	—	—
Saturday	17	—	—	—	—	—

7. During Bright Week, no readings from the Psalter.

The liturgical Psalter also includes the nine biblical canticles (ᾠδή). These nine canticles provide, among other things, the structure of the canon of matins. They consist of prayers taken from both the Old and New Testaments: 1) the Song of Moses (Ex 15.1–19); 2) the Song of Moses (Deut 32.1–43); 3) the Prayer of Hannah (1 Kings 2.1–10); 4) the Prayer of Habakkuk (Hab 3.1–19); 5) the Prayer of Isaiah (Is 26.9–20); 6) the Prayer of Jonah (Jonah 2.3–10); 7) the Prayer of the Three Holy Youths (Dan 3.26–56); 8) the Song of the Three Holy Youths (Dan 3.57–88; and 9) the *Magnificat* and the *Benedictus* (Lk 1.46–55, 68–79).

The Horologion

The Horologion (or the Book of Hours) is the book containing the psalms and prayers selected for the offices of the various hours of the day. It is connected to the daily liturgical cycle. It contains the fixed, unchangeable parts of the divine office.

Although no horologia dating from before the Persian invasion of Palestine (616) have survived, the most ancient Sabaite horologia from the ninth century seem to indicate that the Horologion originated from the "canon of psalmody" (κανὼν τῆς ψαλμῳδίας) followed daily by the monks of Palestine. The *Life of St Sabas the Blessed*, founder of the monastery near Jerusalem which bears his name, tells us that the novices memorized this rule, as well as the entire Psalter, upon joining the monastery. Cyril of Scythopolis writes about St Sabas:

When he received laymen who wished to take their vows, he did not allow
them to live in the Castellion or in a cell in the monastery, but he founded
a small caenobium to the north of the monastery and there assigned men
who were vigilant and hardened by ascesis. He assigned the postulants to
live there *until they had learned the Psalter and the canonical office* and
until they were formed in the monastic discipline.[9]

The Horologion was therefore the only liturgical book used daily for their
canon (rule) of prayer, and which they carried with them when they traveled.[10] As N. Egender explains, "canon here means norm of psalmody; the
Horologion first of all indicates the quantity and arrangement of the Psalter
in the office for use by the reader."[11]

The Horologion thus develops as an adaptation of the Psalter for use in
the daily office, containing psalms and prayers arranged for the different
hours. The Horologion and the Psalter are thus closely linked. There even
exist liturgical books called the "Continuous Psalter," which consist of the
Psalter in the first part, and the Horologion in the second.[12]

We can see on the basis of the schema of the ancient Sabaite Horologion,
which matches the description given by John Cassian of the prayer rule
of the Palestinian monks,[13] that the Palestinian Horologia began the daily
cycle with the daytime services, which were then followed by the nighttime
offices. This differs from the order of services in the other liturgical books
(Octoechos, Menaia, Triodion, Pentecostarion, and Typikon), in which the
sequence of daily services always begins with vespers. Later Palestinian
Horologia always begin with the *mesonyktikon* (midnight office), the first
service upon rising, and conclude with the *apodeipnon* (compline), the last
service before going to bed.

On the whole, the structure of the liturgical offices in the Sabaite Horologia differs little from that in the Studite Horologia. This can be explained
by the fact that that the Palestinian monks, having fled as a result of the

[9]Cyrille de Scythopolis, *Vie de saint Sabas*, 28 [113, 9], A.-J. Festugière, trans., *Les
Moines d'Orient*, III/2 (Paris, 1962), 39.
[10]A. Dmitrievskii, "Chto takoe κανὼν τῆς ψαλμωδίας, tak neredko upominaemyi v
zhizneopisanii prepod. Savvy Osviashchennago?" *RukSP* 38 (1889): 72–73; M. Arranz, *Oko
Tserkovnoe—Istoriia Tipikona* (Rome, 1998), 56.
[11]N. Egender, "Le texte de l'horologion," in *La Prière des heures –Ὡρολόγιον* (Chevetogne, 1975), 52.
[12]For the expression "Continuous Psalter," see ibid., 51–52.
[13]Jean Cassien, *Institutions cénobitiques*, Book 3, J.-C. Guy, tr., SC 109, (Paris, 1965),
90–117.

Arab invasions during the second half of the seventh century, and settling first on Mount Olympus in Bithynia, and later, during the second wave of iconoclasm (815–843), at the Stoudion Monastery in Constantinople, had already introduced the Palestinian Horologion. This first synthesis of Palestinian monastic usages with those of the imperial capital is today referred to as the "Studite reform."[14]

Nonetheless, Studite Horologia, such as the Grottaferrata Horologion,[15] kept the psalm refrain from the Constantinopolitan Psalter. The Sabaite Horologia were, however, different from the Studite ones in a number of details. In general terms, the Sabaite Horologia are characterized by their ascetical rigor, faithful to the ancient traditions of eastern monasticism, as can be seen from the strict fasting rules, the continuity of liturgical hours, which are never omitted on feast days, the existence of intermediary hours, the more extensive reading of psalm kathismata at matins, and a greater amount of hymnography at vespers and matins.[16]

The first printed edition of the Horologion was published in Venice in 1509 by the Cretan Z. Kalliergis, on the basis of a manuscript from the library of Albert Pio of Modena. A revised edition was published in Venice in 1832 by the Athonite monk Bartholomew of Koutloumousiou, with the approval of Patriarch Constans I of Constantinople. This edition, with a number of abbreviations, served as the basis for the 1900 edition of the patriarchal press of Constantinople, as well as for the various Athens editions.

In our days, we distinguish the Small Horologion, which contains only the daily office, from the Great Book of Hours, which, in addition to the daily office, also contains a menologion (a liturgical calendar) that includes the troparia and kontakia of the saints and feasts of the entire year, as well as a number of canons and akathist hymns.

The first Slavic edition appeared in 1491 in Krakow, then in 1493 in Venice. Subsequently, several editions were published in Kiev, Moscow, Belgrade, and Warsaw. As a general rule, it was the publication of printed texts that led to the fixation and standardization of the daily office.

---

[14]T. Pott, *Byzantine Liturgical Reform* (Crestwood, NY: SVS Press, 2010), 115–18; M. Arranz, *Kak molilis' Bogu drevnie vizantiitsy* (Leningrad, 1979), 19, 151.

[15] Ὡρολόγιον (Grottaferrata, 1950).

[16]Skaballanovich, *Tolkovyi Tipikon* 1, 416–17, 422.

The Octoechos

The Octoechos is a liturgical book containing *hymnography*, arranged in eight sections called "tones" or "modes." To each of these "tones" correspond specific melodies, which are used for the hymns. The term "Octoechos" derives from the Greek word ὀκτώηχος, meaning "eight tones." The Octoechos is the liturgical book associated with the *daily liturgical cycle*. Thus the Great Octoechos, or Parakletike (Παρακλητική), contains the hymnody for each day of the week. Since there are eight tones, the hymnography of the Great Octoechos covers a cycle of eight weeks. Each week begins with the Sunday office. Because the liturgical day begins in the evening, each weekly cycle begins with the hymnography of Saturday night vespers. The theme of these hymns is connected to the saints or events commemorated each day of the weekly cycle:

Themes of the weekly cycle	
Day of the week	**Theme**
Sunday	Resurrection of Christ
Monday	Angelic powers, and repentance
Tuesday	St John the Baptist and Forerunner, and repentance
Wednesday	The Holy Cross, and the Mother of God
Thursday	Holy Apostles, and St Nicholas of Myra in Lycia
Friday	The Holy Cross, and the Mother of God
Saturday	All the saints and deceased

The Small Octoechos is an abbreviated version of the Great Octoechos and contains only the hymnography for Sunday in a cycle of eight weeks (eight tones). But it is precisely this part which is the most ancient and which properly bears the title of Octoechos. With the addition of the hymnography for ordinary days, the Octoechos comes to be called the Parakliteke.

The Octoechos is used during the entire year. We begin to use it with Tone 8 on the Monday following the Sunday of All Saints (the first Sunday following Pentecost). Thus Tone 1 begins on the second Sunday after Pentecost. The tones then follow one another in order. When the cycle of eight tones is complete, we begin again with Tone 1. On the tenth Sunday after Pentecost, we begin again with Tone 1, and so on until the end of Great

Lent. Over the course of a year, the Octoechos is sung in its entirety up to six times.

The origin of the Octoechos

The Octoechos is very ancient, and the expression "to sing according to the *Octoechos* [or according to the eight tones,]"[17] is much more ancient than the liturgical book itself. This manner of singing originates in a musical system of eight tones that dates to Greek antiquity.[18] Each of these modes had a dominant note, the starting point for the scale. The national mode was the Dorian. Two other modes, imported from Asia, played an important role in the music of antiquity: the Phrygian and the Lydian. The fourth was called Mixolydian. These four fundamental modes from Greek antiquity each had modes associated with them called "plagal," because they were modeled after the fundamental modes. Thus the eight modes from Greek antiquity went in pairs: Dorian and Hypodorian; Phrygian and Hypophrygian; Lydian and Hypolydian; Mixolydian and Hypomixolydian. The scale of each mode began on a different note, and each had a different dominant note that gave it a particular character. Plato tells us that the Greeks attributed a specific character to each mode, such as the expression of a feeling or a state of the soul. Thus the Dorian mode was reserved for noble music and for certain tragedies; the Phrygian mode for the dithyramb, a liturgical chant in honor of Dionysus, and for military songs; the Lydian mode, considered to be inferior, eventually fell out of use. It is said that the Mixolydian mode wakens the human soul by inducing first joy, and then suffering.

Ancient Greek music thus served as the basis for Christian music and, consequently, for so-called "Byzantine" music. This is how the eight modes or tones (τῶν ὀκτὼ ἤχων) were elaborated and then served as the usual designation of the hymnography which is now contained in the liturgical book called by this name. Byzantine music, just as ancient Greek music, therefore consists of four fundamental tones and four plagal tones, based on the eight ancient modes.[19] We should note, however, that this theory of the Hellenistic origin of Byzantine music is in question, and that some historians insist on a Syrian origin, not only of hymnography, but also of music.

---

[17]Jean Rufin, *Plérophories*, F. Nau, ed., PO 8 (Paris, 1912), 179–80.

[18]On the genesis of this musical system, see E. Werner, *The Sacred Bridge* (London and New York, 1958), 373ff.

[19]Skaballanovich, *Tolkovyi Tipikon* 2, 109–11.

Correspondence of the eight tones	
Tone 1 [=Dorian]	Tone 1 plagal or Tone 5 [=Hypodorian]
Tone 2 [=Lydian]	Tone 2 plagal or Tone 6 [=Hypolydian]
Tone 3 [=Phrygian]	Tone 3 plagal or Tone 7 [=Hypophrygian]
Tone 4 [=Mixolydian]	Tone 4 plagal or Tone 8 [=Hypomixolydian]

Christian hymns composed according to the eight modes followed not only the musical modes elaborated in Greek antiquity, but also precise metrical structures. For the hymns found in our contemporary liturgical books, in their original Greek, are not simply prosaic texts, but follow very precise rules of Greek poetry, which regulate not only the number of syllables, but also accentuation.[20]

During the twentieth century, there were numerous debates about the origin of the Octoechos. A. Baumstark developed a theory according to which Severus of Antioch was the author of a first Octoechos in the sixth century.[21] This theory was taken up by J. Jeannin and J. Puyade,[22] and it persisted until 1982, when A. Cody refuted it and proposed a Palestinian origin for the Octoechos.[23] More recently, P. Jeffery defended the Hagiopolite origin of the Octoechos.[24] In a recent article, S. Frøyshov moves in the same direction in advancing the hypothesis of a Judeo-Christian origin of a system not only of eight tones, but also of eight weeks, which would in fact be the echo in the annual cycle of the weekly ogdoad.[25] According to him,

[20]Skaballanovich, *Tolkovyi Tipikon* 1, 369–70; J. Getcha, "L'utilisation des automèles en tant que lien entre les différentes fêtes de l'économie du salut dand le rite byzantin," in *L'Hymnographie. Conférences Saint-Serge. 46ᵉ Semaine d'études liturgiques* (Rome, 2000), 201–08.

[21]A. Baumstark, *Festbrevier und Kirchenjahr der syrischen Jakobiten* (Paderborn, 1910), 45–48.

[22]J. Jeannin and J. Puyade, "L'Octoëchos syrien," *Oriens Christianus* 3 (1913): 82–104 and 277–98; J. Jeannin, "L'Octoëchos syrien," *DACL* 12/2 (Paris, 1936), cols. 1888–99.

[23]A. Cody, "The Early History of the Octoechos in Syria," in N. Garsoian, T. Mathews, and R. Thomson, eds., *East of Byzantium: Syria and Armenia in the Formative Period* (Washington, DC, 1982), 89–113.

[24]P. Jeffery, "The Earliest Octoechoi: The Role of Jerusalem and Palestine in the Beginnings of Modal Ordering," in P. Jeffery, ed., *The Study of Medieval Chant, Paths and Bridges, East and West. In Honour of Kenneth Levy* (Woodbridge, 2001), 147–209; P. Jeffery, "Octoechos," in *New Grove Dictionary of Music and Musicians*, 18 (2001), 370–73.

[25]On the ogdoad, see J. Daniélou, *The Bible and the Liturgy* (Notre Dame, IN, 1956), 262–86; J. Daniélou, "Le dimanche comme huitième jour," in B. Botte, ed., *Le Dimanche*, LO 39 (Paris, 1965), 61–89.

the earliest Christian community, having replaced a weekly cycle of seven days with an eight-day cycle, also replaced the cycle of seven weeks with an eight-week cycle, which led to the appearance of a system of eight modes in the cathedral rite of Jerusalem, probably dating to the second half of the fourth century.[26] The discovery and publication of the *Old Iadgari* should shed new light on the issue. The *Old Iadgari*, a Georgian version of the ancient Jerusalem hymnal, dating to the fifth century, is the most ancient "Octoechos" we have.[27] These hymns were sung in the ancient liturgy of the Anastasis (Holy Sepulcher) in Jerusalem. They are indeed the ancestor of our current Octoechos, though there are a number of differences. This hymnal consists of two parts: the first contains the Sunday hymnography arranged in eight tones.[28] Here we recognize the primitive form of the hymns for the Sunday office in our Octoechos. The second part contains hymnography for the feasts of the liturgical year, which serves as the primitive stratum of the hymns of the other liturgical books: the Triodion, Pentecostarion, and Menaia.

C. Renoux estimates that these hymns should be dated to the fourth or fifth century, as they reflect the Christology of this era. He goes so far as to suggest that Cyril of Jerusalem (end of the 4th century) may be one of the composers, and that Hesychius of Jerusalem (beginning of the 5th century) probably cites from existing hymns in his homilies.[29]

The development of the Octoechos

We must admit that the redaction of the contemporary liturgical books is relatively late. It comes following the organization of the various annual liturgical cycles. Initially, the arrangement of liturgical hymns was on the basis of their hymnographic genre. Thus the Hirmologion brought together (and continues to do so) the hirmoi of the canons; the Kontakarion the kontakia; the Sticherarion the stichera; the Sticherokathismatarion the

---

[26]S. Frøyshov, "The early Development of the Liturgical Eight-Mode System in Jerusalem," *SVTQ* 51 (2007): 139–78.

[27]M. Van Esbroeck, "Le plus ancien Hymnaire," *Bedi Kartlisa* 39 (1981): 54–62; A. Wade, "The Oldest Iadgari, the Jerusalem Tropologion, V–VIIIc.," *OCP* 50 (1984): 451–56; C. Renoux, "Une Hymnographie ancienne conservée en géorgien," in *L'Hymnographie. Conférences Saint-Serge. 46ᵉ Semaines d'études liturgiques*, BELS 105 (Rome, 2000), 137–51.

[28]A French translation has been published by Father Athanase Renoux: C. Renoux, *Les Hymnes de la Résurrection, I. Hymnographie liturgique géorgienne*, Sources liturgiques 3 (Paris, 2000).

[29]Ibid., 42–49.

kathisma-troparia chanted after the matins psalmody, as well as other troparia (apolytikia and hypakoi); the Tropologion the hymns (troparia) for the canons and the Beatitudes. These ancient books, in rather rough fashion, assembled the liturgical material for the office, i.e., all the hymns that *could* be sung, and not those that *had to be* sung. These hymns were subsequently edited and arranged according to the different liturgical cycles and in the order in which they are used in our contemporary books: the Octoechos, the Triodion, the Pentecostarion, and the Menaia. According to the manuscripts which are known to us, it would seem that this new generation of liturgical books first appeared in the thirteenth century and became universal from the fifteenth century.[30]

The most ancient element of our Octoechos consists of the three resurrectional stichera, composed to accompany the psalm verses of "Lord, I call . . ." at vespers on Saturday night, the aposticha stichera at the same service, and the four resurrectional stichera at the lauds in Sunday matins. Indeed, we find the original version of several of these hymns in the *Old Iadgari*. For example, the first sticheron in tone 1 for "Lord, I call . . ." at Great Vespers— "Receive our evening prayer"—is textually identical to the first sticheron in tone 1 for "Lord, I call . . ." in the Georgian manuscript *Sin. 18*.[31]

Subsequently, additional stichera, referred to as "anatolika," sung at Saturday evening vespers and at lauds in Sunday matins, were added. It was often thought that the epithet *anatolikos* suggested the name of an author— either a fifth-century patriarch of Constantinople, or a Studite monk from the ninth century, or again Anatolios of Thessalonica (10th century). This, however, cannot be the case, because several of these hymns can already be found in the *Old Iadgari*. For example, the first "Anatolian" sticheron at "Lord, I call . . ." at Great vespers on Saturday evening in tone 1—"Rejoice, O heavens, sound the trumpets, you foundations of the earth . . . ," is identical to the fourth sticheron in tone 1 in *Sin. 18*.[32] This name could therefore simply be an allusion to the Orient (in the etymological sense of the word), thus referring to Christ as "The Orient from on high" (cf. Zech 6.12).[33]

---

[30]C. Hannick, "Le texte de l'Oktoechos," in *Dimanche. Office selon les huits tons. La prière des Églises de rite byzantin*, vol. 3 (Chevetogne, 1868), 40–43.

[31]C. Renoux, *Les Hymnes de la Résurrection*, 97–98.

[32]Ibid., 100.

[33]C. Hannick, "Le texte de l'Oktoechos," 44–45; Petridès, "Anatolika," *DACL* I, col. 1940; C. Emereau, "Hymnographi byzantini," *Échos d'Orient* 21 (1922): 265–66.

A third layer of hymns was uncovered thanks to the acrostic which united them: "ΙΩΑΝΝΟΥ Α<μήν>." These are 24 aposticha stichera, referred to as "alphabetical" at Saturday evening vespers, which are followed by a theotokion. These have been attributed to St John of Damascus, which is highly probable.[34] We note in passing that the custom of concluding a series of hymnographic strophes with one called a "theotokion," in honor of the Mother of God, seems to have been initiated by St John Damascene.[35]

The attribution of the totality of the Octoechos to St John of Damascus, which appears in our printed versions, has been refuted by liturgical historians. St John Damascene who, according to some was a presbyter at the Church of the Anastasis in Jerusalem, and a monk at the St Sabas Monastery near Jerusalem according to others,[36] was rather one of the first editors of the Octoechos, who organized earlier liturgical material of Jerusalem provenance and added new material of his own composition (aposticha stichera and resurrectional canons). Subsequently, more hymns were added.

The Jerusalem stratum of the Octoechos was later supplemented by a Constantinopolitan layer. Thus, the resurrectional kontakia and their oikoi are of Constantinopolitan provenance, though their attribution to Romanos the Melode cannot be confirmed with certainty.[37] It is possible to see the hand of Studite monks in a number of compositions. The "antiphons of degrees" (*anabathmoi*), sung before the resurrectional gospel at Sunday matins, were composed by Theodore the Studite during his exile (794–797), if one accepts the interpretation of Nicephoras Callistos Xanthopoulos (14th century).[38]

These hymns constitute the core of the Small Octoechos (the Octoechos properly speaking, distinct from the Parakletike). To these were added the matins canons for weekdays. They were composed in the ninth century by Joseph the Hymnographer (†883) and Theophanes Graptos, Metropolitan of Nicea (†843),[39] who are connected with the origin of the Great Octoechos, or Parakletike.

[34]C. Hannick, "Le texte de l'Oktoechos," 47.

[35]W. Christ and M. Paranikas, *Anthologia graeca carminum christianorum* (Leipzig, 1871), LXI.

[36]Regarding St John of Damascus, see C. Hannick, "Le texte de l'Oktoechos," 55–58.

[37]However, certain of these kontakia are indeed found in editions of Romanos' works.

[38]N.D. Ouspensky, "Chin vsenoshchnogo bdeniia na Pravoslavnom Vostoke i v Russkoi Tserkvi," *BT* 18 (1978): 86–87, note 115; O. Strunk, "The Antiphons of the Oktoechos," *Journal of the American Musicological Society* 13 (1960): 50–67.

[39]C. Hannick, "Le texte de l'Oktoechos," 39, 47–53.

The exaposteilaria, found in an appendix to the Octoechos, and linked to the cycle of 11 resurrectional gospels, are attributed to Emperor Constantine VII Porphyrogenitos (913–959), while the gospel stichera (*eothina*) are attributed to his father, Emperor Leo VI, the Wise (996–913).[40]

Among the more recent compositions added to the Great Octoechos are three stichera to the Mother of God composed by Paul of Amorion (10th century), sung at Saturday evening vespers when there are no stichera from the Menaion (which no longer happens, as the Menaia now contain hymnography for every day of the year). These are found only in Slavic printed editions. To the same hymnographers belongs the hymnody of small vespers on Saturday evening. Similarly, we find in Slavic editions a canon to the Mother of God for each day of the week at apodeipnon (compline). These canons, attributed to Emperor Theodore Laskaris Doukas (†1259), possibly originate from an ancient book of hymns to the Mother of God, called a Theotokarion.[41] Finally, the Sunday mesonyktikon (midnight office) contains a canon to the Holy Trinity, of significant theological value, ascribed to Metrophanes of Smyrna (second half of the 9th century). These canons begin to appear in manuscripts from the thirteenth century, but their use seems to become common only from the fifteenth century.

Editions of the Octoechos

Only with the first printed editions of the Octoechos in the fifteenth century did the text stabilize and become what it is today. The first printed editions were Slavic: Krakow, 1492, and Cetinje, 1494. The first Greek edition did not appear until the sixteenth century, in Venice in 1521. The Greek editions from Venice and Rome reveal little variance, which indicates that the text had stabilized by the sixteenth century. In contrast, the Grottaferrata edition (1734), prepared by the monk Philip Vitali on the basis of Italo-Greek manuscripts presents numerous variants. The modern Slavic

[40]C. Hannick, "Le texte de l'Oktoechos," 53; H.J.W. Tillyard, "Eothina Anastasima. The Morning Hymns of the Emperor Leo," *Annual Brit. School Athens* 30 (1928–1930): 86–108; 31 (1931): 115–47.

[41]The Theotokarion edited by St Nikodemos the Hagiorite and containing a canon of repentance to the Mother of God for each day according to the eight tones, compiled from various ancient hymnographers, is always chanted (and sometimes read) either at the apodeipnon or at the conclusion of vespers in many Athonite monasteries. In other monasteries, these canons from the Theotokarion, which is greatly beloved by the faithful in their private prayers, are sung at orthros (matins) on the feast of "celebrated" saints, instead of the canon from the Paraklesis prescribed by the Typikon.

editions, generally based on the 1873 Moscow edition, contain notes indicating variances between the Greek and Slavic versions. Many hymns lost in Greek editions were kept in Slavic ones. However, a critical edition of the Octoechos, including all the variants contained in the manuscripts, is yet to be completed.

The Menaia

The Menaia (μηναῖον, from μήν = month) are the liturgical books containing the *hymnography* for the *annual cycle of fixed feasts*. In our day, we have twelve Menaia which contain the hymnography for the office of fixed feasts and saints celebrated on each day of the year. There is therefore one volume per month, beginning with the month of September.

The ecclesiastical year begins on September 1. This is an ancient Constantinopolitan custom. In ancient times, the year in Constantinople began on September 23. This date marked, from its institution by Emperor Constantine (in 313), the beginning of the indiction, i.e., the establishment of the annual land tax. This date was chosen because it commemorated the birth of Augustus which, already before Constantine, marked the beginning of the year in a large part of the Orient. With the adoption of the Roman calendar in Constantinople and the suppression of the cult of Augustus, September 23 was stripped of all civil significance. As a result, the beginning of the indiction was shifted to a more convenient date, September 1. It is estimated that this change was made on September 1, 462.[42]

In the Slavic tradition, we also find a General Menaion, which contains common texts for the offices of different categories of saints: apostles, martyrs, monastics, hieromartyrs, hosiomartyrs, Hierarchs, etc. The General Menaion is useful when the church needs to celebrate the office for a saint who does not have a proper service, or if the monthly Menaion is not available. These anonymous common services also exist in some ancient Greek editions, but are rare. They have been published in a recent edition of the *Anthologion* in Thessalonica (1993), but they are rarely used in Greek practice.

---

[42]J. Getcha, "Le système des lectures bibliques du rite byzantin," in *La Liturgie, interprète de l'Écriture. I. Les lectures bibliques pour les dimanches et fêtes. Conférences Saint-Serge. 48ᵉ Semaines d'études liturgiques* (Rome, 2002), 44. We note that, according to Grumel, *Chronologie*, 124, the beginning of the Byzantine year was originally in March.

The Russian tradition also has supplementary Menaia containing hymnography for saints (typically Russian saints or those recently canonized), which has not yet been included in the monthly Menaia. In the Greek tradition, there have appeared numerous pamphlets with offices for local saints.[43]

Finally, we should also mention Menaia used for reading (Menologia or Synaxaria), which are collections of the lives of saints arranged according to the liturgical calendar. Although they are not technically liturgical books, they can nonetheless be utilized in the office.

The origin of the Menaia

The Menaia appeared relatively late. Initially, the hymnography for fixed feasts was contained in other books. For example, the ancestor of our "Octoechos," the *Old Iadgari*, the Georgian version of the ancient hymnal of Jerusalem, dating to the fifth century, contains in its second part hymns for fixed feasts.[44] It is generally believed that it was the synaxaria—lists of saints commemorated on each day of the year—that were at the origin of the development of Menaia.[45] These synaxaria can already be found in the earliest lectionaries, like the fifth-century *Armenian Lectionary*, an Armenian version of the ancient liturgical calendar of Jerusalem. It is the Constantinopolitan Synaxarion,[46] containing the list of synaxes for the feasts of various saints from September 1 to August 31, though with a number of additions, that has today become the official "calendar" of the Orthodox Church and that serves as the basis for the Menaia. This calendar has supplanted the ancient Palestinian calendar,[47] as well as the Antiochian and Alexandrian calendars.

[43]See L. Petit, *Bibliographie des acolouthies grecques*, Analecta Bollandiana 16 (Brussels, 1926).

[44]A. Wade, "The Oldest Iadgari, The Jerusalem tropologion, V–VIIIc.," *OCP* 50 (1984): 451–56.

[45]H. Leclercq, "Ménées," in *DACL*, vol. XI (Paris, 1933), cols. 409–10. On the terminology, see J. Noret, "Ménologes, Synaxaires, Ménées. Essai de clarification d'une terminologie," *Analecta Bollandiana* 86 (1968): 21–24.

[46]H. Delehaye, *Propylaeum ad Acta sanctorum Novembris. Synaxarium Ecclesiae Constantinopolitanae e codice Sirmondiano nunc Berolinensi, adjunctis synaxariis selectis* (Brussels, 1902).

[47]G. Garitte, *Le Calendrier palestino-géorgien di Sinaïticus 34*, Subsidia Hagiographica 30 (Brussels, 1958).

The first Constantinopolitan Menaia essentially contained Studite hymnography. The earliest manuscripts of the Studite Menaia date to the eleventh century. With the spread of the Sabaite Typikon in the fourteenth and fifteenth centuries, the Constantinopolitan Synaxarion was expanded with the addition of commemorations for other, later saints. The most ancient extant manuscripts of Menaia of Jerusalem redaction are from the twelfth century. As for Slavic Menaia, they contain material for the commemoration of Bulgarian, Serbian, and Russian saints, which are not found in Greek Menaia. Menaia therefore bear a distinctly local character. For example, South-Italian Menaia contain a large amount of Greek hymnography, mostly of Studite redaction, which does not appear on the printed editions of the Greek Menaia.[48] The earliest printed edition dates to 1551. The editors of the printed Menaia thus made arbitrary selections; and the spread of printed Menaia, as that of all the other printed liturgical books, greatly reduced regional diversity by imposing a unified text. There exist today two corrected editions of the Greek Menaia: that of Constantinople in 1843, whose Synaxarion was revamped on the basis of the Synaxarion of Nikodemos the Hagiorite; and that of Venice, whose Synaxarion remains in conformity with earlier editions.[49]

The Menaia are the most living liturgical books of the Orthodox Church, because their content is always expanding through the addition of hymnography for newly-canonized saints. With respect to this, we could mention the edition of the Menaia in twenty-four volumes undertaken by the Russian Orthodox Church under Patriarch Pimen beginning in 1978. This edition, despite its use of secular printing fonts (*grazhdanka*) and of new orthography, has the merit of including all the known offices for saints of Russian, South-Slavic, and Greek origin, both ancient and more recent. Similarly, in the Greek tradition, editions of the Menaia by *Apostolike Diakonia* have introduced a number of modern saints, such as Nektarios of Aegina. However, even this edition, as with the other editions of the Menaion, does not meet the actual needs of the Church, and it is still necessary to use countless small pamphlets that reflect the local character of the ordo in each parish or community.

---

[48]See I. Schiro, *Analecta hymnica graeca e codicibus eruta Italiae inferioris*, vols. I–XII (Rome, 1966–1980).

[49]Arkhiepiskop Sergii (Spaskii), *Polnyi mesiatseslov vostoka*, vol. 1 (Vladimir, 1901), 204–21.

The Content of the Menaia

Menaia contain hymnography for the saints or feasts for each day of the month. The hymns are arranged in the order in which they are sung in the office, beginning with vespers (or small vespers when a vigil is prescribed) and concluding with the Divine Liturgy.

Depending on the solemnity of the day, there can be more or less hymnographic material. When it is a simple commemoration without festivity, the hymnography may be limited to three stichera at vespers and a canon at matins. For feasts of greater importance, more material is included.

Appendices to the Menaia provide theotokia which are to be sung following the troparia and stichera. Slavic Menaia contain four appendices:

1. Theotokia to accompany Sunday and festal stichera;

2. Theotokia to accompany stichera on weekdays;

3. Theotokia to accompany the troparia on Sunday and feast days;

4. Theotokia to accompany troparia on weekdays.

Note that the second appendix is absent from contemporary Greek Menaia, which instead provide a fixed theotokion and a staurotheotokion in the text of the office.

Editions of the Menaia

It was the sixteenth-century printed editions of the Menaia that stabilized the core texts we use today. The first printed Greek editions were the work of Andrew and James Spinelli in Venice between 1528 and 1596, and reprinted from 1596 to 1607. The 1873 Venice edition was reprinted several times. There is also a Roman edition dating to 1888–1902. In Russia, the first edition of the common Menaia appeared during the era of Patriarch Job (1589–1605). The first Russian printed edition of the Menaia was published in Moscow from 1610 to 1630.

Just as with the Octoechos, we regret that there is not yet a critical edition of the Menaia containing all the variants found in the manuscripts. In the nineteenth century, Bartholomew of Koutloumousiou prepared a revised edition of the Menaia which is still used, but it contains numerous errors and lacunae. A systematic revision using a good selection of manuscripts, not to speak of a critical edition, is most desirable—but who could under-take such a monumental task?

The Triodion and Pentecostarion

The Triodion (or Lenten Triodion) and the Pentecostarion (or "Flowery" Triodion) are the liturgical books containing the *hymnography* and the *biblical readings* for the *moveable annual cycle*, the Paschal cycle. Because the date of Pascha was set by the First Ecumenical Council (Nicea, 325) as the first Sunday following the first full moon of spring, the cycle which depends on this feast varies from year to year.

The Triodion covers a period of ten weeks preceding the feast of Pascha (three preparatory weeks, six weeks of Great Lent, and Holy Week). The Pentecostarion covers a period of eight weeks following Pascha (seven weeks of paschaltide, and the octave of Pentecost). The ancient Russian books, however, divided the paschal cycle into two periods of nine weeks each, which meant that the Pentecostarion began with Lazarus Saturday, just before Holy Week, which is what gave the name "Flowery Triodion" (*tsvetnaia triod'*) to this book, connected to Palm Sunday. Indeed, originally the Triodion consisted of a single book containing the hymnography of Great Lent and the fifty days of Pascha, as the *Triodion Barberini 484* testifies.[50]

The origin and development of the Triodion and Pentecostarion

Just as we have seen with the Octoechos and the Menaia, prior to the appearance of systematic books organizing the hymnography according to the various liturgical cycles and in the order of their use in the office (Octoechos, Triodion, Pentecostarion, and Menaia), the liturgical hymns were arranged according to their hymnographic genre: Hirmologion, Kontakarion, Sticherarion, Sticherokathismata:rion, Tropologion, Prophetologion (collection of Old Testament readings). These ancient books contained in generally rough fashion liturgical material that *could* be sung, rather than what *had to be* sung.[51] Thus the first Triodia were in fact collections of canons with thee odes (tri-ode) used during Great Lent and the fifty-day paschal season, to which were added, in appendices, troparia-kathismata and stichera.[52]

---

[50]Karabinov, *Postnaia Triod'*, 212.
[51]Ibid., 54–55; Hannick, "Le texte de l'Oktoechos," 40–43, 47.
[52]Karabinov, *Postnaia Triod'*, 205.

It would appear that the Prophetologion was the precursor to the Triodion. Indeed, the prophetic readings during Great Lent were accompanied by special troparia for the prophecies, prokeimena, as well as other hymns which were subsequently incorporated into the Triodion. It is evidently the Holy Week readings which form the most ancient part of the book.[53]

The hymnography contained in the Triodion was composed between the fifth and the fourteenth centuries. Certain hymns in the Triodion and Pentecostarion, often very ancient, can also be found in the Octoechos, from which they derive. Some are already found in the *Old Iadgari* from the fifth century, which points to a Jerusalem, or more generally Palestinian, origin of the Triodion and Pentecostarion. Here, among others, we find hymns attributed to St John of Damascus, St Andrew of Crete, St Cosmas of Maiouma, St Theophanes Graptos, St Stephen the Sabaite. This is the first stratum of the Triodion and Pentecostarion, dating to between the fifth and ninth centuries, before St Theodore the Studite.[54]

The second stratum consists of Constantinopolitan, or, more precisely, Studite, hymnography, dating to the ninth to tenth centuries. Here we find compositions by the Studites St Theodore and his brother Joseph. To them belong the series of three-ode canons used at matins during Great Lent. There exists as well a series of three-ode canons attributed to Joseph the Hymnographer for the paschal period, today read during compline. These canons have survived only in the Slavic books and are absent from the Greek editions. We should also mention hymns from this period attributed to Cassia, as well as other Contantinopolitan hymnographers including Christopher, Sergios Logothetos, Georgios Papias, and the Emperor Leo the Wise. Some of these hymns have come down to us labeled "Byzantine" (βυζαντίνου).[55]

A third stratum consists of hymnography dating to the tenth to fifteenth centuries, which is mostly anonymous. We should mention here hymns composed by Emperor Constantine Porphyrogenitos and Symeon Metaphrastes,[56] as well as the entries in the Synaxarion by Nicephoros Callistos Xanthopoulos (†1335), a presbyter in Hagia Sophia who became a monk before his death. He is the author of a large *Church History* and other rather verbose works which are, nonetheless, important because they are compilations of tradition. These texts were included in the offices of the Triodion

[53]Ibid., 54–64.
[54]Ibid., 77–122.
[55]Ibid., 122–96.
[56]Ibid., 196–204.

and Pentecostarion only very late, while initially they were found in appendices to the Triodion or simply in separate collections. They are a commentary about the event being celebrated, at times inspired by apocryphal writings. They tend to imitate the hagiographic texts found in the synaxaria (menologia).[57]

The redaction of the Triodion and Pentecostarion

As we have just seen, the Triodion and Pentecostarion are a compilation of texts assembled over a period of ten centuries and which underwent considerable redaction before reaching their contemporary form. According to Nicephoras Callistos Xanthopoulos, Theodore and Joseph the Studites were the first editors of the Triodion and Pentecostarion. Nonetheless, as I. Karabinov notes, the Triodia of the tenth and eleventh centuries are so varied in both form and content that it is impossible to establish a genealogy on the basis of a single original.[58] In fact, there exist four types of Triodia. The true redactors of our contemporary Triodion and Pentecostarion were the copyists who arranged the various hymns, included originally in various collections of hymnography according to type, into systematic books. Only in the thirteenth and fourteenth centuries did Triodia and Pentecostaria in their current form appear.[59]

The content of the Triodion and Pentecostarion

The Triodion is divided into three sections: the preparatory period, the period of Great Lent, and Holy Week. This is the arrangement already familiar to St John of Damascus in the eighth century, except that for him, the preparatory period was only one week long.[60] Only in the twelfth century does the three-week preparatory period appear.[61] Each Sunday during the Triodion marks a particular commemoration, based on the Lectionary of

[57] Arkhiepiskop Filaret (Gumilevskii), *Istoricheskii obzor pesnopevtsev i pesnopeniia Grecheskoi Tserkvi* (St Petersburg, 1902), 363–64; Karabinov, *Postnaia Triod'*, 203.

[58] Ibid., 205.

[59] Ibid., 205–16.

[60] John of Damascus, *On the Sacred Fast* [PG 95, 699D]. French translation by V. Conticello in: θυσία αἰνέσεως. *Mélanges liturgiques offerts à la mémoire de l'archevêque Georges Wagner*, Analecta Sergiana 2, J. Getcha and A. Lossky, eds (Paris, 2005), 92–93. On the evolution of Great Lent in the Byzantine world, see J. Getcha, "La pratque du jeûne pendant la quarantaine paschale d'après le Triode byzantin," in ibid., 95–112.

[61] Karabinov, *Postnaia Triod'*, 23.

the Great Church of Constantinople. Nevertheless, the ancient structure of the Triodion, based on the Sunday gospel readings from the Jerusalem Lectionary, which was followed in Constantinople before the imposition of the *lectio continua* of Mark, can still be discerned in present-day Triodia in the themes developed in the iodiomela.[62]

The following table summarizes the different themes developed by the Triodion:

Themes of the Sundays of Great Lent		
Period	Ancient Triodia (Jerusalem Lectionary)	Contemporary Triodia (Constantinople Lectionary)
Preparatory period		1. Sunday of the Publican and the Pharisee
		2. Sunday of the Prodigal Son
		3. Meatfare Sunday
		4. Cheesefare Sunday
Great Lent	1. Sunday of the Holy Prophets	1. Sunday of Orthodoxy
	2. Sunday of the Prodigal Son	2. Sunday of St Gregory Palamas
	3. Sunday of the Publican and the Pharisee	3. Sunday of the Veneration of the Cross
	4. Sunday of the Good Samaritan	4. Sunday of St John Climacus
	5. Sunday of the Rich Man and Lazarus	5. Sunday of St Mary of Egypt
	6. Palm Sunday	6. Palm Sunday
Holy Week		

As for the Pentecostarion, it begins with the Sunday of Pascha and contains the 50-day paschal period and the octave of Pentecost. The theme of each Sunday is carried through an entire week, until the following Saturday. Each Sunday has a particular theme, connected to the gospel reading assigned for the Sunday liturgy and developed in the hymnography, as we can see in the following table:

[62]On this subject see G. Bertonière, *The Sundays of Lent in the Triodion: The Sundays Without a Commemoration*, OCA 253 (Rome, 1997).

The Fifty Days of Pascha	First Sunday: Pascha
	Second Sunday of Pascha: Thomas Sunday (Antipascha)
	Third Sunday of Pascha: Sunday of the Myrrhbearing Women
	Fourth Sunday of Pascha: Sunday of the Paralytic
	Fifth Sunday of Pascha: Sunday of the Samaritan Woman
	Sixth Sunday of Pascha: Sunday of the Blind Man
	Seventh Sunday of Pascha: Sunday of the Fathers of Nicea
The Octave of Pentecost	Eighth Sunday of Pascha: Pentecost
	First Sunday after Pentecost: Sunday of All Saints

Thus, the Sunday of the Publican and the Pharisee opens the moveable (paschal) cycle, and the Sunday of All Saints brings it to a close. In the middle comes the feast of feasts—Pascha, the Resurrection of the Lord.

The Typikon

The Typikon is the book containing all the rubrics regulating the liturgical celebrations. Considered by many to be the supreme arbiter concerning all questions having to do with liturgical worship and the observance of fasts, it has been described by some as the "eye of the Church."[63] In the sense that "the lamp of the body is the eye" (Mt 6.22), the Typikon appears as the revealer of the Church, guiding her members who desire to adhere to the ecclesial community and its rule of liturgical prayer. Since that time, fidelity to the prescriptions of the Typikon is experienced as fidelity to the Church.[64]

[63] The expression "Eye of the Church" (Sl. *Oko tserkovnoe*) comes from the name given to the Typikon edited by the monk Athanasios Vysotsky in 1401 in Constantinople, at the Peribleptos Monastery of the Mother of God. This Typikon was subsequently introduced in Russia, where it functioned as a model for the Sabaite Typikon until the liturgical reforms of Nikon and Joachim during the second half of the 17th century.

[64] A. Lossky, *Le Typikon byzantin: edition d'une version grecque partiellement inedited; analyse de la partie liturgique* (unpublished doctoral dissertation) (Paris: St Sergius Institute, 1987), vol. 1, 16.

According to I. Mansvetov, the Typikon is the most recent among the liturgical books, because it implies the existence of all the other books it seeks to regulate:

> The ordo of the Church, as a systematic indicator (or regulator) of the order of the offices of the daily cycle, of the Triodion and the Menologion, is one of the latest ecclesiastical books, and it was formed at the moment when these three cycles had been formed, and when each had taken its definitive shape. [...] The complete Typikon appeared as the result of the complications which arose in practice at the celebrations of the services based on different liturgical books, and the concurrence of the daily office with the content of the Triodion and the Menaia."[65]

Among the typika, it is necessary to distinguish between the foundational typika (τυπικὸν κτητορικόν)—a document enumerating the functional and organizational rules of a community—and, on the other hand, the liturgical typika, whose aim is to describe the celebration of the liturgical office throughout the year.[66] Generally, the latter consist of three parts (general guidelines or a general description of the services, a Synaxarion or menologion = fixed cycle, and a Triodion = moveable cycle), to which may be added appendices.

As we know, before the invention of the printing press each monastery or church had its own Typikon (ordo) and resolved liturgical issues in its own way. While differences between the various typika were not that numerous, liturgical scholars have discerned three large families of typika: Constantinopolitan (of the Great Church), Studite, and Sabaite (or Hagiopolite).[67]

The Typikon of the Great Church

The Typikon of the Great Church was developed in the church of Hagia Sophia in Constantinople and was used, until the fourteenth century, in secular (i.e., cathedral churches—καθολικαί) and parish churches everywhere in Byzantium and Russia. We must note, however, as E. Velkovska has

---

[65]Mansvetov, *Tserkovnyi Ustav*, 1.

[66]Lossky, *The Typikon byzantin*, vol. 1, 11–12.

[67]In the development of these typika, see M. Arranz, "Les grandes étapes de la liturgie byzantine: Palestine-Byzance-Russie. Essau d'aperçu historique," *Liturgie de l'Église particulière et liturgie de l'Église universelle*, BELS 7 (Rome, 1976), 43–72; K. Kern, *Liturgika. Gimnogrfiia i eortologiia* (Moscow, 2000²), 130–42.

done, that the designation "typikon," originally used for monastic rules, has been applied to this document only by modern editors. Indeed, this document is in fact a synaxarion.[68] In general, the liturgical offices celebrated according to the cathedral tradition of Constantinople are referred to as the "asmatic office," or "sung office" (ἀσματικὴ ἀκολουθία). This expression comes from Symeon of Thessalonica. He explains that the adjective "asmatic" means that, at these celebrations, "nothing is said that is not sung (χωρὶς μέλους) except for the prayers of the priest and the petitions of the deacon."[69] The asmatic office essentially consisted of the antiphonal singing of psalms following the Psalter of the Great Church, which was divided into antiphons.

This "cathedral" office differed completely from the Palestinian monastic office which was adopted by the Studite monks. It must have developed in the church of Hagia Sophia in Constantinople, built under Justinian between 532 and 538, and subsequently became a model for the other secular churches in the Byzantine Empire.

It is evident that the asmatic office underwent its own evolution. However, the circumstances of the origin of its ordo are unknown. It is not impossible that it was inspired largely by the liturgical worship of the cathedral of the Anastasis in Jerusalem, which is described by Egeria at the end of the fourth century. But we know nothing more about its evolution. The two extant manuscripts of the Typikon of the Great Church (from Patmos and from Jerusalem)[70] witness to the practice of the Great Church of Constantinople in the tenth century. I. Mansvetov notes correctly that "We do not know what the sung office was in its original form."[71] In studying the asmatic office, liturgical scholars generally refer to the description given by Symeon of Thessalonica in his treatise *On Sacred Prayer*.[72] However, we must realize that the description of this office by our Byzantine author reflects fifteenth-century practice, when the sung office was on its last breath.[73] And it is on the basis of these late documents that the sung office has been studied by

---

[68]E. Velkovska, "Sistema na vizantiiskite i slavianskite bogosluzheni knigi v perioda na b"znikvaneto im," in V. Gjuzelev and A. Miltenova, eds., *Medieval Christian Europe: East and West. Tradition, Values, Communications* (Sofia, 2002), 225.

[69]Symeon of Thessalonica, *On Sacred Prayer*, PG 155, 624.

[70]Dmitrievskii, *Opisanie*, vol. 1, Τυπικά, part 1, 1–110; Matéos, *Typicon*, I.

[71]I. Mansvetov, "O pesnennom posledovanii," *PTSO* 4 (1880): 973.

[72]Symeon of Thessalonica, *On Sacred Prayer*, PG 155, 628.

[73]Mansvetov, "O pesnennom posledovanii," *PTSO* 3 (1880): 752, 755.

numerous liturgists, including I. Mansvetov,[74] M. Skaballanovich,[75] I. Lisitsyn,[76] M. Arranz,[77] and O. Strunk.[78]

The Studite Typikon

If, for the celebration of the office, the cathedral and parish churches in the
Byzantine Empire and Russia used the Typikon of the Great Church of Constantinople until the fifteenth century, the office celebrated in monasteries
was different in that it was based on a monastic typikon. Urban monasteries
generally followed a typikon based on the Studite tradition. These monastic
offices used the Palestinian Psalter, as well as a large quantity of hymnography originating from Jerusalem (or Palestine).

This monastic rite, called the Studite office, appeared after what modern
liturgists have called the "Studite reform." This reform occurred at Stoudion,
the most famous among the Constantinopolitan monasteries, founded in
463 by the patrician Stoudios near the Church of St John the Forerunner, in
which foundation the "*akoimetoi*" monks (the "non-sleepers") initially settled. During the second half of the seventh century, Palestinian monks flee-
ing the Arab invasions emigrated first to Mount Olympos in Bithynia and
introduced Palestinian customs in this area. Later, during the second wave
of iconoclasm (815–843), these monks from Bithynia settled at Stoudion
at the invitation of St Theodore the Studite. As a result, the Studite monks

---

[74]Mansvetov, "O pesnennom posledovanii, *PTSO* 3 (1880): 752, 797; 4 (1880): 792–
1028.

[75]Skaballanovich, *Tolkovyi Tipikon* I, 372–93.

[76]Lisitsyn, *Pervonachal'nyi Slaviano-Russkii Tipikon*, 3–160.

[77]M. Arranz, "La liturgie des heures selon l'ancien Euchologue byzantin," in *Euchologia: Miscellanea liturgica in originating from onore di P. Burkhard Neunhauser*, Studia Anselmiana 68, Analecta Liturgica 1 (Rome, 1979), 1–19; "La liturgie des Présanctifiés de l'ancien
Euchologue byzantin," *OCP* 47 (1981): 331–88; "L'office de l'Asmatikos Hesperinos ('Vêpres
chantées') de l'ancien Euchologue byzantin," *OCP* 44 (1978): 107–30, 391–412; "L'office de
l'Asmatikos Orthros ('Matines chantées') de l'ancien Euchologue byzantin," *OCP* 47 (1981):
122–57; "Les prières presbytérales de la 'Pannychis' de l'ancien Euchologue byzantin et la
'Pannikhida' des défunts," *OCP* 40 (1974): 314–43; 41 (1975): 119–39; "Les prières presbytérales de la Tritoektî de l'ancien Euchologue byzantin," *OCP* 43 (1977): 70–93, 335–54; "Les
prières presbytérales des matines byzantines," *OCP* 37 (1971): 406–36; 38 (1972): 64–114;
"Les prières presbytérales des petites heures dans l'ancien Euchologue byzantin," *OCP* 39
(1973): 29–82; "Les prières sacerdotales des vêpres byzantines, *OCP* 37 (1971): 85–124; "Le
sacerdoce ministeriel dans les prières secretes des vêpres et des matines byzantines," *Euntes
docete* 24 (1971): 186–219.

[78]O. Strunk, "The Byzantine Office at Hagia Sophia," *DOP* 9–10 (1955–1956): 175–
202.

adopted the Palestinian Horologion and in this way carried out an initial synthesis between Palestinian monastic customs and the liturgical traditions of the imperial capital.[79] As M. Arranz explains,

> In taking charge of the Monastery of Soudion in Constantinople after the iconoclastic crisis, Theodore the Studite did not restore the office of the ancient non-sleepers, but introduced the office he knew, that of the Monastery of St Sabas, near Jerusalem. The entire monastic tradition of the Byzantine West (Athos, Georgia, Russia, South-Italy) followed the Studite usages and customs, fully conscious, however, of their connection through this to the traditions of the Lavra of St Sabas, which were themselves derived from the traditions of the holiest church in the universe, the Anastasis or Holy Sepulcher in Jerusalem.[80]

Nevertheless, it is important to point out that the Studites accepted the cenobitic Palestinian tradition, and not the anchorite Palestinian one.[81]

It is assumed that during the eleventh to the fourteenth centuries, the version of the Studite Typikon by Patriarch Alexios of Constantinople was used in Russia. This assumption is based on the fact that the majority of extant manuscripts from this period reflect the usages of the Studite Typikon rather than those of the Great Church.[82] A. Pentkovskii, following I. Karabinov, has demonstrated that the Typikon of Alexios the Studite indeed reflects the Studite tradition, over against the opinions of Dmitrievskii and Lisitsyn, who considered it to be a foundational typikon (*ktitorikon*).[83]

---

[79]T. Pott, "La réforme stoudite," in *La Réforme liturgique byzantine: Étude du phenomena de l'évolution non spontanèe de la liturgie byzantine*, BEL 104 (Rome, 2000), 108–09; M. Arranz, *Kak molilis' Bogu drevnie vizantiitsy* (Leningrad, 1979), 19, 151.

[80]M. Arranz, "La liturgie des heures selon l'ancien Euchologue byzantin," in *Euchologia: Miscellanea liturgica in onore di P. Burkhard Neunhauser*, Studia Anselmiana 68, Analecta Liturgica 1 (Rome, 1979), 2.

[81]A. Dobroklonskii, *Prepodobnyi Feodor Studit, ispovednik i igumen Studiiskii* (Odessa, 1913), 421–32; J. Leroy, "La réforme stoudite," in *Il monachesimo orientale*, OCA 153 (Rome, 1958), 188–201; A. Pentkovskii, "Studiiskii ustav i ustavy studiiskoi traditsii," *MP* 5 (2001): 72.

[82]M. Zheltov and S. Pravdoliubov, "Bogosluzhenie RPTs X–XXvv.," *PE*, vol. RPTs (Moscow, 2000), 486.

[83]A. Dmitrievskii, "Bogosluzhenie v Russkoi Tserkvi v pervye piat' vekov," *PS* 2 (1882): 139; Lisitsyn, *Pervonachal'nyi Slaviano-Russkii Tipikon*, 175–209 (see especially note 79, pp. 207–08); I.A. Karabinov, "Otzyv o trude protoiereia M. Lisitsyna 'Pervonachal'nyi Slaviano-Russkii Tipikon. Istoriko-arkheologicheskoe issledovanie, SPb, 1911,'" in *Sbornik otchetov o premiiakh i nagradakh, prisuzhdaemykh Rossiiskoi Akademiei Nauk, VII*, otchety za 1912 g. (Petrograd, 1918), 339–47; Pentkovskii, *Tipikon*, 21–41 (see especially pp. 35–36).

The Typikon of Alexios the Studite was the version of the Studite Typikon composed in 1034 by Patriarch Alexios of Constantinople (1025–1043), formerly a monk at Stoudion, for the Monastery of the Dormition of the Mother of God, which he founded near Constantinople. It was precisely this version of the Studite Typikon that was translated into Slavonic and introduced after 1051 by St Theodosius at the Monastery of the Caves in Kiev, and which, from there, spread to most Russian monasteries.[84]

The Sabaite Typikon

The Sabaite or Hagiopolite Typikon in turn reflects the liturgical tradition of Palestinian monasteries. It is linked to the figure of St Sabas the Sanctified (†532), the founder of a large monastery located eighteen kilometers (approximately eleven miles) from Jerusalem in the Kedron Valley.[85] St Sabas likely received this rule from St Euthymios the Great, St Theoktistos, and St Chariton, well-known Palestinian ascetics. After the destruction of the monastery during the Arab invasions, the Palestinian liturgical tradition was restored by St Sophronios, Patriarch of Jerusalem, and St John of Damascus, a priest at the Anastasis who, later, settled in the monastery.

The most ancient version of the Sabaite Typikon comes to us through the manuscript *Sinai gr. 1094* (12–13th century).[86] It is in fact from the twelfth century that the Sabaite Typikon began gradually to replace the Studite Typikon. Thus it appears during this era on Mt Athos with St Sava of Serbia, and comes to influence the Typikon of the Evergetis, a monastery in Constantinople founded in 1048.[87] It is approximately during this period that the "chapters of Mark" appear in Sabaite typika—rubrics attributed to a

[84]M. Zheltov and S. Pravdoliubov, "Bogosluzhenie RPTs X–XXvv.," *PE*, vol. RPTs (Moscow, 2000), 486–87; A. Pentkovskii, "Studiiskii ustav i ustavy studiiskoi traditsii," *MP* 5 (2001): 70–71.

[85]See N. Egender, "La formation et l'influence du Typikon liturgique de Saint-Sabas," in *The Sabaite Heritage in the Orthodox Church from the 5th Century to the Present*, J. Patrich, ed., Orientalia Lovaniensa Analects 98 (Louvain, 2001), 209–16; and from the same volume the study of C. Hannick, "Hymnographie et hymnographes sabaïtes," 217–28.

[86]Edited by A. Lossky, *Le Typikon byzantin: edition d'une version grecque partiellement ineditée; analyse de la partie liturgique* (unpublished doctoral dissertation) (Paris: St Sergius Institute, 1987).

[87]On the liturgical Typikon of Evergetis, see R. Taft, "The Synaxarion of Evergetis in the History of Byzantine Liturgy," in M. Mullet and A. Kirby, eds., *The Theotokos Evergetis and Eleventh-Century Monasticism*, 274–93. The liturgical Typikon of the Evergitis Monastery is in the process of publication: R.H. Jordan, *The Synaxarion of the Monastery of the Theotokos Evergetis*, Belfast Byzantine Texts and Translations 6.5 (Belfast, 2000).

certain Sabaite monk Mark, who became a priest in Constantinople before being Bishop of Otranto in southern Italy (9th–10th century). He sought to resolve problems stemming from the coincidence of several feasts and commemorations, which were originally intended to accompany the synaxarion in the Studite typika.[88]

The Sabaite Typikon, though based on the Palestinian Horologion (just like the Studite Typikon), differs in a number of ways from the Studite Typikon:

Comparison between the Studite Typikon and the Sabaite Typikon

Studite Typikon	Sabaite Typikon
No vigil (agrypnia)	Vigil (agrypnia)
No small vespers	Small vespers
No sung Great Doxology	Great Doxology sung on feast days
Predominance of Studite hymnography	Predominance of Sabaite hymnography
Predominance of Studite saints	Predominance of Palestinian saints
No lesser hours on Sundays and feast days	Lesser hours read even on Sundays and feast days
Fewer readings from the Psalter	More readings from the Psalter
Presanctified liturgies on weekdays	Presanctified liturgies on Wednesday and Friday
Shorter offices	Longer offices
No "Chapters of Mark"	"Chapters of Mark"

At the end of the fourteenth century, the Sabaite Typikon was disseminated throughout the Byzantine world by Patriarch Philotheos of Constantinople, together with his *Diataxis*. M. Arranz proposes on his part that this reform, marked by the *Diataxis tes Hierodiakonias* of Patriarch Philotheos, which is in fact a description of the vigil service (*agrypnia*), "only canonized a situation that had its origins already several centuries earlier: at the moment when when one began to celebrate the Palestinian monastic office while keeping the ancient Euchologion of Constantinople."[89] In Russia, the Sabaite Typikon was disseminated by the "liturgist metropolitan,"[90] Cyprian Tsamblak

[88]Mansvetov, *Tserkovnyi ustav*, 216–22.

[89]M. Arranz, "Les prières presbytérales des matines byzantines," *OCP* 38 (1972): 80.

[90]The expression comes from M. Arranz in: Palestine-Byzance-Russie. Essai d'aperçu

(1330–1406), a spiritual son of Patriarch Philotheos, who thus became the initiator of a true liturgical reform aimed at aligning the liturgical practice of secular and monastic churches.[91] From that point onward, the Sabaite Typikon became the sole and unique regulator of what was to become "the Byzantine Rite." In spreading Athonite hesychasm, he also spread the office as Philotheos had arranged it in the Great Lavra on Mt Athos.

In the fifteenth century, Symeon of Thessalonica explains that the Sabaite Typikon has spread almost everywhere because of its patristic, and therefore universal, authority:

> In these monasteries and in almost all the churches, they follow the ordo of the Typikon of Jerusalem, of the monastery of St Sabas, because it can be carried out by a single person, since it was composed by monks. This *diataxis* is very necessary and patristic. It is indeed our divine Father Sabas who recorded it after receiving it from Saints Euthymios and Theoktistos, they who received it from their predecessors and from Chariton the Confessor. This *diatyposis* of St Sabas which, as we have learned, disappeared after the destruction of the site by the barbarians, was restored with great care by our father among the saints, Sophronios, Patriarch of the Holy City; and again after him our divine father theologian John of Damascus renewed it and transmitted it in written form.[92]

This description by Symeon is clearly an exaggeration, for the ancient Fathers did not pass on a liturgical typikon but an ascetical way of life. Nonetheless, he underscores the rootedness of the typikon in the patristic tradition.

The first printed Greek edition of the Sabaite Typikon appeared in 1545.[93] The Slavic editions of 1610, 1633, and 1634 contributed to the definitive implantation of this liturgical tradition in Russia. The definitive edition of the Sabaite Typikon in Russia dates to 1682.[94]

---

historique," *Liturgie de l'Église particulière et liturgie de l'Église universelle*, BELS 7 (Rome, 1976), 71.

[91] See my doctoral thesis, J. Getcha, *La réforme liturgique du métropolite Cyprien de Kiev* (Paris: Cerf, 2010); as well as my article, "Le Psautier de Cyprien: un témoin de l'évolution de la liturgie byzantine en Russie," *Bolletino della badia greca di Grottaferrata* III s. 4 (2007): 33–47.

[92] Symeon of Thessalonica, *On Sacred Prayer*, PG 155, 556D.

[93] M. Arranz, "Les grandes étapes de la liturgie byzantine," 68; according to Mansvetov, the first Venetian edition dates to 1577. Mansvetov, *Tserkovnyi Ustav*, 249.

[94] M. Arranz, "Les grandes étapes de la liturgie byzantine," 71–72; Mansvetov, *Tserkovnyi Ustav*, 323ff.

The modern Greek Typikon

Though the Sabaite Typikon remains in use to our day in churches of the Russian tradition and in Greek monasteries, a new "parish" typikon appeared in the nineteenth century and has spread throughout the Greek-speaking world and the Balkans. It is the work of Constantine, Protopsaltis of the Great Church of Constantinople, and first appeared in 1838. Two further editions came out: one in 1851, another in 1868. This modern typikon is built upon a Sabaite base, but, for pastoral reasons, it incorporates a certain number of Studite and asmatic practices. Thus vigils were suppressed. Consequently, matins is always celebrated in the morning. The *artoklasia* can be performed either at the conclusion of vespers, or at the end of matins. The reading of the matins Gospel can be shifted to after the eighth ode of the canon. Rubrics for the Feast of Annunciation have been greatly simplified,[95] often at the cost of arbitrary innovations which are today criticized by liturgical scholars. In general, it can be said that not all liturgists approve of this reformed typikon.

The Euchologion and Hieratikon

Whereas the Psalter, the Horologion, the Octoechos, the Menaia, the Triodion, and the Pentecostarion are liturgical books employed by chanters and readers and contain the texts of psalms, hymns, and prayers prescribed for the various liturgical offices, the Euchologion and Hieratikon are the liturgical books used by the bishop, priest, and deacon and contain the texts of the various litanies and priestly prayers.

The Byzantine Euchologion

The Byzantine Euchologion is the book which today contains the texts of prayers and hymns connected to the performance of the varied sacramental and particular actions of the Church. In the manuscript tradition, the euchologia form a corpus of texts that is highly variable, and the manuscripts vary greatly from one to the other. In addition to services like baptism, penance, ordination, funerals, monastic profession, the blessing of water, the consecration of churches and antimensia, one also finds the office of footwashing and other services of this type, the services of the daily cycle,

---

[95]Lossky, *Le Typikon byzantin*, 107–10; Mansvetov, *Tserkovnyi Ustav*, 257–65.

and many other services which are today unknown or lost. With the development of the printing press, the content became more stable. One of the first editions was that of the French Dominican, Jacques Goar; the famous *Euchologion sive ritual graecorum* (Venice, 1647; reprinted in Paris is 1730), which he published on the basis of two Italo-Greek manuscripts: the *Barberinum Sancti Marci* from Florence (better known as *Barberini 336*) and the *Codex Bessarionis* (also known as Grottaferrata Γ.β.1). The first manuscript dates to the eighth century and is a copy of a Constantinopolitan Euchologion made in southern Italy.[96] The second, long considered to date to the eleventh or twelfth century and as having belonged to the Byzantine legate Bessarion at the Council of Florence, who later became a cardinal and honorary abbot of the Greek Monastery of Grottaferrata near Rome in 1462, is in fact a thirteenth-century manuscript.[97] The Goar edition was for a long time considered as a reference source, until the nineteenth century, when manuscript research revealed its lacunae. The Russian liturgical scholar A. Dmitrievskii showed that, of the 162 euchologies he examined, no two are identical in either content or size.[98] This tremendous variety in the rites contained in the manuscripts witnesses to the evolution of liturgical practice and makes practically impossible the publication of a single, critical edition of the Byzantine Euchologion.

The two manuscripts which form the basis for Goar's edition are called "patriarchal" euchologies, because they contain rites of ordination, consecration of chrism, dedication of churches, and imperial coronation—all reserved for patriarchal, or at least episcopal, celebrations. Euchologies that do not contain these rites are generally called "presbyteral" euchologia, as is the case with the Euchologion of Porfirii Uspenskii, a tenth-century Italo-Greek Euchologion brought to Russia from Sinai in 1850 by this great Byzantinist, and kept today in St Petersburg.

In the Slavic world, it is the *Trebnik* of Metropolitan Peter Moghila of Kiev, published in Kiev in 1646, which still reigns. The particularity of this Euchologion is that it is not simply the translation into Church Slavonic of a Greek euchology, but that it contains new euchological creations authored

[96]*Eucologio Barberini gr. 336*, S. Parenti and E. Velkovska, eds., BELS 80 (Rome, 2000²), 19–20.
[97]S. Parenti and E. Velkovska, "A Thirteenth Century Manuscript of the Constantinopolitan Euchology: Grottaferrata _._. 1., alias of Cardinal Bessarion," *Bolletino della badia di Grottaferrata* III s. 4 (2007): 175–96.
[98]Dmitrievskii, *Opisanie*, vol. 2, Εὐχολόγια, i–vii.

by the Metropolitan on the basis of the Latin *Rituale* of Pope Paul V. Later, a *Trebnik* was published in Moscow in 1687, which took into account the liturgical reform of Patriarch Nikon (1654), based on Greek liturgical books printed in Venice.

Since the appearance of the printing press, there has been a tendency to distinguish between the *Hieratikon* (or *Sluzhebnik*), which contains prayers for the divine office and the eucharistic liturgies, from the *Euchologion* (or *Trebnik*), which contains the prayers and other texts for other services of sacramental character. In addition, the prayers and ceremonies proper to episcopal celebration are contained in the *Archieratikon* (or *Chinovnik*).[99]

The origin and development of the Euchologion

The Euchologion is of Constantinopolitan origin. For this reason, the liturgical offices contained in the Euchologion originally followed the ordo of the Typikon of the Great Church of Constantinople and not that of the Palestinian Horologion. As a result, the Euchologion was revised when the Palestinian Horologion was introduced and spread. This is particularly obvious with respect to the priestly prayers of vespers and matins.

These prayers derive from the ancient asmatic ("sung") office and were intended originally to accompany the various antiphons and liturgical actions; they typically concluded the diaconal litanies, as remains the case today with the presbyteral prayers at the Divine Liturgy and other sacraments. For example, the vesperal service in Constantinople consisted of two parts: the first, celebrated in the narthex, consisted of a series of eight antiphons, accompanied by eight diaconal *synaptes* (litanies) and eight presbyteral prayers.[100] The second part contained three antiphons that concluded with a small synapte and a presbyteral prayer. This second part consisted of a prokeimenon, litanies, a prayer of inclination, and the dismissal prayer. To this second part could be added a third, consisting of a *lite*, with prayers for catechumens or the faithful.[101] The service of matins, which consisted of

---

[99]On this last book, see Haberti, Ἀρχιερατικόν *sive Liber pontificalis ecclesiae graecae* (Paris, 1643).

[100]M. Arranz, "Les prières presbytérales des petites heures dans l'ancien Euchologue byzantin, *OCP* 39 (1973): 80.

[101]Concerning asmatic vespers, see I. Mansvetov, "O pesnennom posledovanii," *PTSO* 4 (1880): 975–96; Skaballanovich, *Tolkovyi Tipikon* 1, 377–82; M. Arranz, "L'office de l'Asmatikos Hesperinos ('Vêpres chantées') de l'ancien Euchologue byzantin," *OCP* 44 (1978): 107–30, 391–419.

three sections, similarly began in the narthex with the psalmody consisting of eight antiphons which concluded with a small synapte and a presbyteral prayer. Then came the entrance into the nave of the church, accompanied by an entrance prayer. The second part consisted of Psalm 50, the biblical canticles, the lauds (Pss 148–150), and the great doxology. During the great doxology, the celebrants entered the sanctuary and came back out with the gospel book, which was then read from the ambo. The second part concluded with litanies, the prayer of inclination, and the dismissal prayer.[102]

M. Arranz has studied these prayers in detail and has clearly shown their connection to the sung office.[103] As A. Dmitrievskii affirms: "Until the appearance among us in Russia of the Jerusalem ordo, we cannot find in any liturgical book of our ancient Church any indication that, during the *hexapsalmos*, any prayer at all should be read."[104]

The initial synthesis of the Constantinopolitan and Palestinian offices occurred during the "Studite reform," when the Studites adopted the Palestinian Horologion. At that time, the presbyteral prayers of the sung office were spread throughout the office. Dmitrievskii was one of the first to point out that these prayers correspond by their content, on the one hand, with various moments in matins (e.g., the great synapte, Ps 50, the lauds, etc.), and, on the other hand, with the various litanies of the matins office with their *ekphoneses*.[105] Thus these prayers originally had titles, such as these: "prayer at the reading of the gospel," "prayer for Psalm 50," "prayer at the lauds," "prayer at the doxology"—all of which gradually disappeared as their reading was shifted to during the hexapsalmos by the *Diataxis* of Patriarch Philotheos in the fourteenth century.[106] As Arranz explains:

This preponderance of the Typikon of Stoudion was erased before a new Sabaite wave which, without breaking totally with the innovations of the monks of the Polis [Constantinople], nevertheless pushed the monks

[102]On asmatic matins, see I. Mansvetov, "O pesnennom posledovanii," *PTSO* 4 (1880): 996–1011; Skaballanovich, *Tolkovyi Tipikon* 1, 382–86; M. Arranz, "Les prières presbytérales des matines byzantines," *OCP* 37 (1971): 406–36; 38 (1972): 64–114; M. Arranz, "L'office de l'Asmatikos Orthros ('Matines chantées') de l'ancien Euchologue byzantin," *OCP* 47 (1981): 122–57.

[103]M. Arranz, "Les prières presbytérales des matines byzantines," *OCP* 37 (1971): 406–36; 38 (1972): 64–114; "L'office de l'Asmatikos Orthros ('Matines chantées') de l'ancien Euchologue byzantin," *OCP* 47 (1981): 122–57.

[104]A. Dmitrievskii, "Utrenniia molitvy," *RukSP* 42 (1886): 181.

[105]Ibid., 186–92.

[106]Ibid., 182–83; Skaballanovich, *Tolkovyi Tipikon* 2, 205–08.

in the direction of a return to the more austere sources of the rural and desert monasteries. Paradoxically, it was this second-wave Sabaite office that went on to replace the Studite office, as well as the ancient *asmatikos akolouthia*, i.e., the office of the secular churches.[107]

Consequently, the reform that resulted from the spread of the Sabaite Typikon during the fourteenth century caused these presbyteral prayers to disappear from various places in the office, only to be regrouped into a single bloc intended to be read silently by the priest while the gathered assembly listens to Psalm 103 at vespers and the hexapsalmos at matins. The reason for this may be a certain "faithfulness" to the Palestinian office, which did not initially know these prayers. This reform can appear somewhat paradoxical when one thinks that the priest must go out in front of the holy doors and perform a liturgical action at a time when all are supposed to be silent and attentive. Regarding this, A. Dmitrievskii openly considered this new arrangement of the prayers as incorrect.[108] M. Arranz, on the other hand, considers that this reform undertaken by the *Diataxis* of Patriarch Philotheos only

> canonized a situation which had already existed for several centuries, during which one began to celebrate the Palestinian monastic office while keeping the ancient Euchologion of Constantinople. [...] And it is the authority of this Euchologion which therefore guaranteed the survival of these prayers from vespers and matins in a *congealed* state.[109]

The case of the repartition of the priestly prayers in the office is but one example among others witnessing to the evolution undergone by the Constantinopolitan Euchologion when it was confronted with the Palestinian office. But there are others as well, which we cannot address here.[110]

The content of the Hieratikon

In order to celebrate the liturgical services (the divine office and the eucharistic liturgies), the celebrant uses the Hieratikon, in which he finds the text

---

[107]M. Arranz, "Les prières presbytérales des matines byzantines," *OCP* 38 (1972): 85.

[108]A. Dmitrievskii, "Utrenniia molitvy," *RukSP* 42 (1886): 186.

[109]M. Arranz, "Les prières presbytérales des matines byzantines," *OCP* 38 (1972): 80.

[110]On the transformations in the Euchologion during the 17th century, see N.D. Uspenskii, "Kolloziia dvukh bogoslovii v ispravlenii russkikh bogosluzhebnykh knig v XVII veke," *Bogoslovskie Trudy* 13 (1975): 148–71.

of litanies and priestly prayers. Indeed, the modern Euchologion, ever since the appearance of the printing press, is used only for the celebration of the various sacraments and blessings. In order to show the usual content of this liturgical book in all its variety, we compare the tables of contents of three modern editions, Greek, Slavonic, and French:

Comparison of three modern editions of the Hieratikon		
Hieratikon, Athens 1995	**Sluzhebnik, Moscow 2004**	**Hiératikon, Rome 1986**
		I.
Order of Vespers	Order of Vespers	Order of Vespers
Order of Great Compline		Order of Compline
Order of the Midnight Office		Order of the Midnight Office
Order of Matins	Order of Matins	Order of Matins
Order of the Vigil		Menologion (calendar)
		II.
Ordo of the Divine Liturgy	Ordo of the Divine Liturgy	Preparation
Liturgy of St John Chrysostom	Liturgy of St John Chrysostom	Liturgy of St John Chrysostom
Entrance verses, kontakia, apolytikia	Prayers after communion	Prayers after communion
	Dismissals	
Liturgy of St Basil the Great	Liturgy of St Basil the Great	Liturgy of St Basil the Great
Liturgy of the Presanctified	Liturgy of the Presanctified	Liturgy of the Presanctified
Order for communion	Blessing of kollyvo	
Veneration of the Holy Cross		
Service of the great blessing of water		
Service of kneeling		
Doxologies		
Lite for the deceased (Trisagion)	*Lite* for the deceased	*Lite* for the deceased (Trisagion)
	Various prayers	
	Prokeimena	
Menologion (Synaxarion)	Menologion	Menologion (Calendar)
		Prayers of absolution

The Epistle and Gospel Books

For the reading of biblical texts in the services, liturgical lectionaries are used. We possess today two books: the Epistle Book (ἀπόστολος) and the Gospel Book (εὐαγγέλιον). While the Gospel Book contains the pericopes (liturgical sections) from the gospel read at matins and the liturgy, the Epistle Book contains the pericopes from the Book of Acts and the Epistles read at the liturgy. The Old Testament readings, once contained in the Prophetologion (προφητολόγιον), are today found in the printed Menaia, Triodion, or Pentecostarion. But there remain no fewer than existed in the past, and the study of the Prophetologia would be very useful for determining the history of the Byzantine system of biblical readings.[111]

The origin of the Epistle and Gospel Books

The system of biblical readings of the Byzantine rite seems to be the heir of a synthesis of two great traditions, from Jerusalem and Constantinople. Very complex in appearance, it is the result of centuries-long evolution. The influence of the Great Lectionary of the Church of Jerusalem (5th–8th centuries)[112] on the ancient liturgy of Constantinople is generally admitted. The contemporary system of readings in the Byzantine rite, however, rather resembles the organization of readings in the Armenian Lectionary,[113] the most ancient known lectionary from Jerusalem, dating to the first half of the fifth century. The biblical readings appointed today for the Byzantine rite are essentially those found in the Typikon of the Great Church (9th century).

It is considered that the readings for Saturdays and Sundays are the most ancient. According to some scholars, they date as early as to the second

---

[111]On the subject of the Prophetologion, see A. Rahlfs, *Die alttestamentlichen Lektionen der griechischen Kirche*, Nachtichten von der Kgl. Gesellschaft der Wiss. zu Göttingen, Phil.-hist. Kl. (Göttingen, 1915); G. Zuntz, "Das byzantinische Septuaginta-Lektionar," *Classica et Mediaevalias* 17 (1956): 183–98; C. Höeg and G. Zuntz, "Remarks on the Prophetologion," in *Quantulacumque. Studies Presented to Kirsopp Lake by Pupils, Colleagues and Friends*, eds. R.P. Casey, S. Lake, and A.K. Lake (London, 1937), 221. On the Constantinopolitan lectionary, see E. Velkovska, "Lo studio dei lezionari bizantini," *Ecclesia Orans* 13 (1996): 253–71; A. Alekseev, *Bibliia v bogosluzhenii. Vizantiisko-slavianskii lektsionarii* (St Petersburg, 2008).
[112]*Le Grand Lectionnaire de l'Église de Jérusalem*, ed. M. Tarchnisvili, CSCO 188–189, 204–205, Scriptores Iberici 9–10, 13–14, (Louvain, 1959–1960).
[113]*Le Codex Arménien Jérusalem 121*, ed. A. Renoux, I. PO XXXV, I, No. 163 (Turnhout, 1969); II. PO XXXVI, 2, No. 168 (Turnhout, 1971).

century,[114] according to others to the fourth century,[115] while still other
believe that the system appeared in the seventh to eighth centuries.[116] The
weekday readings would have been added during the eighth and ninth centuries, during the "Studite reform." The series of Sunday readings seems to
be distinct from the one for Saturdays, which lags a little behind; and it is
thus likely that it was organized after that for Sundays, and as a complement
to it. Karabinov, in his study on the Triodion, established firmly that, at least
for the Lenten period, the Constantinopolitan system of readings, comple-
menting the other periods of the year that used Matthew, Luke, and John,
in the eleventh century replaced the selected readings of Jerusalem origin.
Could the same have happened for other times in the liturgical year?

The Byzantine lectionaries from the eighth to the fourteenth centuries
are usually classed in two categories: "complete" (type *l* e) containing, for
the period from Pentecost to Great Lent, readings for each day of the week,
and "short" (type *l* esk), containing, for the same period, readings only for
Saturdays and Sundays.[117] The existence of two main types of lectionaries
(*l* e and *l* esk: complete and short) is not surprising. Indeed, up until the
reform of Patriarch Philotheos of Constantinople in the fourteenth century,
after which the sung office fell out of use, there were in Constantinople and
throughout the empire, and even among the Slavs, two different types of
daily offices: one used in secular churches and following the Typikon of
the Great Church, the other used by the monks, which followed either the
Studite or Sabaite ordo. Further, as M. Arranz and J. Mateos explain, the
Great Church of Constantinople did not have a daily eucharistic liturgy, but
only on feasts of the Lord and of saints, during paschaltide, Saturdays, and
Sundays, at the stational commemoration of saints, and on fast days.[118] This

---

[114]C.-R. Gregory, *Textkritik des Neuen Testamentes*, vol. 1 (Leipzig, 1900), 336.

[115]A. Wikgren, "Chicago Studies in the Greek Lectionary of the New Testament," in
Biblical and Patristic Studies in Memory of Robert Pierce Casey (Fribourg, 1963), 120–21; B.
Metzger, "Greek Lectionaries and a Critical Edition of the Greek New Testament," in *Die
alter Übersetzungen des Neuen Testaments, die Kirchenväterzitate und Lektionare* (Berlin,
1972), 495–96.

[116]K. Aland and B. Aland, *The Text of the New Testament. An Introduction to the Critical
Editions and the Theory and Practice of Modern Textual Criticism* (Leyde, 1987), 165.

[117]Pentkovskii, "Lektsionarii i chetveroevangeliia v vizantiiskoi i slavianskoi liturgicheskikh traditsiiakh," 4. See K. Aland, *Kurzgefasste Listed et griechischen Handschriften
des Neuen Testaments*, vol. 1: *Gesamtübersicht* (Berlin, 1963), 24. In the sigla used, *l* designates a lectionary, "e" means "*ephemeros*" (daily), "sk" signifies "*sabbato-kyriake*" (Satur-
day-Sunday).

[118]Matéos, "Λειτουργία," in *Typicon* II, 302.

explains the necessity of praying for catechumens at sung vespers and matins, as well as the reason for which these two services may be considered as the linchpins of the communal prayer of the ancient Byzantines.[119] In addition, this also explains why the Typikon of the Great Church did not need to have readings for weekdays between Pentecost and Great Lent, because if a eucharistic liturgy was celebrated one of those days, a reading from the Menologion was used, or an appropriate "common" reading.[120] On the basis of these facts, we can imagine that the "complete" lectionaries (*l* e) belonged with the monastic office, while the "short" lectionaries (*l* esk) were used for the office in cathedral and secular churches.

Further, if the celebration of daily eucharistic liturgies in the monasteries of Constantinople is the result of the Studite reform, which preferred the Palestinian ordo over that of the Great Church, one could assume that the short system of readings (*l* esk) was supplemented in the ninth century to produce the complete system of the "*l* e" type.

The Content of the Epistle and Gospel Books

The Epistle and Gospel Books contain the New Testament readings and can be organized in two different ways. On the one hand, there are the "lectionaries" properly speaking, or *aprakos*, which contain the texts of the readings arranged liturgically for each day and solemnity of the year. On the other hand, there are liturgical Epistle and Four-Gospel books which present the complete text as it appears in a modern edition of the New Testament, but indicating in the margins the different readings, the beginning and end of pericopes, and eventually passages to be omitted, an indication of the day of the year or the feast being celebrated, and introductory phrases.

Indeed, for the readings from the New Testament in the Byzantine rite, besides the usual references based on chapter and verse number, there exists also a system of numbering by pericope. For example, the Gospel of Matthew is divided and numbered into 116 pericopes, the Gospel of Mark into 71 pericopes, Luke's Gospel into 114 pericopes, and John's Gospel into 67 pericopes. As for the Epistle Book, it is divided in its totality into 335 pericopes.

[119]M. Arranz, "L'office de l'Asmatikos Orthros ('Matines chantées') de l'ancien Euchologue byzantin," *OCP* 47 (1981): 135 and 156–57.
[120]Pentkovskii, "Lektsionarii i chetveroevangeliia v vizantiiskoi i slavianskoi liturgicheskikh traditsiiakh," 11.

Because these pericopes are intended for liturgical reading, and because they are often taken out of their own context in the New Testament, introductory phrases are essential. They specify who is speaking to whom, on what occasion, and where. Most often, we find: "In those days . . . ," "The Lord said to his disciples . . . ," "The Lord said to the Jews who came to him . . . ," "The Lord said . . . ," "The Lord said this parable . . . ." The text is sometimes adapted for oral recitation: pronouns are replaced by nouns, verb tense is changed. And sentences concluding a pericope are also sometimes adapted or amplified for better effect.[121] For example, the gospel pericope for the twenty-eighth Sunday after Pentecost concerning those invited to the banquet who refuse to come (Lk 14.16–25) concludes with a verse taken from the parallel text from Mt 22.14 ("For many are called, but few are chosen"), which was thus added to the text from Luke. These are some of the textual liberties taken in Byzantine lectionaries to ensure a better oral transmission of the text—but which risks surprising and discouraging biblicists who may be caught unawares!

Contrary to the organization of the Jerusalem lectionaries, which present the year beginning from the Nativity of Christ, the Byzantine lectionaries are divided into three parts. The pericopes of the *aprakoi* lectionaries are distributed within the three parts, and the index of the Gospel and Epistle Books is divided into three sections. The first part contains the readings for the moveable cycle (connected to the feast of Pascha). It covers all the weeks of the year, beginning with Easter Sunday, and concludes with Holy Saturday. We should note in passing that this first part begins with Pascha, while in the typika this period begins with the Lenten Triodion. The second part is called the "menologion" and consists of a calendar of feasts and saints commemorated over the twelve months of the year. In this section, therefore, one finds biblical readings belonging to the sanctoral (fixed) cycle, in those cases where they are prescribed. Finally, a third section contains readings referred to as "common," i.e., for different occasions and for the various categories of saints. It is here, for example, that we would find readings assigned for baptism, for funerals, for the dedication of a church, for a canonized bishop, etc. In the Gospel Book, one generally finds an appendix containing pericopes for Holy Week. This is explained by the fact that several of the Holy Week readings are "composite," in other words, consisting

[121]K. Aland and B. Aland, *The Text of the New Testament* (Grand Rapids, MI, 1987), 166.

of selected verses taken from all four gospels, which would make reading these pericopes from the Gospel Book practically impossible. This is why it was deemed useful to add the composite texts as an appendix, as we find in the *aprakoi*.

We should also be aware of the existence of two systems of reading that lie behind the choice of pericopes. As in other lectionary traditions, Byzantine lectionaries reflect the two classical types of reading: continuous reading (*lectio continua*) and selected reading. Byzantine lectionaries generally select continuous reading for the synaxarion. For example, Genesis is read almost in its entirety during Great Lent, and the Acts of the Apostles and the Gospel of John are read continuously during the 50 days of Pascha. We will return to this.

Selected reading dominates the pericopes of the menologion and the "common" readings. Readings can be selected for a number of reasons. The most obvious is the choice of a text that describes the event being celebrated. This is the case, for example, with the epistle reading on the day of Pentecost (Acts 2.1–11) or the Gospel reading for Christmas (Mt 2.1–12). It is also possible to choose a pericope because of the explicit mention of a saint: this is the case, for example, for the feast of the Apostle James, Brother of the Lord (Gal 1.11–19) on October 23, because he is mentioned in the final verse ("But I saw none of the other apostles except James the Lord's brother"). A pericope may also be selected on the basis of typology. This is the case for most of the Old, as well as New, Testament passages read on feasts of the Mother of God, whether the pericope about Jacob's ladder (Gen 28.10–17), read at vespers, or the pericope about Martha and Mary (Lk 10.38–42; 11.27–28), which present two "types" of the Mother of God. Finally, a reading can also be chosen on the basis of location, particularly if this selection was originally made in the context of a stational liturgy. This is the case, for example, with the reading on Easter Monday (Acts 1.12–17) describing the group of the apostles and the replacement of Judas: this reading, though it also fits within a continuous reading, was chosen because of a station held at the Church of the Holy Apostles in Constantinople on that day. We should note as well that the choice of prokeimena preceding the biblical readings at the eucharistic liturgies during the great week of Pascha is explained by the choice of stations in Constantinople indicated in the Typikon of the Great Church.[122]

---

[122]Matéos, *Typicon* II, 96ff.

The eleven Resurrection Gospels

The Gospel Book contains a cycle of eleven resurrection or morning gospels (εὐαγγέλια ἀναστάσιμα or ἑωθινά), which are read in turn at Sunday matins. This series, found in the Typikon of the Great Church,[123] was taken from the series of eleven gospels read in Jerusalem during the week of Easter,[124] and which more or less determined their number,[125] as it appears in the following table:

Resurrectional Gospels		
Armenian Lectionary	Great Lectionary of the Church of Jerusalem	Typikon of the Great Church
Paschal vigil: Mt 28.1–20	Paschal vigil: Mt 28.1–20	1) Mt 28.16–20
Night of Pascha: Jn 20.1–18	Night of Pascha: Jn 20.1–18	2) Mk 16.1–8
Pascha morning: Mk 16.2–8	Pascha morning: Mk 16.1–8	3) Mk 16.9–20
Pascha evening: Jn 20.19–25	Pascha evening: Jn 20.19–25	4) Lk 24.1–12
Monday: Lk 23.50–24.12	Monday: Lk 23.54–24.12	5) Lk 24.21–35
Tuesday: Lk 24.13–35	Tuesday: Lk 24.36–40	6) Lk 24.36–53
Wednesday: Lk 24.36–40	Wednesday: Lk 24. 13–35	7) Jn 20. 1–10
Thursday: Mt 5.1–12	Thursday: Mt 5.1–12	8) Jn 20.11–18
Friday: Jn 21.1–14	Friday: Jn 21.1–14	9) Jn 20.19–31
Saturday: Jn 21.15–25	Saturday: Jn 21.15–25	10) Jn 21.1–14
Sunday: Jn 1.1–17	Sunday: Jn 1.1–17	11) Jn 21.14–25
Sunday evening: Jn 20.26–31	Sunday evening: Jn 20.26–31	

We note that this cycle of eleven gospel pericopes in the Constanopolitan lectionary is the expansion of a more ancient cycle of eight gospel pericopes in the Jerusalem Lectionary.[126] The fact that the reading of a resurrectional

[123]Ibid., II, 170–75. Concerning the two series of eleven gospels, see Janeras, *Le Vendredi saint dans la tradition liturgique byzantine. Structure et histoire des ses offices*, 122; Pott, *La Réforme liturgique byzantine*, 149.

[124]Renoux, II, 308–25; *Le Grand Lectionnaire de l'Église de Jérusalem*, ed. M. Tarchnisvili, CSCO 189, Scriptores Iberici 10, 113–20.

[125]Pott, *La Réforme liturgique byzantine*, 149–50; S. Janeras, "Ivangeli dominicali della ressurezione nella tradizioni liturgiche agiopolita e byzantina," in G. Farnedi, ed., *Paschale Mysterium. Studi in memoria dell'abate prof. Salvatore Marsili (1910–1983)* (Rome, 1986), 64–66.

[126]Ibid., 55–69.

gospel at Sunday matins is of Hagiopolite origin should not surprise us, because we have the witness to such a reading in the Sunday morning office from Egeria in the fourth century. In effect, she tells us that "the bishop stands inside the screen, takes the Gospel Book, comes to the door, and himself reads the account of the resurrection of the Lord."[127] This fact supports the opinion of Father M. Arranz, who asks himself "whether the Sunday gospel is not a relatively recent innovation in Constantinople, and whether it comes from the Palestinian monastic office, as the verse from Psalm 150.6 seems to suggest."[128] It is therefore very likely that the eleven resurrectional gospels, of Jerusalem origin, were adopted by the Sabaite tradition, then introduced in Constantinople in the Studite reform, and from there influenced the Typikon of the Great Church.

Continuous reading of the New Testament

For the continuous reading of the New Testament, we must refer to the section of the lectionaries containing the synaxarion. As we have already seen, Byzantine lectionaries have divided the year into four general periods. The first begins with Easter and continues to Pentecost. The second falls between Pentecost and the New Year. The third begins at the New Year and lasts until the Triodion cycle begins. The fourth covers the period of the Triodion.

FROM PASCHA TO PENTECOST

The Byzantine tradition has chosen to read continuously the Acts of the Apostles and the Gospel of John during the paschal season, which concludes with Pentecost. It must be said that the Book of Acts was already read in Jerusalem during the same period. This continuous reading begins with the reading of the Prologue of John's Gospel (Jn 1.1–17) on Easter day, a selection read in the Jerusalem tradition on the Sunday following Easter. We note three exceptions to the rule concerning the continuous reading of the gospel: on Easter Tuesday, we read the pericope from Luke (Lk 24.12–35) about the disciples on the road to Emmaus, which is the reading assigned for that day by the Armenian Lectionary,[129] a witness to the Jerusalem liturgy in

---

[127]Egérie, *Journal de voyage* 24, 10.

[128]M. Arranz, "L'office de l'Asmatikos Orthros ('Matines chantées') de l'ancien Euchologue byzantin," *OCP* 47 (1981): 154.

[129]Renoux II, 316–17.

the first half of the fifth century; the pericope from Mark (Mk 15.43–16.8) read on the third Sunday of Easter describes the burial and the empty tomb, and it is in fact a reading chosen because of the commemoration that Sunday of the myrrhbearing women, Joseph of Arimathea, and Nicodemus; and finally the pericope from Luke (Lk 24.36–53), read on Ascension Thursday, a reading clearly chosen in connection with this feast.

FROM PENTECOST TO THE NEW YEAR

Following Pentecost, the Byzantine liturgy prescribes the continuous reading of the Epistle to the Romans and the Gospel of Matthew up until the seventeenth Sunday after Pentecost. The continuous reading of Romans concludes on the sixth Monday after Pentecost and is followed by the reading of 1 Corinthians, which is completed on the tenth Wednesday after Pentecost, after which 2 Corinthians is read. However, on the sixth, seventh, eighth, ninth, and tenth Saturdays after Pentecost, pericopes from Romans are read, on the eleventh to the nineteenth Saturdays passages from 1 Corinthians are appointed, as well as for the tenth to the thirteenth Sundays after Pentecost (simply because the Saturday cycle lags behind that of weekdays and Sundays). Let us also note that, with the continuous readings on weekdays, the Gospel of Matthew concludes on the eleventh Sunday after Pentecost and is followed by the Gospel of Mark, which begins on Monday of the twelfth week. Nevertheless, we continue to read Matthew's Gospel on Saturdays and Sundays until the New Year. The epistle readings are thus taken from the Epistles to the Romans and 1and 2 Corinthians on Saturdays and Sundays, to which Galatians and Ephesians are added on weekdays.

We can therefore see that the organization of the readings for Saturdays and Sundays follows a continuous reading independent of the weekday readings, which appeared only later, as we have already said, because it is not found in the Typikon of the Great Church, but came about through the monastic office, which later spread everywhere.[130]

FROM THE NEW YEAR TO THE TRIODION CYCLE

The Typikon of the Great Church prescribed the continuous reading of the Gospel of Luke, beginning on the New Year.[131] With the adoption of

---

[130]P.-M. Gy, "La question du système des lectures de la liturgie byzantine," in *Miscellànea Liturgica in onore di Sua Eminenza il cardinal Giacomo Lercaro* (Rome, 1967), 254–55.

[131]Matéos, *Typicon* II, 90–91.

the Roman calendar in Constantinople and the suppression of the cult of Augustus, September 23 was stripped of all civil significance. As a result, a new, more convenient date was selected for the beginning of the indiction: September 1. Thus the Typikon of the Great Church maintains the practice dating to the first half of the fifth century, in which September 1 marks the beginning of the indiction (beginning of the civil year), while September 23 remains the beginning of the ecclesiastical year. It is estimated that this change took place during the second half of the fifth century, probably beginning on September 1, 462. The commemoration of the Conception of John the Baptist, chronologically the first of the gospel mysteries, was placed in Byzantium on September 23, at the beginning of the ecclesiastical year (coinciding with the birthday of Augustus), and not on September 24, nine months before the birth of John the Baptist (June 24), the date on which it was celebrated in the West. As a result, with the New Year began the continuous reading of the Gospel of Luke, which begins with the account of the conception of John the Baptist (Lk 1. 5–25). However, little by little, the beginning of the civil year also came to be sanctified with special readings (1 Tim 2.1–7; Lk 4.16–22) toward the first half of the eighth century. In addition, the institution of new feasts, particularly the Nativity of the Mother of God (Setember 8)—an event that chronologically precedes the conception of John the Baptist and is anterior to it in the Mystery of Salvation—also contributed to the lessening of the importance of September 23, which eventually ceased to mark the New Year, which was eventually celebrated on the beginning of the indiction, September 1.[132]

These factors caused a problem regarding when to begin reading the Gospel of Luke. Some began it on the Monday following the Sunday after the Feast of the Exaltation of the Cross (September 14), which more or less corresponds to September 23. This practice is already attested in the eleventh century by the Byzantine-Georgian Lectionary (*Sinai Georg. 74*), which places the beginning of the Lukan readings not after the New Year, but on the Sunday after the Exaltation of the Cross.[133] This practice was widespread in the East among churches following Greek practice, in which the gospel lectionaries contained, in an appendix, the tables of Emmanuel Glyzonios that established for each paschal year the proper day for begin-

---

[132]Matéos, *Typicon* I, 55. See also V. Grumel, *Traité d'études byzantines*, I. *La Chronologie* (Paris, 1958), 193–203.

[133]G. Garrite, "Analyse d'un Lectionnaire byzantino-géorgien des évangiles—Sin. Géorg. 74," *Le Muséon* 91 (1978), fasc. 1–2, p. 211.

ning the lections from Luke. In these gospel lectionaries, the enumeration of the Lukan pericopes is independent of the enumeration of the pericopes from Matthew and Mark, which begins from Pentecost.[134] The tables of Glyzonios were established in the seventeenth century and were introduced into the Greek gospel lectionaries initially by the Patriarchate of Jerusalem during the first half of the eighteenth century.[135] The Russian Church, for its part, long ignored this practice and began reading the Gospel of Luke beginning only on the Moday of the eighteenth week after Pentecost. Nevertheless, eventually the Church of Russia did adopt this practice of beginning to read from the Gospel of Luke on the Monday after the Sunday following the Exaltation of the Cross, independently of the cycle of weeks after Pentecost. That practice was introduced in 1957 on the initiative of the bishop-liturgist Athanasii (Sakharov). However, the introduction of this custom sowed confusion among the Russian clergy, and it was not taken into account in the 1959 edition of the calendar of the Church of Russia.[136] Several years later, the Russian Church took up this practice again and keeps it to the present.[137]

This transition from the Gospel of Matthew to that of Luke is called by liturgical experts the "Lukan jump." As a result, in our days the period from the Exaltation of the Cross until the beginning of the Triodion is rather confused among the Orthodox, since there are now three distinct practices of biblical reading during this time: some do not observe the "Lukan jump"; others observe the "Lukan jump" without altering the order of epistle readings; still others observe the "Lukan jump" and adapt the epistle readings—something that has no historical foundation, but which has for a number of years been done in the Church of Russia. In addition, since the Orthodox follow two different calendars (differing from one another by thirteen days), the "Lukan jump" can take place among some one or two weeks earlier than among others. Thus, in our days there can be up to five different systems

[134]A.G. Kravetskii, "Kalendarno-bogosluzhebnaia komissia," *Uchenye zapiski Rossiiskago Universiteta ap. Ioanna Bogoslova* 2 (1996): 199.

[135]P.M. Mironositskii, "O poriadke tserkovnykh chtenii Evangeliia," in *Bogosluzhebnye ukazanie na 1999 god* (Moscow, 1998), 584. Initially published in *Tserkovnye vedomosti* 7 and 9 (1916), and reprinted in *ZhMP* 12 (1956): 16–25.

[136]A.G. Kravetskii, "Kalendarno-bogosluzhebnaia komissia," *Uchenye zapiski Rossiiskago Universiteta ap. Ioanna Bogoslova* 2 (1996): 189–93.

[137]One generally refers to the article by N.D. Uspenskii, "O sentiabr'skoi prestupke evangel'skikh chtenii," in *Pravoslavnyi Tserkovnyi Kalendar' na 1971 god* (Moscow, 1970), 48; reprinted in *Bogosluzhebnye ukazaniia na 2001 god* (Moscow, 2000), 641–42.

of readings from the Exaltation of the Cross to the beginning of the Triodion—very confusing indeed! We could ask ourselves whether it would be simpler to keep to the order of Sundays following Pentecost, which is celebrated on the same day by all the Orthodox, and which would allow for uniform readings on all Sundays throughout the year.

Despite the issues of the "Lukan jump," it remains a fact that, on all the Sundays during this third period of the year, the Gospel of Luke is read. During the week, Luke is read until the twenty-ninth week after Pentecost (twelfth week of Luke) inclusive, and the reading of Mark is taken up again beginning on the thirtieth week after Pentecost (thirteenth week of Luke). As for the epistle readings, on Saturdays and Sundays 1 and 2 Corinthians, Galatians, Ephesians, Colossians, 1 Timothy, and 1 Thessalonians are read according to a very particular distribution. During the week, the readings are much more continuous: we finish the reading of Ephesians and then move on to Philippians, Colossians, Thessalonians, Timothy, Titus, Hebrews, and then the catholic epistles. Here, we can make the same observation as for the preceding period, that the choice of readings for Saturdays and Sundays is independent of—and no doubt more ancient than—the choice of weekday readings, which sought to complete the continuous reading of all the epistles by filling in the gaps which existed between the Saturday and Sunday readings.

In addition to the "Lukan jump," there also exists what is called the "jump of the Baptism of Christ." This jump stems from the fact that the number of weeks in the paschal cycle varies from year to year. Byzantine lectionaries foresee thirty-three weeks after Pentecost, before the beginning of the subsequent Triodion cycle. But there can be as many as 38 weeks from Pentecost to the beginning of the Triodion. It is necessary to fill the void with readings. To do this, we repeat the most recent readings, beginning with the week following the Sunday after Theophany, by attaching the last week of assigned readings (the thirty-third week after Pentecost, or week sixteen of Luke) to the Triodion cycle.[138]

---

[138] At the Monastery of Simonos Petras on Mt Athos, for example, the sequence of epistles is maintained, and if some days remain at the end of the Luke-Mark cycle and the beginning of the Triodion, on the one hand they read all the gospels appointed for the after-feast of Theophany by the Menologion, then the gospels (and eventually the epistles) of those days which were previously omitted because of the occurrence of great feasts. This implies the need for the ecclesiarch to create a small list of these selected readings, but it has the advantage of avoiding repetition and allowing for the readings of important pericopes that have been omitted.

READINGS FROM THE TRIODION

For the period of the Triodion,[139] one must distinguish between the preparatory weeks before the Holy Forty Days and the Holy Forty Days of Lent. The preparatory period consist of three weeks. It begins with the Sunday of the Publican and the Pharisee, on which are read 2 Timothy 3.10–15 and Luke 18.10–14, the pericope which gave the name to this Sunday. In the week that follows, 2 Peter and 1 John are read, together with the Gospel of Mark. On the following Saturday, pericopes from 2 Timothy and Luke are read, and on Sunday, 2 Timothy 2.10–15 and the passage about the Prodigal Son (Lk 15.11–32), which gave the name to this Sunday. The week following (called Meatfare, or ἀποκρέω), readings from the catholic epistles and the Gospel of Mark are continued. Saturday of Meatfare week, 1 Corinthians 10.23–28 (about food offered in sacrifice) and Luke 21.8–36 (on the signs preceding the Second Coming of Christ) are read. On Meatfare Sunday, we read 1 Corinthians 8.8–9, 2 (about food that we eat) and the pericope about the last judgement (Mt 25.31–46), the theme of this Sunday. Finally, the readings for Cheesefare week are taken from the catholic epistles and from the end of the Gospel of Luke, except for Wednesday and Friday, which already follow a Lenten ordo,[140] and Old Testament readings (from Joel and Zechariah) are read at the sixth hour and vespers in anticipation of the fast which is about to begin. On Cheesefare Saturday, we read Romans 14.19–23 (about food) and Matthew 6.1–13 (on alms and prayer), and on Sunday, Romans 13.11–14.4 (about abstinence from food) and Matthew 6.14–21 (about fasting) are read. These last readings are also selected because of the fast which is about to begin. With Cheesefare Week, the continuous reading of the entirety of the New Testament comes virtually to an end because, apart from Saturdays and Sundays, which are the only days during Great Lent that a full eucharistic liturgy is celebrated,[141]

---

[139]We label the "period of the Triodion" as that liturgical period during the year when the liturgy employs the Triodion, the liturgical book containing the hymnography for the period from Sunday of the Publican and the Pharisee (three weeks before the beginning of Great Lent) to Holy Saturday. Thus, it covers the preparatory weeks before the fast, Great Lent, and Holy Week.

[140]On these days, according to the Sabaite ordo in effect today, no eucharistic liturgy is celebrated, but only the office of typika. The Typikon of the Great Church prescribed a Presanctified liturgy on these days, just as during Great Lent.

[141]The expression "full liturgy" (λειτουργία τελεία) is customarily used to refer to a eucharistic liturgy with an anaphora. Thus the Liturgy of Presanctified Gifts, nowadays celebrated on Wednesdays and Fridays during Great Lent, is not a "full liturgy," but simply

and during Holy Week, there are no more readings from the New Testament during Great Lent.

On Saturdays and Sundays during Lent, the New Testament readings are taken from the Epistle to the Hebrews and the Gospel of Mark. The only exception comes on the first Sunday of Great Lent, when John 1.44–52 (on the calling of the first disciples) is read, and it was likely the reading selected for the commemoration of the Holy Prophets, which the Great Church celebrated that day, before the institution of the feast of the Triumph of Orthodoxy, commemorating the final victory over iconoclasm in 843. The epistle reading that same Sunday (Heb 11.24–26, 32–40), on the fulfillment of the prophets by Christ, is equally a reading selected for the same ancient commemoration. However, it is also possible that the reading of the pericope from John may be the vestige of an ancient system of gospel readings from John during Great Lent.[142]

As for the New Testament readings during Holy Week, they were chosen in relation to the passion of Christ and relate the last words of Christ and the last days of his earthly life.

To summarize, we can systematize the continuous reading of almost the entire New Testament in the following table:

The continuous reading of the New Testament in the Byzantine rite			
Period	**Sunday**	**Weekday**	**Saturday**
Pascha – Pentecost	Acts – **John**	Acts – John	Acts – John
Pentecost – New Year	Romans – **Matthew**	Romans – Matthew	Romans – Matthew
Weeks 1–11	Corinthians	Corinthians	Corinthians
Weeks 12–17		Corinthians – Mark	Corinthians – Mark
		Galatians	Ephesians
		Ephesians	

a communion office, because the faithful commune from gifts that were consecrated at the last "full liturgy."

[142]Hieromoine Macaire, *La Mystagogie du temps liturgique dans le Triodion*, 187. See also A. Kniazeff, "La lecture de l'Ancien et du Nouveau Testament dans le rite byzantin," 230–33; Karabinov, *Postnaia Triod'*, 30–31.

New Year – Triodion	Galatians – **Luke**	Ephesians	Corinthians – Luke
Weeks 18–29	Ephesians	Philippians	Galatians
	Colossians	Colossians	Ephesians
		Thessalonians	
		Timothy	
		Titus	
	Timothy	Hebrews	Colossians
Weeks 30–33		James	Thessalonians
Triodion			
Preparatory period	Timothy – Luke	Peter – Mark	Timothy – Luke
	Corinthians – Matthew	John	Corinthians – Luke
		Jude	Romans – Matthew
Great Lent	Romans	—	Hebrews – Mark
	Hebrews – **Mark**		

CHAPTER TWO

The Offices of the Horologion

The daily cycle consists of eight different offices, for which the Horologion contains the fixed elements. These offices, from the rising to the setting of the sun, are as follows: the mesonyktikon or midnight office, matins, the hours (prime, terce, sext, and none), vespers, and the apodeipnon (compline).[1]

In monasteries, the weekday midnight office, compline, and the hours are celebrated in the narthex. During Great Lent, the hours are celebrated in the nave. Matins and vespers are celebrated in the nave during the entire year. In the spirit of the Typikon, the celebrant enters the sanctuary only at specific moments during the office to carry out a particular task. In parish practice, the midnight office and compline are celebrated only rarely, but typically in the nave. The same is also true for the hours.

The Midnight Office (Mesonyktikon)

Schema of the Midnight Office		
Weekdays	**Saturday**	**Sunday**
Initial prayers	Initial prayers	Initial prayers
Ps 50	Ps 50	Ps 50
Kathisma 17	Kathisma 9	Canon to the Holy Trinity from the Octoechos
Nicene Creed	Nicene Creed	Troparia by St Gregory of Sinai
Trisagion . . . Lord's Prayer	Trisagion . . . Lord's Prayer	Trisagion . . . Lord's Prayer
Troparia ["Behold the Bridegroom"]	Troparia ["O uncreated nature"]	Hypakoe in tone of the Octoechos
Kyrie eleison (40 times)	*Kyrie eleison* (40 times)	*Kyrie eleison* (40 times)
Prayer of the Hours	Prayer of the Hours	

[1]See M. Arranz, "L'office divin," *DS* 11 (Paris, 1982), cols. 707–20.

Kyrie eleison (3 times)	Kyrie eleison (3 times)	Kyrie eleison (3 times)
Glory . . . now and ever . . .	Glory . . . now and ever . . .	Glory . . . now and ever . . .
More honorable . . .	More honorable . . .	More honorable . . .
In the name of the Lord . . .	In the name of the Lord . . .	In the name of the Lord . . .
Priest: Master, God, Father all-powerful . . .	Priest: Master, God, Father all-powerful . . .	Prayer of Mark the Monk to the Holy Trinity
2 prayers of St Basil		
Prayer of St Eustratios	Prayer of St Eustratios	
Pss 120 and 133	Pss 120 and 133	
Troparia ("Remember, O Lord")	Troparia ("Remember, O Lord")	
Prayer for the dead ("Remember, O Lord")	Prayer for the dead ("Remember, O Lord")	
Dismissal and mutual forgiveness	Dismissal and mutual forgiveness	Dismissal and mutual forgiveness
Litany	Litany	Litany

The midnight office or mesonyktikon is the first office in the Horologion, and it is celebrated in the middle of the night, before daybreak. According to E. Diakovskii, the mesonyktikon is a nocturnal office that developed in connection with the "canon of psalmody" (κανὼν τῆς ψαλμωδίας) initially as an appendix to the nocturnal psalmody of twelve psalms from the Egyptian monastic tradition described by St John Cassian.[2]

In the Studite tradition, the mesonyktikon is not a communal office, but a rule of nocturnal prayer in one's cell. The Typikon of Alexios the Studite mentions the mesonyktikon explicitly only during Lent, when each monk is expected to read a small office in his cell consisting essentially of kathisma 17.[3] This explains why the Horologia of Studite redaction begin with the office of matins.[4]

[2]E. Diakovskii, "Posledovanie nochnykh chasov," *TKDA* 7–8 (1909): 585–86. On the Egyptian monastic tradition, see John Cassian, *Institutions cénobitiques*, Book 2, 4–6 (SC 109, trans. J.-C. Guy [Paris, 1965], 64–71). On the mesonyktikon, see also I. Fundulis, "Polunoshchnitsa," *Vechnoe* 325 (1975): 9–12.

[3]Pentkovskii, *Tipikon*, 413. M. Skaballanovich is wrong when he claims that the Typikon of Alexios the Studite calls for the use of kathisma 17 at compline. This particular form of compline during Great Lent is distinct from the mesonyktikon mentioned later in the Typikon of Alexios the Studite. See Skaballanovich, *Tolkovyi Tipikon* 1, 431.

[4]E.E. Sliva, "O nekotorykh tserkovnoslavianskikh Chasoslovakh XIII–XIV vv. (Osobennosti sostava)," in *Rus' i iuzhnye slaviane*, ed. V.M. Zagrebin (St Petersburg, 1998), 188–89.

The Sabaite Horologion, on the other hand, has a midnight office that is generally read in the church. In our day, three forms exist: the first for weekdays (from Monday to Friday), the second for Saturdays, and the third for Sundays. The two first types consist of two parts, each consisting of psalms, troparia, and prayers. In the first part of this office, on weekdays, kathisma 17 is read, while on Saturday kathisma 9 is used.

The ancestor of these distinct forms of the midnight office can be found in *Horologion Sinai 865*, dating to the twelfth century.[5] This manuscript has only two forms of the mesonyktikon: one on weekdays with kathisma 17, and the second for Saturdays and Sundays with kathisma 9. The presence of kathisma 17 (Ps 118) in this office can easily be explained by verse 62 of this psalm: "At midnight (μεσονύκτικτον) I rise to praise you." With this verse comes the name of the office. These two primitive forms have an identical structure consisting of four sections, each composed of three troparia and a prayer.

The Sunday midnight office appears only later, beginning in the fifteenth century. It preserved only Psalm 50 from the other forms, and it consists essentially of the Canon to the Holy and Lifegiving Trinity, in the tone of the Octoechos, attributed to Mitrophanes of Smyrna (9th century), of troparia by St Gregory of Sinai (14th century), and of a prayer to the Holy Trinity ascribed to Mark the Monk (5th century). Canons to the Holy Trinity began to appear in manuscripts of the Octoechos beginning in the thirteenth century, but their use does not seem to become common until the fifteenth century. Greek typika of Jerusalem provenance do not mention the Sunday mesonyktikon, no doubt because the celebration of the vigil had led to its elimination.[6]

For the weekday office, contemporary editions of the Horologion usually prescribe the reading of the first prayer of St Basil beginning on September 22 (the day after the *apodosis* of the Elevation of the Cross) until Palm Sunday. In the Slavic Horologia, this rubric applies to both prayers of St Basil. Certain Horologia indicate that the priest reads the prayer with uplifted hands, but in modern Athonite practice both prayers are recited by the reader.

All three variants of this office conclude with a litany and a rite of mutual forgiveness, both of which are also found in the office of compline at the end

---

[5]Skaballanovich, *Tolkovyi Tipikon* 1, 432; see Pentkovskii, *Tipikon*, 403–04, 239, 282.
[6]Skaballanovich, *Tolkovyi Tipikon* 1, 434.

of the day. In this way, monastics begin and end their day by seeking mutual pardon, just as in the ancient monastic practice in Egypt and Palestine.[7]

Daily Matins

Schema of Daily Matins

1. Royal office
2. Hexapsalmos (Pss 3, 37, 62, 87, 102, and 142)
3. Great synapte
4. "God is the Lord" + apolytikion troparion and theotokion
5. Psalmody (kathismata) + kathisma troparion
6. Ps 50
7. Canons
8. Lauds (Pss 148–150)
9. Doxology
10. Synapte with demands
11. Aposticha
12. "It is good to confess the Lord . . . Trisagion – Lord's Prayer
13. Apolytikion troparion and theotokion
14. Ektene
15. First Hour (Prime)

The office of matins (*orthros* = "of the dawn")[8] begins by what is today called the "royal office." It contains Psalms 19 and 20. This short office was grafted onto matins in the fourteenth century. In the Studite tradition, matins customarily began with Psalm 6.[9] So also, according to the ancient Sabaite typika, matins began directly with the initial blessing by the priest and the hexapsalmos.[10] The royal office which today begins matins is thus a late addition which is, in fact, an intercessory office originally intended

[7]See for example Dorotheos of Gaza, *Instructions diverses*, 26 (SC 92, trans. And ed. L. Regnault and J. de Préville [Paris, 2001²], 186–87).

[8]On matins, see I. Fundulis, "Utrenia," *Vechnoe* 326 (1975): 14–19; 327 (1975): 13–18; 328 (1975): 11–14; 329 (1975): 9–21; 330 (1975): 10–16.

[9]A. Dmitrievskii, "Bogosluzhenie v Russkoi Tserkvi v pervye piat' vekov," *PS* 9 (1882): 363; Mansvetov, *Mitropolit Kiprian*, 99.

[10]See for example *Sinai gr. 1094*, f. 3v.–4, edited by Lossky, *Le Typikon byzantin*, 142–43.

for monasteries of imperial foundation. It was later used also to pray for the founders of a church or a monastery.[11] The Typikon of Alexios the Studite prescribed a similar office for each evening, after compline, in the narthex of the Church of St Panteleimon, which contained the tomb of Patriarch Alexios. This office, consisting of three psalms, also began with Psalm 19.[12] In certain monasteries, such as Vatopedi on Mt Athos, the custom has been kept of celebrating a short office of intercession at the tomb of its founders after vespers. To my knowledge, the foundational typikon of the Monastery of the Mother of God *Eleousa*, founded in 1080 by Manuel of Stoumitza (in south-west Macedonia), is the first document to mention a "trisagion for the emperor," with troparia and an ektene by the priest, to be celebrated after the midnight office and just before the opening blessing of matins.[13] We thus see here the origin of this small preamble to matins, during which we pray by name for the rulers in the short litany that follows the psalms and the troparia ("O Lord, save your people"). The choice of the psalms can therefore be explained by the following verses: "O Lord, preserve the king" (Ps 19.10); "In your strength the king rejoices" (Ps 20.2); "For the king trusts in the Lord" (Ps 20.8). This addition to the beginning of matins became common in the fourteenth century, spreading from monasteries of imperial foundation, like the Great Lavra on Mt Athos, during the liturgical reforms brought about by the Hesychasts.

After the opening blessing by the priest, "Glory to the holy, consubstantial, lifegiving, and undivided Trinity . . . ," comes the reading of the hexapsalmos, a highly ancient element from the Palestinian Horologion, and one which was already adopted by the Studites. It consists of Psalms 3, 37, 62, 87, 102, and 142. M. Arranz links the origin of these six psalms to one half of the Rule of the Angel, consisting of 12 psalms, mentioned by St John Cassian.[14] M. Skaballanovich, for his part, traces the origin of the hexapsalmos to the twelve matins psalms mentioned in the Rule of St Benedict.[15] In any case, the hexapsalmos is already cited in the account of John and

[11]M. Arranz, *Oko Tserkovnoe—Istoriia Tipikona* (Rome, 1998), 63; J. Matéos, "Quelques problèmes de l'orthros byzantin," *POC* 11 (1961): 201.

[12]Pentkovskii, *Tipikon*, 414; Mansvetov, *Mitropolit Kiprian*, 98.

[13]See the Rule of Nilus, Bishop of Tamasia, for the Monastery of the Mother of God in Machairas, Cyprus (1210), in *Byzantine Monastic Foundation Documents*, eds. J. Thomas and A.C. Hero (Dumbarton Oaks Studies 35), vol. 3 (Washington, DC, 2000), 1136–37.

[14]Jean Cassien, *Institutions cénobitiques*, Book 2, 4 (SC 109, trans. J.-C. Guy [Paris, 1965], 64–65); M. Arranz, *Oko Tserkovnoe—Istoriia Tipikona* (Rome, 1998), 38.

[15]Skaballanovich, *Tolkovyi Tipikon* 2, 200–01.

Sophronios, which describes the celebration of the vigil in Sinai during the
seventh century.[16]

Rubrics in the Typikon specify that the assigned brother (in current
monastic practice, always the superior or a dignitary, just as for Ps 103 at
vespers) is to read the hexapsalmos in a low voice, with the fear of God and
attention. Just before the description of the ordo of matins, another rubric
specifies even more precisely how it is to be read and how the assembly is to
behave during its recitation:

> At matins, the assigned brother chants the hexapsalmos softly, with qui-
> etude and attention. So also all stand as though they were in the presence
> of God himself and praying because of their sins. The brother must chant
> in a simple and humble voice, in such a way as to be heard by all. No one
> may sneeze or spit or leave his place or move or enter from the exterior
> narthex of the church while the hexapsalmos is being recited, for that
> is a sign of the absence of fear, and of disorder. If someone is bent over
> because of old age or ravaged by sickness and cannot avoid doing what
> we have just described, let him stay outside the church until the end of
> the hexapsalmos, and then enter the church while "God is the Lord" or
> "Alleluia" is slowly sung.

This rubric appears in all the ancient Sabaite typika.[17]

The description of the same office for the first week of Great Lent underlines once more the particular attention due to the hexapsalmos:

> The designated brother begins to read the psalms with attention and fear
> of God, as if he invisibly addressed Him Himself, and prayed for our sins.
> All remain standing. We should not murmur at this point, but listen
> attentively to the psalms that are being read."

We find a similar rubric in the most ancient Sabaite typika, such as *Sinai gr.
1094*.[18] We should note that the hexapsalmos was originally chanted by the

---

[16]M. Arranz, *Oko Tserkovnoe—Istoriia Tipikona* (Rome, 1998), 57.

[17]For example, in *Sinai gr. 1094*, f. 3v.–4r., 71r. (Lossky, *Le Typikon byzantin*, 142 and
244 = Dmitrievskii, *Opisanie*, vol. 3, Τυπικά, h. 2, p. 8). See also *Sinai gr. 1096*, f. 157v. This
last reference was given to me by A. Lossky, who himself examined a microfilm of this
manuscript.

[18]"εἶτα τὸ ἑξάψαλμον μετὰ πάσης προσοχῆς καὶ φόβου θεοῦ, ὡς αὐτῷ συλλαλοῦντες
ἀοράτως καὶ δυσωποῦντες αὐτὸν ὑπὲρ τῶν ἁμαρτιῶν ἡμῶν." *Sinai gr. 1094*, f. 71. See Lossky,
Le Typikon byzantin, 244.

entire community, just like Psalm 103 at vespers. According to one tradition, the Second Coming of Christ will occur during the hexapsalmos.

Thus the chanting of the matins hexapsalmos is distinguished from all other psalmody, for which no such great attention or immobility is prescribed, and during which it is generally permitted to sit. M. Arranz therefore is led to think that the hexapsalmos, as part of the Rule of the Angel,

> is not strictly speaking part of the psalmody of matins. It can be considered as an introduction to orthros. It finds its parallel in the hexapsalmos of Great Compline. [. . .] The hexapsalmos of orthros is possibly one half of this office already known by John Cassian; the other half would be that of the apodeipnon.[19]

After the first three psalms, the typika indicate that the sacristan (*kandelanaptis* or parecclesiarch) lights a candle which he affixes to the holy doors, so that the priest may come there to read the morning prayers. We note that it is not possible to read all the twelve prayers during the second half of the hexapsalmos; thus in practice the priest usually reads the first six prayers inside the sanctuary in front of the altar table, and after "Glory to the Father" he goes out through the north door to read the second six prayers in front of the holy doors. In Greek usage, the priest reads these prayers in front of the icon of Christ. These morning prayers derive from the ancient sung office and were originally destined to accompany the various antiphons and liturgical actions, and to conclude the diaconal litanies, as is still the case today with the presbyteral prayers of the eucharistic liturgy and other sacraments. M. Arranz has studied these prayers in detail and has clearly demonstrated their connection to the sung office.[20]

It is to Patriarch Philotheos of Constantinople (14th century) that we attribute this synthesis of two offices. The first reform occurred when the Studites adopted the Palestinian Horologion. But at that time, the presbyteral prayers of the sung office were distributed throughout the office. Dmitrievskii was one of the first to note that these prayers corresponded, on the one hand, by their content to various moments during matins (for example, the Great Synapte, Ps 50, lauds, etc.), and on the other hand, through their

---

[19]M. Arranz, "Les prières presbytérales des matines byzantines," *OCP* 38 (1972): 91, note 1.

[20]See M. Arranz, "Les prières presbytérales des matines byzantines," *OCP* 37 (1971): 406–36, and 38 (1972): 64–114; "L'office de l'asmatikos orthros (matines chantées) de l'ancien Eucologue byzantin," *OCP* 47 (1981): 122–57.

ekphoneses, to the ekphoneses of the various litanies of the matins office.[21] Thus these prayers originally had titles: "Prayer at the Reading of the Gospel," Prayer at Psalm 50," "Prayer at the Lauds," "Prayer at the Doxology," all of which gradually disappeared once their reading was fixed to during the hexapsalmos by the *Diataxis* of Patriarch Philotheos in the fourteenth century.[22] As Arranz explains:

> This dominance of the Typikon of Stoudion was erased by a new Sabaite wave which, without breaking totally with the innovations of the monks of the Polis [Constantinople], nevertheless pushed the monks to return to the more austere sources of the rural or desert monasteries. Paradoxically, it is this second-wave Sabaite office that was to replace the Studite office, as well as the ancient *asmatikos akolouthia*, i.e., the office of the secular churches.[23]

In this way, the reform that resulted from the spread of the Sabaite Typikon in the fourteenth century led to the disappearance of these presbyteral prayers from various places within the office and their gathering into a block destined to be read silently by the priest while the gathered assembly listens to the hexapsalmos. The reason for this may have been a certain "fidelity" to the Palestinian office, which did not originally have these prayers. Nonetheless, this reform may appear somewhat paradoxical, because it leads to the priest's going out before the holy doors to perform a liturgical action at a moment when all are instructed to stand immobile and attentive to the rule of prayer represented by the reading of the six psalms. Concerning this problem, A. Dmitrievskii openly considered this arrangement of the prayers to be incorrect.[24] M. Arranz suggests that this reform brought about by the *Diataxis* of Patriarch Philotheos did

> nothing but canonize a situation that had its origins already several centuries earlier: at the moment when one began to celebrate the Palestinian monastic office while keeping the ancient Euchologion of Constantinople. [. . .] And it was the authority of this Euchologion that thus guaranteed the survival of these prayers from vespers and matins in a *frozen* state."[25]

[21] A. Dmitrievskii, "Utrenniia molitvy," *RukSP* 42 (1886): 186–92.

[22] Ibid., 182–83; Skaballanovich, *Tolovyi Tipikon*, 205–08.

[23] See M. Arranz, "Les prières presbytérales des matines byzantines," *OCP* 38 (1972): 85.

[24] A. Dmitrievskii, "Utrenniia molitvy," *RukSP* 42 (1886): 186.

[25] Arranz, "Les prières presbytérales des matines byzantines," *OCP* 38 (1972): 80.

Finally, M. Skaballanovich offered the hypothesis that the reading of the presbyteral prayers was assigned during the second half of the hexapsalmos so that the priest himself could at least also listen to one half of the hexapsalmos.[26]

Following the hexapsalmos, during which the priest silently reads the morning prayers, comes the great synapte, which does not appear in the Horologia, but only in the Hieratikon. This litany is recited by the deacon, who stands in front of the holy doors. If there is no deacon, the priest recites it. On ordinary days, in Greek practice, the priest recites the litany in front of the holy doors; but on those days when the gospel is read at orthros, he recites it from inside the sanctuary, in front of the altar table. Then comes the chanting by the canonarch (or the deacon, in Russian practice) of psalm verses with a refrain taken up by the choir. This is the chant "God is the Lord" (Ps 117. 27, 26) which was formerly used only at festal matins, i.e., when the Menaion prescribed a troparion—on other days, "Alleluia" was sung. The development of the annual cycle and of the Menaia led to a reduction in the number of offices using the "Alleluia" (which is used today only on weekdays during Lent and in the funeral service).

The psalm verses of "God is the Lord" and the "Alleluia" are proclaimed by the canonarch, and the choir takes up the refrain: "God is the Lord" or "Alleluia." J. Matéos compares this way of performance with the great prokeimena on the evening of great feasts and on Sundays during Lent.[27] The choir then sings the apolytikion troparion from the Menaion and the theotokion (see the fourth appendix to the Menaion).

Then follows the psalmody (see the table showing the arrangement of the Psalter). After each section of psalmody (kathisma), are sung hymns called "kathismata" or "kathisma troparia," which are found in the Octoechos.

After the psalmody, a reader (the monastic superior in Greek practice) reads Psalm 50, and then the canons are sung. This marks the original beginning of the office of matins, as all the preceding psalmody is in fact the vestige of the nocturnal psalmody of the ancient mesonyktikon (midnight office).[28]

In our day, canons consist of nine odes, but the second is always absent, except during Great Lent. This structure is based on the nine biblical canticles which were once chanted at matins, and which in our time are only

---

[26]Skaballanovich, *Tolovyi Tipikon* 2, 208.
[27]J. Matéos, "Quelques problèmes de l'orthros byzantin," *POC* 11 (1961): 203.
[28]Ibid., 22–24.

chanted during Great Lent. In contemporary practice, during ordinary time, a sufficient number of verses from the biblical ode are chanted before each troparion of the canon to reach the number of fourteen troparia per ode—thus: the hirmos (usually two times), followed by ten verses from the ode preceding each troparion, "Glory to the Father . . . ," troparion, "Now and ever . . . ," theotokion, then the *katabasia,* if one is appointed.

The nine biblical canticles that provide the structure of the canon at matins and which are part of the Palestinian Psalter are: 1) the Canticle of Moses (Ex 15.1–19; 2) the Canticle of Moses (Deut 32.1–43); 3) the Prayer of Hannah (1 Kgs [1 Samuel] 2.1–10); 4) the Prayer of Habakkuk (Hab 3.1–19); 5) the Prayer of Isaiah (Is 26.9–20); 6) the Prayer of Jonah (Jonah 2.3–10); 7) the Prayer of the Three Youths (Dan 3.26–56); 8) the Canticle of the Three Youths (Dan 3.57–88); and 9) the Magnificat and the Benedictus (Lk 1. 46–55, 68–79).

At the daily office, three canons are generally sung (two from the Octoechos and one from the Menaion; if the Menaion has two canons, then one is done from the Octoechos, and two from the Menaion). Each ode begins with the hirmos of the first canon, a hymn that makes the link between the hymnography and the biblical text. Then the troparia of the first, second, and third canons are read, after which the next ode begins. In the practice of the majority of Athonite monasteries (except those that follow the Typikon strictly), only the first, third, and ninth odes are sung; the others are read.

After the third, sixth, eighth, and ninth odes, the hirmos of the third canon is sung as the katabasia. After the third, sixth, and ninth odes, the deacon recites a small synapte, after which the choir chants the appointed hymns. After the eighth ode, the Magnificat (Lk 1.46–55) is sung with the refrain "More honorable than the Cherubim . . ." (which is the hirmos of the ninth ode of the canon on Holy Saturday). This is the only biblical canticle sung daily during the office of matins in contemporary Russian parish practice. We can summarize the structure of the canon in the following schema:

Ode 1	
Canon 1 Hirmos + troparia	[Octoechos]
Canon 2 troparia	[Octoechos or Menaion]
Canon 3 troparia	[Menaion]

Ode 3

Canon 1 Hirmos + troparia	[Octoechos]
Canon 2 troparia	[Octoechos or Menaion]
Canon 3 troparia (katabasia)	[Menaion]

Small synapte [second kontakion, if two are prescribed].
Kathisma troparia from the Menaion.

Ode 4

Canon 1 Hirmos + troparia	[Octoechos]
Canon 2 troparia	[Octoechos or Menaion]
Canon 3 troparia	[Menaion]

Ode 5

Canon 1 Hirmos + troparia	[Octoechos]
Canon 2 troparia	[Octoechos or Menaion]
Canon 3 troparia	[Menaion]

Ode 6

Canon 1 Hirmos + troparia	[Octoechos]
Canon 2 troparia	[Octoechos or Menaion]
Canon 3 troparia (katabasia)	[Menaion]

Small synapte. Kontakion [and ikos] from the Menaion

Ode 7

Canon 1 Hirmos + troparia	[Octoechos]
Canon 2 troparia	[Octoechos or Menaion]
Canon 3 troparia	[Menaion]

Ode 8

Canon 1 Hirmos + troparia	[Octoechos]
Canon 2 troparia	[Octoechos or Menaion]
Canon 3 troparia (katabasia)[28]	[Menaion]

Magnificat

Ode 9	
Canon 1 Hirmos + troparia	[Octoechos]
Canon 2 troparia	[Octoechos or Menaion]
Canon 3 troparia (katabasia)	[Menaion]
Small synapte. Photagogikon or exaposteilarion from the Octoechos and the Menaion.	

While it is customary on ordinary days to sing the hirmos of the third canon as the katabasia after the third, sixth, eighth, and ninth odes, the singing of katabasiai on Sundays and feast days is different. It depends on the period in the liturgical year. On those days, a katabasia is sung after each ode, as indicated in the following table:

The singing of katabasia on Sundays and feast days

1. From Sep 1 to Sep 21: Hirmoi of the Canon of the Exaltation of the Cross (tone 8).
2. From Sep 22 to Nov 20: Hirmoi of the Canon to the Mother of God (tone 4) ["I shall open my mouth"].
3. From Nov 21 to Dec 31: Hirmoi of the Canon of Christmas (tone 1).
4. From Jan 1–14: Hirmoi of the Canon of Theophany (tone 2).
5. From Jan 15 to the leavetaking of the Feast of the Presentation of Christ (Hypapante): Hirmoi of the Canon of the Presentation (tone 3).
6. From the leavetaking of Hypapante to July 31: Hirmoi of the Canon to the Mother of God (tone 4) ["My mouth will open"], except during the period covered by the Triodion and Pentecostarion, when katabasiai prescribed by these books are used.
7. From Aug 1–6: Hirmoi of the Canon of the Exaltation of the Cross (tone 8).
8. From Aug 7–13: Hirmoi of the Canon of the Transfiguration (tone 4).
9. From Aug 13–23: Hirmoi of the Canon of the Dormition (tone 1).
10. From Aug 24–31: Hirmoi of the Canon of the Exaltation of the Cross (tone 8).

[29]N.B.: the katabasia of the eighth ode is always preceded by the final verse of the eight biblical canticle: "We praise, bless and worship the Lord, singing and exalting him through all ages." So also at the eight ode, instead of "Glory to the Father . . . ," we say: "Let us bless the Father, the Son, and the Holy Spirit, now and ever . . . ."

Following the canon, on non-festal days, the lauds and doxology are read. It is important to know that the Horologion has two different texts of lauds and the doxology:

Non-festal office	Festal office
Palestinian redaction	Constantinopolitan redaction
Lauds read:	Lauds sung:
	Let every breath praise the Lord. (Ps 150.5)
Praise the Lord from the heavens. (Ps 148.1)	Praise the Lord from the heavens. (Ps 148.1)
Refrain (R): *To you, O God, belongs praise.*	Refrain (R): *To you, O God, belongs praise.*
Praise the Lord from the heavens, Praise him in the highest. (Ps 148.1)	Praise the Lord from the heavens, Praise him in the highest. (Ps 148.1)
R: *To you, O God, belongs praise.*	R: *To you, O God, belongs praise.*
Praise him all his angels. Praise him all his hosts. (Ps 148.2)	Praise him all his angels. Praise him all his hosts. (Ps 148.2)
R: *To you, O God, belongs praise.*	R: *To you, O God, belongs praise.*
Praise him sun and moon, etc. (Pss 148, 149, and 150)	Praise him sun and moon, etc. (Pss 148, 149, and 150)
	To the last verses of Ps 150, stichera of lauds are added.
To you belongs glory, O Lord our God . . .	
Glory to you, who have shown us the light . . .	Glory to you, who have shown us the light . . .
Doxology read:	Great Doxology sung:
Glory to God in the highest . . .	Glory to God in the highest . . .
Every day I will bless you . . .	Every day I will bless you . . .
	Vouchsafe, O Lord
O Lord, you are our refuge from generation to generation . . .	O Lord, you are our refuge from generation to generation . . .
Vouchsafe, O Lord	
	Trisagion

Note here that the singing of the Great Doxology,[30] in its Constantinopolitan redaction, is preceded by a more festive form of the lauds, which are then sung in the tone of the first sticheron. The lauds begin with the final verse of Psalm 150: "Let every breath praise the Lord" (Ps 150.5), after which we sing the first part of the first verse of Psalm 148 with the non-psalmic refrain: "To you, O God, belongs praise." This structure with a refrain to open lauds recalls the performance of antiphons in the sung office with their refrains,[31] particularly of the lauds in asmatic matins.[32] Moreover, in this office of the Great Church, the lauds preceded the reading of the gospel. M. Arranz notes in this regard that the final verse of Psalm 150, which serves as the refrain for lauds in the sung office, led to the formation of a doublet in the form of a fixed prokeimenon consisting of verses 6 and 1 of Psalm 50 and situated just before the matins gospel—when the reading of this gospel was placed just before Psalm 50 in matins of the Sabaite office.[33] In addition, the introductory verse to the doxology, "Glory to you, who have shown us the light," was also originally a refrain for lauds in the sung office.[34] The synthesis of Palestinian and Constantinopolitan usages is anterior to the fourteenth century. The most ancient version of the Sabaite Typikon, *Sinai gr. 1094* (12th–13th century) already mentions this festive and sung structure of the lauds, indicated by the expression "πᾶσα πνοή."[35] Let us note that the absence of troparia for "πᾶσα πνοή" in the monastic office was questioned in the seventh century in the *Account of John and Sophronios*.[36]

However, with the diffusion of the neo-Sabaite Typikon at the end of the fourteenth century, the Constantinopolitan redaction of the Great Doxology, preceded by lauds performed in the style of the sung office, became the rule for festal days and replaced the Jerusalem redaction of this doxology and the reading of the lauds, a practice that was then kept only on non-festal days.

[30]On the text of the Great Doxology, see A. Gastoué, "La grande doxologie. Étude critique," *Revue de l'Orient chrétien* 4 (1989): 280–90.

[31]Lisitsyn, *Pervonachal'nyi Slaviano-Russkii Tipikon*, 85.

[32]N.D. Uspenskii, "Chin vsenoshchnogo bdeniia na Pravoslavnom Vostoke i v Russkoi Tserkvi," *BT* 19 (1978): 43.

[33]M. Arranz, "Les prières presbytérales des matines byzantines," *OCP* 38 (1972): 90, note 2.

[34]D. Balfour, "La réforme de l'Horologion," *Irénikon* 7 (1930): 175.

[35]*Sinai gr. 1094*, f. 18v., 35r., 56r., 64r., 65v., 84r. [edited by Lossky, *Le Typikon byzantin*, 165, 189, 221, 233, 236, 260].

[36]Jean et Sophrone, *Narration* II, 40, p. 253.

On ordinary days, after the doxology, the priest recites the synapte with demands (for a deacon does not customarily serve at non-festal matins). Then is said the psalmic prayer, "It is good to give thanks to the Lord" (Ps 91.2–3). The trisagion prayers are then added: "Holy God, Holy Mighty, Holy Immortal . . . ," "Glory . . . now and ever . . . ," "Most Holy Trinity . . . ," "*Kyrie eleison*," "Glory . . . now and ever . . . ," "Our Father . . . ." Then the apolytikion troparion is sung, which is found in the Menaion (at the conclusion of vespers) with the appropriate theotokion (see the fourth appendix to the Menaia).

The priest then recites the ektene (or "augmented litany"), and the first part of the dismissal:

Priest: Wisdom!

Choir: Master, bless!

Priest: He is blessed, He who is, Christ our God, always, now and ever, and unto ages of ages.

Choir: Confirm, O God, the holy Orthodox faith and Orthodox Christians, unto ages of ages.

The reader then begins reading the first hour, starting directly with "O come let us worship . . . ." It is only at the end of the first hour that the priest will say: "Glory to you, O Christ our God and our hope, glory to you!" The choir: "Glory . . . now and ever . . . *Kyrie eleison* (3 times), Master bless!" And the priest once again: "May Christ our true God, through the prayers . . . ."

To summarize, we can say that there are five types of matins services, which we will examine later in detail:

1) Matins with "Alleluia" (celebrated today essentially on weekdays during Great Lent);

2) Matins for the deceased with "Alleluia" (celebrated on those days when we commemorate the dead);

3) Daily matins with "God is the Lord," the doxology read in its Hagiopolite form, aposticha, and eventually stichera at lauds;

4) Matins with the Great Doxology, "God is the Lord," with both the lauds and Great Doxology sung, but no gospel reading;

5) Festal matins (when there was an entrance at vespers), with "God is the Lord," the *polyeleos*, a gospel reading, sung lauds and Great Doxology (this is done on Sundays and at vigils).

The Hours

Schema of the Hours

---

1. Initial prayers [if the hour is read apart from another office]
2. O come, let us worship . . .
3. Three psalms
4. Troparion [or troparia]
5. Theotokion for the hour
6. Psalm prayer
7. Trisagion . . . Our Father
8. Kontakion
9. *Kyrie eleison* (40 times)
10. You who at all times and at every hour . . .
11. *Kyrie eleison* (3 times). Glory . . . now and ever . . . More honorable than the Cherubim . . . In the name of the Lord, bless father!
12. Prayer

The term "hour" is used in the Horologion to designate any office prescribed to be celebrated at a specific hour of the day or night.[37] In our day, the term is used for four offices: prime, terce, sext, and none. In addition to these, the Great Horologion also contains four so-called "intermediary" hours. There is also a short office called the "typika."

Each hour consists of three psalms. The selection of many of these psalms is already attested to in the ancient Horologion *Sinai gr. 863*. This manuscript, however, contained six to eight psalms per office. In our case, the three-psalm structure is a particularity of the Palestinian monastic office.[38] John Cassian

[37]E. Diakovskii, "Posledovanie nochnykh chasov," *TDKA* 7–8 (1909): 546. See also R. Taft, *The Liturgy of the Hours in East and West* (Collegeville: Liturgical Press, 1986); N. Egender, "La prière des Heures," in *La Prière des Églises de rite byzantin*, vol. 1 (Chevetogne, 1975); Mgr Cassien and B. Botte, *La Prière des Heures*, LO 35 (Paris, 1963); I. Fundulis, "Chasy," *Vechnoe* 331 (1976): 6–12.
[38]E. Diakovskii, "Posledovanie nochnykh chasov," *TDKA* 7–8 (1909): 551.

witnesses to the celebration of hours containing three psalms at monasteries in Palestine and Mesopotamia.[39] According to him, this practice was an attenuation of "the perfection and rigorous and inimitable discipline of the Egyptians."[40] Indeed, Cassian affirms the Egyptian origin of the rule of twelve psalms, or "the Rule of the Angel." He says that there in Egypt,

> Some even thought that in the daily office of prayers—that is, terce, sext, and none—it was necessary to harmonize the number of psalms and of prayers with the number of the hours at which these homages are rendered to God [i.e., three psalms and prayers at terce, six at terce, nine at none]. For others, it pleased them to apply the amount of six to each assembly during the day.[41]

The three-psalm structure thus reflects Palestinian practice. Troparia for the day (from the Menologion) follow the psalms on those days when "God is the Lord" is sung at matins, or the troparion of the hour accompanied by psalm verses on those days when "Alleluia" is used. After this, each hour has a theotokion. This is followed by a short psalmic prayer consisting of verses from psalms or biblical canticles, and the trisagion prayers. After the Lord's Prayer comes the kontakion for the day (from the Menologion) or kontakia for the hour, then *Kyrie eleison* (40 times), the prayer of the hours ("You, who at all times and at every hour . . ."), and each hour concludes with a prayer specific to it.

In addition to these four offices, there exist intermediary hours (μεσώριον; *mezhdochasie*). As M. Skaballanovich explains, these are characteristic of the Jerusalem ordo. These are already attested in the twelfth century in the Typikon of Chio-Mgvin (1172), and one finds them in Horologia from Sinai in the twelfth and thirteenth centuries.[42] Diakovskii explains that this comes from a desire to make the number of offices correspond to the twenty-four hours of the day.[43] According to him, the rule of twelve psalms, or the "Rule of the Angel," originating from the Pachomian monasticism in Egypt, as John Cassian tells us,[44] led to the development of a rule of twelve

---

[39]Jean Cassien, *Institutions cénobitiques*, Book III, 3, 1, J.-C. Guy, tr., SC 109, (Paris, 1965), 94–95.

[40]Ibid., Book III, 1 (pp. 92–93).

[41]Ibid., Book II, 2, 2 (pp. 58–61).

[42]Skaballanovich, *Tolkovyi Tipikon* 1, 422–23.

[43]E. Diakovskii, "Posledovanie nochnykh chasov," *TDKA* 7–8 (1909): 551.

[44]Jean Cassien, *Institutions cénobitiques* Book II, 4–6 (SC 109, pp. 64–71).

psalms recited not only at night, but also by day. Thus the monks followed a rule of twenty-four psalms for the twenty-four hours of the day. This phenomenon lies at the origin of the practice observed, among others by the "Non-Sleeper" monks in Constantinople. In an attempt to synthesize the Egyptian monastic tradition with the Palestinian, the rule of twelve psalms by day came to be added to the four daily, three-psalm offices. Because of the impossibility of simultaneously fulfilling both the daily offices and the rule of twelve psalms, the latter rule was divided into four short, three-psalm offices that were to be read by each monk in his cell, thus creating a parallel structure, called "intermediary hours," to the four offices of the hours that were read in church.[45] The study of E. Diakovskii has amply demonstrated the diversity among the ancient manuscript horologia in the choice of psalms used at these intermediary hours. This can be explained by the fact that there were different rules of psalmody for day and night.[46]

The intermediary hours follow a three-psalm model in which the choice of psalms is exactly as it appears in the Horologion *Sinai gr. 865* from the twelfth century.[47] The psalmody is followed by troparia specific to each intermediary hour. After these, *Kyrie eleison* is recited. In Studite practice, "*Kyrie eleison*" was said thirty times at the end of each hour. With the introduction of the Sabaite Typikon, the number rose to forty. Each intermediary hour concludes with a prayer specific to it.

The Typikon suppresses the intermediary hours during the festal periods of the year. This suppression lightens the rhythm of the liturgical offices and gives the monks a certain amount of rest during these festal seasons. We find such an attenuation in the period from Christmas until the end of Epiphany, during Bright Week, and during the week of Pentecost. However, these intermediary hours are no longer celebrated today. Some Athonite typika recommend their use only during the Nativity Fast, when the saint of the day has no doxastikon, and when Alleluia is sung at matins, but this rule rarely applies.

As for the office of typika, it is an ancient communion office originally used by Palestinian anchorites, as attested in *Sinai gr. 863*, a ninth-century manuscript Horologion.[48] In our days, this office is generally omitted,

---

[45]Diakovskii, "Posledovanie nochnykh chasov," *TDKA* 7–8 (1909): 560–61, 578–79. Ibid., 561–67.

[46]Ibid., 561–67.

[47]Ibid., 565–66.

[48]See J. Matéos, "Un horologion inédit de Saint-Sabas," *Studi e testi* 233 (Vatican, 1964), 54–55.

except during Great Lent and on non-liturgical days. On Mt Athos, however, it is read every day, removing those parts of it used in the celebration of the eucharistic liturgy. Indeed, certain parts of this monastic office came to be attached to the Divine Liturgy of the Constantinopolitan cathedral Euchologion, such as the psalms and Beatitudes which replaced the antiphons of the eucharistic liturgy (Pss 102 and 145), as well as the chant "Blessed be the name of the Lord" (Ps 112.2) and Psalm 33 at the end of the liturgy. For, as J. Matéos recalls,

> According to the Evergetes Typikon, the monasteries that followed the Studite rule did not chant the typika at the liturgy, but after none, when the monks received the antidoron. This is an intermediary practice between the ancient communion office and the more recent office, which has lost all connection to the Eucharist.[49]

According to some fourteenth-century liturgical manuscripts, the service of the typika was chanted after the sixth hour on non-fasting days, and after the ninth hour on fast days. This represents an innovation with respect to the Studite tradition, in which the ninth hour always preceded the typika.[50]

Thus this typika office seems to come before the monks take their first meal of the day.[51] In the first case, Psalms 102 and 145 are sung, followed by the Beatitudes. When they are sung at the liturgy, the typika begin with the final words of the Beatitudes: "Remember us . . . ." followed by the troparia ("The heavenly choir . . .") and the Creed. Then the prayer of "absolution" ("Erase, remit, pardon" –ἄνες, ἄφες, συγχώρησον),[52] the Lord's Prayer, and the kontakion of the day. Then "*Kyrie eleison*" (12 times), the prayer to the Holy Trinity, "Blessed be the name of the Lord," Psalm 33, and the final dismissal.

---

[49]Ibid., 68. According to N. Uspenskii, the typika were celebrated at Evergetes only on those days when the eucharistic liturgy was not celebrated. See N. Uspenskii, "Liturgiia Prezhdeosviashchennykh Darov. Istoriko-liturgicheskii ocherk," *BT* 15 (1975): 154.

[50]E.E. Sliva, "O nekotorykh tserkovnoslavianskikh Chasoslovakh XIII–XIV vv. (Osobennosti sostava)," in *Rus' i iuzhnye slaviane*, ed. V.M. Zagrebin (St Petersburg, 1998), 188.

[51]Just as with the fasting practices observed by John Cassian among the Palestinian monks: Jean Cassien, *Conférences*, XXI, 11, SC 64 (Paris, 1959), 86.

[52]On this prayer and its connection with the typika, see A. Wade, "La prière ἄνες, ἄφες, συγχώρησον. La pratique palestinienne de demander l'absolution pour la communion solitaire et quotidienne. *Lex orandi* pour une orthopraxis perdue?," in θυσία αἰνέσεως. *Mélanges liturgiques offerts à la mémoire de l'archevêque Georges Wagner*, eds. J. Getcha and A. Lossky, *AS* 2 (Paris, 2005), 431–35.

During Great Lent, the order of the typika is as follows. After the ninth hour, the Beatitudes are sung. Then the troparia are read, the Creed, the prayer of absolution, the Lord's Prayer, and "*Kyrie eleison*" (40 times). After this, "More honorable than the Cherubim . . . ," accompanied by the exclamation of the priest, the prayer of St Ephrem with its prostrations, and then vespers.

Daily Vespers

Schema of Daily Vespers

---

1. Psalm 103
2. Great synapte
3. Psalmody (kathisma)
4. Small synapte
5. Lucernarium ("Lord, I call")
6. O Gladsome Light
7. Evening prokeimenon
8. Vouchsafe, O Lord
9. Synapte with demands
10. Aposticha
11. Canticle of Symeon
12. Apolytikion troparion and theotokion
13. Ektene
14. Dismissal

The liturgical day begins with vespers. The Church has inherited this arrangement of the hours of the day and night from antiquity, in which the night was considered as the first part of the day. We can already see this in Genesis, in which we read: "There was evening and there was morning, one day" (Gen 1.5). So also in the psalms: "Evening and morning and at noon I utter my complaint and moan, and he will hear my voice" (Ps 54.18).[53]

After the initial blessing ("Blessed is our God") and the verses ("Come, let us worship"), vespers begins with Psalm 103 in accordance with the Palestinian tradition. The psalm is usually read by the presider. Because by means

[53]I. Fundulis, "Utrenia," *Vechnoe* 334 (1976): 3.

of this psalm vespers begins the daily liturgical cycle, this psalm is some-times called the "preliminary psalm," or "psalm of introduction," or simply referred to as the "first psalm" (προοιμιακὸν ψαλμόν; *pervonachal'nyi psa-lom* or *pervyi psalom*). In the sung office of Constantinople, vespers began with Psalm 85. In the Palestinian monastic office, Psalm 85 is read at none.[54] In the sung office, Psalm 103 followed Psalm 85 at vespers on Sunday eve-ning.[55] We do not know precisely when this psalm entered into the ordo of Palestinian vespers. The *Account of John and Sophronios* does not mention it.[56] According to Mateos, the first allusion to it appears in the seventy-third of the *Great Catecheses* of Theodore the Studite (8th century).[57] It is, however, well-attested in the ninth-century Horologion, *Sinai gr. 863*. In the modern printed Horologia, verses 19, 20, and 24 of the psalm are repeated at the end. The ancient Horologion, *Sinai gr. 863*, however, does not indicate the repetition of these verses.[58]

During Psalm 103, the priest silently recites the presbyteral prayers taken from the Constantinopolitan Euchologion, a reform introduced in the four-teenth century through the *Diataxis* of Patriarch Philotheos.[59] These prayers were destined originally to accompany the various antiphons and liturgi-cal actions of sung vespers (*Typikon of the Great Church*), in which they typically concluded the diaconal litanies. Following upon A. Dmitrievskii, M. Arranz, who also studied the prayers of the lucernarium (εὐχὰς τοῦ λυχνικοῦ –*svetil'nichnyia molitvy*), has clearly demonstrated their connec-tion to the sung office.[60] These prayers from the sung office were first intro-duced into the Palestinian monastic office by the Studites; they were read at various moments during the celebration. Their number, however, var-ies from manuscript to manuscript in the ancient Studite liturgical sources from the fourteenth century.[61]

[54]O. Strunk, "The Byzantine Office at Hagia Sophia," *DOP* 9–10 (1955–1956): 184.

[55]M. Arranz, "L'office de l'Asmatikos Hesperinos," *OCP* 36 (1970): 261.

[56]Jean et Sophrone, *Narration* I, 5, p. 251.

[57]J. Matéos, "La synaxe monastique des vêpres byzantines," *OCP* 36 (1970): 261.

[58]See J. Matéos, "Un horologion inédit de Saint-Sabas," *Studi e testi* 233 (Vatican, 1964), 69.

[59]J. Goar, Ἐυχολόγιον *Sive Rituale Graecorum Complectens* (Paris, 1647), 2–3.

[60]See A. Dmitrievskii, "Vecherniia molitvy," *RukSP* 33 (1888): 494–507; 36 (1888): 20–32; M. Arranz, "Les prières sacerdotales des vêpres byzantines," *OCP* 37 (1971): 85–124; "L'Office de l'asmatikos hesperinos (vêpres chantées) de l'ancien Euchologue byzantin," *OCP* 44 (1978): 107–30, 391–419.

[61]A. Dmitrievskii, "Vecherniia molitvy," *RukSP* 33 (1888): 496–97.

As a result, in a movement consisting of both reform and synthesis, there was a certain desire to return to the simplicity of the Palestinian office, which did not contain these presbyteral prayers. This led to the grouping of the prayers into one block and to their silent reading reserved exclusively to the priest, and to their being inaudible to the assembly.

Vespers then continues with the great synapte and the psalmody, consisting of one kathisma from the Psalter. Then follows the singing of the lucernarium—the evening psalms (140, 141, 129, and 116), the first of which formed part of the evening office already in the ancient Jewish Temple. It contains an allusion to the incense offered during the evening prayer and asks that this prayer may rise to God like incense.[62] It is attested as well in the *Account of John and Sophronios* (7th century) by the expression: "Κύριε ἐκέκραξα."[63] We note the presence of a refrain for the first two verses of Psalm 140:

Lord, I call upon you, hear me. (Ps 140.1)

Ref: *Hear me, O Lord.*

Lord. I call upon you, hear me. Receive the voice of my prayer when I call upon you. (Ps 140.1)

Ref: *Hear me, O Lord.*

Let my prayer rise like incense before you, and let the lifting up of my hands be an evening sacrifice. (Ps 140.2)

Ref: *Hear me, O Lord.*

This structure with a refrain recalls once again how the antiphons of the sung office were performed with their various refrains.[64] We know as well that "Hear me, O Lord" (Ἐπάκουσόν μου, Κύριε) was one of the ten refrains inserted between verses of the Constantinopolitan Psalter.[65] This manner of performance recalls particularly the way that Psalm 140 was performed in the office of sung vespers, in which it formed the last (τελευταίον)[66] of the eight antiphons of vespers.[67]

---

[62]I. Fundulis, "Vechernia," 8.

[63]Jean et Sophrone, *Narration* I, 6, p. 251.

[64]Lisitsyn, *Pervonachal'nyi Slaviano-Russkii Tipikon*, 85.

[65]O. Strunk, "The Byzantine Office at Hagia Sophia," *DOP* 9–10 (1955–1956): 185.

[66]M. Arranz, *Oko Tserkovnoe—Istoriia Tipikona* (Rome, 1998), 52; "L'Office de l'asmatikos hesperinos (vêpres chantées) de l'ancien Euchologue byzantin," *OCP* 44 (1978): 400.

[67]See the example taken from a Slavic antiphonary by N.D. Uspenskii, "Chin vsen-

Stichera are intercalated between the final verses of the vesperal psalms (141, 129, and 116). The Sabaite Typikon normally prescribes up to ten stichera at the lucernarium, in contrast with the Studite tradition that only called for a maximum of eight. Indeed, ten stichera are indicated at the resurrectional vespers on Saturday evening, eight at great vespers on the eve of major feasts, and six on ordinary days. We usually take three stichera from the Octoechos and three from the Menaion, unless instructed otherwise. When the vespers service has an entrance, the Menaion provides an idiomelon doxastikon, and the dogmatikon theotokion from Sunday is sung.

Vespers then continues with the evening hymn, "O Gladsome Light" (Φῶς ἱλαρόν), a hymn already referred to by St Basil as very ancient. Some attribute it to the martyr Athenagenes, but this is the result of a misunderstanding. The text of St Basil, upon which this attribution is based, indeed clearly distinguishes between the "ancient" lucernarium hymn, "whose author no one knows," from the hymn composed by the holy martyr Athenogenes, "which he left to his disciples as a farewell speech as he was hastening to the stake."[68] This hymn is attested in the *Account of John and Sophronios* (7th century),[69] whose complete text can be found in the Horologion *Sinai gr. 863* from the ninth century.[70] The Jewish tradition, in which is rooted the prayer of the very first Church of Jerusalem, also had the practice of offering thanks for the artificial light that was lit at sunset. The Book of Exodus in the Old Testament already witnesses to the fact that the Jews observed a ritual connected to the evening light: at the evening sacrifice, when the lights were lit, incense was offered to the Lord. The incense did not have the banal sense it has today (of "incensing" objects), but was used only to symbolize the offering that rises toward God. The lamps were lit from a candle that burned permanently inside the Tent of the Covenant (see Lev 24.1). It is interesting

---

oshchnogo bdeniia na Pravoslavnom Vostoke i v Russkoi Tserkvi," *BT* 19 (1978): 21. Indeed, the performance of "Κύριε ἐκέκραξα" in the Great Church was far more complicated, with refrains varying according to the day of the week in a two-week cycle. See O. Strunk, "The Byzantine Office at Hagia Sophia," *DOP* 9–10 (1955–1956): 195, 201–02.

[68] St Basil, *On the Holy Spirit* 29, 73, B. Pruche, tr., SC 17 (Paris, 1945), 250–51.

[69] Jean et Sophrone, *Narration* I, 7, p. 251. See M. Arranz, *Oko Tserkovnoe—Istoriia Tipikona* (Rome, 1998), 57.

[70] J. Matéos, "Un horologion inédit de Saint-Sabas," *Studi e testi* 233 (Vatican, 1964), 56, 70–74. On the "Φῶς ἱλαρόν" see E.R. Smothers, "Φῶς ἱλαρον," *Recherches de sciences religieuses* 19 (1929): 266–83; A. Tripolitis, "Φῶς ἱλαρον—Ancient Hymn and Modern Enigma," *VC* 24 (1970): 189–90. See also my article: J. Getcha, "Φῶς ἱλαρον. Doxologie vespérale de la sainte Trinité," in *Le Feu sur la terre. Mélanges offerts au Père Boris Bobrinskoy pour son 80ᵉ anniversaire*, AS 3 (Paris, 2005), 93–99.

to note that this evening ritual was preserved by the Jews even after the destruction of the Temple of Jerusalem: the Talmud reminded them that it is God himself that they praised and glorified in performing this ritual.[71] The Church of Jerusalem inherited this tradition, and after the construction of the Anastasis complex around 335, it became customary to keep a lamp burning permanently in the Holy Sepulcher, from which all the other lamps were lit at the proper moment in the Lucernare, as Egeria attests, though without mentioning the Φῶς ἱλαρὸν.[72] This custom, originating from both Jewish and pagan antiquity, was thus taken up by the ancient Christian tradition. Tertullian (c. 160–c. 225), in speaking of a Christian meal, indicates that, after the light is brought in, each Christian is to stand and sing a hymn to God, either taken from the Holy Scriptures or inspired from his heart.[73] The *Apostolic Tradition*, attributed to St Hippolytus of Rome (c. 215) indicates that at the evening office the deacon brings a lamp, and the bishop says a prayer of thanksgiving to God for the illumination from the immaterial light through his only-begotten Son, our Lord, Jesus Christ.[74] St Gregory of Nyssa (c. 330–c. 395), in the *Vita* that he composed of his sister, St Macrina, also mentions a hymn connected to the bringing of the light during the evening prayer.[75] It is therefore in this ancient custom of giving thanks during the lighting of the lamps at sunset that the hymn Φῶς ἱλαρον was composed and became the hymn of Byzantine vespers.

Then follow the various evening prokeimena, one for each day of the week, which are found in the Horologion. Each prokeimenon consists of two psalm verses pronounced by the deacon or the canonarch, with the first verse serving as the refrain sung by the choir after each verse pronounced by the deacon or canonarch. The prokeimenon is in fact a remnant in the contemporary services of the ancient practice of reciting an entire psalm with its response.

The prayer, "Vouchsafe, O Lord," follows, already attested to at this point in the service by the *Account of John and Sophronios* (7th century),[76] and

---

[71]N. Uspensky, "Orthodox Vespers: A Liturgical History," in *Evening Worship in the Orthodox Church* (Crestwood, NY: SVS Press, 1985), 14–15.

[72]Égérie, *Journal de voyage* 24, 4 (SC 296, pp 238–39).

[73]Tertullien, *Apologétique* XXXIX, 18, J.P. Waltzing, ed. and tr., Les Belles Lettres; Classique en poche 34 (Paris, 1998), 183.

[74]B. Botte, *La Tradition apostolique de saint Hippolyte* (Münster, 1963), 64–67.

[75]Grégoire de Nysse, *Vie de sainte Macrine* 22 and 25, P. Maraval, ed. and tr., SC 178, (Paris, 1971), 212–13, 226–27.

[76]Jean et Sophrone, *Narration* I, 7, p. 251. See M. Arranz, *Oko Tserkovnoe—Istoriia Tipikona* (Rome, 1998), 57.

whose complete text appears in the Horologion *Sinai gr. 863* from the ninth century.[77] This prayer is composed almost exclusively of biblical verses: Daniel 3.26, Psalm 32.22; Psalm 118.12; Psalm 137.8.[78] It is followed by the synapte with demands, with the people's response, "Grant this, O Lord," after which comes a prayer of inclination (see the Hieratikon). This prayer, recited by the priest, is the ancient prayer of dismissal with which he blesses the people before the conclusion of the office.

The Horologion then provides psalm verses which, on weekdays, are intercalated between the aposticha stichera from the Octoechos. However, when stichera are appointed from other books, then those other books also provide special verses. The aposticha stichera were once connected to the *lite* (procession) that took place every day at the Anastasis in Jerusalem at the end of vespers, from the basilica to Golgotha.[79]

Then the Canticle of Symeon (Lk 2.19–32) is recited. As Fountoulis suggests, it is possible that this canticle was chosen in connection with the dismissal of vespers.[80] To this canticle are added the trisagion prayers: "Holy God, Holy Mighty, Holy Immortal . . . ," "Glory . . . now and ever . . . ," "Most holy Trinity," "*Kyrie eleison*," "Glory . . . now and ever," "Our Father." We then sing the dismissal troparia (*apolytikia*), which are found in the Menaia, together with the appropriate theotokion, found in an appendix at the end of the Menaion.

The deacon (or priest) then recites the ektene, and the priest does the dismissal:

Deacon: Wisdom!

Choir: Father, bless!

Priest: He is blessed, He who is, Christ our God, always, now and ever, and unto ages of ages.

Choir: Confirm, O God, the holy Orthodox faith and Orthodox Christians, unto ages of ages.Priest: Most holy Theotokos, save us!

Choir: More honorable than the Cherubim, and more glorious that the Seraphim, without corruption you gave birth to God, the Word. True Theotokos, we magnify you.

---

[77]J. Matéos, "Un horologion inédit de Saint-Sabas," *Studi e testi* 233 (Vatican, 1964), 58, 75.

[78]I. Fundulis, "Vechernia," *Vechnoe* 335 (1976): 3–4.

[79]I. Fundulis, "Vechernia," *Vechnoe* 334 (1976): 6. See the description of the office of vespers in Egeria's account.

[80]I. Fundulis, "Vechernia," *Vechnoe* 334 (1976): 8.

Priest: Glory to you, O Christ our God, glory to you!

Choir: Glory . . . now and ever . . . *Kyrie eleison* (3 times). Father bless!

Priest: May Christ our true God, through the prayers . . .

We shall see later that there are three types of vespers: daily vespers, great vespers (with an entrance) celebrated on feast days, and small vespers.

Compline (Apodeipnon)

The Schema of Compline	
Great Compline	**Small Compline**
I.	
1. Initial prayers	1. Initial prayers
2. Pss 4, 6, 12, 24, 30, 90	
3. God is with us	
4. Troparia ("The day is past")	
5. Creed	
6. Prostrations ("Most Holy Mother of God")	
7. Trisagion . . . Lord's Prayer	
8. Troparia ("Illumine my eyes")	
9. *Kyrie eleison* (40 times)— ekphonesis by priest	
10. Prayer ("O Lord, Lord, you deliver us")	
II.	
1. Pss 50, 101, and Prayer of Manasses	2. Ps 50
2. Trisagion . . . Lord's Prayer	
3. Troparia ("Have mercy on us, O Lord")	
4. *Kyrie eleison* (40 times)— ekphonesis by priest	
5. Prayer (Lord God, all-powerful Father")	

III.

1. Pss 69 and 142	3. Pss 69 and 142
2. Doxology (Palestinian redaction)	4. Doxology (Palestinian redaction)
	5. Creed
	6. It is meet in truth
3. Trisagion . . . Lord's Prayer	7. Trisagion . . . Lord's Prayer
4. May the God of powers be with us	8. Troparia
5. *Kyrie eleison* (40 times)	9. *Kyrie eleison* (40 times)
—You who at all times	—You who at all times
—Ekphonesis by priest	—Ekphonesis by priest
6. Prayer of St Ephrem	
7. Trisagion . . . Lord's Prayer	
8. Prayer to the Mother of God by Paul of Evergetes	10. Prayer to the Mother of God by Paul of Evergetes
9. Prayer to Christ by the monk Antiochus	11. Prayer to Christ by the monk Antiochus
10. Dismissal. Exchange of forgiveness and litany	12. Dismissal. Exchange of forgiveness and litany

Compline is said after the evening meal, as the etymology of the Greek word "ἀπόδειπνον" indicates.[81] This office is very ancient, as it is already attested to from the fourth century by St Basil and St John Cassian.[82] Nevertheless, it is obvious that it has developed greatly through the centuries. In the Horologion, we find two types of apodeipnon: the first is called "great" compline, the second is "small" compline.

"Great" compline contains three parts, each different in both content and length. "Small" compline greatly resembles the third part of "great" compline. According to E. Diakovskii, we should consider the first part of "great" compline as the original apodeipnon. The other parts are in fact a series of offices that were originally independent and which became attached to it for diverse reasons. For example, we find the ancestor of the second part of "great" compline in the Horologion *Sinai gr. 868* (13th–14th century), where this part is called the "intermediary hour of the apodeipnon."[83] As for "small" compline, it corresponds in the Horologion *Sinai*

---

[81]J. Pargoire, "Apodeipnon," *DACL* I, 2 (Paris, 1907), col. 2579.

[82]Ibid., cols. 2579–82.

[83]E. Diakovskii, "Posledovanie nochnykh chasov," *TKDA* 7–8 (1909): 581.

gr. 866 to the third part of "great" compline, except for the one that is read during Great Lent.[84] Thus, according to E. Diakovskii and M. Skaballanovich, we must seek the origin of these appendices to compline in the ordo of twelve psalms, which explains the kinship between certain psalms, troparia, and prayers which are found both in compline and in the intermediary hours of the day.[85] A. Raes suggested the hypothesis that the second part of the contemporary "great" compline is a vestige of the pannychis, which no longer exists, but is similar to the office commemorating the dead and known today as the *pannychida*. In Constantinople, the service of pannychis was either tied to vespers or preceded matins. The Evergetes Typikon (12th century) in fact specifies that the pannychis on weekdays was not tied to vespers, but that its canon was recited at compline. Similarly, Raes believes that the third part of compline was originally a short office for the dead.[86]

According to Pétridès, at the Monastery of St Sabas compline was recited by the monks in their cells, while in cenobitic Palestinian monasteries it was read by the monks in the church.[87]

Today, "great" compline is recited only during Great Lent and on the eves of Christmas and Theophany. On other days, "small" compline is read. But this was not always the case. As A. Dmitrievskii explains, the Studite ordo had three types of compline. Studite typika do not specify the ordo of ordinary compline, but we can deduce that it corresponded to the first part of our "great" compline, which was also celebrated during Great Lent.[88] The "small" compline of the Studites began with the reading of the last of the six psalms belonging to the first part of our "great" compline, Psalm 90 ("He who dwells in the shadow of the Most High"). This type of compline was used by the Studites from Ascension to the Sunday of All Saints,[89] the eve of Sundays and of feasts of the Lord, and the eve of the feasts of major saints.[90] The third type of compline, even more abbreviated, began directly with the singing of "God is with us." It was celebrated by the Studites on the evening

[84]Ibid., 583.
[85]Ibid., 584–85; Skaballanovich, *Tolkovyi Tipikon* 1, 425ff.
[86]A. Raes, "Les complies dans les rites orientaux," *OCP* 17 (1951): 138.
[87]S. Pétridès, "Apodeipnon," *DACL* I, 2 (Paris, 1907), col. 2583.
[88]See Pentkovskii, *Tipikon*, 240.
[89]See ibid., 271
[90]For example, on the eve of the Saturday of St Theodore the Recruit, because of the feast of the saint: Pentkovskii, *Tipikon*, 240. Concerning compline on the eve of feasts of the Mother of God, see ibid., 280.

of Holy Friday,[91] from Monday of Antipascha until Ascension,[92] as well as on the eve of certain feasts of the Mother of God.[93] Dmitrievskii explains that this Studite practice survived until the Sabaite Typikon was introduced in Russia during the fifteenth century. Following the introduction of the Sabaite Typikon, the contemporary "small" compline was read (in one's cell) on those days when there was a vigil, or if there was the commemoration of a saint with a polyeleos, from Thomas Sunday until the Sunday of All Saints, from December 24 to January 14, and on Meatfare and Cheesefare Sundays. The Studite "small" compline, which began with Psalm 90, was read throughout the year, except during fasting periods and days with "Alleluia," on which "great" compline was indicated.[94]

The Horologion specifies that, during the first week of Great Lent, we begin "great" compline with Psalm 69, after which the Great Canon of St Andrew of Crete is sung. In contemporary practice, at least among the Slavs, the other canons read during Great Lent follow the doxology in the third part.[95]

The first part consists of six psalms (4, 6, 12, 24, 30, 90). Let us note that the last, Psalm 90, always appears among the psalms of "great" compline in both the Byzantine and Latin traditions. After these six psalms, we sing the verses of the prophecy of Isaiah (8. 9–11, 12–15, 18; 9. 2, 6) with the refrain "For God is with us" (Is 8.9) intercalated after each verse. It appears that this chant goes back to the fourth century and was in fact an antiphon introduced by St Basil in Caesarea.[96] Then follow three symmetrical troparia in honor of the three divine persons, beginning with: "The day is past," then a troparion in honor of the Holy Trinity ("The bodiless nature of the Cherubim"). After these troparia, the Creed is recited. Then a series of verses, each repeated two times and sung alternately by the two choirs. While one

[91]See ibid., 254.

[92]See ibid., 262, 271.

[93]See ibid., 280.

[94]A. Dmitrievskii, "Bogosluzhenie v Russkoi Tserkvi v pervye piat' vekov," *PS* 7–8 (1882): 357–59. We note in passing that Dmitrievskii distinguishes "great" compline from ordinary compline, which, in our humble opinion, should not be. Consequently, he defines four types of compline among the Studites rather than three.

[95]Even if the contemporary Greek printed Horologion calls for the singing of the Great Canon after Ps 69 at the beginning of "great" compline (Ὡρολόγιον τὸ μέγα [Athens, 1995³], 200), today's (Constantinopolitan) practice has shifted it to after the doxology, at the end of the third part. S. Pétridès, "Apodeipnon," *DACL* I, 2 (Paris, 1907), col. 2583.

[96]Ibid., col. 2583; Brightman, *Liturgies Eastern and Western* (Oxford, 1896), vol. 1, 570.

choir chants the verse, the other makes a prostration. Because of the numerous prostrations, the prostrations during the trisagion that follows are suppressed. After the Lord's Prayer, the appointed troparia are sung.

The Horologion gives two series of troparia which are to be sung alternately, according to the day of the week. After the benediction by the priest, the prayer of St Basil is read—"Lord, Lord, who have delivered us from all arrows flying by day"—in which we ask the Lord for a peaceful rest free of evil imaginings.

The second part of compline then begins. It consists of Psalms 50 and 101 and the Prayer of Manasses, the trisagion prayers, and penitential troparia ("Have mercy on us, O Lord, have mercy on us"). After the benediction by the priest, the Prayer of St Mardarios, a fourth-century martyr, is read—a prayer that is also recited at the midnight office and at the end of the third hour.

Following this prayer, we begin the third part of compline, consisting of Psalms 69 and 142. During the first week of Great Lent, Psalm 69 is omitted here because it was already recited at the beginning of the office. Then we read the doxology in its Palestinian redaction ("Glory to God in the Highest," "Lord, you were for us a refuge from generation to generation," and "Vouchsafe, O Lord"). As we noted above, in contemporary practice this is the moment at which a canon may be read. On Mt Athos, the akathistos to the Mother of God, which is recited on every day of the year, is read at this point. Then follow the trisagion prayers. The verses of Psalm 150 are sung with the refrain "O God of hosts, remain with us" (Ps 45.7). The verses of this antiphon are alternated by the two choirs. This antiphon is followed by several troparia. After the forty-fold "*Kyrie eleison*," the prayer of the hours ("You who at all times" and the benediction by the priest, we say, on fast days, the Prayer of St Ephrem with prostrations and the trisagion prayers. Then, following the benediction by the priest, are recited the Prayer of St Paul, founder of the Evergetes Monastery in Constantinople—"Immaculate, spotless"—and the Prayer of St Antiochus, author of the *Pandects* (7th century)—"And give us, Master, as we go to sleep." Then comes the final dismissal with the rite of forgiveness just as at the midnight office. During Great Lent, instead of the final dismissal, the priest reads the prayer "O most merciful Master," while the entire assembly lies prostrate on the floor. After the rite of forgiveness, the priest recites the final ektene.

The ordo of "small" compline essentially follows that of the third part of "great" compline. S. Pétridès supposes that this service appeared toward the thirteenth century.[97] St Symeon of Thessalonica witnesses to the fact that, at the beginning of the fifteenth century, one distinguished this "small" compline from "great" compline, which was at that time only chanted on week nights during Great Lent.[98] However, according to A. Dmitrievskii, during the fourteenth century our "small" compline was supposed to be read (in one's cell) on those days when there was a vigil, when there was the commemoration of a saint with the polyeleos, from Thomas Sunday to the Sunday of All Saints, from December 24 to January 14, and on Meatfare and Cheesefare Sundays.[99] On other days, "great" compline was read.

As we have said, the service of "small" compline greatly resembles the third part of "great" compline. It begins with Psalms 50, 69, and 142, followed by the doxology in its Palestinian recension and by the Creed. The Creed is taken from the first part of "great" compline, while Psalm 50 is borrowed from the second part. The canon comes after the doxology and the Creed, and it is followed by the hymn to the Mother of God—"It is truly meet." After the trisagion prayers, we sing either the troparia of the day, or the kontakion of the feast, or, on Saturday night, the hypakoe of the tone of the week. At one time, these same troparia were also sung at "great" compline when the latter was celebrated outside of Great Lent. "O God of powers" was then reserved for Great Lent. After the forty-fold *Kyrie eleison* came the prayer of the hours ("You who at all times") and the benediction of the priest, followed by the Prayer of St Paul of Evergetes—"Immaculate, spotless"—the Prayer of St Antiochus—"And give us, Master, as we go to sleep." Then the final dismissal is made.

[97]S. Pétridès, "Apodeipnon," *DACL* I, 2 (Paris, 1907), col. 2587.

[98]Symeon of Thessalonica, *On sacred prayer*, 343 (PG 155, col. 620).

[99]See A. Dmitrievskii, "Bogosluzhenie v Russkoi Tserkvi v pervye piat' vekov," *PS* 7–8 (1882): 359.

CHAPTER THREE

The Offices in the Menaion

Different Degrees of Solemnity

In the menologia contained in the liturgical Psalter, the Horologion, or the Hieratikon, we find a mark beside each daily commemoration throughout the year indicating the degree of solemnity and consequently the type of office that must be celebrated.

Slavic liturgical books	Greek liturgical books
No sign = non-festal, daily office	
℮ (black) = (daily) office with six stichera	† = great doxology at matins
℮ (red) = office with great doxology	✢ = readings at vespers and gospel at matins
✚ (red) = office with polyeleos	⳨ = resurrectional office sung with the office of the feast if it falls on Sunday
⳨ (red) = vigil (agrypnia)	✝ = only the office of the feast is sung, even if it falls on Sunday
⊕ (red) = great feast = vigil (agrypnia)	

Thus these signs indicate not merely the degree of solemnity, but also the shape of the office. During the liturgical year, therefore, we see the following:

1) Ordinary days. The daily, non-festal office is celebrated.

2) Days with "celebrated" saints. The great doxology is sung at matins in its Constantinopolitan recension. Generally, when this solemnity falls on a fast day, wine and oil are permitted at table.

3) Feast days. Great vespers is celebrated with an entrance and readings. At matins, following the singing of the polyeleos, the gospel is read, and the great doxology is sung in its Constantinopolitan version. If the feast falls on a fast day, oil and wine are permitted. At the great

feasts of the Lord or the Mother of God, as well as for the major saints, a vigil is celebrated. The ancient typika contained, in addition to those on Sundays, an average of one to two vigils per month. In the Slavic tradition, however, which has in practice reduced the vigil service to an office lasting two to three hours, the number of vigils prescribed in the Menologion has increased greatly. It is therefore recommended, in order to preserve the spirit of the Typikon, to celebrate vigils only for major and local saints, and to have only the office with the polyeleos for other celebrated saints. When a great feast of the Lord or the Mother of God coincides with a fast day, fish, wine, and oil may be permitted.

We will now see how this arrangement of the liturgical year affects the structure of the office.

The Ordo of Vespers in the Different Categories

Daily vespers	Office with great doxology	Office with polyeleos
1. Ps 103	1. Ps 103	1. Ps 103
2. Great synapte	2. Great synapte	2. Great synapte
3. Psalmody	3. Psalmody	3. "Blessed is the man"
4. Small synapte	4. Small synapte	4. Small synapte
5. "Lord, I call"	5. "Lord, I call"	5. "Lord, I call"
		6. Entrance
6. Gladsome light	6. Gladsome light	7. Gladsome light
7. Evening prokeimenon	7. Evening prokeimenon	8. Evening prokeimenon
		9. Readings from prophets
		10. Ektene
8. Vouchsafe, O Lord	8. Vouchsafe, O Lord	11. Vouchsafe, O Lord
9. Synapte with demands	9. Synapte with demands	12. Synapte with demands
10. Aposticha	10. Aposticha	13. Aposticha
11. St Symeon's Prayer	11. St Symeon's Prayer	14. St Symeon's Prayer
12. Apolytikion and theotokion	12. Apolytikion and theotokion	15. Apolytikion and theotokion
13. Ektene	13. Ektene	
14. Dismissal	14. Dismissal	16. Dismissal

The office with great doxology follows the same order at vespers as the daily office, according to the Palestinian ordo. We should note, however, the theotokion following "Lord, I call" is the Sunday theotokion in the tone of the doxastikon. At the aposticha, stichera from the Menaion are sung, if any are indicated, and the ordinary daily theotokion. After the apolytikion troparion, the Sunday theotokion in the tone of the troparion is sung.

At the office with polyeleos, except on Saturdays and Sundays, nothing is sung from the Octoechos. Vespers follows the order of great vespers. As distinct from daily vespers, instead of the regular sequential kathisma, the first stasis of kathisma 1 is sung ("Blessed is the man"). At "Lord, I call," either six or eight stichera are sung, as indicated in the Menaion. It should be noted that the theotokion following "Lord, I call" is the Sunday theotokion in the tone of the doxastikon. During the singing of this theotokion, the small entrance takes place. The deacon carries the censer, preceded by an acolyte with a candle, and followed by the priest. They exit the sanctuary and stand in front of the holy doors of the iconostasis. When the theotokion is ended, the deacon exclaims: "Wisdom! Let us attend!" We then sing the hymn, "O Gladsome Light." After the evening prokeimenon, three readings from the prophets (*paremiai*) follow, as indicated in the Menaia. The ektene follows. At the aposticha, stichera from the Menaion are sung, and then the Sunday theotokion in the tone of the doxastikon. After the apolytikion troparion, the Sunday theotokion in the tone of the troparion is sung.

The Ordo of Matins in the Different Categories

Daily matins	Matins with great doxology	Matins with polyeleos
1. Royal office	1. Royal office	1. Royal office
2. Hexapsalmos	2. Hexapsalmos	2. Hexapsalmos
3. Great synapte	3. Great synapte	3. Great synapte
4. "God is the Lord" + Apolytikion and theotokion	4. "God is the Lord" + Apolytikion and theotokion	4. "God is the Lord" + Apolytikion and theotokion
5. Psalmody	5. Psalmody	5. Psalmody
	6. Small synaptes	6. Small synaptes
6. Kathisma-troparia	7. Kathisma-troparia	7. Kathisma-troparia

		8. Polyeleos (with selected psalm and magalynarion)
		9. Small synapte
		10. Kathisma-troparion
		11. Anabathmoi ("From my youth"
		12. Prokeimenon + "Let every breath"
		13. Gospel
7. Ps 50	8. Ps 50	14. Ps 50
		15. Troparia idiomela
		16. "O Lord. Save your people"
8. Canons	9. Canons	17. Canons
9. Lauds read	10. Lauds sung ("Let every breath")	18. Lauds sung ("Let every breath")
10. Doxology read	11. Great doxology sung	19. Great doxology sung
	12. Apolytikion and theotokion	20. Apolytikion and theotokion
	13. Ektene	21. Ektene
11. Synapte with demands	14. Synapte with demands	22. Synapte with demands
12. Aposticha		
13. "It is good to confess the Lord"		
Trisagion . . . Lord's Prayer		
14. Apolytikion and theotokion		
15. Ektene		
	15. Dismissal	23. Dismissal
16. First hour	16. First hour	24. First hour

At matins with a great doxology, after "God is the Lord" and the apolytikion troparion, the Sunday theotokion in the tone of the troparion is sung. After each section of the Psalter, the priest recites the small synapte, and, if any are appointed, the kathisma-troparia from the Menaion are sung. For the canon, generally two canons from the Octoechos and one from the Menaion are used. The katabasia may be festal, as prescribed in the Menaion. The exaposteilaria from the Octoechos are not read. Matins concludes following the Constantinopolitan ordo: the lauds are sung in the tone of the first sticheron and begin with the words "Let everything that has breath praise the Lord." Four stichera from the Menaion are sung with the lauds. The theotokion is generally sung in the tone of the doxastikon. The theotokion is usually found in the second appendix to the Menaion, except for the theotokion "O Mother of God, you are the true vine" (tone 6), which appears in the Horologion at the third hour. The great doxology is sung, followed by the trisagion. After the apolytikion troparion, the Sunday theotokion in the tone of the troparion is sung. Following the ektene and the synapte with demands, the priest does the full dismissal before prime begins.

At matins with the polyeleos, after "God is the Lord" and the apolytikion troparion, the Sunday theotokion in the tone of the troparion is sung. After each section of the Psalter, the priest recites the small synapte, and the kathisma-troparia from the Menaion are sung.

After the psalmody, the polyeleos is sung. N. Uspenskii traced the history of the polyeleos as follows.[1] The term seems to have appeared originally in the seventh-century Canonarion from Jerusalem,[2] but it may refer to Psalm 117, in which the expression "for his mercy endures forever" appears repeatedly (Ps 117. 1–4, 29). He suggests that the polyeleos, signifying the singing just as today of Psalms 134 and 135, is connected to the person of St Theodore the Studite. It was Theodore who elaborated a system of singing the *Alleluia* according to the eight tones as a refrain to the kathismata of the Palestinian Psalter. Indeed, in this Psalter, Psalms 134, 135, and 136 form the first "stasis" (or glory) of kathisma 19. The frequent repetition of the words "for his mercy endures forever" (ὅτι εἰς αἰῶνα τὸ ἔλεος αὐτοῦ) in Psalm 135 gave the name of πολυελέος to this group of psalms. The Typikon of Alexios the Studite indeed describes the performance of the polyeleos (*mnogomilostive*), which it also calls the first "glory" of kathisma 19, following the elaborated system of singing Alleluia in the different tones.[3] From Stoudion, the polyeleos was likely introduced into the sung office of Constantinople. The Dresden manuscript of the Typikon of the Great Church indeed mentions it at the sung matins on the feast of the Elevation of the Cross.[4] From Constantinople, the polyeleos would have been

---

[1] See N.D. Uspenskii, "Chin vsenoshchnogo bdeniia na Pravoslavnom Vostoke i v Russkoi Tserkvi," *BT* 18 (1978): 85–86, note 115.

[2] See K. Kekelidze, *Ierusalimskii kanonar' VII veka* (Tbilisi, 1912), 94.

[3] Pentkovskii, *Tipikon*, 405.

[4] A.A. Dmitrievskii, *Drevneishie patriarshie tipikony. Sviatogrobskii, Ierusalimskii i Velikoi Konstantinopol'skoi Tserkvi* (Kiev, 1907), 281.

adopted in the patriarchal liturgy of Jerusalem, where it preceded kathisma 17 and served as the third kathisma.[5] From the patriarchal liturgy of Jerusalem, it entered into Palestinian monastic practice. It first appears in the Georgian Sabaite Typikon of Chio-Mgvina, which, however, contains only Psalm 135.[6] Other typika indicate the singing of other selected psalms following the polyeleos. According to Uspensky, these additional psalms came in time to replace Psalm 136, and then were themselves gradually replaced by "selected" psalm verses. Consequently, Psalm 136, originally part of the polyeleos, survived in contemporary practice only at the vigils on the Sunday of the Prodigal Son, and on Meatfare and Cheesefare Sundays. Such is the history of the polyeleos as traced by N. Uspenskii. J. Matéos, however, believed that the polyeleos belonged originally to the ancient cathedral vigil of Jerusalem, as described by Egeria. He sees the source of the three psalms constituting the polyeleos (Pss 134, 135, and 136)[7] in the three psalms preceding the incensation and the reading of the gospel in Egeria.[8] According to Lisitsyn, the polyeleos originated from the sung office. He argues that, because Symeon of Thessalonica did not mention it, he considered it to be an appendix to kathisma 17 (Ps 118), whose performance he described in detail. In his study, Lisistsyn provides extracts from the Slavic Kontakarion from the Monastery of the Annunciation, which describes the performance of the polyeleos in the style of the sung office, with several refrains other than "Alleluia."[9] In this case, it is possible that the polyeleos was imported from the Anastasis to the Great Church of Constantinople, and that from these it was passed on first to the Studite typika, and then to the Sabaite.

Following the polyeleos, a selected psalm is sung. This consists of psalm verses selected according to the theme of the feast. Sung after Psalms 134 and 135 of the polyeleos, they were composed by Nicephoros Blemmydes (†1272). In Greek practice, they are normally sung as is, followed by the "Alleluia" refrain. Among the Russians, they intercalate the magalynarion. After the selected psalm, a small synapte is recited, followed by the kathisma-troparion.

[5]See A. Papadopoulos-Kerameus, Ἀνάλεκτα ἱερουσαλυμιτικῆς στυχολογίας, vol. 2 (St Petersburg, 1894), 5.
[6]K. Kekelidze, *Ierusalimskii kanonar' VII veka* (Tbilisi, 1912), 318.
[7]J. Matéos, "La vigile cathédrale chez Égérie," OCP 27 (1961): 281–312, especially 303 and 307.
[8]Égérie, *Journal de voyage* 24, 10 (SC 296, pp. 244–45).
[9]Lisistsyn, *Pervonachal'nyi Slaviano-Russkii Tipikon*, 78–83.

Then the first antiphon of the anabathmoi in tone 4 ("From my youth") is sung. We will return to the history of the anabathmoi when we speak of the vigil.

The prokeimenon, always in tone 4, is found in the Menaion. It is followed by "Let us pray to the Lord, *Kyrie eleison*," and the ekphonesis by the priest: "For you are holy, O our God . . . ," and then the verses "Let every breath praise the Lord." The priest reads the gospel indicated in the Lectionary or the Menaion. The Typikon indicates that the gospel is to be read at the altar. However, in customary practice, it is read by the priest either from the middle of the church, in front of the icon of the feast or the saint (in Russian practice), or from the ambo, facing the people (in Greek practice). After the gospel, Psalm 50 is read, and then we sing in tone 6: "Glory to the Father . . ."; "Through the prayers of St *N.*, O merciful Lord, cleanse us from our many sins"; "Now and ever . . ."; "Through the prayers of the Mother of God, cleanse us from our many sins"; "Have mercy on us, O God, according to your great mercy . . ."; and then the sticheron after Psalm 50 indicated in the Menaion. The deacon then recites the prayer "O Lord save your people" (see the Hieratikon), which is followed by the ekphonesis of the priest: "Through the mercies and kindnesses . . . ."

The canon is chanted in a festive manner. First comes the canon to the Mother of God (six troparia), and the one or two canons from the Menaion (eight troparia in all). The katabasia is festal. The remainder of the service follows the same order as matins with the great doxology.

The Vigil (Agrypnia)

Sunday vigil	Festal vigil
1. Glory to the holy, consubstantial . . .	1. Glory to the holy, consubstantial . . .
2. Come, let us worship	2. Come, let us worship
3. Ps 103, sung with refrains	3. Ps 103, sung with refrains
4. Great synapte	4. Great synapte
5. Blessed is the man (kathisma 1, 3 antiphons)	5. Blessed is the man (kathisma 1, antiphon 1)
6. Small synapte after each antiphon	6. Small synapte
7. Lord, I call	7. Lord, I call
8. Entrance	8. Entrance

9. Gladsome light	9. Gladsome light
10. Evening prokeimenon	10. Evening prokeimenon
	11. Old Testament readings (paremiai)
11. Ektene	12. Ektene
12. Vouchsafe, O Lord	13. Vouchsafe, O Lord
13. Synapte with demands	14. Synapte with demands
14. *Lite* idiomela	15. *Lite* idiomela
15. *Lite* petitions	16. *Lite* petitions
16. Aposticha	17. Aposticha
17. St Symeon's Prayer	18. St Symeon's Prayer
18. Apolytikion troparion (3 times) ("Mother of God and Virgin")	19. Apolytikion troparion (3 times for feast of the Lord and the Mother of God; 2 times for saints + "Mother of God and Virgin")
19. Artoklasia (blessing of loaves) [Great reading]	20. Artoklasia (blessing of loaves) [Great reading]
20. Hexapsalmos	21. Hexapsalmos
21. Great synapte	22. Great synapte
22. God is the Lord + apolytikion troparion and theotokion	23. God is the Lord + apolytikion troparion and theotokion
23. Psalmody	24. Psalmody
24. Small synaptes	25. Small synaptes
25. Kathisma-troparia	26. Kathisma-troparia
26. Polyeleos or kathisma 17	27. Polyeleos (with selected psalm and megalynarion)
27. Evlogitaria	
28. Small synapte	28. Small synapte
29. Hypakoe of the tone of the week	29. Kathisma-troparion
30. Anabathmoi of the tone of the week	30. Anabathmoi in tone 4 ("From my youth")
31. Prokeimenon in tone of the week + "Let every breath"	31. Festal prokeimenon + "Let every breath"
32. Matins gospel (resurrectional)	32. Festal gospel
33. Having beheld the resurrection	
34. Ps 50	33. Ps 50
35. Idiomelon	34. Idiomelon
36. O Lord, save your people	35. O Lord, save your people

37. Canons	36. Canons
38. Lauds sung ("Let every breath")	37. Lauds sung ("Let every breath")
39. Great doxology sung	38. Great doxology sung
40. Resurrection troparion (special)	39. Apolytikion troparion and theotokion
41. Ektene	40. Ektene
42. Synapte with demands	41. Synapte with demands
43. Dismissal	42. Dismissal
44. First hour	43. First hour

The celebration of the vigil is a particularity of the Sabaite Typikon. It was the fourteenth-century reform by Patriarch Philotheos of Constantinople, and then in Russia by Metropolitan Cyprian, that spread this Palestinian practice. It had earlier been adopted in the Byzantino-Slav world by the Athonite monks —thus requiring a new redaction of the liturgical books. This new redaction was necessary because, among other things, it was needed to add the office of small vespers, celebrated before the evening meal with which it is closely connected and which precedes the celebration of the vigil.[10]

As N. Uspenskii notes, the service of small vespers is the creation of this reform era, whereas the much more ancient Sabaite Typikon is at this time spread among the cenobitic monasteries and secular churches. In the ancient tradition of the Monastery of St Sabas, small vespers did not exist, and the vigil lasted from the setting to the rising of the sun. For the cenobitic monks, unlike for the anchorites, coming to church was no great effort, nor was going to the refectory following the dismissal of vespers. Consequently, at the time of the spread of the Sabaite Typikon in the fourteenth century, in both the Greek and Slavic worlds, the vigil began at a later hour: small vespers was celebrated at the usual time of vespers, after which the meal took place in the refectory, and the artoklasia lost its original purpose of substituting for the evening meal and became a purely liturgical rite.[11]

This reform also led to the addition into the liturgical books of troparia idiomela (sometimes referred to as stichera, even if there are no psalm verses) for the *lite* (procession) of vespers, as well as of rubrics concerning

---

[10]See N.D. Uspenskii, "Pravoslavnaia Vechernia," *BT* 1 (1960): 49–50.

[11]N.D. Uspenskii, "Chin vsenoshchnogo bdeniia na Pravoslavnom Vostoke i v Russkoi Tserkvi," *BT* 18 (1978): 90. See also the review of this article by M. Arranz, "L'office de veillée nocturne dans l'Église grecque et l'Église russe," *OCP* 42 (1976): 117–55, 402–25.

the patristic readings, not to mention the reform at the conclusion of festal matins with the lauds and the great doxology in their Constantinopolitan recension.

According to most redactions of the Sabaite Typikon, vigils are celebrated on the eve of Sundays and great feasts, as well as on the eve of other feasts as determined by the monastic superior. In contemporary practice the vigil, which usually consists of vespers and matins, is composed instead of great compline and matins three times a year: on the eves of Christmas, Theophany, and Annunciation (in the modern reformed Greek tradition, this practice was unfortunately abandoned for Annunciation).

The vigil begins with the singing of Psalm 103. N. Uspenskii, who dedicated an entire study to the history of the vigil and reviewed a number of liturgical manuscripts, explains that there are variations in the performance of Psalm 103 in Russia with respect to the Sabaite Typikon. First, he affirms that this psalm was never sung in its entirety, and that only selected verses were used, accompanied by refrains such as: "Blessed are you, O Lord," "For glorious are your works, O Lord," "Glory to you, O Lord, who created all"—which certainly recalls the influence of the sung office on the reformed Sabaite office. Further, the Russians never knew the famous *anoixantaria*, which developed largely in the Athonite vigil for feasts of the Lord, of the Mother of God, and of certain major saints, such as the Holy Archangels, Peter and Paul, Demetrios, or the patronal feast.[12] These reflect the influence of the sung office, and the highly ornate compositions of the anoixantaria (by John Koukouzelos) exist since the fourteenth century.

Just as in Studite practice,[13] the Sabaite Typikon calls for the singing of the first kathisma ("Blessed is the man") on the eve of Sundays and great feasts. In Greek practice, when the anoixantaria are sung, kathisma 1 is omitted. On Saturday evening, the first kathisma is to be sung in its entirety, divided into three parts (called "antiphons" in the Slavic liturgical books), with a small synapte following each part. On the eve of feasts, only the first antiphon (the first stasis) of kathisma 1 is sung. This kathisma is sung with the refrain "Alleluia." This too recalls how the odd-numbered antiphons were performed in the sung office.[14] Further, one could think that the use

---

[12]N.D. Uspenskii, "Chin vsenoshchnogo bdeniia na Pravoslavnom Vostoke i v Russkoi Tserkvi," *BT* 18 (1978): 16.

[13]See Pentkovskii, *Tipikon*, 403–04, 239.

[14]O. Strunk, "The Byzantine Office at Hagia Sophis," *DOP* 9–10 (1955–1856): 185, 200; N.D. Uspenskii, "Chin vesnoshchnogo bdeniia na Pravoslavnom Vostoke i v Russkoi

of the term "antiphon" to designate the first stasis of the kathisma derives
from Constantinopolitan terminology, unless it reflects an archaic Jerusalem terminology about which Egeria speaks.[15]

At "Lord, I call," ten stichera are sung on Sunday and eight on feast days.
The Menaion always contains a doxastikon for feast days. The theotokion
that concludes this series of stichera is from Sunday of the tone of the doxastikon, or from the feast for a great feast of the Lord or the Mother of God.

The entrance that takes place after the lucernarium is a particularity of
great vespers. It takes place as well at the vespers which precede the Liturgy of St Basil, at the eves of Christmas and Theophany, at Annunciation,
Holy Thursday and Holy Saturday, at great vespers that conclude with the
Presanctified Liturgy on feast days during Great Lent, as well as at vespers
on Sunday evenings during Great Lent and the evening of great feasts. As
Uspenskii explains, the entrance at vespers was borrowed by the Sabaite
Typikon from the Typikon of the Great Church, where it was part of sung
vespers. Uspenskii underlines that the entrance became particularly solemn
in the Russian Church because of the participation of all the diocesan clergy
at the entrance of vespers in cathedrals.[16]

Another fundamental element of the vigil is the *lite* (procession) at vespers.[17] This is one element that distinguishes the vigil from great vespers,
even if in our day in parish practice, the *lite* is sometimes celebrated during
great vespers, without a vigil. Originally, the *lite* was the procession to the
Cross, described by Egeria, which took place every day at the conclusion
of vespers in the Anastasis in Jerusalem.[18] This procession was maintained
in Palestine, chiefly at the Monastery of St Sabas, at which the monks went
to the different churches in the monastery and, finally, to the tomb of the
founder. The procession was accompanied with the singing of idiomela and
with litanies.[19] In our day, the *lite* is generally restricted to a procession,

Tserkvi," *BT* 18 (1978): 10–20; N.D. Uspenskii, "Pravoslavnaia Vechernia," *BT* 1 (1960):
44–45.

[15]On the term *"antiphonae"* in Egeria, see Égérie, *Journal de voyage* (SC 296, p. 235,
note 5).

[16]N.D. Uspenskii, "Pravoslavnaia Vechernia," *BT* 1 (1960): 46–47; N.D. Uspenskii,
"Chin vsenoshchnogo bdeniia na Pravoslavnom Vostoke i v Russkoi Tserkvi," *BT* 18 (1978):
21–23.

[17]A. Lossky, "La litie, un type de procession liturgique byzantine, extension du lieu du
culte," in *Les Enjeux spirituels et théologiques de l'espace liturgique. Conférences Saint-Serge.
51ᵉ semaine d'études liturgiques*, BELS 135 (Rome, 2005), 165–77.

[18]Égérie, *Journal de voyage* (SC 296, pp. 240–41).

[19]N.D. Uspenskii, "Pravoslavnaia Vechernia," *BT* 1 (1960): 38; N.D. Uspenskii, "Chin

accompanied by the singing of idiomela, to the narthex, where the petitions of the *lite* are done.

Closely linked to the *lite* is the rite of artoklasia, the blessing of the loaves.[20] As Uspenskii explains, this rite originated in Palestine, at the Monasteries of St Euthymios and St Sabas, at which the vigil was very long and easily took up all night, from the setting of the sun until dawn. The monks therefore needed some refreshment at a point in the office. During the procession of the different churches in the monastery, the priest would stop at the bakery, where he blessed the dough and the loaves which the sacristan (*ekklesiastikos*) then cut into pieces and distributed to the brethren.[21] From here comes our artoklasia, at which we bless five loaves and, with them, also wheat, wine, and oil—no doubt as a result of the allusion made in Psalm 4.7–9 and customarily read at the blessing of the meal, referring to the miracle of the multiplication of the loaves in the Gospel, as the text of the prayer itself indicates. The bread and wine are then distributed in the assembly during the "great reading" (customarily, a patristic reading), which is supposed to take place between vespers and matins. It is significant that the distribution of this blessed bread and wine originates from the evening meal, and that it marks the beginning of the eucharistic fast. Thus the ancient Sabaite typika, like *Sinai gr. 1096*, note the "beginning from this hour, no one who desires to commune of the Most Pure Mysteries may drink water."[22]

We have said that the distribution of bread and wine occurs during the "great reading" that serves as the link between vespers (or great compline) and matins. This reading, generally referred to by the term ἀνάγνωσις,[23] can be from the life of a saint, a patristic homily, or a book of the Bible.

After being refreshed and having listened to the inspiring reading, the faithful assist at the matins service, which begins with the hexapsalmos. It

vsenoshchnogo bdeniia na Pravoslavnom Vostoke i v Russkoi Tserkvi," *BT* 18 (1978): 69–77.

[20]S. Parenti, "Vino e olio nelle liturgie byzantine," in *Olio e vino nell'alto medioevo*, Settimana di Studio della Fondazione Centro italiano di studi sull'alto medioevo LIV (Rome, 2007), 1283–85.

[21]N.D. Uspenskii, "Chin vsenoshchnogo bdeniia na Pravoslavnom Vostoke i v Russkoi Tserkvi," *BT* 18 (1978): 69–75.

[22]"Ἀπὸ δὲ τῆς ὥρας ἐκείνης οὐκ ἔχει ἐξουσίαν πίνειν ὕδωρ ὁ τῶν ἀχράντων μυστηρίων μετασχεῖν βουλόμενος"; Dmitrievskii, *Opisanie*, vol. 3, Τυπικά, Pt. 2, 23–24.

[23]On this term, see A. Lossky, "Le système des lectures patristiques prescrites au cours de l'année liturgique par les Typica byzantins: une forme de predication integrée dans l'office divin," in *La Prédication liturgique et les commentaries de la liturgie. Conférences Saint-Serge. 38ᵉ Semaine d'études liturgiques*, BELS 65 (Rome, 1992), 138.

should be stated that we find other patristic readings assigned in matins at a vigil. The typika, for example, mention readings after the kathismata, after the polyeleos, after the third ode of the canon, or even after the sixth ode. These patristic readings can be homilies—often, the orations of St Gregory the Theologian are read, or biblical commentaries, for example those by St John Chrysostom.

The distinctive elements of festal matins at a vigil are, of course, the polyeleos and the reading of the gospel. At the Saturday evening vigil, the polyeleos is sometimes replaced by kathisma 17 (sometimes referred to by the term "ἄμωμοι" Slav. "*neporochni*," "blameless"—referring to Psalm 118. In order to determine which to use, it is necessary to consult the arrangement of the Psalter at different times of the year. In Greek practice, Psalm 118 is always read on Sunday, unless there is a vigil in honor of a saint (or the Mother of God), in which case it is replaced by the polyeleos.

Psalm 118 (or kathisma 17) is a very ancient element in matins.[24] St John Cassian mentions it in his description of the Palestinian monastic liturgy.[25] But it appears as well in the matins of secular churches. In the sung office of the Great Church of Constantinople, this psalm was sung on every day of the year, including even the day of Pascha.[26] Symeon of Thessalonica mentions it in his description of sung matins, in which the movement from the narthex to the nave takes place between the second and third parts of Psalm 118.[27] According to Uspenskii, this psalm was a fundamental element of festal matins in the archaic form of the Jerusalem ordo. To the psalm were added specific refrains in honor of the feast or the saint.[28] M. Arranz tells us that Psalm 118 later belonged to the psalmody for Saturday in the monastic tradition, while it belonged to the sung matins of Sunday in the cathedral rite.[29] The presence of this psalm at the matins office of both Saturday and Sunday has inspired the composition of the evlogitaria (εὐλογητάρια)—a series of troparia for the Saturday office in memory of the dead, or in honor

[24]N.D. Uspenskii, "Chin vsenoshchnogo bdeniia na Pravoslavnom Vostoke i v Russkoi Tserkvi," *BT* 18 (1978): 85, note 114.

[25]Jean Cassien, *Institutions cénobitiques*, Book 3, ch. 3, 10, J.-C. Guy, tr., SC 109 (Paris, 1965), 102–03.

[26]Dmitrievskii, *Opisanie*, vol. 1, Τυπικά, Pt. 1, 135; Matéos, *Typicon* II, 92–93.

[27]Symeon of Thessalonica, *On sacred prayer*, PG 155, col. 640; Lisitsyn, *Pervonachal'nyi Slaviano-Russkii Tipikon*, 78–80, note 87; I. Mansvetov, "O pesnennom posledovanii," *PTSO* 4 (1880): 1006.

[28]N.D. Uspenskii, "Chin vsenoshchnogo bdeniia na Pravoslavnom Vostoke i v Russkoi Tserkvi," *BT* 18 (1978): 95.

of the Resurrection on Sunday, and whose refrain is Psalm 118.12—"Blessed are you O Lord, teach me your statutes."[30] In contemporary practice, the evlogitaria in honor of the Resurrection are sung at every resurrectional vigil, regardless of whether Psalm 118 or the polyeleos is sung.

The anabathmoi (ἀναβαθμοί, *stepenny*) are an element of both the vigil and of the matins with polyeleos. These are antiphonal hymns, arranged according to the eight tones of the Octoechos, that were composed on the basis of the gradual psalms (Pss 119–133). According to Uspenskii, who bases himself on the interpretation of Nicephoros Callistos Xanthopoulos (14th century), the anabathmoi may have been composed by Theodore the Studite during his exile (794–797).[31] These hymns were intended to accompany the gradual psalms which inspired them, and these psalms eventually replaced Psalm 118. Indeed, we can see that, for tones 1 and 5, the author was inspired by Psalms 119, 120, and 121; for tones 2 and 6, by Psalms 122, 123, and 124; for tones 3 and 7, by Psalms 125, 126, and 127; and for tones 4 and 8, by Psalms 128, 129, and 130. At Stoudion, therefore, the anabathmoi, composed of psalms and hymns, replaced Psalm 118 and were sung following the two kathismata and the patristic reading, after which the prokeimenon was sung and the gospel read.[32] The Typikon of Alexios the Studite indeed mentions this ordo for major feasts.[33] With the spread of the Sabaite Typikon in the fourteenth century, the liturgical reform kept only the hymnography, and left out the psalms that originally inspired the hymns. At the same time, a fourth antiphon, inspired by Psalm 132, was added to the anabathmoi in tone 8, which were originally indicated for feasts that fell on days other than Sunday.[34] Ever since, the anabathmoi have been sung at festal matins after the polyeleos or Psalm 118, before the

[29]M. Arranz, "Les prières presbytérales des matine byzantines," *OCP* 38 (1972): 97, note 1.

[30]N.D. Uspenskii, "Chin vsenoshchnogo bdeniia na Pravoslavnom Vostoke i v Russkoi Tserkvi," *BT* 18 (1978): 78–79.

[31]Ibid., 86–87, note 115. On the anabathmoi, see O. Strunk, "The Antiphons of the Oktoechos," *Journal of the American Musicologist Society* 13 (1960): 50–67.

[32]N.D. Uspenskii, "Chin vsenoshchnogo bdeniia na Pravoslavnom Vostoke i v Russkoi Tserkvi," *BT* 18 (1978): 87. See also Dmitrievskii, *Opisanie*, vol. 1, Τυπικά, Pt. 1, 229.

[33]See, for example, the description of matins for the Nativity of the Mother of God (September 8): Pentkovskii, *Tipikon*, 279. The description of matins for the Exaltation of the Cross contains a indication concerning the singing of the anabathmoi during the year: ibid., 282.

[34]N.D. Uspenskii, "Chin vsenoshchnogo bdeniia na Pravoslavnom Vostoke i v Russkoi Tserkvi," *BT* 18 (1978): 87.

prokeimenon and the gospel reading. On Sundays, the anabathmoi are sung in the tone of the week, while on feast days, we sing the first antiphon of the anabathmoi in tone 4 from the Octoechos. As for the Typikon of Alexios the Studite, on feast days, it prescribes: "anabathmoi, tone 4."[35] Is this the same thing—which would, in this case, reflect an evolution with respect to the practice of St Theodore—or is Alexios referring to the special festal antiphon which is to be sung in tone 4, the antiphon that was later added to tone 8 (or plagal tone 4), for which it later becomes the fourth antiphon? Or is he simply calling for the singing of the anabathmoi entirely in tone 4? The rubric in the same Typikon, concerning the matins of Ascension, indicates that the anabathmoi of tone 5 are to be sung,[36] which would lead us to opt for one of the latter two hypotheses.

After the anabathmoi follow the prokeimenon and the psalm verses "Let every breath" (Ps 150.5,1), and then the gospel reading. We have already spoken above about this doublet of the lauds that comes before the reading of he gospel. These psalm verses are already mentioned in the Typikon of Alexios the Studite in the descriptions of the matins of several great feasts and Sundays.[37] This doublet can be explained by the fact the lauds precede the gospel reading in the sung office of the Great Church of Constantinople. We have seen above the explanation given by M. Arranz concerning the final verse of Psalm 150, which became a kind of fixed prokeimenon preceding the matins gospel, when the reading of this gospel was shifted from the end of the service to just before Psalm 50.[38]

The fourteenth-century Sabaite ordo therefore inherited the system of readings from the Lectionary of the Great Church, which had already been adopted by the Studites in the ninth century. In an appendix to the Typikon of the Great Church, we find the matins prokeimena in eight tones, and the eleven morning, or resurrectional, gospels, as well as the prokeimena and gospel readings for the matins of great feasts.[39] The history of the eleven morning gospels (εὐαγγέλια ἑωθινά) seems to indicate that the Great Church of Constantinople borrows them from the Church of Jerusalem: the series of eleven gospels in fact takes up the gospel readings in Jerusalem

---

[35]See, for example, Pentkovskii, *Tipikon*, 282.

[36]Ibid., 269.

[37]Ibid., 247, 269, 271, 272, 282, 308, 317, 358, 363.

[38]M. Arranz, "Les prières presbytérales des matine byzantines," *OCP* 38 (1972): 90, note 2.

[39]Matéos, *Typicon* II, 170, 180.

during the week of Pascha.[40] Egeria witnesses to the Jerusalem practice of
reading the Resurrection gospel at the Sunday morning office in the fourth
century.[41] M. Arranz asked himself "whether the Sunday gospel is a recent
innovation in Constantinople, and whether it derives from the Palestinian
monastic office."[42] We should, however, remember, that the reading of the
resurrectional gospels originates not in the monastic vigil of the anchorites,
but in the Anastasis in Jerusalem. As Matéos explains,

> We must be aware that the Sunday vigil practiced at St Sabas was not
> exactly the same as that of St Nilus the Solitary [on Sinai]. At St Sabas,
> the resurrectional gospel was read, but not in the eremitic office. This is
> because the monks who lived near Jerusalem adopted the offices of the
> cathedral.[43]

Thus the eleven resurrectional gospels, of Jerusalem origin, were adopted
by the Great Church of Constantinople, where they were read after lauds,
at the end of sung matins, preceded by a prokeimenon, as is still the case
today in the matins of Holy Saturday. Subsequently, they found a place in
the neo-Sabaite office, before Psalm 50, but still preceded by a prokeimenon
and the verse from Psalm 150.6.

We will say nothing more about the ordo of the vigil, because what follows corresponds to the normal order of matins, except to say that the singing of the great doxology in its Constantinopolitan redaction (in which the
order of verses differs from that of the Jerusalem version) was an innovation
introduced with the spread of the Sabaite Typikon in the fourteenth century.
The singing of the great doxology is preceded by a more festive rendering of
the lauds, which are chanted in the tone of the first sticheron of lauds. The
lauds begin with the final verse of Psalm 150 ("Let every breath praise the
Lord" [Ps 150. 5]), after which we sing the first part of the first verse of Psalm
148 with the non-psalmic refrain, "For to you, O Lord, is due a song." This

[40]See J. Getcha, "Le système des lectures bibliques du rite byzantin," in *La Liturgie, interprète de l'Écriture, I. Les lectures bibliques pour les dimanches et fêtes. Conférences Saint-Serge.
48ᵉ Semaine d'études liturgiques*, BELS 119 (Rome 2002), 39–41.
[41]"The bishop stands inside the barrier, he takes the gospel book, goes to the entrance,
and himself reads the account of the resurrection of the Lord" (Égérie, *Journal de voyage*
24, 10 (SC 296, pp. 244–45).
[42]M. Arranz, "L'office de l'asmatikos orthros (matines chantées) de l'ancien Eucologue
byzantin," *OCP* 47 (1981): 154.
[43]J. Matéos, "La psalmodie variable dans l'office byzantin," in *Societas Academica
Dacoromana, Acta philosophica et theologica*, vol. 2 (Rome, 1964), 338.

structure with a refrain at the beginning of lauds on festal days recalls the way of performing the antiphons of the sung office with their refrains,[44] and especially of the lauds of the sung office.[45] In this office of the Great Church, lauds precede the reading of the gospel. M. Arranz notes in this regard that the final verse of Psalm 150, which served as a refrain at lauds in the sung office, led to the development of a doublet in the form of a fixed prokeimenon, consisting of verses 6 and 1 of Psalm 150 and preceding the matins gospel when the reading of this gospel was shifted to just before Psalm 50 in Sabaite matins.[46] In addition, the introductory verse for the doxology ("Glory to you, who have shown us the light") was itself also originally a refrain at the lauds in the sung office.[47] It is important to note that this synthesis between Palestinian and Constantinopolitan usages occurred before the fourteenth century. The most ancient version of the Sabaite Typikon, *Sinai gr. 1094* (12th–13th century) already mentions this festal and chanted structure of the lauds, referred to by the expression "πᾶσα πνοή."[48]

In addition, the anointing that should normally take place in the narthex after the dismissal of matins is, in contemporary practice, performed after the gospel reading (among the Russians) or during the lauds (in Greek practice). This anointing is a characteristic part of all vigils in the Sabaite tradition and occurred in the narthex. The going out into the narthex following the matins dismissal is a vestige of the ancient *lite* that took place at the Monastery of St Sabas at the end of matins and which followed the reverse order of the vesperal *lite*. The monks left the church through the narthex, went to the tomb of St Sabas, and then processed to the other churches in the monastery, as we can see in the most ancient version of the Sabaite Typikon, *Sinai gr. 1096*.[49]

Most of the rubrics that are based on the *Diataxis* of Patriarch Philotheos mention only anointing with holy oil from the lamp and say nothing about

---

[44]Lisitsyn, *Pervonachal'nyi Slaviano-Russkii Tipikon*, 85.

[45]N.D. Uspenskii, "Chin vsenoshchnogo bdeniia na Pravoslavnom Vostoke i v Russkoi Tserkvi," *BT* 18 (1978): 43.

[46]M. Arranz, "Les prières presbytérales des matine byzantines," *OCP* 38 (1972): 90, note 2.

[47]D. Balfour, "La réforme de l'Horologion," *Irénikon* 7 (1930): 175.

[48]*Sinai gr. 1094*, f. 18v., 35r., 56r., 84r. (edited by A. Lossky, *Le Typikon byzantin*, 165, 189, 221, 233, 236, 260).

[49]Dmitrievskii, *Opisanie*, vol. 3, Τυπικά, Pt. 2, 24. About the matins *lite*, see N.D. Uspenskii, "Chin vsenoshchnogo bdeniia na Pravoslavnom Vostoke i v Russkoi Tserkvi," *BT* 18 (1978): 80–81; Skaballanovic, *Tolkovyi Tipikon* 2, 322–24.

going out into the narthex.[50] As Uspenskii explains, "The veneration of the icon of the saint and the anointing with oil from his lamp have replaced the going out into the narthex."[51]

Nonetheless, a *lite* around the monastery has remained in the rubrics of most Menaia and Triodia, at the third hour of the day, on Annunciation and Palm Sunday. The *Diataxis* of Philotheos indicated the same for these two days, as well as during the week of Easter.[52] But these processions are also partially inherited from the Typikon of the Great Church, which called for a *lite* from the Church of Chalchoprateia to the Forum of Constantine on Annunciation, to the Church of the Forty Martyrs on Palm Sunday, and on Easter Monday from the Forum to the Church of the Holy Apostles.[53]

The Saturday Office

The Saturday services contain certain particularities, because Saturday marks the "conclusion of the tone." For this reason, at "Lord, call" and after the apolytikion troparion, the Sunday Theotokia are always sung in the tone of the week, and not in the tone of the doxastikon or of the preceding troparion. In general, the texts from the Menaion precede those of the Octoechos.

The Octoechos calls for the commemoration of all the saints and of the dead on Saturday. Two ordos exist.

The Saturday office with "God is the Lord"

In this case, the office for the dead from the Octoechos is omitted. If the Menaion office is simple, it is converted into a service with six stichera. Thus at vespers at "Lord, I call" we sing six stichera from the Menaion and the theotokion in the tone of the week. At the aposticha, three stichera for the holy martyrs appointed for "Lord, I call are sung, together with the nor-

[50]J. Goar, *Euchologion sive Rituale Graecorum* (Venice, 1730), 8; N.D. Uspenskii, "Chin vsenoshchnogo bdeniia na Pravoslavnom Vostoke i v Russkoi Tserkvi," *BT* 18 (1978): 96–97.

[51]Ibid., 97.

[52]J. Goar, *Euchologion sive Rituale Graecorum* (Venice, 1730), 8; N.D. Uspenskii, "Chin vsenoshchnogo bdeniia na Pravoslavnom Vostoke i v Russkoi Tserkvi," *BT* 18 (1978): 97.

[53]A.A. Dmitrievskii, *Drevneishie patriarshie tipikony. Sviatogrobskii, Ierusalimskii i Velikoi Konstantinopol'skoi Tserkvi* (Kiev, 1907), 306–08, 119–20, 173; Matéos, *Typicon* I, 254–55; II, 66–67, 96–99; N.D. Uspenskii, "Chin vsenoshchnogo bdeniia na Pravoslavnom Vostoke i v Russkoi Tserkvi," *BT* 18 (1978): 99–100 (notes 51–53).

mal aposticha verses, rather than those for the dead. After the apolytikion troparion follows the Sunday theotokion in the tone of the week.

At matins, after "God is the Lord," the apolytikion troparion is sung, followed by the Sunday theotokion in the tone of the troparion, since the Sunday theotokion in the tone of the week will be sung after the first kathisma-troparion from the Octoechos. After each section of the psalmody (kathismata 16 and 17), the small synapte is said. At the canon, the canon from the Menaion is read first, then the canon of the saint to whom the church is dedicated, if it is dedicated to a saint. In churches dedicated to the Lord or to the Mother of God, the canon for the feast of the church is read first, then the canon from the Menaion. If the Menaion has two saints' commemorations, then the two canons for the saints are read, and the canon for the church is omitted. In third position comes the canon for all the saints, from the Octoechos. At the aposticha, we sing three stichera for the holy martyrs, which are appointed in the Octoechos for lauds, together with the verses normally appointed for the aposticha, and not the stichera for the dead. After the apolytikion troparion, the usual theotokion is sung, taken from the fourth appendix to the Menaion, in the tone of the apolytikion troparion.

The Saturday office with "Alleluia"

If we decide to commemorate the dead on a Saturday, the office is done with "Alleluia." In this case, at "Lord, I call" in vespers we sing three stichera from the Menaion and then three stichera for the martyrs from the Octoechos, and then the theotokion in the tone of the week. At the aposticha, stichera for the dead are sung, with specific verses. As the apolytikion troparion, we sing the two Saturday troparia and the specific theotokion. These are found in the Horologion, in the series of weekday troparia.

At matins, instead of "God is the Lord" we sing the "Alleluia" with special verses for the dead. We then sing the same apolytikia troparia as at vespers. After the first section of the Psalter (kathisma 16), the small synapte is said, followed by the kathisma troparion from the Octoechos. Then comes the second section from the Psalter (kathisma 17) in two parts, with special refrains from the funeral service. These are found in the chanter's book (the Hirmologion). After the first part of kathisma 17, the synapte for the dead is said, and then we intone the second part of kathisma 17. The kathisma concludes with the singing of the evlogitaria for the dead, which are found in both the Hirmologion and the Horologion. During this chant, the priest incenses the entire church. Then he recites the synapte for the dead. At the canon, we first read the canon from the Menaion (six troparia), then the canon for the saint to whom the church is dedicated, if it is named after a saint. In churches dedicated to the Lord or to the Mother of God, the canon for the feast of the church is read first, than that of the saint from the Menaion. If the Menaion contains commemorations for two saints, the two canons for the saints are read, and the canon for the church is omitted. In third place comes the canon for all the saints from the Octoechos. The canon for the dead from the Octoechos is sung during the office for the dead which is celebrated between vespers and compline. This is the service, originally a private office, which we know as the pannykhida. At lauds, which are read, we insert four stichera for the martyrs from the Octoechos. Then, as for the daily office, follows the reading of the doxology. At the aposticha, stichera for the dead from the Octoechos are sung, together with their specific verses. At the end of the service, we sing the same apolytikia troparia for the dead as at vespers.

The Combination of Services from the Menaia and the Sunday Office

The ordo of the Sunday vigil varies depending on the degree of solemnity of the saint's commemoration in the Menaion, and on the number of commemorations in the Menaion. The Sunday office found in the Octoechos always takes precedence. However, depending on the degree of solemnity for the saint in the Menaion, the number of stichera or troparia from the Menaion may increase, at the expense of those from the Octoechos. At matins, no more than four canons may be used. For this reason, if the Menaion prescribes two canons, the second canon from the Octoechos (for the Cross and the Resurrection) is omitted.

The combination of the services from the Menaion with those from the Octoechos, based on the signs in the Typikon, is summarized in the following charts:

Non-festive offices in the Menaion

Office from the Menaion without sign		Office from the Menaion with six stichera	
One office	Two offices	One office	Two offices
Lord, I call:	**Lord, I call:**	**Lord, I call:**	**Lord, I call:**
7 Octoechos	4 Octoechos	6 Octoechos	4 Octoechos
3 Menaion	3 + 3 Menaion	4 Menaion	3 + 3 Menaion
Glory: Menaion	Glory: Menaion	Glory: Menaion	Glory: Menaion
Now and ever:	Now and ever:	Now and ever:	Now and ever:
Sunday theotokion	Sunday theotokion	Sunday theotokion	Sunday theotokion
Stichera at *lite*:	**Stichera at *lite*:**	**Stichera at *lite*:**	**Stichera at *lite*:**
of the church	of the church	of the church	of the church
		Glory: Menaion	Glory: Menaion
		Now and ever:	Now and ever:
		Sunday theotokion	Sunday theotokion
Aposticha:	**Aposticha:**	**Aposticha:**	**Aposticha:**
Octoechos	Octoechos	Octoechos	Octoechos
Glory: Menaion	Glory: Menaion	Glory: Menaion	Glory: Menaion
Now and ever:	Now and ever:	Now and ever:	Now and ever:
Sunday theotokion	Sunday theotokion	Sunday theotokion	Sunday theotokion
At the artoklasia:	**At the artoklasia:**	**At the artoklasia:**	**At the artoklasia:**
Mother of God and Virgin (3 times)	Mother of God and Virgin (3 times)	Mother of God and Virgin (3 times)	Mother of God and Virgin (3 times)
God is the Lord:	**God is the Lord:**	**God is the Lord:**	**God is the Lord:**
Sunday troparion (twice)	Sunday troparion troparion 1 from Menaion	Sunday troparion (twice)	Sunday troparion troparion 1 from Menaion
Glory: troparion from Menaion	Glory: troparion 2 from Menaion	Glory: troparion from Menaion	Glory: troparion 2 from Menaion
Now and ever:	Now and ever:	Now and ever:	Now and ever:
Sunday theotokion	Sunday theotokion	Sunday theotokion	Sunday theotokion

After each kathisma:	**After each kathisma:**	**After each kathisma:**	**After each kathisma:**
small synapte and kathisma troparia from Octoechos	small synapte and kathisma troparia from Octoechos	small synapte and kathisma troparia from Octoechos	small synapte and kathisma troparia from Octoechos
Canons:	**Canons:**	**Canons:**	**Canons:**
Octoechos (Resurrection) 4	Octoechos (Resurrection) 4	Octoechos (Resurrection) 4	Octoechos (Resurrection) 4
Octoechos (Cross and Resurrection) 3		Octoechos (Cross and Resurrection) 3	
Octoechos (Mother of God) 3	Octoechos (Mother of God) 2	Octoechos (Mother of God) 2	Octoechos (Mother of God) 2
Menaion 4	Menaion (1) 4	Menaion 6	Menaion (1) 4
	Menaion (2) 4		Menaion (2) 4
Lauds:	**Lauds:**	**Lauds:**	**Lauds:**
Octoechos 8	Octoechos 8	Octoechos 4	Octoechos 4
		Menaion 4	Menaion 4

Festal Offices in the Menaion

Doxology	Polyeleos	Vigil	Feast of Mary
Lord, I call:	**Lord, I call:**	**Lord, I call:**	**Lord, I call:**
6 Octoechos	4 Octoechos	4 Octoechos	4 Octoechos
4 Menaion	6 Menaion	6 Menaion	6 Menaion
Glory: Menaion	Glory: Menaion	Glory: Menaion	Glory: Now and ever: Menaion
Now and ever:	Now and ever:	Now and ever:	
Sunday theotokion	Sunday theotokion	Sunday theotokion	
	Prophetic readings for saint	Prophetic readings for saint	Prophetic readings for saint
Stichera at *lite*:	**Stichera at *lite*:**	**Stichera at *lite*:**	**Stichera at *lite*:**
of the church	of the church	of the church	Menaion
Glory: Menaion	Glory: Menaion	Glory: Menaion	
Now and ever:	Now and ever:	Now and ever:	
Sunday theotokion	Sunday theotokion	Sunday theotokion	

Aposticha:	Aposticha:	Aposticha:	Aposticha:
Octoechos	Octoechos	Octoechos	Octoechos
Glory: Menaion	Glory: Menaion	Glory: Menaion	Glory: Now and ever: Menaion
Now and ever:	Now and ever:	Now and ever:	
Sunday theotokion	Sunday theotokion	Sunday theotokion	

At the artoklasia:	At the artoklasia:	At the artoklasia:	At the artoklasia:
Mother of God and Virgin (3 times)	Mother of God and Virgin (3 times)	Mother of God and Virgin (twice)	troparion from Menaion (3 times)
		troparion from Menaion (once)	

God is the Lord:	God is the Lord:	God is the Lord:	God is the Lord:
Sunday troparion (twice)	Sunday troparion (twice)	Sunday troparion (twice)	Sunday troparion
			Glory: Now and Ever
Glory: troparion from Menaion	Glory: troparion from Menaion	Glory: troparion from Menaion	troparion from Menaion
Now and ever: Sunday theotokion	Now and ever: Sunday theotokion	Now and ever: Sunday theotokion	

After each kathisma:	After each kathisma:	After each kathisma:	After each kathisma:
small synapte and kathisma troparia from Octoechos	small synapte and kathisma troparia from Octoechos	small synapte and kathisma troparia from Octoechos	small synapte and kathisma troparia from Octoechos
Anabathmoi in tone of the Octoechos	Anabathmoi in tone of the Octoechos	Anabathmoi in tone of the Octoechos	Anabathmoi in tone of the Octoechos
Prokeimenon in tone of Octoechos and Resurrection gospel	Prokeimenon in tone of Octoechos and Resurrection gospel	Prokeimenon in tone of Octoechos and Resurrection gospel	Prokeimenon and festal gospel from Menaion

Canons:	Canons:	Canons:	Canons:
Octoechos (Resurrection) 4	Octoechos (Resurrection) 4	Octoechos (Resurrection) 4	Octoechos (Resurrection) 4
Octoechos (Cross and Resurrection) 2	Octoechos (Cross and Resurrection) 2		
Octoechos (Mother of God) 2	Octoechos (Mother of God) 2	Octoechos (Mother of God) 2	Octoechos (Mother of God) 2
Menaion 6	Menaion 6	Menaion 6	Menaion 6

Lauds:	Lauds:	Lauds:	Lauds:
4 Octoechos	4 Octoechos	4 Octoechos	4 Octoechos
4 Menaion	4 Menaion	4 Menaion	4 Menaion

At a feast of the Lord, the entire service is taken from the Menaion, and nothing from the Octoechos (that is, the Sunday office is suppressed).

Great Feasts

Great feasts, pre-feasts, and after-feasts

We have twelve great feasts in the Byzantine liturgical year. Some are in honor of the Lord, the others in honor of the Mother of God. Each feast is preceded by a pre-festal period which, through special hymnography, prepares us, and is followed by a post-festal period during which we repeat the festal hymnography. During the pre- and post-festal periods, the special hymnography from the Menaion replaces the hymnography from the Octoechos. The final day in the post-festal period is referred to as the "after-feast." On this day, the festal office is repeated in its entirety in the form of an office with a doxology (which, therefore, has no entrance, no prophetic readings, no *lite* at vespers, and no polyeleos or gospel reading at matins). Indeed, in the conscience of the church, as it appears also in the lighting of the lamps during the office on Mt Athos, the after-feast has the degree of a feast without the polyeleos or the gospel reading at matins.

On the day of the feast and at the leavetaking, the Magnificat is not sung at matins at the ninth ode of the canon. So also at the eucharistic liturgy on the day of the feast and during the post-festal period, the hymn to the Mother of God ("It is truly meet") is replaced with the refrain and hirmos of the ninth ode of the canon from matins. We note, however, that in Greek practice, this rule applies only on the day of the feast and the after-feast; on the other days, "It is truly meet" is sung at the liturgy.

On the feasts of the Lord, special antiphons are sung at the eucharistic liturgy. In Greek practice, special antiphons are also used on feasts of the Mother of God, even though the Typikon calls for the typika antiphons. On the evening of these feasts, there is an entrance at vespers, followed by a great prokeimenon that replaces the evening prokeimenon from the Horologion.

In addition to having a post-festal period, the feasts of Christmas, Theophany, and the Exaltation of the Cross have a Saturday and a Sunday before the feast, as well as a Saturday and Sunday after the feast, for which special readings are prescribed at the Divine Liturgy.

Great feasts of the Lord		
Pre-feast	Feast	Post-feast
5 days	**Nativity of Christ**	6 days
Beginning on	December 25	After-feast:
December 20		December 31
4 days	**Theophany**	8 days
Beginning January 2	January 6	After-feast: January 14
	Entrance of Christ	
	into Jerusalem	
	(7 days before Pascha)*	
1 day	**Ascension**	8 days
	(40 days after Pascha)*	
	Pentecost	8 days
	(50 days after Pascha)*	
1 day	**Transfiguration**	7 days
August 5	August 6	After-feast: August 13
	Exaltation of the	
1 day	**Holy Cross**	7 days
September 13	September 14	After-feast: September 21

*Feasts of the moveable annual cycle. See the Triodion and Pentecostarion

Great feasts of the Mother of God		
Pre-feast	Feast	Post-feast
	Nativity of the	
1 day	**Mother of God**	4 days
September 7	September 8	After-feast: September 12
	Entrance of the Mother	
1 day	**of God into the Temple**	4 days
November 20	November 21	After-feast: November 25
	Hypapante	
1 day	(The Holy Encounter)	7 days
February 1*	February 2	After-feast: February 9*
1 day	**Annunciation**	1 day
March 24*	March 25	March 26*
1 day	**Dormition**	8 days
August 14	August 15	After-feast: August 23

*May be reduced, depending on the Triodion

Particularities of services during the pre-feast and post-feast

During the pre- and post-festal periods, except on Sundays, all the offices are celebrated on the basis of the Menaion. The Octoechos is not used on those days: the usual hymnography from the Octoechos, including the usual Theotokia, is replaced by the hymnography for the pre- or post-festal days. On Sundays, the services use both the Octoechos and the Menaia. It is useful, therefore, to follow the "Chapters of Mark" found in the Menaion or the Typikon.

The celebration of vespers and matins during pre- and post-festal periods, except on Sundays

One saint's office in the Menaion	Two saints' offices in the Menaion
Lord I call:	**Lord I call:**
3 feast	3 first saint
3 saint	3 second saint
Glory: saint	Glory: saint
Now and ever: feast	Now and ever: feast
Aposticha:	**Aposticha:**
feast	feast
Glory: saint	Glory: saint
Now and ever: feast	Now and ever: feast
Troparia:	**Troparia:**
saint	First saint
Glory: Now and ever: feast	Glory: second saint
	Now and ever: feast
God is the Lord:	**God is the Lord:**
troparion of the feast	troparion of the feast
	troparion of the first saint
Glory: saint	Glory: of the second saint
Now and ever: feast	Now and ever: feast
After each kathisma:	**After each kathisma:**
kathisma troparia of the feast	kathisma troparia of the feast
Canons:	**Canons:**
feast 8 troparia	feast 6 troparia
saint 4 troparia	first saint 4 troparia
	second saint 4 troparia

The Nativity of Christ and Theophany

Historical remarks

The celebration of the services for Christmas and Theophany traces its origin to their ancient celebration in Jerusalem. In the fourth century in the Church of Jerusalem, the Epiphany (manifestation) of the Lord was one of two fundamental festal cycles of the church year. It consisted of a forty-day period beginning with the Feast of Epiphany, celebrated on January 6,[54] commemorating the Nativity of Christ, and lasting eight days. This period concluded with the Feast of Hypapante (Encounter) on the 40th day after Epiphany, on February 14.

Egeria speaks of this cycle in chapter 25 of her account, but a folio is unfortunately missing in the only manuscript we have. In it, we can only read the description of a procession toward Jerusalem, a little before dawn, then a morning office at the second hour in the Church of the Resurrection (the Anastasis).

The Armenian Lectionary attests, in the first chapter, that on the eve of Epiphany, on January 5, a vigil was celebrated at the "Place of the Shepherds," near Bethlehem. According to tradition, this was the place where the shepherds were when the angels told them about the birth of Christ. This office consisted of eleven Old-Testament readings. In the morning, the liturgy mentioned by Egeria was celebrated in the Church of the Resurrection in Jerusalem.

The Feast of Epiphany in Jerusalem commemorated the birth of Christ. Unlike other eastern churches, the Church of Jerusalem did not know on January 6 a double celebration of the birth and baptism of Christ. It is only from the account of the anonymous pilgrim from Plaisance, who in approximately 560–570 assisted at a pilgrimage at the shore of the Jordan River, that we find the first mention in the Church of Jerusalem of a celebration of the baptism in the Jordan.[55] As for the blessing of the waters, C. Renoux notes that it is only in much later versions of the Armenian Lectionary that it is mentioned, after the morning office in the Holy Sepulcher.[56]

---

[54]As witnessed in the Armenian Lectionary: Renoux, II, 211.

[55]"Itinéraire du Pelerin de Plaisance," § 11 in P. Maraval, *Récits des premiers pèlerins chrétiens au Proche-Orient (ive–viie siècle)* (Paris, 1996), 213.

[56]He refers to manuscripts *Jerusalem 12, 22, 95, and 122,* all dating to the fourteenth century. They are unfortunately not published, but are mentioned in Renoux, II, 217, note 5.

All the eastern churches, except the Church of Jerusalem, celebrated the birth and the baptism of Christ on the same day, January 6, before the introduction of the December 25 feast, which is of Roman origin. The latter was the Christianization of the pagan feast of the winter solstice.[57] A sermon by St Gregory the Theologian, proclaimed in 379 or 380, shows that in Constantinople already in the fourth century they celebrated the birth on December 25 and the baptism on January 6.[58] And a sermon preached in Antioch by St John Chrysostom toward 386 shows that the same thing took place in Antioch a few years later.[59]

We know that the Feast of Epiphany was celebrated as early as the second century by Gnostic sects: this is what we learn from Clement of Alexandria in his *Stromateis*, where he writes that the disciples of Basilides, a second-century Gnostic from Alexandria, celebrated the baptism of Christ on either the 10th or 6th of January.[60] Indeed, several of these Gnostic sects taught that the divine Christ never fully entered into carnal existence, but only temporarily into the man Jesus, precisely at the moment of baptism. In Jerusalem, it was these heretical Judeo-Christians who inherited and developed this Gnostic syncretism. And it was precisely in this Judeo-Christian system that the baptism of Christ had an important place.[61] It is doubtless in this context of opposing Gnostic and Ebionite tendencies, as well as because of the Arian controversies that shook the Church in the fourth century and into which the Ebionites were eventually absorbed, that the Great Church of Jerusalem desired to emphasize certain feasts. This is precisely the position taken by R. Taft when he speaks of the Christmas-Epiphany cycle:

> These feasts were introduced in the fourth century for apologetic reasons, and not out of any "historicizing" desire to celebrate the anniversary of the birth and baptism of Jesus. An examination of the sources

[57]B. Botte, *Les origins de la Noël et de l'Épiphanie* (Louvain, 1932), 32ff. See also N.D. Uspenskii, "Istoriia i znachenie prazdnika Rozhdestva Khristova v drevnei Tserkvi," *ZhMP* 12 (1956): 38–47.

[58]Grégoire de Nazianze, Discours 38 et 39 (PG 36, cols. 312–360) (=SC 358, pp. 104–97). See J. Mossey, *Les Fêtes de Noël et d'Épiphanie d'après les sources littéraires cappadociennes du ive siècle* (Louvain, 1965), 9–10.

[59]John Chrysostom, *Oratio in Nativitatem* (PG 49, cols. 351–62). See J. Mossey, *Les Fêtes do Noël et d'Épiphanie d'aprè les sources littéraires cappadociennes du ive siècle* (Louvain, 1965), 22–23; B. Botte, *Les origins de la Noël et de l'Épiphanie* (Louvain, 1932), 24.

[60]Clement of Alexandria, *Stromata* I, 21 § 146, 1 (SC 30 [Paris, 1951], 150).

[61]J. Daniélou, *Théologie du judéo-christianisme* (Paris, 1991²), 284.

concerning the origin and meaning of these two feasts shows that both celebrations had the same object: it is the manifestation of God in Jesus, and not the events, which was manifested and which provided the scenario for the liturgical anamnesis.[62]

Thus, as R.-G. Coquin has underlined, "January 6 has become the feast of Nicene orthodoxy."[63] The latter also sees this as the reason for shifting Great Lent from the period following the Feast of Epiphany to the period before the Feast of Easter.[64]

The celebration of the unique mystery of the Nativity may be one of the possible reasons for the very late introduction in Palestine of the Roman feast on December 25, though it already existed in Constantinople.[65] It was only at the end of the episcopate of Juvenal (422–458), after the Council of Chalcedon, that there was a first attempt, between 454 and 456,[66] to adapt the practice of Jerusalem to that of the other local churches by temporarily introducing the Western feast of December 25. Consequently, Epiphany became the feast of the baptism. But this attempt did not persist after Juvenal's death, and it was only after a letter from Emperor Justinian, from around 560,[67] that the practice of the Church of Jerusalem was aligned with that of the other churches. It is interesting to note that it is precisely in the Georgian Lectionaries of the eighth century, which witness to the Jerusa-

[62]R. Taft, "Historicisme: Une conception à revoir," *La Maison Dieu* 147 (1981): 80.

[63]R.-G. Coquin, "Une réforme liturgique au Concile de Nicée?," in *Comptes rendus de l'Académie des Inscriptions et Belles-Lettres* (Paris, April-June 1967), 188–89.

[64]Ibid., 189–90.

[65]J. Lemarié, *La Manifestation du Seigneur*, LO 23 (Paris, 1957), 43.

[66]According to L. Perrone, "Vie religieuse et théologie en Palestine durant la première phase des controverses christologique," *POC* 27 (1977): 229. Botte opted rather for the year 430: B. Botte, *Les origines de la Noël et de l'Épiphanie* (Louvain, 1932), 19–20. Perrone sees in this effort by Juvenal a certain way of balancing the human birth with the divine manifestation, in accordance with the dogma of Chalcedon: "We can also ask ourselves whether the celebration of the feast was inspired by the desire better to emphasize the human reality of the birth of Christ with respect to the manifestation of the glory of God in Chrust. [. . .] This would seem to confirm, on the one hand, a later dating and would, on the other hand, explain why Juvenal's innovation enjoyed so little success and was suppressed some time after his death" (p. 231). Indeed, this innovation, susceptible to accusations of Nestorianism, could not long have survived in Jerusalem, where there was a strong monophysite influence; on this subject, see M. van Esbroeck, "La lettre de l'empereur Justinien sur l'Annonciation et la Noël," *Analecta Bollandiana* 86 (1968): 351–52.

[67]M. van Esbroeck, "La lettre de l'empereur Justinien sur l'Annonciation et la Noël," *Analecta Bollandiana* 86 (1968): 351–52; *idem*, "Encore la lettre de Justinien," *Analecta Bollandiana* 87 (1969): 442–44.

lem rite of the end of the fifth century, that we find the first mentions of a celebration of the baptism of Christ.[68]

It should be noted that three of the eleven readings used at the vigil of Epiphany in Jerusalem were borrowed from the paschal vigil. There was therefore from the beginning a link between the Epiphany and the paschal celebrations: in addition to these three readings, the structure of the vigils and the organization of the services during the octave curiously resemble each other. We should underline as well that many of the texts read in the Jerusalem office for Epiphany correspond to those appointed in the Byzantine rite and remain today a part of the Orthodox services for Christmas.

Finally, section nine of the Armenian lectionary attests that "on the eighth day, we gather at the Holy Anastasis on the day of the circumcision of our Lord Jesus Christ." Renoux notes that this was not yet an independent feast, but a commemoration taking place on the eighth day of the octave of Epiphany, serving as a conclusion of the feast.[69] Indeed, this ninth section of the Lectionary concludes with the notice: "The canon of synaxes for holy epiphany is completed."

The offices for the Nativity of Christ

THE PRE-FEAST

The pre-feast of Christmas begins on December 20. We should note, however, that this feast, just like Pascha, is preceded by a forty-day fast, during which the Typikon prescribes that the office be said with "Alleluia," just as during Great Lent, except on days with a polyeleos. This reinforces the parallel between Christmas and Easter, and the Nativity is often referred to as "the winter Pascha."[70] According to the Sabaite Typikon as it has been applied on Mt Athos, the offices with "Alleluia" during these fasting periods should be celebrated only on those days when the saint of the day has no doxastikon in the Menaion. As this happens only rarely, the office with "Alleluia" has in practice been forgotten. Beginning with the Feast of the Entrance of the Mother of God into the Temple (November 21), at festal matins the hirmoi

---

[68]Renoux, II, 183.

[69]Ibid., 223, note 1. The Feast of the Circumcision, still according to Renoux, appears in the West in the 6th century and is mentioned in the Georgian version of the Jerusalem Lectionary (5th–8th century) and in the Typikon of the Great Church of Constantinople (10th century). It is therefore likely that the Feast of the Circumcision originates in Jerusalem.

[70]T. Spassky, "La pâques de Noël," *Irénikon* 30 (1957): 289–306.

of the Christmas canon by Cosmas of Maioum are sung as the katabasia ("Christ is born glorify him"). Similarly, during this period certain theotokia at festal services are replaced by hymnography from Christmas (see, for example, the services for the holy Apostle Andrew on November 30, or for St Nicholas on December 6). The Feast of the Nativity is preceded by two preparatory Sundays—the Sunday of the Forefathers and the Sunday of the Fathers or of the Genealogy—each having its proper hymnography and special readings at the liturgy. The Saturday before Christmas similarly has special readings at the liturgy. We should note that it is hard to tell the difference between these last two Sundays; and originally there was, in fact, only one Sunday of the Forefathers: the Sunday before Christmas.

During the pre-festal period properly speaking (December 20–24), not only are the hymns from the Octoechos replaced by those for the pre-feast from the Menaion, but, just as during Holy Week, canons are prescribed for small compline. These canons are modeled on those of Holy Week, as we can see from their acrostics,[71] the hirmoi that are used,[72] and the parallelisms developed in the troparia.[73]

THE *PARAMONE*

The *paramone* (a term indicating keeping vigil, waiting, referring to the eve of the feast) is a strict fast day. The services are modeled on those of Holy Friday and Holy Saturday. However, we shall see that the order of the services is changed if the eve falls on a Saturday or a Sunday which, in accordance with Apostolic Canon 64, cannot be fast days.[74]

THE ROYAL HOURS

In contemporary practice, after the matins of December 24, the first hour is not read. Just as on Holy Friday, prime, terce, sext, and none are all read together, one after the other, forming what is called the "great" or "royal"

[71]The acrostics, respectively, are: December 20—*On the second [day]* (=Monday); December 21—*I sing on the fourth [day]* (=Wednesday); December 22—*I sing the long hymn of Holy Thursday*; on December 23—*[Canon] before Saturday*; December 24—*Today, I sing the Holy Saturday*.

[72]For example, on December 24, which corresponds to Holy Saturday, the hirmoi imitate those of the canon of Holy Saturday ("By the waves of the sea").

[73]For example, see the parallels between Herod seeking to kill Christ and the betrayal of Christ by Judas (December 21), the manger and the table of the Mystical Supper (December 22), Christ in the manger and Christ in the tomb (December 24).

[74]See P.-P. Joannou, *Discipline générale antique* (Fonti, fasc. 9), vol. 1, 2 (Rome, 1962), 41.

hours. At each hour, there is a reading from the prophets, the epistle, and the gospel. The Menaion assigns particular psalms (adapted to the theme of the feast), which replace those from the Horologion, as well as a series of stichera.

In the ancient Studite tradition, as it is found in the Typikon of Alexios the Studite, we see that the eve was a day of feasting: the hours were suppressed, as were prostrations and obediences. In contrast, in the Sabaite tradition it was a strict fast day. The Sabaite typika call for the reading of the hours at the seventh hour of the day, as called for in contemporary practice. If the eve falls on a Saturday or a Sunday, the great hours are celebrated on the preceding Friday, because they are linked to a non-liturgical day of strict fasting.

Today, these great hours are called "Royal." This can cause some confusion, since this office originally had nothing in common with the imperial or patriarchal office and was not known in Constantinople. The office of great hours is of Jerusalem provenance, where it was initially known as "the service of twelve troparia." The authorship of the twelve troparia, which were distributed among the four hours, three per hour, is customarily ascribed to St Sophronios, Patriarch of Jerusalem (†644). From Palestine, this office was in the twelfth century introduced in Constantinople at the Monastery of Evergetis. The Typikon of Evergetis indeed refers to this service, which was usually celebrated between the third and the sixth hour.[75] Subsequently, as E. Diakovskii points out, under the influence of the Sabaite Palestinian ordo, other typika gradually adopted this service of twelve troparia by inserting them into the hours.[76] This service even found its way to the Great Church of Constantinople, and we have a description of it in the *Treatise on the Offices* by Pseudo-Kodinos.[77] From there, it spread to Russia at the same time as the Sabaite Typikon.

Consequently, the spread of the Sabaite Typikon at the end of the fourteenth century necessarily led to a correction in the Menaia by introducing, to the eve of Christmas, and also of Epiphany, the service of great hours, with its prescribed readings and hymnography.

---

[75] *The Synaxarion of the Monastery of the Theotokos Evergetis* (text and translation by R.H. Jordan), "Belfast Byzantine Texts and Translations" 6.5 (Belfast, 2000), 320–29.

[76] E. Diakovskii, "Tsarskie chasy Rozhdestva Khristova i Bogoiavleniia," *TDKA* 12 (1908): 487–88.

[77] Pseudo-Kodinos, *Traité des offices* IV (Introduction, text, and translation by J. Verpaux), "Le Monde byzantin" 1 (Paris, 1966), 189–220.

VESPERS AND THE LITURGY OF ST BASIL

Because the eve of Christmas is a day of strict fasting comparable to Holy Saturday, the Typikon prescribes the celebration of the Liturgy of St Basil following vespers, which begin at the seventh hour of the day.

However, if the eve falls on Saturday or Sunday, then the Liturgy of St John Chrysostom is celebrated at the usual hour. The Liturgy of St Basil is then celebrated on the day of the feast itself, at the customary hour.

The Menaion calls for the singing of eight stichera for the feast at "Lord, I call." After the entrance with the gospel book, the evening prokeimenon follows (Horologion), and then a series of eight prophetic readings, recalling the 15 readings on Holy Saturday. After the third reading, the holy doors of the iconostasis are opened, and we sing a series of troparia ("In secret you were born in a cave"). In the same way, another series of troparia is sung after the sixth reading ("You shone forth from the Virgin, O Christ"). After the eighth reading, the deacon recites the small synapte, after which follow the Trisagion and the usual order of the Divine Liturgy of St Basil, which was once the liturgy of the feast when the liturgy was celebrated in the evening.

THE FEAST OF CHRISTMAS

THE FESTAL VIGIL

Because vespers was celebrated at the seventh hour of the day, the vigil consists of great compline and matins. This consequently leads to the reading of compline in the church, following the Sabaite tradition. After the first trisagion, the troparion of the feast is sung instead of the troparia from the Horologion. After the second trisagion, the kontakion of the feast is sung, replacing the troparia from the Horologion. The *lite* and the artoklasia follow the doxology. Thus, after the doxology of compline, we continue directly with the vespers that were interrupted by the Liturgy of St Basil, and the vigil continues normally with the idiomela of the *lite* and the festal aposticha stichera (see the Menaion). The hexapsalmos of matins follows. We should note, however, that if the eve falls on Saturday or Sunday, the Liturgy of St John Chrysostom is celebrated at its usual time in the morning, and vespers comes at its normal hour, concluding with the reading of the epistle and the gospel, followed by the ektene, the prayer "Vouchsafe, O Lord," and the synapte with demands. The vigil, in this case, begins with great compline. On the day of the feast, the Liturgy of St Basil is celebrated in the morning.

At matins, the small synapte is said after each section of the psalmody (as at all vigils), and the kathisma troparia are sung. Then follows the singing of the polyeleos and the selection of psalm verses of Nicephoras Blemmydes, accompanied (among the Russians) by the megalynarion. After these verses, we sing "Glory . . . now and ever . . . ,: accompanied (among the Greeks) by a highly ornate Trinitarian troparion. A small synapte and the kathisma troparia from the Menaion follow. Then comes the first antiphon of the anabathmoi in tone 4, the festal prokeimenon (see the Menaion), then "Let every breath" and the reading of the festal gospel. After Psalm 50 and its troparia, we sing the idiomelon from the Menaion. The festal canon is sung with twelve troparia. The first canon, attributed to Cosmas of Maioum, has the acrostic "Christ becomes man while remaining God, as he was." The first hirmos ("Christ is born, glorify him") repeats the opening words of Sermon 38 of St Gregory the Theologian.[78] The second canon is ascribed to St John of Damascus. After the third ode, the hypakoe of the feast is sung; after the sixth ode, the festal kontakion and ikos. At the ninth ode, the Maginificat is not sung, and the megalynaria of the feast precede the troparia as on all great feasts (see the Menaion). The exaposteilarion of the feast is then sung three times. The lauds ("Let everything that breathes") are sung with four stichera and the doxastikon and theotokion of the feast. The great doxology is followed by the troparion of the feast, and the vigil concludes with the customary litanies.

At each of the hours, the troparion and kontakion of the feast are read.

THE DIVINE LITURGY

At the Divine Liturgy of St John Chrysostom (or of St Basil the Great, if the eve falls on Saturday or Sunday), the festal antiphons are sung (see the Menaion). After the entrance and the entrance verse, we sing the troparion and kontakion of the feast. Instead of the trisagion, we sing "As many as have been baptized into Christ."[79] As on all feasts of the Lord, the prokeimenon before the epistle, the verses for the Alleluia, the epistle and gospel readings,

[78]Gregoire de Nazianze, *Discours 38*, 1 (SC 358, p. 105).
[79]This chant at the liturgy is explained by the fact that this feast was modeled after Epiphany, at which baptisms were performed in Constantinople as on Easter day. See Matéos, *Typicon* II, 158 and 184.

and the koinonikon are all festal, and the hymn to the Mother of God ("It is truly meet") is replaced by the hirmos of the ninth ode of the canon.

If Christmas falls on a Wednesday or a Friday, the regular fast is suppressed. In addition, fasting is eliminated during the days following the feast, until the eve of Epiphany.

THE AFTER-FEAST OF CHRISTMAS

THE SYNAXIS OF THE MOTHER OF GOD

On the day following Christmas, we celebrate the synaxis of the Mother of God. At "Lord, I call," three stichera from the vespers of the feast are sung, on 6, followed by the sticheron "Glory to God in the highest." As on the evening of any feast of the Lord, there is an entrance and a great prokeimenon ("Who is so great a God as our God?"). At the aposticha, the idiomela stichera of the feast are sung, and after the Lord's Prayer, the troparion of the feast. At small compline, we read the canon of St Euthymios of Sardis, whose feast falls that day. At matins (with doxology), the hymnography is taken entirely from the feast (see the Menaion). The kontakion of the feast is sung after the third ode of the canon, and the kontakion and ikos for the synaxis of the Mother of God are sung after the sixth ode. At the liturgy, in Greek practice, the typika antiphons are followed by "As many as have been baptized," and not the trisagion.

OTHER DAYS DURING THE AFTER-FEAST

The after-feast of Christmas continues until December 31. The offices combine material for the feast with that for the saint of the day in the Menaion.

At vespers, three stichera for the feast and three stichera for the saint are sung. All the Theotokia are replaced by idiomela for the feast. The aposticha stichera are taken from the Menaion.

At matins, after each section of the psalmody the kathisma troparion of the feast is sung. After Psalm 50, one of the canons of the feast is done with six troparia, and then four troparia for the canon of the saint of the day in the Menaion. After the third ode, the kontakion and ikos are said, then the kathisma troparion of the saint of the day, all from the Menaion, "Glory . . . now and ever . . . ," and the kathisma troparion for the feast; after the sixth ode, the kontakion and ikos of the feast; and after the ninth ode, the exaposteilarion of the feast. At the aposticha, the stichera are taken for the feast.

SATURDAY AND SUNDAY AFTER CHRISTMAS

The Byzantine Lectionary calls for special readings at the eucharistic liturgy on Saturday after Christmas. The office, however, combines material from the feast with that for the saint of the day in the Menaion.

The Menaion contains an office for the Sunday following Christmas, at which the righteous Joseph the Betrothed, King David, and James, the Brother of the Lord are commemorated. This office is combined with the regular Sunday office (from the Octoechos, in the tone of the week) and that of the feast (see the Menaion), and the saint of the day is omitted.

We should note that if Christmas falls on a Sunday, there is only one Saturday and one Sunday between Christmas and Theophany. The office for Sunday after Christmas is then sung on December 26. The readings appointed for Saturday after Christmas are then read on the leavetaking of the feast, together with the readings for the Saturday before Theophany. The readings for Sunday after Christmas are done on December 26. The readings for Sunday before Theophany are read on January 1, before those for the Circumcision in the ordo.

If Christmas falls on a Monday, then there is only one Saturday and one Sunday between Christmas and Epiphany. Saturday then falls on December 30, and the readings of the Saturday following Christmas and the Saturday before Theophany are done together. The office appointed for the Sunday after Christmas is sung on the leavetaking. On that day, the readings for the Sunday following Christmas are done. The readings for the Sunday before Theophany are done on January 1, before those for the Circumcision.

If Christmas falls on a Tuesday, then there are two Saturdays and one Sunday between Christmas and Theophany. The readings for Saturday after Christmas are read on December 29. The office for Sunday after Christmas is chanted on December 30, and the readings for Sunday after Christmas are also read that day. The readings assigned to the Sunday before Theophany are read on January 1, before those for the Circumcision. The readings for Saturday before Theophany are done on January 5.

If the Nativity of Christ falls on a Wednesday, Thursday, or Friday, then there are two Saturday and two Sundays between Christmas and Theophany, and there is no difficulty.

If Christmas falls on a Saturday, then there are two Sundays, but only one Saturday, between Christmas and Epiphany. The readings for Saturday after Christmas are read on Friday, December 31, the day of the leavetaking. The readings for the Saturday before Theophany are taken on January 1, follow-ing those for the Circumcision.

On December 31, the leavetaking of Christmas, the office for the feast is repeated in its entirety (except for the prophetic readings, the *lite*, the poly-eleos, and the matins gospel). The office for St Melanie (commemorated on December 31) is done by anticipation on December 30.

As we have seen, the leavetaking in Jerusalem originally took place on the eighth day, which also commemorated the Circumcision of the Lord (on the eighth day after birth). In our day, this eighth day (January 1) coincides with the feast of St Basil the Great, for which the Sabaite Typikon prescribes a vigil. This explains why the leavetaking was moved up by one day. The office for St Basil is combined with the office for the Circumcision. Even though the Circumcision is a feast of the Lord, the rubrics for this day give priority to the commemoration of St Basil.

The offices of Theophany

THE PRE-FEAST

For the historical reasons enumerated above, the feast of Theophany, just as its twin feast of Christmas, is also modeled on the feast of Easter. It is preceded by a Saturday and a Sunday that have, as we have just seen, special readings for the eucharistic liturgy.

During the pre-festal period properly-speaking (January 2–6), not only is the customary hymnography from the Octoechos replaced by hymns for the pre-feast from the Menaion, but special canons are appointed for small compline, just as during Holy Week. These canons, just as was the case with the canons for the pre-feast of Christmas, are modeled on the Holy Week canons, as we can see from their acrostics[80] and hirmoi.[81]

---

[80]The acrostics, respectively, are: January 2—*On the second [day]* (=Monday); January 3—*I sing on the fourth [day]* (=Wednesday); January 4—*I sing the long hymn of Holy Thurs-day*; January 5—*And today, I sing the Great Saturday*.

[81]For example, on January 5, which corresponds to Holy Saturday, the hirmoi imitate those of the canon of Holy Saturday ("By the waves of the sea").

THE *PARAMONE*

The eve of Theophany, just as the eve of Christmas, is a day of strict fasting. However, as we have seen in the case of the eve of Christmas, the order of services changes if the eve falls on a Saturday or Sunday, for the same reasons.

THE ROYAL HOURS

After the matins of January 5, the first hour is not read. Just as on Holy Friday, prime, terce, sext, and none are read together, one after the other, and form what are called the "great" or "royal" hours. At each hour, a passage is read from the prophets, the epistle, and the gospel. The Menaion appoints special psalms, which replace the regular psalms from the Horologion, as well as a series of stichera. If the eve falls on a Saturday or a Sunday, the great hours are celebrated on the preceding Friday.

VESPERS AND THE LITURGY OF ST BASIL

Because the eve is strict fast day comparable to Holy Saturday, the Liturgy of St Basil appointed for this day follows vespers, which begin at the fifth hour of the day. However, if the eve falls on a Saturday or a Sunday, the Liturgy of St John Chrysostom is celebrated at the normal time, followed by vespers at the usual hour. The Liturgy of St Basil is then celebrated on the day of the feast, at the customary time.

The Menaion calls for the eight stichera idiomela, attributed to St John of Damascus, at "Lord, I call." After the entrance with the gospel book, the evening prokeimenon is said (Horologion), followed by a series of 13 prophetic readings, recalling the 15 readings on Holy Saturday. After the third reading, the holy doors of the iconostasis are opened, and a series of troparia are sung ("You appeared to the world"). So also after the sixth ode, when we sing another series of troparia ("To the sinners and the Publicans"). After the thirteenth reading, the deacon recites the small synapte, the trisagion is sung, and the Divine Liturgy follows according to the normal order.

After the prayer behind the ambo at the end of the Divine Liturgy, there is a procession to a river or a spring, or to the baptistery or the narthex, to celebrate the office of the great blessing of water (see the Euchologion or the Menaion).[82] In our day, it is customary to repeat the great blessing of

[82]On the blessing of water on Theophny, see V. Prilutskii, *Chastnoe bogosluzhenie v Russkoi Tserkvi* (Kazan', 1912[1]; Moscow, 2000[2]), 134–51; M. Vidalis, "La bénédiction des

water on the day of Theophany itself. However, this was originally done only once, on the eve of the feast,[83] as even our contemporary liturgical books indicate. This duplication can be explained, it seems, because in Palestinian monasteries the monks went down to bless the Jordan River.

We should note, however, that if the eve falls on a Saturday or a Sunday, the eucharistic liturgy is celebrated at the usual hour in the morning. Vespers follows at its usual hour, concluding with the reading of the epistle and the gospel, the ektene, the prayer "Vouchsafe, O Lord," and the synapte with demands, after which the great blessing of water is celebrated.

THE FEAST OF THEOPHANY

THE VIGIL OF THE FEAST

Because vespers was already celebrated at the fifth hour of the day, the vigil consists of great compline and matins. After the first trisagion, the troparion of the feast replaces the troparia from the Horologion. After the second trisagion, the kontakion of the feast is sung instead of the troparia from the Horologion. After the doxology come the *lite* and the artoklasia, as at Christmas. The hexapsalmos of matins follows.

At matins, after each section of the psalmody, the small synapte is recited and the kathisma troparia from the Menaion are sung. Then comes the singing of the polyeleos and the selected verses accompanied, in Russian practice, by the megalynarion. The deacon then intones the small synapte, after which the kathisma troparia from the Menaion are sung. After the first antiphon of the anabathmoi in tone 4 comes the prokeimenon of the feast (See the Menaion), then "Let every breath" and the reading of the festal gospel. After Psalm 50 and its troparia, the idiomelon from the Menaion is sung. The canons of the feast are sung with twelve troparia. The first canon, attributed to Cosmas of Maioum, has the acrostic "Baptism—the purification from sins of those who are born on earth." The second canon is attributed to St John of Damascus. After the third ode, the hypakoe is read; after the sixth ode, the kontakion and ikos of the feast. At the ninth ode, the Magnificat is not sung, but the megalynaria of the feast (see the Menaion), followed by the troparia of the ode. After ode 9—the exaposteilarion of the feast. The lauds

eaux de la fête de l'Épiphanie selon le rite grec de l'Église orthodoxe," in *La Prière liturgique. Conférences Saint-Serge. 47ᵉ semaine d'études liturgiques*, BELS 115 (Rome 2001), 237–57; M. Zheltov, "Vodoosviashchenie," *PE*, vol. IX (Moscow, 2005), 142–44.

[83]Mansvetov, *Tserkovnyi ustav*, 154–57; M.S. Zheltov and S. Pravdoliubov, "Bogosluzhenie RPTs X–XX vv.," *PE*, vol. RPTs (Moscow, 2000), 489.

("Let everything that has breath") are sung, followed by four stichera attributed to St Germanos of Constantinople, the doxastikon, and the theotokion of the feast, and then the great doxology and the troparion of the feast. Vigil concludes with the usual litanies. In Greek usage, after the conclusion of matins the second blessing of water, more solemn, is celebrated, at which is read the first prayer (in fact, a homily) of St Sophronios of Jerusalem.

At each of the hours, the troparion and kontakion of the feast are read.

THE DIVINE LITURGY

At the Divine Liturgy of St John Chrysostom (or of St Basil the Great, if the eve falls on a Saturday or Sunday), the antiphons of the feast are sung (see the Menaion). After the entrance and the entrance verse, the troparion and kontakion are sung. Instead of the trisagion, we sing "As many as have been baptized into Christ."[84] As is the case with all feasts of the Lord, the epistle prokeimenon, the Alleluia verses, the epistle and gospel readings, and the koinonikon are all festal. The hymn to the Mother of God ("It is truly meet") is replaced by the hirmos of the ninth ode of the canon.

If the feast of Theophany falls on a Wednesday or a Friday, the fast is eliminated.

THE AFTER-FEAST OF THEOPHANY

THE SYNAXIS OF THE GLORIOUS PROPHET, FORERUNNER, AND BAPTIST JOHN

The day after Theophany, we celebrate the synaxis of the glorious Prophet, Forerunner, and Baptist John. At "Lord, I call," we sing three stichera for the feast and 3 for the Forerunner, followed by a doxastikon for the Forerunner and an idiomelon for the feast. As on the evening of any feast of the Lord, there is an entrance and the singing of a great prokeimenon: "Our God, in heaven and on earth." At the aposticha, the idiomela stichera of the feast are sung, and after the Lord's Prayer, the troparia for the Forerunner and for the feast. At matins (with doxology), we sing entirely from the offices of the feast and of the Forerunner (see the Menaion). After the third ode of the canon, we sing the kontakion of the feast; after the sixth ode, the kontakion and ikos

---

[84]The singing of "As many as have been baptized" is explained by the fact that baptisms were oerformed on this day in Constantinople as on Easter day. See Matéos, *Typicon* II, 184, 186.

for the Forerunner. At the liturgy, the typika antiphons are sung, as well as the trisagion instead of "As many as have been baptized."

THE OTHER DAYS OF THE AFTER-FEAST

The after-feast of Theophany lasts until January 14. The services combine the office of the feast with that of the saint of the day in the Menaion.

At vespers, we sing three stichera for the feast and 3 for the saint at "Lord, I call." All the Theotokia are replaced by idiomela from the feast. The aposticha stichera are taken from the Menaion.

At matins, after each section of the psalmody, we sing the kathisma troparion of the feast. After Psalm 50, we sing one of the two canons for the feast with six troparia, and then four troparia from the canon of the saint of the day in the Menaion. After the third ode, we sing the kontakion, ikos, and kathisma troparion from the saint in the Menaion, followed by the kathisma troparion of the feast; after the sixth ode, the kontakion and ikos of the feast; at the ninth ode, the Magnificat; and after the ninth ode, the exaposteilarion of the feast. At the aposticha, the festal stichera are sung.

SATURDAY AND SUNDAY AFTER EPIPHANY

The Byzantine Lectionary appoints special readings at the eucharistic liturgies of the Saturday and Sunday following Theophany. The office is that for the feast combined with that for the saint in the Menaion on Saturday, and on Sunday, in addition, the resurrectional office from the Octoechos.

THE LEAVETAKING OF THEOPHANY

On January 14, the leavetaking of Epiphany, the office for the feast is repeated in its entirety (except for the prophetic readings, the *lite*, the polyeleos, and the matins gospel). The office for the holy Fathers martyred on Sinai and at Raithou (commemorated on January 14) is done by anticipation on January 13.

CHAPTER FOUR

The Services of the Triodion

The Preparatory Period of the Triodion

Sunday of the Publican and the Pharisee

ORIGIN

The Triodion cycle begins with the Sunday of the Publican and the Pharisee, taking its name from the parable which is read on this day at the Divine Liturgy (Lk 18.10–14). This reading appears at this moment for the first time in the Typikon of the Great Church (950–959) as the appointed reading for the thirty-third Sunday after Pentecost. In the Jerusalem tradition, it was part of the pericope assigned for the third Sunday of Great Lent, as we can see in the Georgian Lectionary, as well as in other lectionaries of this tradition.[1] This explains why we find the theme of the Publican and the Pharisee in the hymnography of the fourth week of Great Lent, thus alluding to the theme of the gospel once read in Jerusalem on the preceding Sunday.[2] This seems to indicate that the Sunday of the Publican and the Pharisee was added quite late to the preparatory cycle of the Triodion. And in fact, in eleventh-century Evangelia, this reading has no real connection to the Triodion, since a rubric there indicates that if the period from one Pascha to another is very long, then the pericope about the Canaanite woman can be inserted between this Sunday and the next. Nonetheless, in these documents the Sunday of the Publican and the Pharisee is also called the "Sunday before the Prodigal" (πρὸ τοῦ ἀσώτου). In the twelfth-century Evangelia, this Sunday is in its present place as the beginning of the Triodion cycle. The reason for this connection to the Triodion cycle, and especially to the Sunday of the Prodigal Son, is not so much the theme of the parable as it

---

[1]See the comparative table in G. Bertonière, *The Sundays of Lent in the Triodion: The Sundays Without a Commemoration*, OCA 253 (Rome, 1997), 46–47.

[2]Ibid., 77.

is the desire to differ from the strict fast observed by the Armenians during the week between these two Sundays.

THE SUPPRESSION OF THE FAST

Indeed, during the entire week that follows this first Sunday of the Triodion, fasting is eliminated. The rubrics explain the reason for this:

> It must be known that, during this week of fasting, the accursed Armenians observe a defiled fast called *artzibouri*. In order to vanquish their shame, we free ourselves from fasting. During the entire week, beginning from Monday, we eat cheese and eggs, thus rejecting and overcoming this practice.[3]

We do not find this rubric in the Studite tradition, as it appears in the Typikon of Alexios the Studite. However, it appears in all the Sabaite Typika, as well as in Triodia of Hagiopolite redaction.[4] This highly polemical rubric is aimed at refuting the Armenian practice of a fast called *artzibouri* (ἀρτζιβούρη) in transliteration from the Greek. The actual name of this fast, *arachavor* (*arajawor*), in Armenian, literally means "before the days." It designates a period of fasting before Great Lent, introduced, according to current historical knowledge, by the Armenians during the eighth century in memory of the fast of St Gregory the Illuminator, who spent thirteen years "in the deep pit."[5] The tradition of the Armenian Church claims that the fast originates during the era of St Gregory the Illuminator himself. According to Nersess the Gracious, St Gregory the Illuminator, once he got out of the pit, introduced this five-day fast, forbidding the consumption of any kind of food.[6]

However, before the eleventh century we find no trace of any written polemics against the Armenians on the subject of this fast. The source of the polemics about the *artzibouri* fast is found in the "Discourse against the

---

[3]Typikon, ch. 49, 6th remark.

[4]See for example *Sinai gr. 1094*, f. 66v (edited by Lossky, *Le Typikon byzantin,* 237); *Typikon* (Moscow, 1906), 393.

[5]A. Renoux, *Le Lectionnaire de Jérusalem en Arménie. Le Casoce,* II, PO 48, fasc. 2, No. 214 (Turnhout, 1999), 106 [20]. On the establishment of this fast in the eighth century, see A. Renoux, "Samuel Kamrjajerec'i: le Traité sur l'arajawor," in *From Byzantium to Iran: In Honor of Nina Garsoian* (Atlanta, 1997), 469–72. See also I. Mansvetov, *O postakh pravo-slavnoi vostochnoi Tserkvi* (Moscow, 1886), 46–47. Mansvetov thinks that this fast may have been observed already from the time of St Gregory the Illuminator.

[6]Karabinov, *Postnaia Triod',* 24.

Armenians," an apocryphal Greek text attributed to the Armenian Catholicos Isaac III (*c.* 635–*c.* 705),[7] according to which he called on the Armenians
to accept the decisions of the Council of Chalcedon. We do know that Isaac
was called to Constantinople by Justinian II in 689–690, where he accepted
the doctrine about the two natures, and that his stance was rejected by the
clergy in Armenia.[8] In the discourse attributed to him, Catholicos Isaac
attacks a certain Sergios who, he claims, was one of the chief proponents of
monophysitism. The latter purportedly had a dog named Artzibour, whom
he also used as a messenger. After his dog was eaten by wolves, Sergius
introduced a fast in memory of his dog, thus giving the name to the fast.[9]
As Mansvetov explains,

> As incredible as it was when first invented, with the obvious aim of dis-
> crediting and profaning in the eyes of non-Armenians the famous Arme-
> nian fast, which was also a characteristic of this sect (of Sergians), this
> falsehood was nevertheless received favorably and even found a place in
> the Typikon.[10]

Later, Nikon of the Black Mountain (*c.* 1025–*c.* 1088) noted in the fourteenth discourse of his *Taktikon* that nothing on this subject was written in
the decrees of the holy councils.[11] Along with Nicholas Grammatikos, he
sought to soften the polemical tone by explaining that the elimination of
the Wednesday and Friday fast during this week was instituted simply to
distinguish the Orthodox from the Armenians.[12]

The placement of this rubric in the Sabaite Typika can be explained by
the fact that there were Armenians and monophysites living in Palestine,
and that the Chalcedonian Christians, seeking to distinguish themselves,
adopted this rubric. Later, with the spread of the Sabaite Typikon, this rubric
spread throughout the Orthodox world and, to this day, has a quasi-doc-
trinal character.[13]

---

[7]Isaac, Armenian Catholicos, *Oratio 1 contra Armenios,* 14 (PG 132, cols. 1197ff). Par-
tial translation into Russian in I. Mansvetov, *O postakh pravoslavnoi vostochnoi Tserkvi*
(Moscow, 1886), 60–64.

[8]B. Coulie, "Isaak III, catholicos d'Arménie," in *Dictionnaire d'histoire et de géographie
ecclésiastiques,* vol. 26 (Paris, 1997), cols. 75–77.

[9]Isaac, Armenian Catholicos, *Oratio 1 contra Armenios,* 14 (PG 132, col. 1203).

[10]I. Mansvetov, *O postakh pravoslavnoi vostochnoi Tserkvi* (Moscow, 1886), 49.

[11]Karabinov, *Postnaia Triod',* 24.

[12]I. Mansvetov, *O postakh pravoslavnoi vostochnoi Tserkvi* (Moscow, 1886), 52–53.

[13]Ibid., 52.

THE ORDO OF THE OFFICE

The Triodion contains only the office for Sunday, and nothing for the week that follows. As a general rule, during the period of the Triodion, the Sunday office (until Palm Sunday) uses only the Octoechos and the Triodion. The Menaion is put aside, except in the case of saints for whom there is a vigil or the polyeleos. The other saints' offices are either delayed or anticipated at compline on weekdays.

At "Lord, I call" at vespers, three stichera are added to those of the Octoechos, as is a doxastikon. Note that the tones of the Octoechos continue to succeed one another during the entire period of the Triodion, until the end of Great Lent. There is also a doxastikon for the *lite*, and another for the aposticha.

Beginning on this Sunday, and until Palm Sunday, penitential troparia are sung after Psalm 50 (which is read after the gospel) at Sunday matins: "Open to me the doors of repentance . . . ," "Lead me on the path of salvation . . . ," "Meditating on the many sins I have committed . . ." These texts replace those customarily sung. The period of repentance is thus set in motion by the hymnography. The use of these hymns seems to go back only to the fourteenth century, even if the last of them is found in twelfth-century manuscripts at the matins of Holy Tuesday.[14]

A canon from the Triodion with six troparia is added to the canons from the Octoechos (of the Resurrection, four troparia; of the Cross and the Resurrection, two troparia; of the Mother of God, two troparia). After the third ode, the two kathisma troparia from the Triodion are sung, and, after the sixth ode, the kontakion and ikos from the Triodion. Beginning from this Sunday and until the Sunday of All Saints, it is prescribed the read the synaxaria attributed to Nicephoras Kallistos Xanthopoulos, which were only included very late in the offices of the Triodion and Pentecostarion, while originally they were found either in an appendix to the Triodion or simply in separate collections. These texts consist of a commentary about the event being celebrated, which is at times inspired by apocryphal writings. They tend to imitate the hagiographic texts contained in the synaxaria (menologia).[15] Following the ninth ode, an exaposteilarion from the Triodion is added to the gospel exaposteilarion.

[14]Karabinov, *Postnaia Triod'*, 201–03.

[15]Arkhiepiskop Filaret (Gumilevskii), *Istoricheskii obzor pesnopevtsev i pesnopeniia Grecheskoi Tserkvi* (St Petersburg, 1902), 362–64; Karabinov, *Postnaia Triod'*, 203.

At lauds, the Triodion provides four stichera, the first two of which are repeated from "Lord, I call" of vespers and are added to four stichera from the Octoechos, as well as a doxastikon. The gospel idiomelon (*eothinon*), which is commonly sung at this point, is sung during the period of the Triodion after the dismissal of matins, before the first hour. During the singing of this idiomelon, the Typikon calls for a procession to the narthex, where the *Catecheses* of St Theodore the Studite are supposed to be read. Following the reading, the troparion of St Theodore is sung, and prime is read. In the practice of many monasteries where the catechesis of St Theodore is read on every Sunday of the year at the end of the midnight office, the eothinon idiomelon is read after the Lord's Prayer at the midnight office, or at the first hour.

At each of the hours, only one kontakion, from the Triodion, is read. The same is done at the liturgy, eventually in addition to the kontakion for a church dedicated to the Mother of God or to a saint. No kontakion from the Octoechos is sung, but only that from the Triodion.

Sunday of the Prodigal Son

ORIGIN

The second Sunday of this preparatory period is the Sunday of the Prodigal Son. It begins the week of Meat-Fare (ἀποκρέω), the last week during which the laity may eat meat. As for the monastics who never eat meat, they enjoy a bit of rest before the beginning of the Lenten ascetical effort, as the rubrics of the Typikon prescribe that the Alleluia office is not sung. The intermediate hours are omitted. One of the matins kathismata is omitted and shifted to vespers. At compline, the intercessory canons to the Theotokos are also omitted. The same is done during Cheese-Fare week, except on Wednesday and Friday, when the Alleluia office is prescribed.[16]

It seems that this second preparatory week was introduced in Constantinople in addition to Cheese-Fare week, which was known in Palestine and attested to by St John of Damascus.[17] The ninth- and tenth-century Constantinopolitan Evangelia indicate that there is a Sunday "before *apokreo*" (πρὸ τῆς ἀποκρέου).[18] In the Typikon of the Great Church, this Sunday inaugurates the moveable cycle. The reading for this day is the parable of

---

[16]*Typikon*, ch. 49, Sunday of the Prodigal Son, 1st remark.
[17]John of Damascus, *On the Sacred Fast*, 5 (PG 95, col. 69D).
[18]Karabinov, *Postnaia Triod'*, 23.

the Prodigal Son (Lk 15.11–32), prescribed in the Jerusalem tradition for the second Sunday of Great Lent, as we can see in the Georgian Lectionary and other lectionaries in this tradition.[19] This explains why we again find the theme of the Prodigal Son in the hymnography of Thursday evening and Friday morning during the third week of Great Lent, clearly alluding to the theme of the gospel once read in Jerusalem on the preceding Sunday.[20]

In this way the Constantinopolitan Lectionary introduced specific readings, whose theme was a preparation for the forty-day fast. Indeed, after a continuous reading of the Gospel of Luke, for the Sundays of the Publican and the Pharisee and the Prodigal Son, we take a step backward: from section 94 we go back to sections 89 and 79, and for the two Sundays that follow (Meat-Fare and Cheese-Fare), we shall see that the readings are taken from the Gospel of Matthew. We can clearly see, therefore, a tendency to choose, during this preparatory period, gospel readings preparing the faithful for the fast.[21]

THE ORDO OF THE OFFICE

Once again, the Triodion contains only the office for this Sunday, and nothing for the week that follows.

At "Lord, I call" at vespers, two stichera, each sung twice, are added to six from the Octoechos, as well as a doxastikon. There is also a doxastikon for the *lite* and one for the aposticha.

At matins, Psalm 136 ("By the waters of Babylon") is added to the two polyeleos psalms (Pss 134 and 135). We should note that in Greek practice, Psalm 136 is sung with the polyeleos only on Meat-Fare and Cheese-Fare Sundays. As we saw in the preceding chapter, this psalm was originally an integral part of the polyeleos, whose origin is tied to the person of St Theodore the Studite. Theodore also elaborated a system of chant in eight tones, in which the word "Alleluia" served as a refrain to the kathismata of the Palestinian Psalter. And indeed, in the Palestinian Psalter, Psalms 134, 135, and 136 formed the first stasis of kathisma 19. The frequent repetition of the phrase "For his mercy endures for ever" (ὅτι εἰς αἰῶνα τὸ ἔλεος αὐτοῦ) in Psalm 135 subsequently gave the name polyeleos to this group of psalms. The Studite Typika, like the Typikon of Alexios the Studite, for example,

---

[19]See the comparative table in G. Bertonière, *The Sundays of Lent in the Triodion: The Sundays Without a Commemoration*, OCA 253 (Rome, 1997), 46–47.

[20]Ibid., 77.

[21]Karabinov, *Postnaia Triod'*, 23.

indeed describe the chanting of the polyeleos as that of the first stasis of kathisma 19.[22] In the Georgian Sabaite Typikon of Chio-Mgvin, however, only Psalm 135 is included in the polyeleos.[23] In other Typika, we find other selected psalms at the end of the polyeleos. According to Uspenskii, these psalms at first replaced Psalm 136, and were then themselves replaced with "selected" psalm verses, elaborated during the thirteenth century by Nikephoras Blemmydes.[24] As a result, Psalm 136, originally part of the polyeleos, survived in contemporary practice only in the vigil of Sunday of the Prodigal Son, as well as at the vigils of Meat-Fare and Cheese-Fare Sundays, as we shall see. J. Matéos, for his part, believes that the polyeleos originally belonged to the ancient cathedral vigil in Jerusalem, as it is described by Egeria. In the three psalms preceding the incensation and the reading of the gospel in Egeria,[25] he sees the source of the three psalms constituting the polyeleos (Pss 134, 135, and 136).[26]

As was done on the preceding Sunday, penitential troparia are sung after Psalm 50. Similarly, a canon from the Triodion with six troparia is added to the canons from the Octoechos (of the Resurrection, four troparia; of the Cross and the Resurrection, two troparia; of the Mother of God, two troparia). After the third ode, the kathisma troparion from the Triodion is sung, and, after the sixth ode, the kontakion and ikos from the Triodion. Then comes the reading from the Synaxarion of Nicephoras Kallistos Xanthopoulos. After the ninth ode, an exaposteilarion from the Triodion is added to the gospel exaposteilarion. At lauds, three stichera from the Triodion are added to five stichera from the Octoechos, as well as a doxastikon.

Saturday of the dead during Meat-Fare week

ORIGIN

Saturday of Meat-Fare week is dedicated to the memory of "our fathers and brothers, all the Orthodox Christians who fell asleep throughout the ages." This is a universal commemoration of all the dead, which we shall find again

---

[22]Pentkovskii, *Tipikon*, 405.

[23]K. Kelelidze, *Liturgicheskie gruzinskie pamiatniki* (Tbilissi, 1908), 318.

[24]N.D. Uspenskii, "Chin vsenoshchnogo bdeniia na Pravoslavnom Vostoke i v Russkoi Tserkvi," *BT* 18 (1978): 85–86 (note 115); Karabinov, *Postnaia Triod'*, 199.

[25]Égérie, *Journal de voyage*, 24, 10 (SC 296, pp. 244–45).

[26]J. Matéos, "La vigile cathédrale chez Égérie," *OCP* 27 (1961): 281–312, especially 303 and 307.

on the Saturday before Pentecost. Thus we find such a commemoration and the beginning and the end of the moveable cycle.

The first indication of this universal commemoration of the dead on Saturday of Meat-Fare week appears in the Typikon of the Great Church (9th–10th century). It is possible that it was instituted in connection with the commemoration on Meat-Fare Sunday of the last judgement. The Typikon St Alexios the Studite (11th century) describes an ordo of the office very similar to what we celebrate today.[27]

Bishop Afanasii (Sakharov) believed that, during these two days, the Church prayed in a more intense way for the repose of all the dead, familiar and stranger, known and unknown, of every age and circumstance, of all times and all peoples, of all who have died since the beginning of the world. According to him, this is the reason the Church put aside the commemoration of saints from the Menaion, in order to dedicate itself fully to prayer for the dead.[28] Indeed, in contrast with other Saturdays, when the commemoration of the dead follows the glorification of all the saints, here the memorial of the dead takes up the entire focus of the liturgical celebration.

The order of the office on this Saturday, modeled on the office for the dead on Saturday, has a number of peculiarities, for the reasons we just enumerated. Only the Triodion and the Octoechos are used, with the office from the Menaion shifted to compline.

If this Saturday falls on the patronal feast of the church, or with the Feast of the Entrance into the Temple (February 2), the Typikon indicates that the office for the dead is not eliminated, but celebrated in the ossuary (or shifted to the preceding Saturday), while the festal office is celebrated in the church.

THE ORDO

At vespers (celebrated in monasteries either in the ossuary or the cemetery), at "Lord, I call" three stichera (in honor of the martyrs) are sung from the Octoechos in the tone of the week, and three stichera from the Triodion. The doxastikon is from the Triodion and then, as on every Friday evening, follows the Sunday theotokion from the Octoechos in the tone of the week. There is no entrance. The evening prokeimenon is replaced by "Alleluia" in tone 8,

[27] A.A. Lukashevich, "Vselenskie subboty," in *Pravoslavnaia Entsiklopedia* IX (Moscow, 2005), 565–66.
[28] Episkop Afanasii (Sakharov), *O pominovenii usopshikh po ustavu Pravoslavnoi Tserkvi* (St Petersburg, 1995), 37.

with the verses for the dead ("Blessed are those whom you have chosen," and "Their souls shall dwell with the righteous"). At the aposticha, the stichera from the Octoechos are sung in the tone of the week, with special verses for the dead. The doxastikon and theotokion are taken from the Triodion. After the Lord's Prayer, the troparion for the dead is sung in tone 8 ("In the depth of the wisdom" and its theotokion: "In you we have our refuge").

The Triodion prescribes that, after the dismissal of vespers, a panikhida (the office for the dead) be celebrated in the narthex, at which the canon from the dead from the Octoechos is sung in the tone of the week. According to the ancient Typika and in contemporary monastic practice, this panikhida is celebrated either in the ossuary or the monastic cemetery.

At matins, we sing "Alleluia" in tone 8, with the verses for the dead ("Blessed are those whom you have chosen," and "Their souls shall dwell with the righteous"), then the troparion for the dead twice—"In the depth of the wisdom"—and its theotokion: "In you we have our refuge." As on every Saturday, kathismata 16 and 17 are read. After the first kathisma, we sing the kathisma troparia from the Octoechos. As at offices for the dead, kathisma 17 is interspersed with refrains and divided into two stanzas. The priest (accompanied by the deacon) leaves the sanctuary and goes to the table for the dead (where candles for the dead are lit, and where the *kollyvo* and other offerings are deposited), which the deacon incenses continuously while silently reading the diptychs of the dead. After the first stanza (Ps 118.1–93), the synapte for the dead is recited. Then the second stanza of kathisma 17 (Ps 118. 94–176) is read, after which the evlogitaria troparia are sung ("The assembly of the saints," etc.). At this time, in Russian practice, the priest, preceded by the deacon with a candle, incenses the entire church. After the evlogitaria, the synapte for the dead is said once again, and the kathisma troparion ("Give rest with the just") from the Triodion is sung. The priest and deacon return into the sanctuary.

Psalm 50 is read, and we begin to sing the canon. We sing six troparia from the canon of the dedication of the church (the feast or the saint after whom the church is named), and then eight troparia from the Triodion canon. We note that the Triodion canon contains ode 2, which is sung with eight troparia. After the third ode, the customary small synapte is said, and we sing the kathisma troparion and its theotokion from the Triodion. After the sixth ode, during the katabasia, the priest and the deacon again go to the table for the dead. The synapte for the dead is said once again. Then the kontakion for the dead is sung ("With the saints give rest"). During this hymn, the deacon incenses the table on all four sides, then the iconostasis, the priest, and the faithful. The celebrants then return to the sanctuary. At the ninth ode, the Magnificat is sung as usual. After the ninth ode follow the customary small synapte, and then the exaposteilaria and theotokion from the Triodion.

At lauds, which are read, four stichera from the Triodion are sung, and then a doxastikon and theotokion, both from the Triodion as well. The doxology is read. At the aposticha, the stichera for the dead from the Octoechos are sung in the tone of the week, with verses for the dead ("Blessed are those whom you have chosen," and "Their souls shall dwell with the righteous"). The doxastikon and theotokion are taken from the Triodion. After the Lord's Prayer, the troparion for the dead is sung in tone 8 ("In the depth of the wisdom" and its theotokion: "In you we have our refuge"). Then matins concludes as on ordinary days. At the hours and the eucharistic liturgy, the troparion and kontakion for the dead are sung. At the liturgy, the theotokion is added: "In you we have our refuge."

Meat-Fare Sunday, the Last Judgment

ORIGIN

The third Sunday of the preparatory period is Meat-Fare Sunday (ἀποκρέω), the last day on which lay people may eat meat.

This Sunday is also called "Sunday of the Last Judgment," in reference to the gospel pericope appointed that day by the ninth to tenth-century Typikon of the Great Church (Mt 25.31–46). In earlier times, however, other readings were used. For example, the Georgian Lectionary had the reading of Mt 6.34–7.21.[29] We can therefore conclude that the hymnography for this Sunday found in the Triodion is of Constantinopolitan origin and cannot antedate the ninth to tenth centuries.

THE ORDO

As was the case with the two previous Sundays, only the Octoechos and the Triodion are used. At vespers, the Triodion contains four stichera for "Lord, I call," to which six are added from the Octoechos, as well as a doxastikon.

---

[29]See the comparative table in G. Bertonière, *The Sundays of Lent in the Triodion: The Sundays Without a Commemoration*, OCA 253 (Rome, 1997), 46–47.

There are also a doxastikon and a theotokion for the *lite* stichera, and a doxastikon for the aposticha.

At matins, as on the preceding Sunday, Psalm 136 ("By the waters of Babylon") is added to the two psalms of the polyeleos (Pss 134 and 135). The penitential troparia are also sung after Psalm 50. The Triodion canon is sung with eight troparia, to which are added two canons from the Octoechos (of the Resurrection, four troparia; and of the Mother of God, two troparia). After the third ode, we sing a kathisma troparion from the Triodion, and after the sixth ode, the kontakion and ikos from the Triodion. Then follows the reading from the Synaxarion of Nicephoras Kallistos Xanthopoulos. After the ninth ode, a photagogikon from the Triodion is added to the gospel exaposteilarion. At the lauds, four stichera from the Triodion are added to five stichera from the Octoechos, as well as a doxastikon. The last three stichera are accompanied by verses from the Triodion.

At the hours, only the kontakion from the Triodion is read. So also at the Liturgy, except that the kontakion of the church (if the church is dedicated to the Mother of God or a saint) is eventually added—but the kontakion from the Octoechos is not sung.

Particularities during Cheese-Fare Week

ELIMINATION OF THE FAST

The week that follows Meat-Fare Sunday is Cheese-Fare Week. After meat is no longer allowed, this is now the last week during which eggs and cheese may be consumed. This week is therefore also a week of relaxation before the strenuous efforts of Great Lent. Fasting is eliminated on Wednesday and Friday, as the rubric in the Triodion indicates:

> We do the same during Cheese-Fare Week, except that on Wednesday and Friday we do the office with Alleluia. Thus the brethren get a little rest. Observing the fast until the ninth hour and making prostrations, after vespers we eat cheese and eggs on these two days, keeping the rule of our Father among the saints, the Confessor Nicephoras of Constantinople, who says that it is fitting for the monks to fast on Wednesday and Friday of Cheese-Fare and to eat cheese and eggs after the dismissal of vespers. Whoever deviates from this rule will fall prey to the teaching of the Jacobites and to the Quartodeciman heresy.[30]

[30] *Triod' postnaia* (Moscow, 1992), 48v.

This last rubric, which may at first glance seem contradictory, comes from
the Sabaite Typika.[31] As for the Typikon of Alexios the Studite, it says:

> For it is not fitting to fast on Wednesday and Friday of Cheese-Fare
> Week. [...] After the conclusion of vespers, having entered the refec-
> tory, we eat eggs, cheese, and fish. [...] We even drink three cups of
> wine, because this was transmitted from above by the Fathers in order to
> refute certain heresies.[32]

All these rubrics refer to various heresies and to a canon attributed to Patriarch St Nicephoras of Constantinople.

In order to understand to what polemics these rubrics refer, it is necessary to know that the duration of Great Lent has evolved in the Christian
East. In Jerusalem, a fast of six weeks was observed originally, or the equiva-
lent of 40 days before Pascha.[33] Later, the practice evolved to eight weeks,
with five days of fasting per week, because, in accordance with Apostolic
Canon 64, one did not fast on Saturday or Sunday.[34] This new practice was
observed by the western pilgrim Egeria during her stay in the Holy City
between 381 and 384, as we can see in her journal.[35] John Cassian, on the
other hand, speaks of the fast as a tithe of the days of the year.[36] This leads
us to conclude that, at the beginning of the fifth century, Palestine shifted
from an eight-week to a seven-week fast.

In the sixth century, St Dorotheos of Gaza takes up the calculation of St
John Cassian of the fast as a tithe of the year, which he considers to be of
apostolic provenance. He explains how the Fathers later added an eighth,
supplementary week.[37] This practice was also observed in Antioch at the

---

[31]See, for example, *Sinai gr. 1094*, f. 68v. (Edited by Lossky, *Le Typikon byzantin*, p. 240);
Typikon (Moscow, 1906), 401.

[32]Pentkovskii, *Tipikon*, 374.

[33]See S. Verhelst, "Histoire ancienne de la durée du carême à Jérusalem," *Questions
liturgiques* 84 (2003): 23–50.

[34]See P.-P. Joannou, *Discipline générale antique* (Fonti, fasc. 9), vol. 1, 2 (Rome, 1962),
41.

[35]Égérie, *Journal de voyage*, 27, 1 (SC 296, pp. 257–59).

[36]"Therefore, if from seven weeks you take away the Saturdays and the Sundays, there
remain thirty-five days dedicated to fasting. Add to this the great vigil on Saturday, during
which we continue the fast until cockcrow, at the first hours of the Sunday of the Resurrection: and you have not only thirty-six days, but, in counting the nighttime as the tithe for
the other five days, you reach a total which lacks nothing." Jean Cassien, *Conférences XXI*,
25 (trans. E. Pichery, SC 64 [Paris, 1959], 100).

[37]"It is the Fathers who later agreed to add another week, both to practice in advance

same time, since Severus of Antioch (†538) gives a spiritual interpretation for the eight weeks of fasting.[38]

We know as well that an eighth week of additional fasting was introduced during the seventh century by Heraclius (610–641). Indeed, after the victory of Heraclius over the Persians in 629, he agreed to punish those Jews in Jerusalem who had collaborated with the Persians and who had persecuted Christians, as long as these Christians agreed to fast an extra week before Great Lent. But this practice was quickly abandoned.[39]

During the eighth century, however, there was a controversy in the East about whether the fast should last seven or eight weeks. In his treatise on fasting, St John of Damascus divided the eight weeks before Pascha into three parts: a preparatory week, the six-week forty-day fast, and Holy Week.[40] We should be aware that the custom of fasting for eight weeks was kept among the Monophysites (Severians and Copts), which explains why the Chalcedonians wanted to distinguish themselves. A canon attributed to Patriarch Nicephoras of Constantinople (*c.* 758–*c.* 829), a confessor of Orthodoxy, states that one must not fast during this eighth week in order to mark oneself off from the Monophysites.[41]

The rubrics we cited above do in fact mention the Jacobites and the Tetradites or Quartodecimans, who were Severian Monophysites, as distinct from the Quartodecimans of the first centuries.[42] Jacob Bardaeus (*c.* 500–*c.* 578),

and properly to dispose those who will dedicated themselves to the effort of fasting, and to honor these fasts through the holy number 40, which the Lord himself spent in fasting." Dorothée de Gaza (6th century), *Oeuvres spirituelles*, XV, 159 (trans. L. Regnault and J. de Préville, SC 92 [Paris, 1963], 446).

[38]"After having given these explanations, let us return to speak about what we proposed, and let us see why we fast only during these forty days. Why?—In order to prepare ourselves for this eighth and first day, this important and resplendent [day], this day of the Lord. Indeed, those who purify eight times these five senses by means of which sin enters, I mean hearing, sight, touch, taste, and smell, fast for forty days in order to reach the joyful day, this eight and first day, for the number five, in returning eight times, completes the number forty." Sévère d'Antioche, *Homélie cathédrale* XV, 15 (PO 38, fasc. 2, no. 175 [Turnhout, 1976], 428–29). See also Karabinov, *Postnaia Triod'*, 16.

[39]Ibid., 24.

[40]John of Damascus, *On the Sacred Fast* (PG 95, col. 699D). French translation by V. Conticello in: θυσία αἰνέσεως. *Mélanges liturgiques offerts à la mémoire de l'archévêque Georges Wagner*, "Analecta Sergiana" 2, eds., J. Getcha and A. Lossky (Paris, 2005), 92–93. On the evolution of Great Lent in the Byzantine world, see J. Getcha, "La pratique du jeûne pendant la quarantaine paschale d'après le Triode byzantin," in ibid., 95–112; N.D. Uspenskii, "Sviataia Chetyredesiatnitsa. Istoriko-liturgicheskii ocherk," *ZhMP* 3 (1945): 33–38.

[41]Ibid., 21.

[42]Ibid.

head of the Syrian Christians and considered to be the father of the "Jaco-bites," traveled to Constantinople around 528 to plead the Monophysite cause, and then became bishop of Edessa toward 542. Having become the soul of the resistance to the politics and theology of Emperor Justinian, he traveled throughout Egypt and Syria, and even to Armenia and Persia, ordaining thousands of priests, twenty-seven bishops and two patriarchs, and found-ing anti-Chalcedonian churches. For this reason he was considered by his enemies as the founder of the Monophysite or "Jacobite" Church.[43]

The rule of St Nicephoras the Confessor mentioned in these rubrics refers to Canon 32 attributed to Patriarch Nicephoras, stipulating that:

> Monks must fast on Wednesday and Friday of Cheese-Fare. And after the dismissal from the Liturgy of the Presanctified, they must eat cheese where it is available, either at the market, or, in other words, wherever it can be obtained, in order to refute the heresy of the Jacobites and the Tetradites.[44]

We should note that, in the Triodia of Jerusalem redaction, the rubric concerning the time at which cheese and eggs are eaten on Wednesday and Friday of Cheese-Fare has been corrected to reflect Palestinian practice, in which the Liturgy of the Presanctified was not celebrated on these days, as it was when the Typikon of the Great Church of Constantinople was being followed. This new practice spread with the reforms of Patriarch Philotheos and of Metropolitan Cyprian during the fourteenth century. The words in the canon, "after Presanctified" ("μετὰ τῶν προηγιασμένων") were replaced with "after vespers."[45]

THE ORDO OF THE SERVICES DURING CHEESE-FARE WEEK

Beginning with Cheese-Fare Week, the Triodion has an office for each day. From the evening of Meat-Fare Sunday until Saturday of the sixth week of Lent, at vespers, the aposticha stichera from the Octoechos are not sung, but instead the stichera idiomela from the Triodion.[46]

---

[43]J.M. Fiey, "Jacques Baradée," *Dictionnaire d'histoire et de géographie ecclésiastiques*, vol. 26 (Paris, 1997), cols. 626–27; D.D. Bundy, "Jacob Bardaeus," *Le Muséon* 41 (1978): 45–86.

[44]Πηδάλιον (Athens, 1886), 588; D. Cummins, *The Rudder (Pedalion)* (Chicago, 1957), 968. Canon 40 in I.B. Pitra, *Juris ecclesiastici graecorum historia et monumenta*, II (Rome, 1868), 331.

[45]I. Mansvetov, *Mitropolit Kiprian v ego liturgicheskoi deiatel'nosti* (Moscow, 1882), 69.

[46]*Typikon*, ch. 49, note 1.

At matins on each day of this week, the Triodion contains canons with three odes (tri-ode). The canons of the Triodion are preceded by canons from the Menaion. For the odes missing from the Triodion, the Menaion canon is preceded by two canons from the Octoechos. The hirmos is always taken from the first canon, and the katabasia (after the 1st, 3rd, 6th, 8th, and 9th odes) from the second canon.

The most complicated cases are on Wednesday and Friday, when the Triodion contains not only two three-ode canons, but a nine-ode canon (without ode 2). In this case, for each ode where there is a three-ode canon, we read six troparia from the first canon and eight troparia from the two three-ode canons. The troparia of the canon from the Menaion are then read in anticipation during a previous ode. In this case, the number of troparia from the first canon from the Octoechos is reduced from 6 to 4, and that from the Menaion canon augmented from 4 to 6.

The following tables summarize the composition of the canons during Cheese-Fare Week:

Tables summarizing the composition of the canons at matins of Cheese-Fare Week

---

		Monday	
Ode	Octoechos	Menaion	Triodion
1	0	6	8
2	0	0	0
3	6+4	4	0
4	6+4	4	0
5	6+4	4	0
6	6+4	4	0
7	6+4	4	0
8	0	6	8
9	0	6	8

Tuesday

Ode	Octoechos	Menaion	Triodion
1	6+4	4	0
2	0	0	8
3	6+4	4	0
4	6+4	4	0
5	6+4	4	0
6	6+4	4	0
7	6+4	4	0
8	0	6	8
9	0	6	8

Wednesday

Ode	Octoechos	Menaion	Triodion
1	4	3+3	4
2	0	0	0
3	0	0	6+8
4	6	4	4
5	6	4	4
6	4	3+3	4
7	4	3+3	4
8	0	0	6+8
9	0	0	6+8

Thursday

Ode	Octoechos	Menaion	Triodion
1	6+4	4	0
2	0	0	0
3	6+4	4	0
4	0	6	8
5	6+4	4	0
6	6+4	4	0
7	6+4	4	0
8	0	6	8
9	0	6	8

Friday

Ode	Octoechos	Menaion	Triodion
1	6	4	4
2	0	0	0
3	6	4	4
4	4	3+3	4
5	0	0	6+8
6	4	3+3	4
7	4	3+3	4
8	0	0	6+8
9	0	0	6+8

Note that in some places, as at the Monastery of Simonos Petras on Mt Athos, this arrangement is simplified according to the following order: Octoechos, Menaion, Triodion. Thus, when an ode from the Triodion is chanted, the Octoechos canon is eliminated, and the canon from the Menaion is sung first with six troparia, followed by the two Triodion canons:

Monday	Ode 1:	6 Menaion, 8 Triodion
	Odes 3, 4, 5, 6, and 7	10 Octoechos, 4 Menaion
	Odes 8 and 9	8 Menaion, 8 Triodion
Tuesday	Odes 1, 3, 4, 5, 6, and 7	10 Octoechos, 4 Menaion
	Ode 2	8 Triodion
	Odes 8 and 9	6 Menaion, 8 Triodion
Wednesday	Odes 1, 4, 5, 6, and 7	6 Octoechos, 4 Menaion, 4 Triodion
	Odes 3, 8, and 9	4 + 6 + 4 Triodion
Thursday	Odes 1, 3, 5, 6, and 7	10 Octoechos, 4 Menaion
	Odes 4, 8, and 9	8 Menaion, 8 Triodion
Friday	Odes 1, 3, 4, 6, and 7	6 Octoechos, 4 Menaion, 4 Triodion
	Odes 5, 8, and 9	4 + 6 + 4 Triodion

The services on Wednesday and Friday of Cheese-Fare are indeed particular. By anticipation, they follow, with a few exceptions, the ordo of the offices of Great Lent. Thus the vespers of Tuesday evening conclude with prostrations. After the Lord's Prayer, the troparia with prostrations are sung: "O Mother of God and Virgin," "O Forerunner of Christ," "O holy Apostles, intercede for us," as well as "Beneath your compassion" (without a prostration). Instead of the ektene, we say *Kyrie eleison* 40 times, Glory to the Father . . . Now and ever . . . More honorable than the Cherubim . . . In the name of the Lord, bless father! The priest says the blessing: "Christ our God, He who is, is blessed . . ." Then the prayer "O heavenly King . . ." The priest then recites the Prayer of St Ephrem in three sections, each followed by a prostration, then 12 small prostrations, then the Prayer of St Ephrem in its entirety with one prostration. The trisagion prayers are then read once more through the Lord's Prayer. Then *Kyrie eleison* 12 times, and the dismissal: "Glory to you, O Christ our God and our hope, glory to you," etc. Then it is prescribed to read great compline (the troparia sung during Lent are read), accompanied by prostrations and the Prayer of St Ephrem at the end. At the end of the midnight office, the Prayer of St Ephrem is also said, with 16 prostrations.

At matins, "Alleluia" is sung instead of "God is the Lord." After the first section of psalmody, the kathisma troparia from the Octoechos are sung, and after the second section, the kathisma troparia from the Triodion. The canon is done as explained above (see the table). Matins concludes with prostrations. "It is good to confess the Lord" is read one time. After the Lord's Prayer, we read the troparion, "Standing in the temple of your glory." Instead of the ektene, we say *Kyrie eleison* 40 times, Glory to the Father . . . Now and ever . . . More honorable than the Cherubim . . . In the name of the Lord, bless father! The priest says the blessing: "Christ our God, He who is, is blessed . . ." Then the prayer "O heavenly King . . ." The priest then recites the Prayer of St Ephrem in three sections, each followed by a prostration, then 12 small prostrations, then the Prayer of St Ephrem in its entirety with one prostration. The first hour follows. At the hours, the troparia and kontakia of the hours (from the Horologion) are read, rather than sung as during Great Lent, and the Prayer of St Ephrem is recited at he end of each hour, accompanied by 16 prostrations. (At the ninth hour, only 3 prostrations are done with the Prayer of St Ephrem.) At the sixth hour, a prophetic reading from Joel is read, preceded by the troparion of the prophecy and a prokeimenon, and followed by another prokeimenon whose text is found in the Triodion.

On this day, the Divine Liturgy is not celebrated, nor the Liturgy of the Presanctified, as we have seen above. After the ninth hour, the typika are read. At the conclusion of the typika, the Prayer of St Ephrem is recited, with 16 prostrations. Vespers begins immediately.

At vespers on Wednesday evening, there is a prophetic reading from Joel, preceded and followed by a prokeimenon. Vespers conclude with the troparion for the saint of the day and its theotokion, the ektene, after which the Prayer of St Ephrem is said once (with three prostrations), then the prayer "Most holy Trinity," "Blessed be the name of the Lord," Glory . . . now and ever . . . , and Psalm 33. We should note, however, that in Greek practice, vespers on Wednesday and Friday evening follow the customary order. Then follows the dismissal: "Wisdom!"—"It is truly meet . . ."; "O most holy Mother of God, save us!"—"More honorable than the Cherubim"; "Glory to you, O Christ our God and our hope, glory to you," etc. Then small compline is read.

The same ordo is followed on Friday (beginning on Thursday evening), except that the prophecies at sext and at vespers are from Zechariah.

Saturday of Cheese-Fare, memorial of all the holy monks who shone through ascetical efforts

The Typikon calls for the Menaion office falling on Cheese-Fare Saturday to be celebrated at compline on another day of the week, because the Triodion appoints on this day the commemoration "of all our venerable and God-bearing Fathers who have shone through fasting"—an office found in the Triodion and scrupulously observed. The office is doxological, and thus the Octoechos and Menaion are omitted.

At matins, "God is the Lord" is sung, followed by the troparion to the holy monks ("O God of our Fathers") and the Sunday theotokion. The canon of the church (the saint or the feast to which the church is dedicated) is sung with six troparia, and then eight troparia from the canon from the Triodion in honor of the holy monks and holy women. Note that this last canon has its own katabasia and a second ode, signs of antiquity. After the third ode, a kathisma troparion from the Triodion is sung, and after the sixth ode, the kontakion and ikos from the Triodion. Then comes the reading from the Synaxarion of Nicephoras Kallistos Xanthopoulos. After the ninth ode, "It is truly meet" is not sung, because the canon has its own katabasia. After the small synapte, the exaposteilarion from the Triodion is sung. Then "Let every breath" and four lauds stichera from the Triodion, with their doxastikon and theotokion. The great doxology is then sung. At the hours, the troparion and kontakion (for the holy monks) from the Triodion are read. At the liturgy, the troparion and kontakion of the church are added, and two epistles and two gospels are read.

Cheese-Fare Sunday, the expulsion of Adam, forgiveness

The hymnography for the Sunday preceding the beginning of Great Lent is inspired by the creation and the sin of Adam and Eve, connecting the theme of the gluttony of Adam and the forty-day fast of the Lord in the desert. According to the commentary of Xanthopoulos, the origin of this Sunday is very ancient, probably from Palestine.[47]

As on the preceding Sundays, only the Octoechos and the Triodion are used. At vespers, the Triodion supplies four stichera at "Lord, I call," as well as a doxastikon, to which six stichera are added from the Octoechos. The Triodion also contains a doxastikon and theotokion for the *lite*, and a doxastikon and theotokion for the aposticha.

At matins, as at the preceding Sunday, Psalm 136 ("By the waters of Babylon") is added to the two psalms of the polyeleos (Pss 134 and 135). So also, after Psalm 50, the penitential troparia are sung. The canon from the Triodion is sung with six troparia, to which are added the three canons from the Octoechos (of the resurrection, four troparia; of the Cross and the Resurrection, two troparia; and of the Mother of God, two troparia). After the third ode, a kathisma troparion from the Triodion is sung, and after the sixth ode, the kontakion and ikos from the Triodion. Then follows the reading from the Synaxarion of Nicephoras Kallistos Xanthopoulos. After the ninth ode and after "Holy is our God," an exaposteilarion from the Triodion is added to the gospel exaposteilarion. At the lauds, four stichera from the Triodion are added to the five stichera from the Octoechos, and a doxastikon from the Triodion.

At the hours, we read only the kontakion from the Triodion. So also at the liturgy, though eventually the kontakion of the church (if it is dedicated to the Mother of God or a saint) is also sung. The kontakion from the Octoechos is not sung, but only that from the Triodion.

[47]M. Arranz, "Les fêtes théologiques du calendrier byzantin," in *La Liturgie, expression de la foi. Conférences Saint-Serge. XXVᵉ Semaine d'études liturgiques* (Rome, 1979), 37–39.

At the Divine Liturgy on this Sunday (as on the Sundays that follow), two extra lambs are prepared and consecrated for the Presanctified Liturgies on Wednesday and Friday following. During the proskomide, the necessary number of additional lambs is prepared in exactly the same way as the principal lamb. At the liturgy, during the elevation of the gifts (at "Holy things are for the holy"), the priest raises all the lambs together. Then he intincts the lambs that are intended for the Presanctified Liturgies by tracing a sign of the cross on them with the spoon containing the consecrated wine. (Some dip the lamb directly in the chalice, but this practice is not recommended.) These lambs are then placed in an *artophorion* or on a diskos, which then remains on the altar table until the celebration of the Presanctified Liturgy. We should be aware of the fact that, from the origin of the Presanctified Liturgy around the sixth century, and until the ninth century, not only was the consecrated bread preserved, but also a chalice containing the consecrated wine. They were kept on the prothesis table, from which they were again placed on the altar table during the great entrance of the Presanctified Liturgy. As a result of the difficulty and the danger of keeping a chalice full of consecrated wine, the practice of intincting the consecrated bread with the consecrated wine appeared, probably in the ninth century, in southern Italy. Only in the fifteenth century was this practice adopted in Constantinople and in the Byzantine world.[48]

The Office during Great Lent

Particularities of the services during Great Lent

The weekday services during Lent, from Monday to Friday, follow a particular order, different from that of the Saturday and Sunday services. They are referred to by the term "office with Alleluia," whereas the services during ordinary time are labeled by the term "God is the Lord," which is sung at the beginning of matins. The ordo of these services, which we will now describe, minus individual rubrical details, will serve as a model for the totality of Great Lent.

During the week, these offices use only the Triodion and the Menaion. The few necessary hymns from the Octoechos (photagogika and kathisma

---

[48] A. Raes, "La Communion au Calice dans l'Office byzantin des Présanctifiés, *OCP* 20 (1954): 168–69.

troparia) are found in an appendix at the end of the Triodion. The Liturgy
of St John Chrysostom is not celebrated on weekdays, but only on Saturdays
and on the day of Annunciation, while the Liturgy of St Basil is celebrated
on Sundays. On Wednesdays and Fridays, as well as on feast days with polyeleos, the Liturgy of the Presanctified is celebrated.

VESPERS ON SUNDAY EVENING

The services of each week of Great Lent begin with vespers on Sunday evening, which follows a particular order because it serves as a kind of transition between the festal and the Lenten office.

As on every Sunday evening, there is no psalmody (reading from the
Psalter) at vespers (because of the tiredness resulting from the all-night vigil
that was celebrated each week at St Sabas Monastery). At "Lord, I call," ten
stichera are sung: four from the Octoechos, three from the Triodion, and
three from the Menaion.

During the singing of the theotokion, the vespers entrance takes place
with a candle and the censer. The Typika specify that this entrance, which
never occurs except on feast days, occurs on "every Sunday evening during
the holy fast, because of the great prokeimena."[49] This seems to be a relatively recent practice (appearing toward the 14th century), since the more
ancient Sabaite Typika (from the 12th century), as well as the Typikon of
Alexios the Studite, did not indicate an entrance at these vespers and did
not have great prokeimena. The two prokeimena indicated for Sundays of
Great Lent had only one verse.[50]

In contemporary practice, we have two great prokeimena (with three
verses), which are used alternately beginning on Cheese-Fare Sunday: "Do
not turn away your face from your servant" and "You have given your inher-
itance to those who fear your name."[51]

The Typika indicate that prostrations are resumed beginning from the
prayer "Vouchsafe, O Lord."[52] This rubric is in accordance with Canon 90 of
the Council in Trullo, which indicates that there should be no kneeling from

---

[49]See, for example, the *Triodion* (Moscow, 1992), 77; *Typikon* (Moscow, 1906), 405v.

[50]For example, *Sinai gr. 1094*, f. 70v. and 79v. (edited by A. Lossky, *Le Typikon byzantin*,
243 and 253); Pentkovskii, *Tipikon*, 238 and 241.

[51]See the *Triodion* (Moscow, 1992), 77 and 152; *Typikon* (Moscow, 1906), 404v. and
423v.

[52]Pentkovskii, *Tipikon*, 238 and 241; see also, for example, *Typikon* (Moscow, 1906),
405.

the entrance of vespers on Saturday evening until the entrance of vespers on Sunday.[53] It is in fact the custom to cease prostrations beginning with vespers on Friday evening, at which the festal ordo of the office resumes. Beginning with this prayer on Sunday evening, we resume the Lenten ordo. It is, by the way, during this prayer that the priest changes his vestments, passing from a light to a dark color, as also the ornaments in the church.

After the synapte with demands, aposticha from the Triodion are sung. In Greek practice, the first idiomelon is sung very ornately. Vespers conclude with the singing of troparia indicated for the "Alleluia" office, accompanied by prostrations, from the Horologion: "O Mother of God and Virgin," "O Forerunner of Christ," "O holy Apostles, intercede for us," as well as "Beneath your compassion" (without a prostration). Instead of the ektene, we say *Kyrie eleison* 40 times, Glory to the Father . . . Now and ever . . . More honorable than the Cherubim . . . In the name of the Lord, bless father! The priest says the blessing: "Christ our God, He who is, is blessed . . ." Then the prayer "O heavenly King . . ." The priest then recites the Prayer of St Ephrem. On Sunday evening, at the end of vespers, there are only three full prostrations at the Prayer of St Ephrem (and not 16 as during the week). While neither the Typikon of Alexios the Studite nor the ancient Sabaite Typika give any specific instructions,[54] the later Sabaite Typika specify that this prayer is said by each one "raising their hands, standing," and "meditating."[55] In current practice, the prayer is recited by the priest.

The Triodion then indicates that the icons be venerated and the dismissal takes place. In the monasteries on Athos, the veneration of icons, as well as bowing to the community from the center of the church, takes place during the aposticha at every service. In our day, a solemn rite of forgiveness occurs on Cheese-Fare Sunday, modeled on the customary asking for forgiveness at the conclusion of each office. The rite takes place after the dismissal of vespers. On Athos, this rite of forgiveness is generally performed in the refectory, after the evening meal and the reading of compline. The abbot reads a prayer of absolution, and as the monks leave they kiss the small gospel book he holds in his hands, then they ask forgiveness of one another and wish each other a blessed Lent. This rite of forgiveness has given Cheese-Fare Sunday

---

[53]See P.-P. Joannou, *Discipline générale antique* (Fonti, fasc. 9), vol. 1, 1 (Rome, 1962), 226–27.

[54]For example, *Sinai gr. 1094* mentions only three full prostrations: f. 70v. (edited by A. Lossky, *Le Typikon byzantin*, 244).

[55]*Typikon* (Moscow, 1906), 405.

its name of "Forgiveness Sunday." After the dismissal of vespers, a cross and icons of Christ and the Mother of God are placed on lecterns. The superior makes full prostrations before them, venerates them, and then offers the assembly a homily on the theme of forgiveness. He then asks for their pardon, saying: "Bless me, holy fathers, brothers [and sisters], and forgive me, a sinner, all the sins I have committed this day and on all days of my life, in word, deed, or thought, and through all my senses." He then does a full prostration. The assembly responds in turn by making a full prostration, while the second priest says: "May God forgive you, holy father. Forgive us, sinners, and bless us." The superior answers: "May God, through his grace, forgive us and have mercy on us all." The superior then takes the cross in his hands, and the clergy and the faithful approach, venerate the icons and the cross, and ask each other for mutual forgiveness. The Typika do not prescribe any hymns to accompany this rite of forgiveness. However, there are several practices: some sing at this point the repentance troparia ("Open to us the doors of repentance"), while others sing the paschal stichera. On Mt Athos, at Dionysiou and Simonas Petras, the formula "Through the prayers of our holy Fathers" is sung with a highly ornate melody. This rite of forgiveness is rooted in the ancient tradition of the Palestinian monks, who would go out into the desert for all of Great Lent and would return only on Palm Sunday, while some died in the desert and did not return to the monastery for Pascha.[56]

MATINS DURING GREAT LENT

Matins follows the order of the "office with Alleluia." They begin with the royal office and the hexapsalmos. Rubrics in the Triodion emphasize the careful attention that is due to this psalmody by recalling that

> The appointed brother, standing at the proper place, begins to read the psalms with all necessary attention, not rushing and with the fear of God, as if he were invisibly speaking with God himself, and praying for our sins. No one may whisper, or spit, or clear his throat, but he must listen attentively to the psalms read by the reader.[57]

These rubrics are identical to those during ordinary time. They were preserved in the Triodion because of the distinct character of this book, which

[56]Cyril of Scythopolis, *Life of St Euthymius* 5 and 7 (ed. E. Schwartz, *Kyrillos von Scythopolis*, "Texte und Untersuchungen" 49:2 [Leipzig, 1939]. 13 and 15); *Life of St Kyriakos* III, 3 (ibid., 225); *Life of St Sabas* 11, 22, 24–27 (ibid., 94, 106, 109–10).
[57]*Triodion* (Moscow, 1992), 78v.

very early on absorbed the rubrics from the Typikon of St Sabas. We find a similar rubric in the most ancient Sabaite Typika, such as *Sinai gr. 1094*.[58]

After the hexapsalmos, the great synapte is recited and we sing "Alleluia" in the tone of the week, accompanied by four verses from Isaiah. These verses are proclaimed by the canonarch or the deacon in the same way as the verses at "God is the Lord," while the choir responds after each verse with "Alleluia," just as for prokeimena.[59] After the "Alleluia," the triadica troparia, found in an appendix to the Triodion or in the Great Horologion, are sung in the tone of the week. Note that the ending of these troparia varies with the day of the week. The triadica troparia are so called because they conclude with a doxological formula to the Holy Trinity: "Holy, holy, holy are you, O our God." In their content, as also in the case of the verses from the Canticle of Isaiah that accompany the "Alleluia," they make no reference either to fasting or to penitence, which clearly indicates that these two units were constitutive elements of the ordinary, non-festal, office.[60]

Three kathismata from the Psalter are then read, following the arrangement for Great Lent. After the first kathisma, we sing the kathisma troparia from the Octoechos in the tone of the week (see the appendix at the end of the Triodion). After the second and third kathismata, the kathisma troparia from the Triodion are sung. It is interesting to note that, after the first and second kathismata, the Triodion appoints, throughout Lent, patristic readings from the works of St Ephrem, and the *Lausiac History* after the third kathisma.[61] After Psalm 50 (which is preceded by *Kyrie eleison*, three times, Glory . . . Now and ever . . .), the priest recites the prayer "O Lord, save your people," usually read at Sunday matins, followed by the ekphonesis. We note that this part is dropped in contemporary Greek usage.

The ordo of the canon is particular during Great Lent. The biblical canticles are sung in their entirety. This represents a major difference, because in ordinary time we sing only as many verses of the ode as there are troparia, i.e., 10. The first canticle is sung on Monday, the second on Tuesday, the third on Wednesday, the fourth on Thursday, the fifth on Friday; and the eighth and ninth are sung each day. The verses of the biblical ode are inter-

[58]"εἶτα τὸ ἐξάψαλμον μετὰ πάσης προσοχῆς καὶ φόβου θεοῦ, ὡς αὐτῷ συλλαλοῦντες ἀοράτως καὶ δυσωποῦντες αὐτὸν ὑπερ τῶν ἁμαρτιῶν ἡμῶν," *Sinai gr. 1094*, f. 71. See Lossky, *Le typikon byzantin*, 244.

[59]J. Matéos, "Quelques problems de l'orthros byzantin," *POC* 11 (1961): 203.

[60]Ibid., 27–28.

[61]*Triodion* (Moscow, 1992), 79 and 79v.

calated with the canon troparia from the Menaion and Triodion. The entire canon from the Menaion is taken, to which two three-ode canons from the Triodion are added. These three-ode canons consist of: on Monday, odes 1, 8, and 9; on Tuesday, odes 2, 8, and 9; on Wednesday, odes 3, 8, and 9; on Thursday, odes 4, 8, and 9; on Friday, odes 5, 8, and 9. The troparia of these canons are intercalated between verses of the biblical canticle. To do this, it is necessary to follow the arrangement of the biblical canticles in the section of the Hirmologion for Great Lent. For those odes for which there are canons from the Triodion, the hirmos of the Menaion canon is intercalated after the fourteenth verse before the end of the canticle, the ante-penultimate verse being "Glory," and the last being "Now and ever." Then, after each verse, we intercalate the troparia of the canon from the Menaion (6 with the hirmos) and those from the Triodion canon (eight troparia). Note that in Greek practice, most of the time the hirmos of the Menaion canon is sung twice—so as to set the tone in which the ode and the troparia will be sung—and then the entire biblical canticle with the interpolated troparia.[62] The second three-ode canon consists of one or two troparia which are not part of the fourteen troparia. These are preceded by the refrain "Glory to you, our God, glory to you." They are called *perisse* (supplement), in technical terminology. The katabasia is the hirmos of the second canon from the Triodion. Note that the second biblical canticle, considered to be a penitential canticle, is sung in its entirety, after which the troparia of the canons are read with the refrain "Glory to you, our God, glory to you." In Greek practice, the second ode is read and not sung, and then the troparia are sung. For those odes that have only a canon from the Menaion, the other canticles are sung, but only with as many verses as correspond to the number of troparia, as in ordinary time; i.e., only the last four verses of the canticle are used.

After the third ode come the small synapte and the kathisma troparion from the Menaion. After the sixth ode follows the small synapte, and then we sing the martyrikon in the tone of the week (see the appendix at the end of the Triodion). Note that the kontakion, as well as the exaposteilarion and the apolytikion troparion are omitted here on the days when "Alleluia"

[62]Note that if the Menaion contains the memorials of two saints, and that there are consequently two canons, they are then sung with the hirmos of the canon and six troparia: the hirmos of the first canon, two troparia of the first canon together, the third troparion of the first canon (the theotokion of the first canon is omitted), two troparia from the second canon together, the third troparion of the second canon, and the theotokion of the second canon. We should note that, in Greek practice, during Great Lent two canons from the Menaion are never sung.

is sung. After the ninth ode come a small synapte and then the Trinitarian photagogikon according to the tone and the day of the week (see the appendix at the end of the Triodion). Note also that the ending of the photagogikon changes depending on the day of the week.

The lauds are read in the Palestinian redaction ("Praise the Lord from the heavens"), as well as the doxology, also in the Hagiopolite version. After the synapte with demands, the aposticha from the Triodion are sung. The psalm prayer, "It is good to confess the Lord," is read twice. After the Lord's Prayer, the reader or canonarch reads the troparion (read, and not sung): "Standing in the temple of your glory." Instead of the ektene, we say *Kyrie eleison* forty times, Glory to the Father . . . Now and ever . . . More honorable than the Cherubim . . . In the name of the Lord, bless father! The priest says the blessing: "Christ our God, He who is, is blessed . . ." Then the prayer "O heavenly King . . ." The priest then recites the Prayer of St Ephrem in three sections, each followed by a prostration. Then we do twelve small prostrations, each time repeating "O God, cleanse me, a sinner." The ancient Typika specify that "all should do the prostrations in the same way."[63] Then the Prayer of St Ephrem is repeated a second time, after which we do a full prostration. Then the first hour is read.

THE HOURS

The hours are read with the troparia and kontakia from the Horologion appointed for the days on which the office is done with "Alleluia" (the troparia and kontakia are sung). The troparia are done with psalm verses and accompanied by prostrations. At the end of each hour, the Prayer of St Ephrem is said twice, with 16 prostrations, except at the ninth hour, when the Prayer is said only once, with three prostrations.

Except for prime, which is read immediately following matins, the other hours are read all together, one after the other. The office of the hours begins at the third hour of the day. For each of the hours, the monk appointed to light the lamps strikes the large simandron (*kopanon*) or rings one of the bells the number of times corresponding to the hour: three times for terce, six times for sext, nine times for none.

After the theotokion at terce, sext, and none, a reading from the *Ladder* of St John Climacus is appointed. This reading, customary in Sabaite Typika, is not mentioned in the Typikon of Alexios the Studite, which instead

[63]See *Sinai gr. 1094*, f. 72r. (edited by Lossky, *Le Typikon byzantin*, 245).

prescribes a reading at matins after the kathismata from the writings of St Ephrem of Syria.[64]

At sext, before this reading, a prophecy from Isaiah is read, preceded by a troparion of the prophecy and a prokeimenon, and followed by another prokeimenon. These troparia for the prophecy, prokeimena, and readings come from the Constantinopolitan Prophetologion, which served as the skeleton for the edition of our modern Triodion. They were intended for the office of tersext (τριτοέκτι, terce-sext) in the sung office. This office was primarily celebrated in the Great Church on those days when there was no eucharistic liturgy. During Great Lent, this office was destined essentially for the catechesis of catechumens, which explains the presence of a biblical reading which was no doubt originally followed by a sermon.[65] In this way, the cycle of readings from tersext of the Great Church was inserted into the hours of the Palestinian Horologion.

The typika that follow the ninth hour begin directly with the singing of the Beatitudes. On the days when the Presanctified Liturgy is not celebrated (Monday, Tuesday, and Thursday), following the Prayer of St Ephrem and its 16 prostrations, there is no dismissal, and vespers begins immediately. On those days when there is a Presanctified Liturgy (Wednesday and Friday), following the Prayer of St Ephrem, the typika conclude as follows: the trisagion through the Lord's Prayer, Kyrie eleison (12 times), and the prayer "O most holy Trinity." Then the dismissal: "Wisdom!"—"It is truly meet . . ."; "Most holy Theotokos, save us!"—"More honorable than the Cherubim"; "Glory to you, O Christ God, our hope, glory to you," etc.

VESPERS ON WEEKDAYS

The simandron or bell is struck twelve times. Vespers begins with Psalm 103 and the great synapte. During Great Lent, kathisma 18 is always used at vespers. At "Lord, I call," we sing three stichera from the Triodion and three from the Menaion. The theotokion is taken from the second appendix

---

[64]*Typikon* (Moscow, 1906), 410; Pentkovskii, *Tipikon*, 238, 239. *Sinai gr. 1094* (12th century) mentions a reading taken from the *Paterikon*: see *Sinai gr. 1094*, f. 73r. (edited by Lossky, *Le Typikon byzantin*, 246).

[65]M. Arranz, "Les prières prebytérales de la Tritoekti de l'ancien Euchologue byzantin," *OCP* 43 (1977): 335–36, 341–43; Matéos, *Typicon*, I, xxiv. The ancient Jerusalem liturgy also had a similar practice: see J. Getcha, *Les Grandes Fêtes dans l'Église de Jérusalem entre 381 et 431* (unpublished master's thesis defended at the Orthodox Theological Institute of St Sergius) (Paris, 1998), 54; Égérie, *Journal de voyage* 46 (SC 296, pp. 306–11); Renoux, II, 95–99.

to the Menaion. There is no entrance. Instead of the evening prokeimenon from the Horologion, a prokeimenon from the Triodion precedes the first reading (from Genesis). After this reading, a second prokeimenon from the Triodion is sung, followed by the second reading (from Proverbs). Then the presider or the reader recites the prayer "Vouchsafe, O Lord," and the priest says the synapte with demands.

The aposticha are sung from the Triodion. After St Symeon's Prayer and the trisagion prayers, the troparia from the Horologion are sung, accompanied by prostrations: "O Mother of God and Virgin," "O Forerunner of Christ," "O holy Apostles, intercede for us," as well as "Beneath your compassion" (without a prostration). In Greek practice, this theotokion is read by the reader or canonarch. Instead of the ektene, we say *Kyrie eleison* 40 times, Glory to the Father . . . now and ever . . . More honorable than the Cherubim . . . In the name of the Lord, bless father! The priest says the blessing: "Christ our God, He who is, is blessed . . ." Then the prayer "O heavenly King . . ." The priest then recites the Prayer of St Ephrem in three sections, each followed by a prostration, then 12 small prostrations, then the Prayer of St Ephrem in its entirety with one prostration. The trisagion prayers are then read once more through the Lord's Prayer. Then *Kyrie eleison* 12 times, and the prayer "Most holy Trinity," "Blessed be the name of the Lord" (3 times), Glory . . . now and ever . . . Psalm 33. Then the dismissal: "Wisdom!"—"It is truly meet . . ."; "Most holy Theotokos, save us!"—"More honorable than the Cherubim"; "Glory to you, O Christ our God and our hope, glory to you," etc.

THE PRESANCTIFIED LITURGY

At the end of vespers of Monday of the first week of Lent, the Triodion specifies:

> We have not received [from our Fathers] the practice of celebrating the Presanctified [Liturgy] until Wednesday, for it is fitting for all the brothers to fast according to tradition. Those who are able keep the fast until Friday.[66]

This rubric modified the practice that existed at the time when the Church followed the Typikon of the Great Church and the Typikon of Alexios the Studite, both of which called for the daily celebration of the Presanctified

[66] *Triodion* (Moscow, 1992), 88v.

Liturgy on weekdays of Great Lent. The Typikon of Alexios the Studite even indicated a meal in the refectory after the Presanctified Liturgy on the first Monday of Lent.[67] This Constantinopolitan practice was established by Canon 52 of the Council in Trullo, which states:

> On the days of Great Lent, except on Saturdays, Sundays, and the holy day of Annunciation, no liturgy may be celebrated except that of the Presanctified Gifts.[68]

As M. Arranz explains,

> In the seventh century, the reception of communion must have been considered as breaking the fast; also, because the eucharistic liturgy (apart from the great vigils of Christmas, Epiphany, and Easter, as well as the completely exceptional day of Holy Thursday) was celebrated only during the morning hours, Canon 52 of Trullo, while admitting the exception of Annunciation, fixes the time of communion from the Presanctified gifts at the end of the day, even after vespers, to ensure the seriousness of the fast during Great Lent.[69]

In this way, the fast was broken not after the third hour, as on festal days, but after the ninth hour, in accordance with the ancient monastic tradition followed on fast days.[70] The Palestinian tradition (preserved at the Monastery of St Sabas and at the coenobium of St Euthymios) would, however, adopt an even more rigorous discipline. It sought to prolong the complete fast by forbidding the consumption of any food until Wednesday, or even Friday for those who were able. Consequently, no eucharistic communion was possible before Wednesday or Friday—hence the Sabaite custom of celebrating the Presanctified Liturgy only on Wednesday and Friday. It is in this spirit that we should understand the rubric cited above, which we find already in the most ancient version of the Sabaite Typikon, *Sinai gr. 1094.*[71] We should mention that this custom is still almost universally observed

---

[67]Dmitrievskii, *Opisanie*, vol. 1, Τυπικά, pt. 1, 113; Matéos, *Typicon*, II, 12; Pentkovskii, *Tipikon*, 238, 239.

[68]Canon 52 of the Council in Trullo. See P.-P. Joannou, *Discipline générale antique* (Fonti, fasc. 9), vol. 1, 1 (Rome, 1962), 189.

[69]M. Arranz, "La liturgie des Présanctifiés de l'ancien Euchologue byzantin," *OCP* 47 (1981): 388. On the history of the Presanctified Liturgy, see N.D. Uspenskii, "Liturgiia prezhdeosviashchennykh darov. Istoriko-liturgicheskii ocherk," *BT* 15 (1976): 146–84.

[70]See John Cassian, *Conferences*, XX, 11 (SC 64 [Paris, 1959], 85–86).

[71]*Sinai gr. 1094*, f. 76r. (edited by Lossky, *Le Typikon byzantin*, 249).

in monasteries, where no meal is served until Wednesday following the Presanctified Liturgy, and all the monks who are able neither eat nor drink anything for three days (*trimeri*). Among the laity, the first day of Great Lent is also strictly observed.

The Presanctified Liturgy begins with the office of vespers.[72] The simandron or bell is struck 12 times. After the opening blessing ("Blessed is the Kingdom"), Psalm 103 is read. During this psalm, the priest reads the vesperal prayers, beginning with the fourth, as the first three are read during the psalmody. This poses a liturgical problem about which there is no agreement, as the prayers were originally destined to be distributed throughout the service of vespers, while at Presanctified vespers is interrupted after the entrance and the structure of the eucharistic liturgy takes over. The deacon then says the great synapte. The psalmody of kathisma 18 is split into three parts. At the end of each, the deacon says the small synapte, while the priest reads the first three vesperal prayers and their ekphoneses. During the first stanza, the priest unfolds the antimension on the altar table, on which he places the diskos. He then takes the presanctified lamb from the artophorion on the altar table and places it on the diskos. During the second stanza, he incenses the altar table from all four sides, accompanied by the deacon carrying a candle. During the third stanza, he carries the diskos from the altar to the prothesis table, preceded by the deacon, who carries a candle and continuously incenses the holy gifts. Having arrived at the prothesis table, the deacon pours wine into the chalice, to which he also adds some water. The priest covers the holy gifts, saying only: "Through the prayers of our holy fathers . . . ."

At "Lord, I call," we sing six stichera from the Triodion and 4 from the Menaion. The theotokion is taken from the second appendix to the Menaion. During the theotokion, the priest, accompanied by the deacon who holds the censer, does the small entrance. Instead of the evening prokeimenon, a prokeimenon from the Triodion is sung, followed by the first reading (from Genesis). After the reading comes a second prokeimenon from the Triodion. Then the deacon says "Command," and the priest: "Wisdom. Arise. The light of Christ illumines all." He blesses the assembly, which is prostrate on the ground, with a candle and censer which he holds in his right hand. Then follows the second reading (from Proverbs), after which the reader,

[72]On the Presanctified Liturgy, see I. Fundulis, "Liturgiia Prezhdeosviashchennykh Darov," *Vechnoe* 332 (1976): 2–8.

standing in the middle of the church, chants selected verses from Psalm 140: "Let my prayer arise." This is a remnant of an ancient great prokeimenon from the solemn Lenten office in Constantinople. After each verse sung by the reader, the choir responds with a refrain consisting of the first verse: "Let my prayer arise." During this chant, the priest incenses the altar table, and then the prothesis. At the last refrain, he hands the censer to the deacon, who continues to incense the prothesis, and he kneels before the altar table. It is customary today for all the faithful to kneel during this entire chant. In Greek practice, the faithful perform a small prostration each time the refrain repeats "as an evening sacrifice"; and at the last verse, when the priest incenses from the solea, they do three full prostrations, corresponding to the three prostrations accompanying the Prayer of St Ephrem at the end of vespers—but in Greek practice the priest does not recite the Prayer of St Ephrem.

In Russian practice, following the singing of Psalm 140, the priest recites the Prayer of St Ephrem, accompanied by three prostrations, and the Presanctified Liturgy continues following the ordo in the Euchologion or the Hieratikon. If it is a feast with the polyeleos, the readings of the epistle and gospel are done at this point. If not, then the ektene and the litany for the catechumens follow immediately. Beginning on Wednesday of the fourth week of Great Lent, an additional litany "for those who are preparing for illumination" is added after these two. This concerns those catechumens who, in Constantinople, would be enrolled for baptism on Holy Saturday, and who would, from this point onward, receive more intensive preparation.[73] Two litanies for the faithful follow.

The great entrance takes place during the singing of the hymn "Now the powers of heaven." After the deacon has incensed the sanctuary, the priest goes to the prothesis table, takes the diskos in his right hand and, holding it over the chalice held in his left hand (if there are concelebrants, the first priest holds the diskos) and moves towards the altar, passing through the north deacon's door and entering the sanctuary through the holy doors, saying nothing. The deacon continuously incenses the holy gifts, and the assembly is prostrate on the floor. In Russian practice, the priest again recites the Prayer of St Ephrem, with three prostrations. Then the deacon recites

[73]M. Arranz, "La liturgie des Présanctifiés de l'ancien Euchologue byzantin," *OCP* 47 (1981): 345–46; M. Arranz, "Les sacrements de l'ancien Euchologue constantinopolitain—4," *OCP* 50 (1984): 47–49.

the synapte with demands, after which comes the Lord's Prayer. Communion follows.

In Greek practice, the communion of the clergy follows the typical practice. This is the ancient Byzantine practice. Russian practice, however, follows rubrics that were introduced into the Hieratikon in the seventeenth century, according to which the celebrants commune only from the holy gifts on the diskos. Only those who do not consume the gifts after the communion of the faithful drink from the chalice, as the rubrics indicate that the wine in the chalice is not considered to be consecrated. These rubrics, influenced by scholasticism, are based on the belief that the wine in the chalice is not consecrated by "infusion," when a particle of the holy gifts is placed in the chalice. Byzantine theologians, however, considered that the wine in the chalice was consecrated by contact with the particle of the holy gifts placed into it.[74] During the communion of the clergy, the koinonikon is sung: "Taste and see how good the Lord is." After the communion of the faithful, which takes place as usual, comes the thanksgiving: the litany by the deacon, the prayer of the ambo read by the priest ("O Master, all-powerful"), and then Psalm 33, during which the priest distributes the antidoron saved from the preceding Sunday, and the dismissal.

GREAT COMPLINE

At the ninth hour on Monday, it is prescribed that the monk appointed to light the candles should strike the large simandron twelve times to indicate the beginning of great compline.

On the first four days of the first week of Great Lent, Psalm 69 is read immediately following the opening prayers, and then the penitential Great Canon of St Andrew of Crete is sung, divided into four parts.[75] This hymnographic unit is called the "Great Canon" because it is one of the rare hymnographic compositions to have nine odes, with a troparion to accompany each verse of the nine biblical canticles.[76] It therefore contains 250

[74]N.D. Uspenskii, "Kolloziia dvukh bogoslovii v ispravlenii russkikh bogosluzhebnykh knig v XVII veke," *BT* 13 (1975): 156–66. On this subject, see also N. Karabinov, "Sviataia chasha na liturgii Prezhdeosviashchennykh Darov," *Khristianskoe Chtenie* 1 (1915): 737–53; and the article by a Catholic liturgist: A. Raes, "La Communion au Calice dans l'Office byzantin des Présanctifiés," *OCP* 20 (1954): 166–74. On consecration by infusion or immixing, see M. Andrieu, *Immixtio et Consecratio* (Paris, 1924), 196–243.

[75]*Triodion* (Moscow, 1992), 89.

[76]Indeed, the singing of the biblical canticles was usually spread throughout the week, and the canons generally consisted of only three or four odes. The common practice, which

troparia, each corresponding to nearly every verse of the biblical canticles. The hirmoi of this Great Canon almost literally repeat verses from the biblical canticles, which is not original, but a sign of antiquity, like the presence of the second ode. Three prostrations are done with each troparion as a sign of repentance and contrition—reflecting the spirit of the Great Canon, which is referred to as "penitential."[77] Unfortunately, the prostrations have been abandoned in Greek practice, and the canon is chanted very quickly, as has also happened in Russian parochial practice.

The "Great Canon" (ὁ μέγας κανών) of St Andrew of Crete is sung in its entirety at matins on Thursday of the fifth week of Lent, and in four sections at compline during the first week of Lent, from Monday through Thursday evening.

St Andrew of Crete (660–740) was a monk at the Holy Sepulcher in Jerusalem before being ordained, in 685, to be the deacon at the Great Church of Constantinople, and then a bishop on the island of Crete at the turn of the seventh and eighth centuries. It is during his episcopate that he pronounced the various homilies that have come down to us, and it is also at this time that he composed the various canons attributed to him.[78] In his hymnography, St Andrew of Crete owes a great deal to St Romanos the Melode, by whom he is inspired and whom he sometimes paraphrases: for example, the fourth ode of the Great Canon is a paraphrase of the proemium kontakion, "O my soul," (ψυχή μου) of Romanos, sung today after the sixth ode of the canon.[79]

The Russian liturgist I. Karabinov has shown clearly that the Great Canon was composed by St Andrew of Crete not for a particular liturgical solemnity—for Thursday of the fifth week of Great Lent—but rather, as the Synaxarion of Kallistos Xanthopoulos states, as a spiritual autobiography

no doubt developed later, is to have canons consisting of eight odes, with the second ode sung only during Great Lent.

[77]E. Wellecz, *A History of Byzantine Music and Hymnography* (Oxford, 1961), 204.

[78]On St Andrew of Crete, see G. Bardy, "André de Crète," *DSp* I (1937): cols. 554–55; C. Émereau, "Hymnographi Byzantini," *Échos d'Orient* XXI (1922): 267–71; M. Jugie, "André de Crète," *Catholicisme: Hier, aujourd'hui, demain* 1 (1948): cols. 525–26; Karabinov, *Postnaia Triod'*, 98–107; E. Marin, "André de Crète," *Dictionnaire de théologie catholique* I (1909), col. 1182–84; E. Mercenier, "À propos d'André de Crète," in *Tome commemoratif du Millenium de la Bibliothèque d'Alexandrie* (Alexandria, 1953), 70–78; L. Petit, "André de Crète," *DACL* I, 2 (1907), cols. 2034–41; H. Rahner, "Andreas von Kreta," *Lexikon für Theologie und Kirche* 1 (1957), cols. 516–17; S. Vailhé, "Saint André de Crète," *Échos d'Orient* V (1902): 378–87.

[79]Karabinov, *Postnaia Triod'*, 100; E. Wellecz, *A History of Byzantine Music and Hymnography* (Oxford, 1961), 204–05.

of repentance. Indeed, some think that St Andrew composed this text after having been dragged by Emperor Philippikos into the monothelite heresy. Thus this canon, composed toward the end of his life, reflects his personal experience of sin and conversion.[80] As Karabinov explains:

> In order to facilitate the enumeration of his sins, [Saint Andrew] employs an original method—he turns to a review of all biblical history: the sinful persons and the negative actions give him a pretext to express reproach against his own soul, because it has imitated them; on the contrary, it [the reproach] suggests that he imitate the just and their righteous actions.[81]

The survey of the Old Testament concludes with the eighth ode, the last Old-Testament ode. In the ninth ode, he proceeds to list examples taken exclusively from the New Testament. Thus, it is in a spirit of repentance that the author refers to the great biblical personages, finding in them a reflection of his own experience of sin, and this explains the adjective "penitential" that is used to describe this Great Canon.[82]

Note that the Typikon of Alexios the Studite does not mention the Great Canon at compline during the first week, but only at matins of the fifth week.[83] One of the most ancient manuscripts of the Typikon of St Sabas, *Sinai gr. 1094* (12th century) reflects our contemporary practice, though it indicates that this is a practice of the Palestinian coenobia—while the monks at the Monastery of St Sabas read compline in their cells.[84] Note also that in contemporary Greek practice, the Great Canon is sung at the end of great compline, after the doxology. The current Russian practice has kept the ancient custom of reading the Great Canon at the beginning of great compline, for all the other canons read at this office during Great Lent have also been shifted to following the doxology in the third section. Even if the printed Greek Horologion still calls for the singing of the Great Canon

---

[80]Hieromoine Macaire de Simonos Petras (G. Bonnet), *La Mystagogie du temps liturgique dans le Triodion* (Unpublished thesis, Sorbonne, E.P.H.E., Vᵉ Section [Paris, 1977], 482–83); V. Iljine, "Le mystère de la pénitence et le Grand Carême de saint André de Crète," *Le Messager de l'Exarchat du Patriarche russe en Europe occidentale* 6 (1955): 8–16; J.M. Fountoulis, Λογικὴ λατρεία (Thessalonica, 1970), 56–57.

[81]Karabinov, *Postnaia Triod'*, 104–05.

[82]See my article: J. Getcha,"Le grand canon pénitentiel de Saint André de Crète: une lecture typologique de l'histoire du salut," in *La Liturgie, interprète de l'Écriture. II. Dans les compositions liturgiques, prières et chants*, BEL 126 (Rome, 2003), 105–20.

[83]Pentkovskii, *Tipikon*, 244.

[84]*Sinai gr. 1094*, f. 76r–76v (edited by Lossky, *Le Typikon byzantin*, 249).

after Psalm 69 of great compline,[85] the contemporary (Constantinopolitan) practice also shifts the Great Canon to the third section of great compline, after the doxology.[86]

After the Great Canon, great compline, containing three sections, continues as usual. The first part, consists of six psalms (Pss 4, 6, 12, 24, 30, 90), after which the verses from Isaiah are sung (Is 8. 9–11, 12–15, 18; 9. 2, 6) with the refrain "For God is with us" (Is 8.9) after each verse. It appears that this chant dates back to the fourth century and is in fact an antiphon introduced by St Basil in Caesarea.[87] In the Studite tradition, this chant was given the name of "meth-emon" (μεθ'ἡμῶν), after the first two words of the antiphon: "μεθ'ἡμῶν ὁ θεός"—"God is with us" (Is 8.8). Then we sing three symmetrical troparia honoring the three divine persons, beginning with "The day is past," then a troparion in honor of the Holy Trinity ("The bodiless nature of the Cherubim"). After these troparia, the Creed is recited. Then follow a series of verses, each repeated twice and sung alternately by the two choirs. While one choir sings the verse, the other does a prostration. Because of the many prostrations accompanying these verses, the prostrations at the trisagion which follows are omitted. After the Lord's Prayer, the troparia are sung. There are two sets of troparia, which alternate each day. After the benediction by the priest, the Prayer of St Basil is read—"O Lord, Lord, who have delivered us from every arrow that flies in the day"—in which we ask the Lord for a peaceful rest, free of evil imaginations.

Then the second part of great compline begins. It consists of Psalms 50 and 101, the Prayer of Manasseh, the trisagion followed by the other penitential prayers and troparia ("Have mercy on us, O Lord, have mercy on us . . ."). After the benediction by the priest, the Prayer of St Mardarios, a fourth-century martyr, is read—which is also read at the midnight office and at the end of the third hour.

After this prayer, the third section of great compline begins, consisting of Psalms 69 and 142. During the first week of Great Lent, Psalm 69 is omitted here, as it was read at the beginning of the office, before the Great Canon. After Psalm 142, the doxology is read in its Hagiopolite redaction ("Glory to God in the highest," "O Lord, you were our refuge from generation to generation," and "Vouchsafe, O Lord"). As we have stated above, in current

[85]Ὡρολόγιον τὸ μέγα (Athens, 1995³), 200.
[86]S. Pétridès, "Apodeipnon," *DACL* I, 2 (Paris, 1907), col. 2583.
[87]Ibid., col. 2583; Brightman, *Liturgies Eastern and Western* (Oxford, 1896), vol. 1, 570.

practice this is where the canons are read—even, in Greek practice, the Great Canon. The trisagion prayers follow. After the Lord's Prayer, verses from Psalm 150 are sung with the refrain: "O God of hosts, be with us" (Ps 45.7). The verses of this antiphon are sung alternately by the two choirs. This antiphon is followed by a doxastikon and a theotokion. After *Kyrie eleison* (40 times), the prayer of the hours ("You who at all times"), and the benediction by the priest, the Prayer of St Ephrem is recited with 16 prostrations, then the Prayer of St Paul, founder of the Evergetis Monastery in Constantinople (11th century) ("Immaculate, spotless") and the Prayer of St Antiochos, author of the *Pandects* (7th century) ("And give us, Master, as we go to sleep"), as at small compline. Instead of the customary dismissal, the rubrics indicate that the faithful are prostrate, their faces to the ground (in Greek practice, they simply incline their heads) while the priest says the prayer in a loud voice: "O most merciful Master." Then follows the customary rite of forgiveness, after which each goes to his cell in silence. Rubrics in the Triodion specify that the ecclesiarch must watch that the dismissal of compline take place while it is still day, i.e., before darkness falls,[88] a rubric that also appears in *Sinai gr. 1094*.[89] The rubrics in the Triodion also specify that a total of 300 prostrations are done in church, evening and morning, not including the midnight office.[90]

If a feast with the polyeleos occurs during Great Lent

When a feast with the polyeleos occurs during Great Lent, the services follow a particular pattern that takes account of both the office with polyeleos (with "God is the Lord") and the office with "Alleluia." Almost every year, the feasts of the first and second findings of the head of St John the Baptist (February 24) and of the forty martyrs of Sebaste (March 9) fall during Great Lent. In Greek practice, since the eighteenth century, the feast of St Charalambos (February 10) also has a festal celebration. To these, we could also add the patronal feast of the church, if it falls during this period.

We note, however, that, according to the "Chapters of Mark," if the feast of the first and second finding of the head of St John the Baptist falls during

---

[88]*Triodion* (Moscow, 1992), 95.

[89]*Sinai gr. 1094*, f. 77v. (edited by Lossky, *Le Typikon byzantin*, 251).

[90]*Triodion* (Moscow, 1992), 95. *Sinai gr. 1094* mentions the same number of prostrations on f. 78r. (edited by Lossky, *Le Typikon byzantin*, 251).

the first week of Great Lent, the celebration is moved either to Cheese-Fare Sunday, or to Saturday of the first week.

VESPERS ON THE EVE OF THE FEAST: IF OF SUNDAY EVENING

If the feast falls on a Monday, the eve is then Sunday evening, and, as on all Sundays during Great Lent, vespers marks the transition between the festal and the Lenten offices.

After the great synapte, the first antiphon (stanza) of kathisma 1 ("Blessed is the man") is sung. At "Lord, I call," ten stichera are sung: four from the Triodion and six from the Menaion, then the doxastikon from the Menaion and dogmatikon theotokion. During the singing of the dogmatikon, the vesperal entrance takes place with the candle and censer. The great prokeimenon from the Triodion is sung, and then follow the three Old-Testament readings for the feast (see the Menaion). The prayer "Vouchsafe, O Lord" is then read. After the synapte with demands, we sing the aposticha from the Triodion, with the doxastikon from the Menaion and the Sunday theotokion in the tone of the doxastikon. After the Lord's Prayer, we sing the troparion of the saint (from the Menaion) and the Sunday theotokion in the tone of the troparion. Then, after the ektene, the priest recites the Prayer of St Ephrem once, with only three prostrations, followed by the dismissal.

VESPERS ON THE EVE OF THE FEAST: IF ON MONDAY, TUESDAY, OR THURSDAY EVENING

If the feast falls on a Monday, Tuesday, or Thursday, vespers on the eve is celebrated as follows:

After the great synapte, kathisma 18 is read. At "Lord, I call," six stichera are sung: 3 from the Triodion and 3 from the Menaion, followed by the doxastikon from the Menaion and the Sunday theotokion in the tone of the doxastikon. During the singing of the theotokion, the vesperal entrance takes place with the candle and censer. The first prokeimenon from the Triodion follows, followed by the reading from Genesis, the second prokeimenon from the Triodion, the reading from Proverbs, and then the three Old-Testament readings for the feast from the Menaion. The prayer "Vouchsafe, O Lord" is then read. After the synapte with demands, we sing the aposticha from the Triodion, with the doxastikon from the Menaion and the Sunday theotokion in the tone of the doxastikon. After the Lord's Prayer, we sing the troparion of the saint (from the Menaion) and the Sunday theotokion in the tone of the troparion. Then, after the ektene, the priest recites the Prayer of St Ephrem once, with only three prostrations, followed by the prayer "O most holy Trinity," "Blessed be the name of the Lord" (3 times), Glory . . . now and ever . . . Psalm 33. Then the dismissal: "Wisdom!"—"It is truly meet . . ."; "Most holy Theotokos, save us!"—"More honorable than the Cherubim"; "Glory to you, O Christ our God and our hope, glory to you," etc.

VESPERS ON THE EVE OF THE FEAST: IF ON WEDNESDAY OR FRIDAY EVENING

If the feast falls on Thursday or Saturday, vespers on the eve of the feast is celebrated with the Presanctified Liturgy:

After the dismissal of the typika, vespers begins with the blessing: "Blessed is the Kingdom." After the great synapte, kathisma 18 is read in three sections, each followed by a small synapte. At "Lord, I call," ten stichera are sung: six from the Triodion and four from the Menaion, followed by the doxastikon from the Menaion and the Sunday theotokion in the tone of the doxastikon. During the singing of the theotokion, the vesperal entrance takes place with the candle and censer. The first prokeimenon from the Triodion follows, followed by the reading from Genesis, the second prokeimenon from the Triodion, the reading from Proverbs, and then the three Old-Testament readings for the feast from the Menaion. We then sing the verses from Psalm 140 ("Let my prayer arise") and the Presanctified Liturgy proceeds as usual.

GREAT COMPLINE ON THE EVE OF THE FEAST

On the eve of the feast, great compline is read and not sung, "without prostrations." After the trisagion in the first section, we sing the troparion of the saint (from the Menaion) and the Sunday theotokion. (We note that, in Greek practice, this troparion is sung after the trisagion in the second section: the first part has no troparion, but is read nonetheless.) After the trisagion, the customary penitential troparia are sung ("Have mercy on us, O Lord, have mercy on us . . ."). After the trisagion in the third section, the verses from Psalm 150 ("O God of the powers, be with us") are not sung, and instead the kontakion of the saint is read (from the Menaion), after which the end of small compline follows. After *Kyrie eleison* (40 times), the prayer of the hours ("You who at all times"), and the benediction by the priest, the

Prayer of St Ephrem is recited with 3 prostrations, then the Prayer of St Paul of Evergetis ("Immaculate, spotless") and the Prayer of St Antiochos ("And give us, Master, as we go to sleep"), and the customary small dismissal, as at small compline.

MATINS ON THE DAY OF THE FEAST

After the hexapsalmos, the great synapte is said, and then we sing "God is the Lord," and then the troparion from the Menaion and the Sunday theotokion, followed by the three appointed kathismata from the Psalter. After the first and second kathismata, the kathisma troparia from the Triodion are sung, without small synaptes, and then we read from the writings of St Ephrem. After the third kathisma, the deacon says the small synapte, we sing the kathisma troparia from the Menaion and read the life of the saint. The polyeleos follows (with the megalynarion for the saint and selected psalm verses), and then the small synapte, the kathisma troparia from the Menaion, and the rest of the life of the saint. Then we sing the first antiphon of the anabathmoi in tone 4 ("From my youth"), and the prokeimenon from the Menaion, after which the priest reads the gospel appointed for matins of the feast. After Psalm 50 and the sticheron from the Menaion, the deacon recites the prayer "O Lord, save your people," concluded by the ekphonesis of the priest.

The canon for the saint (from the Menaion) is sung with hirmos and eight troparia, with the katabasiai from the canon for the Mother of God "My mouth will open"). For those odes where there is a three-ode canon (from the Triodion), the canon from the Menaion is sung with six troparia, the Triodion canons with eight troparia, and the katabasia is from the Triodion. After the third ode, there is a small synapte followed by the kathisma troparion from the Menaion. After the sixth ode, there is the small synapte, followed by the kontakion and ikos from the Menaion. After the ninth ode follow a small synapte and the exaposteilarion from the Menaion.

The lauds are read in their Hagiopolite recension ("Praise the Lord from the heavens"), as also the doxology, read in its Palestinian version. In Greek practice, the lauds are sung in their Constantinopolitan version, followed by the troparia for the saint from the Menaion, but the doxology is read in the Hagiopolite version, and not sung in the Constantinopolitan recension. The deacon recites the synapte with demands, and the aposticha from the Triodion are sung, followed by the doxastikon from the Menaion and the

Sunday theotokion in the tone of the doxastikon. Indeed, it is not possible
to omit the idiomela for the aposticha during the period of the Triodion,
because these are the most ancient part of the Triodion and doctrinally the
richest. After the Lord's Prayer, the troparion for the saint is sung with the
Sunday theotokion. The deacon says the ektene, and then the priest recites
the Prayer of St Ephrem ("O Lord and Master of my life") once, with only
three full prostrations. Then the first hour is read.

HOURS AND THE TYPIKA

When the polyeleos has been sung at matins, the bells are not rung for the
hours. The hours are read with the appointed kathismata, but the troparia
and kontakia from the Horologion are not sung. Instead, the troparion and
kontakion for the saint (from the Menaion) are read. At the conclusion of each
hour, the Prayer of St Ephrem is recited once, with only three prostrations.

At sext, the reading from Isaiah is done as indicated in the Triodion, preceded by the singing of the troparion of the prophecy and a prokeimenon,
and followed by another prokeimenon.

The typika are read "rapidly, and not sung," immediately following none.
At the end, the Prayer of St Ephrem is said, with three prostrations, and then
the prayer "O most holy Trinity." The dismissal follows: "Wisdom!"—"It is
truly meet...."; "Most holy Theotokos, save us!"—"More honorable than the
Cherubim"; "Glory to you, O Christ God, our hope, glory to you," etc.

PRESANCTIFIED LITURGY ON THE EVENING OF THE FEAST

On feast days with a polyeleos during Great Lent, only the Presanctified
Liturgy may be celebrated, theoretically on the evening of the feast, in accordance with Canon 52 of the Council in Trullo, which states: "During Great
Lent, except on Saturdays, Sundays, and the holy day of Annunciation, only
the Liturgy of the Presanctified Gifts may be celebrated."[91]

The Presanctified Liturgy begins with the office of vespers. The bell or
simandron is struck 12 times. After the opening blessing, "Blessed is the
Kingdom," Psalm 103 is read. During this psalm, the priest reads the vesperal prayers, beginning with the fourth, as the first three are read during
the psalmody. The deacon then says the great synapte. The psalmody of
kathisma 18 is split into three parts. At the end of each, the deacon says the
small synapte.

[91]Canon 52 of the Council in Trullo. See P.-P. Joannou, *Discipline générale antique*
(Fonti, fasc. 9), vol. 1, 1 (Rome, 1962), 189.

At "Lord, I call," we sing six stichera from the Triodion and 4 for the saint (from the Menaion). We should note that the stichera from the Menaion appointed for vespers on the next day are shifted to lauds at matins of the following day (or simply omitted). The doxastikon from the Menaion is sung, followed by the Sunday theotokion in the same tone. During the theotokion, the priest, accompanied by the deacon carrying the gospel, does the small entrance. After "O Gladsome Light," the prokeimenon from the Triodion is sung, followed by the first reading (from Genesis). After the reading from Genesis, the second prokeimenon from the Triodion is done. Then the deacon says "Command," and the priest: "Wisdom. Arise. The light of Christ illumines all." He blesses the assembly, which is prostrate on the ground, with a candle and censer which he holds in his right hand. Then follows the second reading (from Proverbs), after which the reader, standing in the middle of the church, chants selected verses from Psalm 140: "Let my prayer arise." After the singing of Psalm 140, the priest recites the Prayer of St Ephrem, with three prostrations. The reading of the epistle and the gospel for the feast follows. Then the Presanctified Liturgy continues as usual In addition the regular koinonikon ("Taste and see how good the Lord is"), the koinonikon for the saint is also sung.

Saturday of St Theodore The Recruit

ORIGIN

The first Saturday of Great Lent commemorates the great martyr and saint Theodore the Recruit. This solemnity derives from a miracle connected to the saint that allegedly took place in 361, when the emperor Julian the Apostate ordered the prefect of Constantinople, during the first week of Great Lent, to sprinkle the fruits and vegetables in the market with the blood of victims offered to idols, in order to defile the fast of the Christians. The holy martyr reportedly appeared to Patriarch Eudoxios (360–364) and commanded him that no Christian should buy any food at the market, but that they should make *kollyvo*, i.e., boiled grains of wheat, to feed themselves. In this way, the Christians avoided the stain of idolatry. This, at least, is the explanation found in the Triodion, in the Synaxarion of Nicephoras Kallistos Xanthopoulos read at matins on the first Saturday of Great Lent.[92]

[92]Hiéromoine Macaire de Simonos Petras, *Le Synaxaire*, vol. 3 (Thessalonica, 1990), 157–58. See the synaxarion for the first Saturday of Great Lent: *Triod' postnaia* (reprint: Moscow, 1992), 139–40; *Triode de Carême*, D. Guillaume, tr. (Parma, 1993³), 155–56.

The commemoration of this miraculous intervention by the holy martyr was quickly instituted on the first Saturday of Great Lent. The Studite tradition knew this custom and may have been the first to institute it. Indeed, the Typikon of Alexios the Studite emphasizes the festal character of this Saturday by indicating that, as an exception, on Friday evening of the first week, small compline is read instead of great compline. However, nothing in this Typikon mentions any commemoration of St Theodore at the end of the Presanctified Liturgy, as is indicated in the Sabaite Typika.[93] The latter indicate that, in honor of the saint, oil and wine are permitted in the refectory.

ORDO

At the Presanctified Liturgy on Friday of the first week, ten stichera are sung at "Lord, I call": the idiomelon from the Triodion twice, then four martyrika from the Octoechos and four stichera for the martyr (from the Triodion). The doxastikon for the martyr is sung, followed by the dogmatikon theotokion (because of the Saturday office). During the singing of the theotokion, the priest, accompanied by the deacon carrying the censer, does the small entrance. Instead of the evening prokeimenon, the two prokeimena from the Triodion are used, accompanying the first reading (from Genesis) and the second (from Proverbs). After the reading from Proverbs, the reader, standing in the middle of the church, sings the selected verses from Psalm 140 ("Let my prayer arise"). And the Liturgy of the Presanctified continues as usual.

After the prayer of the ambo at the Presanctified Liturgy, it is appointed to go to the narthex to sing a canon of thanksgiving to St Theodore the Recruit, before the kollyvo prepared in his honor. The reader recites Psalm 142. Then "God is the Lord" is sung, followed by the troparion of the martyr and the Sunday theotokion. Psalm 50 is read (during which the deacon incenses the table on which the *kollyvo* is placed). The canon to St Theodore is then sung. After the sixth ode, the kontakion of the martyr is sung. After the ninth ode, instead of "It is truly meet," the hirmos of the ninth ode is sung once more. The trisagion prayers are read. After the Lord's Prayer, the troparion, kontakion, and theotokion are sung once again. Then the priest reads the prayer of blessing over the *kollyvo*, commemorating the saint and

---

[93]Pentkovskii, *Tipikon*, 240; see Mansvetov, *Tserkovnyi ustav*, 135, 143, 214. Note that the Sabaite Typikon *Sinai gr. 1094* indicates a canon to the Great Martyr Theodore on f. 78v. (edited by Lossky, *Le Typikon byzantin*, 251).

great martyr Theodore. Then follows the usual dismissal of the Presanctified Liturgy.

At matins, "God is the Lord" is sung, followed by the troparion to the holy
martyr and the Sunday theotokion. After the first kathisma, the kathisma
troparion from the Octoechos is sung; after the second kathisma, we sing
the kathisma troparion for the martyr (from the Triodion). After Psalm
50, the canon for the church (for the saint or feast to which the church is
dedicated) is sung with six troparia, and the canon from the Triodion in
honor of the martyr with eight troparia. After the third ode, the kathisma
troparion from the Triodion is sung, after the sixth ode, the kontakion and
ikos from the Triodion. The reading from the Synaxarion of Nicephoras
Kallistos Xanthopoulos follows. After the ninth ode, "It is truly meet" is
not sung. After the small synapte, the exaposteilarion from the Triodion is
read. At lauds, which are read ("Praise the Lord from the heavens"), four
stichera from the Triodion are sung, together with their doxastikon and
theotokion. The doxology in its Palestinian redaction is then read. After the
synapte with demands, the aposticha stichera from the Triodion are sung,
followed by their doxastikon and theotokion. After the Lord's Prayer, we
sing the troparion of the great martyr and the Sunday theotokion. At the
hours, the troparion and kontakion from the Triodion (for the martyr) are
read. On this day, as on all Saturdays of Great Lent, the Liturgy of St John
Chrysostom is celebrated. The troparia and kontakia of both the church and
the martyr are sung.

The first Sunday: the Sunday of Orthodoxy

ORIGIN

For the first Sunday of Great Lent, the Triodion calls for the celebration of
the "Sunday of Orthodoxy." This commemoration was introduced in March
843 to celebrate the final victory over iconoclasm. It was established then
each year to celebrate the triumph of Orthodoxy on the first Sunday of Great
Lent. This celebration was then added to the more ancient commemoration
of the holy prophets Moses, Aaron, David, Samuel, and the other prophets
on that day.[94] The Typikon of Alexios the Studite called for the singing of the

[94]This was still the case in the Sabaite Typikon, *Sinai gr. 1094*, f. 79r. (edited by Lossky,
Le Typikon byzantin, 2512–53). On this subject, see M. Arranz, "Les fêtes théologiques
du calendrier byzantin," in *La Liturgie, expression de la foi. Conférences Saint-Serge. XXV*ᵉ
Semaine d'études liturgiques (Rome, 1979), 39–41.

office for the holy icons combined with the office for the holy prophets.[95] In later Sabaite Typika, however, which reflect the widespread practice at the end of the fourteenth century, the commemoration of the holy prophets has disappeared, and their canon has been moved to compline on Sunday evening.

We should not forget that, after the victory of the hesychasts in 1351, the Sunday of Orthodoxy took on an additional meaning. It commemorated not only the victory over iconoclasm, but the victory over all heresies, including the victory of the hesychast monks over their opponents. We note here that the decisions of the Council of Blachernai (1351), at which the teachings of St Gregory Palamas proved victorious, were added to the *Synodikon of Orthodoxy*, which was no doubt read for the first time in its new redaction on the first Sunday of Lent in 1352.[96] These factors can explain the importance ascribed to the office of the triumph of Orthodoxy and the disappearance of the commemoration of the holy prophets in the Sabaite Typika and the Triodia of Palestinian redaction after the fourteenth century. Only the canon to the prophets survived in the Slavic editions, having been shifted from Sunday matins to compline on Sunday evening.[97] It has disappeared completely from the Greek editions.

ORDO

As on Sundays during the preparatory period, only the Octoechos and the Triodion are used. At vespers, four stichera from the Triodion are sung at "Lord, I call," added to six from the Octoechos, as well as a doxastikon from the Triodion. The Triodion also contains a doxastikon and a theotokion for the *lite*, as well as a doxastikon and a theotokion for the aposticha. At the artoklasia, "Mother of God and Virgin" is sung twice, and the troparion of the feast, "We venerate your most pure icon," is sung once.

At matins, at "God is the Lord," the Sunday troparion is sung twice, followed by the troparion of the feast and the Sunday theotokion. After Psalm 50, the penitential troparia are sung (as on the preparatory Sundays). The Triodion canon is sung with six troparia and is added to the three canons from the Octoechos (of the Resurrection, four troparia; of the Cross and the Resurrection, two troparia; and of the Mother of God, two troparia). The katabasia are taken from the Triodion. After the third ode, a kathisma

[95]Pentkovskii, *Tipikon*, 241.
[96]J. Meyendorff, *Introduction à l'étude de Grégoire Palamas* (Paris, 1959), 152.
[97]See the *Triod' postnaia* (reprint: Moscow, 1992), 152v.–154v.

troparion from the Triodion is sung, and after the sixth ode, the kontakion and ikos from the Triodion. The reading from the Synaxarion of Nicephoras Kallistos Xanthopoulos follows. After the ninth ode and "Holy is the Lord our God," an exaposteilarion from the Triodion is added to the gospel exaposteilarion. At lauds, the Triodion provides four stichera, which are added to five stichera from the Octoechos, as well as a doxastikon (from the Triodion).

At the hours, the Sunday troparion is read, as well as the troparion of the feast and only one kontakion (from the Triodion). So also at the liturgy, where we sing the Sunday troparion, the troparion of the feast, and the kontakion from the Triodion.

On this Sunday, as on all Sundays of Great Lent through the fifth Sunday, we celebrate the Liturgy of St Basil the Great. Two additional lambs are prepared and consecrated for the Presanctified Liturgies on the following Wednesday and Friday.

Memorial Saturdays

ORIGIN

The second, third, and fourth Saturdays of Great Lent are dedicated to the memory of the dead, except if they fall on the feast of a saint with a polyeleos (such as the Finding of the Head of St John the Baptist, or the Forty Martyrs of Sebaste). The Typika specify that if someone dies during Great Lent, no memorial should take place at the normal times (the third, ninth, and 40th days), but they should be postponed to Friday evening, with the eucharistic liturgy for the dead on Saturday. They indicate that the customary commemorations of the dead resume on St Thomas Sunday, a week following Pascha.[98] These rubrics reflect an ancient practice, attested to by Canon 51 of the Council of Laodicea, which instructs that the memory of the martyrs should not be celebrated during the forty days of Lent, but on Saturdays and Sundays.[99] Theodore Balsamon (c. 1140–c. 1195), the great Byzantine canonist, already considered that this canon concerning the commemoration of martyrs applied equally to the commemoration of the dead.[100] From

---

[98]See for example, *Typikon* (Moscow, 1906), 405v.

[99]Canon 51 of Laodicea. See P.–P. Joannou, *Discipline générale antique* (Fonti, fasc. 9), vol. 1, 1 (Rome, 1962), 151.

[100]*Pravila sviatykh pomestnykh soborov s tolkovaniiami* (Moscow, 1880; reprint 2000), 270.

this time, the rule was taken up by the Typika of Hagiopolite redaction.[101] Indeed, the days when the dead were commemorated, on which the eucharistic liturgy was celebrated and agapes were organized, were rather festive days, which did not accord well with the spirit of the fast.[102]

ORDO

At vespers, which are celebrated with the Presanctified Liturgy, ten stichera are sung at "Lord, I call": the idiomelon from the Triodion (twice), four stichera (in honor of the martyrs) from the Octoechos in the tone of the week, and four stichera for the saint from the Menaion. The doxastikon is the idiomelon for the dead taken from the aposticha in the Octoechos. Then, at "Now and ever," as on every Friday night, the dogmatikon theotokion from the Octoechos is sung in the tone of the week. After the entrance follow the readings from the Triodion, preceded by their prokeimena, and then the Presanctified Liturgy as usual.

At matins, the "Alleluia" is sung in tone 2, with the verses for the dead ("Blessed are those whom you have chosen," "Their souls shall rest with the righteous"), then the Saturday troparion twice in tone 2: "Apostles, martyrs, and prophets," "Glory," the troparion for the dead in tone 2: "Remember, O Lord," "Now and ever," and the theotokion: "O holy Mother." As on all Saturdays, kathismata 16 and 17 are read. After the first kathisma, the kathisma troparia from the Octoechos are sung. As at the offices for the dead, kathisma 17 is read with chanted refrains and is divided into two stanzas. The priest (accompanied by the deacon) leaves the sanctuary and goes to the memorial table for the dead (a table at which candles for the dead are lit, and where the kollyvo or other offerings for the dead are placed), which the deacon incenses continuously. After the first stanza (Ps 118.1–93), there is a litany for the dead. Then the second stanza of kathisma 17 follows (Ps 118.94–176), after which the evlogitaria for the dead are sung ("The assembly of the saints," etc.). During these, the priest incenses the entire church, preceded by the deacon with a candle. After the evlogitaria, there is once again the litany for the dead, then the kathisma troparion from the Triodion ("Give rest with the righteous"). The priest and deacon return to the sanctuary.

---

[101]For example, *Typikon* (Moscow, 1906), 405v.
[102]Mansvetov, *Mitropolit Kiprian v ego liturgicheskoi deiatel'nosti*, 122.

Psalm 50 is read, and we begin to sing the canon. In churches dedicated to the Lord or to the Mother of God, the canon of the church (of the feast after which the church is named) is read with six troparia, and the canon of the saint from the Menaion with four troparia. In churches dedicated to a saint, the canon of the saint from the Menaion is read with six troparia, and the canon of the saint of the church with four troparia, Beginning with the sixth ode, the canon of the church is set aside, and we begin with the canon of the saint from the Menaion with six troparia, to which we add the two four-ode canons from the Triodion: that of Joseph the Hymnographer with four troparia, and that of Theodore the Studite with six troparia.

After the third ode, the hirmos of the last canon is sung as the katabasia. After the sixth, seventh, eighth, and ninth odes, the katabasia is the hirmos of the second four-ode canon.

After the third ode, the customary small synapte is said, followed by the singing of the kontakion, (the ikos), and the kathisma troparion from the Menaion and its theotokion. After the sixth ode, during the katabasia, the priest and deacon again go stand before the table for the dead. Then the kontakion for the dead is sung ("With the saints give rest"), during which the deacon incenses the table from all four sides, the iconostasis, the priest, and the faithful. The celebrants then return into the sanctuary. At the ninth ode, the Magnificat is sung as usual. After the ninth ode, the customary small synapte is said, and then follow the exaposteilaria and the theotokion for the day.

At lauds, which are read, we sing four stichera (for the martyrs), a doxastikon (in honor of the dead), and a theotokion from the Octoechos, in the tone of the week. The doxology is read. At the aposticha, we sing the stichera for the dead from the Octoechos in the tone of the week, accompanied by the psalm verses for the dead ("Blessed are those whom you have chosen," "Their souls shall dwell with the righteous"). "It is good to confess the Lord" is read once only. After the Lord's Prayer, we sing the Saturday troparion in tone 2: "Apostles, martyrs, and Prophets," "Glory," the troparion for the dead in tone 2 ("Remember, O Lord"), "Now and ever," and the theotokion ("O holy Mother"). Then matins is concluded as on ordinary days.

At the hours, the troparia are read: "Apostles, Martyrs, and Prophets," "Glory," "Remember, O Lord," and the kontakion for the dead. At the eucharistic liturgy, the troparia are sung: "Apostles, Martyrs, and Prophets," "Remember, O Lord," "Glory," the kontakion for the dead, "Now and ever," and the theotokion ("In you we have a rampart." The prokeimena of Saturday ("Rejoice in the Lord") and for the dead ("Their souls shall dwell") are both done, and the epistles and gospels of the day and for the dead are read.

The second Sunday: Commemoration of St Gregory Palamas

ORIGIN

In our day, the second Sunday of Great Lent is dedicated to the memory of St Gregory Palamas. In the past, however, this Sunday had no specific theme: this is the case in both the Typikon of Alexios the Studite and the Sabaite Typikon, *Sinai gr. 1094.*[103] It is only in the Sabaite Typika and Triodia of Jerusalem redaction after the fourteenth century that we find this commemoration. In fact, we know that the Greek service for St Gregory Palamas was composed by Patriarch Philotheos.[104] The Slavic translation of this service was realized a few years later.

It was for polemical and doctrinal issues that the commemoration of St Gregory Palamas was instituted on the second Sunday of Great Lent, one week after the Sunday of Orthodoxy. Indeed, the synodal decree instituting his feast at the Great Church of Christ on this second Sunday of Lent in February–March 1368 preceded the condemnation in April 1368 of the anti-Palamite monk Prochoros Kydones, ranking the latter with the other heretics: Arius, Nestorius, Barlaam, and Akindynos.[105] We know that, after the victory of hesychasm in 1351, the Sunday of Orthodoxy took on a new meaning. It commemorated not just the victory over iconoclasm, but the victory over all heresies, including the victory over the opponents of the hesychast monks. The decisions of the Council of Blachernai (1351), which marked the victory of the teaching of St Gregory Palamas, were then added to the *Synodikon of Orthodoxy*, which was certainly read for the first time in this new version on the first Sunday of Lent in 1352.[106] It therefore

---

[103]Pentkovskii, *Tipikon*, 242; *Sinai gr. 1094*, f. 80r. (edited by Lossky, *Le Typikon byzantin*, 254). On this subject, see M. Arranz, "Les fêtes théologiques du calendrier byzantin," in *La Liturgie, expression de la foi. Conférences Saint-Serge. XXVe Semaine d'études liturgiques* (Rome, 1979), 42–43.

[104]G.M. Prokhorov, "K istorii liturgicheskoi poezii: gimny i molitvy patriarkha Filofeia Kokkina," *TODRL* 27 (1972): 42–43.

[105]J. Darrouzès, *Les Regestes des Actes du Patriarcat de Constantinople*, vol. I, fasc. V (Paris, 1977), nos. 2540–41, pp. 453–54. See also Karabinov, *Postnaia Triod'*, 50.

[106]J. Meyendorff, *Introduction à l'étude de Grégoire Palamas* (Paris, 1959), 152.

seemed appropriate to commemorate the great hesychast teacher on the following Sunday.

ORDO

As on Sundays during the preparatory period, only the Octoechos and the Triodion are used. At vespers, four stichera from the Triodion are sung at "Lord, I call," added to six from the Octoechos, as well as a doxastikon from the Triodion. The Triodion also contains a doxastikon and a theotokion for the aposticha. At the artoklasia, "Mother of God and Virgin" is sung three times.

At "God is the Lord" in matins, the Sunday troparion is sung twice, then the troparion of the saint and the Sunday theotokion. After Psalm 50, the penitential troparia from the Triodion are sung, as during the preparatory period. The canon of the Resurrection from the Octoechos is sung with four troparia, the first Triodion canon with four troparia, and the second Triodion canon (for the saint) with six troparia. The katabasiai are from the canon to the Mother of God ("My mouth will open"), in preparation for Annunciation. After the third ode, the kontakion and a kathisma troparion, both from the Triodion, are sung; after the sixth ode, the kontakion and ikos of the saint from the Triodion. Then follows the reading from the Synaxarion of Nicephoras Kallistos Xanthopoulos, though the account could not have been composed by him, as he died in 1335—some twenty years before St Gregory Palamas. After the ninth ode, after "Holy is the Lord, our God," an exaposteilarion from the Triodion is added to the gospel exaposteilarion. At the lauds, 5 stichera from the Octoechos are sung and 4 from the Triodion. The last sticheron from the Triodion, an idiomelon, is repeated as the doxastikon.

At all the hours, both the Sunday troparion and that for the saint are read. The two kontakia from the Triodion are alternated: the first at prime and sext, the second (for the saint) at terce and none.

On this Sunday, as on all Sundays of Great Lent through the fifth, the Liturgy of St Basil is celebrated. At this liturgy, two additional lambs are prepared and consecrated for the Presanctified Liturgies on the following Wednesday and Friday. After the entrance, we sing the Sunday troparion, [the troparion of the church, if it is dedicated to the Mother of God or a saint], [the kontakion of the church, if it is dedicated to a saint], the troparion for St Gregory, the kontakion of St Gregory, and the first kontakion from the Triodion. [If the church is dedicated to the Mother of God, then the first kontakion from the Triodion is sung, then the kontakion for St Gregory, and finally that of the church.] The prokeimena of the tone of the week and of the saint are both done, followed by two readings each from the epistle and the gospel: for Sunday and for the saint. The koinonika of both the Sunday and the saint are sung.

The third Sunday: the veneration of the Cross

ORIGIN

The third Sunday of Great Lent is dedicated to the veneration of the lifegiving Cross, connected to the shifting of the veneration of the Cross from mid-Lent, on Wednesday of the fourth week, to Sunday. According to the ancient tradition of Constantinople, this was the Sunday at which catechumens preparing to be baptized on that Easter would be enrolled, accompanied by their sponsors. The Byzantine tradition has to this day preserved the practice of praying for "those preparing for illumination" at a special litany added to the Presanctified Liturgy, following the litany for the catechumens, beginning in the week following the Sunday of the Cross.[107] This Wednesday marks the middle of Great Lent. According to Nicephoras Kallistos Xanthopoulos in his Synaxarion, the Cross is offered to us as a comfort and encouragement in our journey through Great Lent, and it announces the approach of the Passion and Resurrection of the Lord.[108]

As a witness to the Constantinopolitan monastic tradition, the Typikon of Alexios the Studite calls for the Cross, which was taken from the skeuophylakion (the sacristy) after the matins kathismata, to remain on the altar table until the end of the ninth ode of the canon. Then it was solemnly placed on a small table in from of the holy doors for veneration. After the Lord's Prayer at the end of matins, the troparion "Before your Cross" was sung, and everyone venerated the Cross.[109]

In the neo-Sabaite tradition, matins at the Sunday vigil concluded with the great doxology in its Constantinopolitan redaction. It is at this point,

[107]M. Arranz, "Les sacrements de l'ancien Euchologue constantinopolitain—4, IIIe partie: Préparation au baptême," *OCP* 50 (1984): 47–49.

[108]See Hiéromoine Macaire (G. Bonnet), "Le mystère de la croix dans le Carême orthodoxe," *Irénikon* 52 (1979): 34–53 and 200–13; M. Arranz, "Les fêtes théologiques du calendrier byzantin," in *La Liturgie, expression de la foi. Conférences Saint-Serge. XXVe Semaine d'études liturgiques* (Rome, 1979), 43–46.

[109]Pentkovskii, *Tipikon*, 242.

during the final singing of the trisagion, that the Cross is solemnly carried in procession from the altar, where it was placed at the beginning of the vigil, to the middle of the church, to be venerated by the clergy and the faithful.[110]

ORDO

After the ninth hour, before the beginning of the vigil, the priest goes to the sacristy to get the Cross, which has been decorated with flowers, brings it into the sanctuary, preceded by the deacon who incenses, while the clerics sing the troparion and kontakion of the Cross, and places it on the altar table. A lit candle is put in front of it. Note that in our day the Cross is most often transported from the prothesis table in the sanctuary to the altar.

As on Sundays during the preparatory period, only the Octoechos and the Triodion are used. At vespers, four stichera from the Triodion are sung at "Lord, I call," added to six from the Octoechos, as well as a doxastikon from the Triodion. The Triodion also contains a doxastikon and a theotokion for the lite stichera and the aposticha. At the artoklasia, "Mother of God and Virgin" is sung twice, followed by the troparion for the Cross ("O Lord, save your people") once.

At "God is the Lord" in matins, the Sunday troparion is sung twice, then the troparion for the Cross and the Sunday theotokion. After Psalm 50, the penitential troparia from the Triodion are sung, as during the preparatory period. The canon of the Resurrection from the Octoechos is sung with four troparia, of the Mother of God (from the Octoechos) with two troparia, and the Triodion canon, ascribed to St Theodore the Studite, with eight troparia. Note that this canon has the same hirmoi as the paschal canon, and this is why in many places it is sung modeled on that pattern.[111] The katabasiai indicated in the Triodion are sung. After the third ode, we sing the kathisma troparia from the Triodion. After the sixth ode, follow the kontakion and ikos for the Cross, from the Triodion. Then comes the reading from the Synaxarion of Nicephoras Kallistos Xanthopoulos. Following the ninth ode, after "Holy is the Lord, our God," an exaposteilarion from the

---

[110]See *Sinai gr. 1094*, f. 80r. (edited by Lossky, *Le Typikon byzantin*, 255). Compare with: *Typikon* (Moscow, 1906), 72v.–73 (office of the Exaltation), 160v.–161 (office on August 1), 429–429v. (third Sunday of Lent).

[111]V. Talin, "O penii na utrene nedeli krestopoklonnoi irmosov paskhal'nogo kanona," *ZhMP* 3 (1968): 74–76; N.D. Uspenskii,"Eshche neskol'ko slov o penii na utrene nedeli krestopoklonnoi irmosov paskhal'nogo kanona," *ZhMP* 2 (1969): 75–79.

Triodion is added to that for the gospel. At the lauds, we sing four stichera from the Octoechos and 5 from the Triodion. The last sticheron from the Triodion, an idiomelon, is repeated as the doxastikon. During the singing of the lauds, the presiding priest dons all his vestments (as for the celebration of the Divine Liturgy). During the singing of the great doxology, he (accompanied by the deacon) incenses the Cross on the altar table from all four sides, three times. During the singing of the final trisagion, he lifts the Cross on his head and goes out in procession through the north door, stopping in front of the open holy doors. When the trisagion is finished, he proclaims: "Wisdom! Stand upright!" The choir sings the troparion for the Cross three times. As they do so, the celebrant carries the Cross to the center of the church and places it on a table or a lectern. He again incenses the Cross from all four sides, thrice. Then the clergy sing the troparion, "Before your Cross, we bow down in worship, O Master . . . ," three times, taken up by the choir. Everyone in turn then approaches, bows three times, and venerates the Cross. During this time, the choir sings the stichera indicated in the Triodion. Then matins concludes as usual.

At the hours, the Sunday troparion and the troparion and kontakion for the Cross are read.

As on all Sundays of Great Lent through the fifth, we celebrate the Liturgy of St Basil. After the entrance, we sing the Sunday troparion and the troparion and kontakion for the Cross. The prokeimenon is for the Cross.

The veneration of the Cross during the fourth week

ORIGIN

In our day, the Cross remains in the center of the church, or on the right side in front of the iconostasis, until the following Friday. It is prescribed to venerate it solemnly on three other occasions during the week that follows: on Monday, Wednesday, and Friday. At the first hour, the psalm prayer "Direct my steps" is replaced by the troparion "Before your Cross." At this time, the priest leaves the sanctuary through the holy doors and incenses the Cross three times from all four sides. Then everyone comes to venerate the Cross, during the singing of the same stichera used at the veneration at the end of matins on the third Sunday. Instead of the usual kontakion, we sing the kontakion for the Cross. On Friday, the Cross is venerated at the end of the typika, just before it is taken back into the sanctuary.

In the ancient Studite tradition, the Cross did not remain permanently in the middle of the church. Rather, following Sunday matins, a procession with the Cross took place around the monastery, after which it was returned to its place in the skeuophylakion (sacristy). It was then taken out on each day for veneration, from Monday to Friday, at the end of the ninth hour, and then put away each time.[112] Our current practice of solemnly venerating the Cross on Monday, Wednesday, and Friday of the fourth week is a remnant of this ancient practice.

PARTICULARITIES IN THE OFFICES ON MONDAY, WEDNESDAY, AND FRIDAY

In addition to this solemn veneration of the Cross on Monday, Wednesday, and Friday of the fourth week, the office has another peculiarity on Wednesday and Friday. The office for the saint from the Menaion is shifted to compline and is replaced by an office for the Cross. At Tuesday evening vespers, at "Lord, I call," six stichera and one sticheron for "Glory . . . now and ever . . ." are sung, all taken from the Triodion. On Thursday evening, however, after the three stichera from the Triodion, we sing the three stichera for the saint from the Menaion, even if the canon for the saint is not read at matins. At matins, a nine-ode canon for the Cross is sung (the canon for Wednesday is different from that on Friday), to which are added the two three-ode canons. After the third ode, we sing the kathisma troparia for the Cross (from the Triodion). After the sixth ode, we sing the kontakion and ikos for the Cross. After the ninth ode, the photagogikon of the tone and the exaposteilarion for the Cross are sung.

The fourth Sunday: Commemoration of St John Climacus

ORIGIN

The modern editions of the Triodion call for the commemoration of St John of the Ladder on the fourth Sunday of Great Lent. In some manuscripts, we find a rubric in the menologia explaining that the office for St John Climacus is shifted from the day of his feast, March 30, to the fourth Sunday of Great Lent.[113] In the spirit of Canon 51 of the Council of Laodicea, this commemoration, which always fell during Great Lent, was no doubt moved

---

[112]Pentkovskii, *Tipikon*, 243; see Mansvetov, *Tserkovnyi ustav*, 144.

[113]This is the case, for example, in the *Liturgical Psalter* of Metropolitan Cyprian, which I edited: Kiprian, *Psaltir' s vossledovaniem*, f. 242.

to a Sunday to make it more solemn.[114] St John Climacus, an ascetical author from the second half of the sixth century, holds an important place in the Byzantine tradition and is particularly cherished by the hesychastic monks, who no doubt wished to emphasize his memory beginning in the fourteenth century. It is interesting to note that the Typikon of Alexios the Studite does not yet include this celebration.[115] We have already seen that the reading of *The Ladder* of St John Climacus is prescribed at the hours during Great Lent, which explains why the commemoration of this saint is appropriate for this time of the year.

ORDO

As on Sundays during the preparatory period, only the Octoechos and the Triodion are used. At vespers, at "Lord, I call," 7 stichera from the Octoechos are sung, and 3 from the Triodion, as well as a doxastikon from the Triodion. The Triodion also contains a doxastikon for the aposticha. At the artoklasia, "O Mother of God and virgin" is sung three times.

At "God is the Lord" in matins, the Sunday troparion is sung twice, followed by the troparion for the saint and the Sunday theotokion. After Psalm 50, the penitential troparia from the Triodion are sung, as during the preparatory period. The canon of the Resurrection from the Octoechos is sung with four troparia, of the Mother of God (from the Octoechos) with two troparia, the first canon from the Triodion (an ancient canon on the theme of the Good Samaritan—the theme of this Sunday gospel in ancient Jerusalem) with four troparia, and the second Triodion canon (for the saint) with four troparia. The katabasiai are from the canon to the Mother of God ("I will open my mouth"). After the third ode, the kathisma troparia from the Triodion are sung; after the sixth ode, the kontakion and ikos for the saint from the Triodion. Then follows the reading from the Synaxarion of Nicephoras Kallistos Xanthopoulos. After the ninth ode and "Holy is the Lord, our God," an exaposteilarion from the Triodion is added to the gospel exaposteilarion. At the lauds, eight stichera from the Octoechos are sung,

---

[114]Canon 51 of Laodicea orders that martyrs not be commemorated during Great Lent, but that they be commemorated on Saturdays and Sundays. See P.-P. Joannou, *Discipline générale antique* (Fonti, fasc. 9), vol. 1, 1 (Rome, 1962), 151.

[115]Pentkovskii, *Tipikon*, 243, 340; see Karabinov, *Postnaia Triod'*, 50; M. Arranz, "Les fêtes théologiques du calendrier byzantin," in *La Liturgie, expression de la foi. Conférences Saint-Serge. XXVe Semaine d'études liturgiques* (Rome, 1979), 47.

as well as one idiomelon sticheron from the Triodion, which is repeated as the doxastikon.

At the hours, the Sunday troparion and the troparion of the saint are read, and the Sunday kontakion is alternated with that for the saint. On this Sunday, as on all Sundays of Great Lent through the fifth, the Liturgy of St Basil is celebrated. At this liturgy, three additional lambs are prepared and consecrated for the Presanctified Liturgies on the following Wednesday, Thursday (because of the Great Canon), and Friday. After the entrance, we sing the Sunday troparion, [the troparion of the church, if it is dedicated to the Mother of God or a saint], the troparion for the saint, the kontakion of the saint, and the Sunday kontakion [if the church is dedicated to the Mother of God, the Sunday kontakion is sung first, then that for the saint, and finally that for the church; if it is dedicated to a saint, the kontakia are in the following order: Sunday, for the church, for the saint, and for the Mother of God]. The prokeimena of the tone and of the saint are both sung, and we read two epistles and two gospels: for Sunday and for the saint. The koinonika of both the Sunday and the saint are sung.

Thursday of the Great Canon

ORIGIN

An important event during Great Lent is Thursday of the Great Canon, which falls during the fifth week and is already attested to in the Typikon of Alexios the Studite.[116] According to I. Karabinov, the reading of the Great Canon was, during the eleventh century, set for the fifth week of Lent, no doubt in memory of an earthquake that occurred in Constantinople on March 17, 790, during the reign of Constantine VI.[117] This may explain why the Typikon of the Great Church does not mention it. Note that the custom of singing the Great Canon on Thursday of the fifth week is more ancient than that of singing it during the first week.

ORDO

At Presanctified Liturgy on Wednesday, at "Lord, I call," in addition to the usual six stichera from the Triodion, we sing 24 additional stichera for the Great Canon, which are attributed to St Andrew of Crete in Slavic Triodia,

[116]Pentkovskii, *Tipikon*, 243–44.
[117]Karabinov, *Postnaia Triod'*, 34–35.

but which were in fact composed by Symeon Metaphrastes in the tenth century, as the Greek Triodion indicates. These stichera, which begin with the 24 letters of the Greek alphabet, each conclude with the phrase "O Lord, before I perish completely, save me!" The Presanctified Liturgy then continues as usual.

After the dismissal of the Presanctified Liturgy, the Typikon indicates that the monks should eat food boiled with oil and drink wine, "because of the strenuousness of the vigil of the Great Canon."[118] The Typikon of Alexios the Studite called for the same. Because of the effort to come, small compline is read in the cells. If Annunciation falls on Thursday of the fifth week, the Great Canon is on Monday or Tuesday evening in anticipation.

Matins, which is generally celebrated either on Wednesday evening or during the night from Wednesday to Thursday, follows the order of an "office with Alleluia." It begins with the royal office and the hexapsalmos. After the hexapsalmos, the great synapte is recited and "Alleluia" is sung in the tone of the week, followed by the Trinitarian troparia.

Then a single kathisma is read (kathisma 8). Note that the arrangement of the Psalter is particular during the fifth week of Great Lent. After the psalmody, the kathisma troparia from the Octoechos are sung in the tone of the week. We then read the first half of the life of St Mary of Egypt, attributed to St Sophronios of Jerusalem. Psalm 50 follows (preceded by *Kyrie eleison* 3 times, Glory . . . now and ever . . .). The prayer "O Lord, save your people," exceptionally, is not read this day.

Then the Great Canon begins, without the biblical canticles. To each ode of the Great Canon, the Triodion has added troparia in honor of St Mary of Egypt and a troparion in honor of St Andrew of Crete. The troparia of the Great Canon are each preceded by the verse: "Have mercy on me, O God, have mercy on me!"—and should normally be accompanied by three full prostrations. The troparia for St Mary of Egypt are preceded by: "O venerable Mother Mary, pray to God for us!"; and those for St Andrew: "O venerable Father Andrew, pray to God for us!" At the fourth, eighth, and ninth odes, the Great Canon is preceded by two three-ode canons. The refrain for these is: "O holy apostles, pray to God for us!" At each ode, the hirmos of the Great Canon is sung. These hirmoi are also the katabasiai for the third, sixth, eight, and ninth odes.

---

[118] *Triodion* (Moscow, 1992), 394v. Compare this rubric with *Sinai gr. 1094*, f. 8iv. (edited by Lossky, *Le Typikon byzantin*, 257).

After the third ode, the small synapte is said, and the kathisma troparia from the Triodion are sung. Then the second half of the life of St Mary of Egypt is read. After the sixth ode follow the small synapte and the kontakion from the Triodion, ascribed to St Romanos the Melode ("My soul, my soul, arise"), with its ikos. The Synaxarion of Nicephoras Kallistos Xanthopoulos is then read, followed by the Beatitudes, accompanied by prostrations and troparia. At the ninth ode, the Magnificat is sung with its refrain "More honorable than the Cherubim." After the ninth ode, there is a small synapte, and then the Trinitarian photagogikon in the tone of the week.

In the spirit of the Triodion, the office concludes like an ordinary Lenten office. The great Canon is in fact inserted into the structure of the ordinary office with "Alleluia," with the biblical canticles omitted for practical reasons. The lauds are therefore read in their Hagiopolite recension ("Praise the Lord from the heavens"), as is the doxology. The deacon says the synapte with demands, and the aposticha from the Triodion are sung. The psalm prayer ("It is good to confess the Lord") is, exceptionally, read only once. After the Lord's Prayer, the troparion, "Standing in the temple of your glory," is read. In some places, exceptionally, the deacon says the ektene. Following the ekphonesis by the priest, we find diverse practices: some recite the Prayer of St Ephrem with 16 prostrations, other with just three, while others omit it, which does not fit the spirit of the Triodion. The same happens at the conclusion of each hour. This reflects different practices, intended to compensate for the large number of prostrations during the Great Canon. The Typikon is silent on the subject, thus indicating that the normal Lenten practice should be observed. Then the first hour is read.

The hours are read "quickly, because of the effort at the vigil." The troparia are read, together with the psalmody appointed for the fifth week. Instead of the kontakia from the Horologion, the kontakion from the Great Canon is used: "My soul, my soul, arise."

At the typika, the Beatitudes are read. The kontakion is from the Great Canon ("My soul, my soul, arise") The typika conclude as usual before the Presanctified Liturgy: "*Kyrie eleison*" (40 times), and the prayer: "O most holy Trinity." Then follows the dismissal: "Wisdom!"—"It is truly meet . . ."; "Most holy Theotokos, save us!"—"More honorable than the Cherubim"; "Glory to you, O Christ God, our hope, glory to you," etc.

Exceptionally, the Presanctified Liturgy is celebrated on Thursday of the fifth week because of the Great Canon. It follows the usual order.

At the evening meal, oil and wine may be consumed "because of the effort at the vigil." We note that, on Mt Athos, only wine is served that day.

Saturday of the Akathist

ORIGIN

Saturday of the fifth week has another important solemnity, which brings the week to an end. Its origin is not very clear, as is also the case with the Akathist.[119] In its form, it resembles a kontakion, a form of hymnography containing 24 poetical stanzas, each beginning with a letter of the Greek alphabet. On this last point, the first kontakion ("O invincible leader of triumphant hosts") does not begin with the letter "A" (to which corresponds the first ikos, "The angel standing before . . ."), and consequently it may have been added later to the Akathist hymn. This kontakion alludes to the liberation of Constantinople from danger through the intercession of the Mother of God ("I, your city, freed from danger, offer thanks to you, O Mother of God . . .").

According to the Synaxarion of Nicephoras Kallistos Xanthopoulos, the solemnity on the fifth Saturday of Great Lent was introduced in connection with the liberation of Constantinople from Persian and Arab occupation in 626, during the reign of Emperor Heraclius and Patriarch Sergius, and then in 672–678 and in 716. According to the "Account about the Akathist" contained in some Triodia, the celebration is connected to the liberation in 626. According to the *Chronicle* of G. Amartolos, the Akathist is linked to the event of 678.[120] However, according to various chronologies, this liberation occurred in July or August, and so the link with the celebration on the fifth Saturday is not evident. A. Papadopoulos-Kerameus believes that this solemnity originates from the liberation of Constantinople from Slavic occupation in 860, at the time of Patriarch Photius.[121] Here again, according to the chronologies, this event occurred in June and does not even coincide with the Triodion. In 1904, P. von Winterfield discovered a Latin translation of the Akathist, dating to the ninth century, which he

---

[119]On the origin of this celebration, we summarize here the study of Karabinov, *Post-naia triod'*, 35–50. On the origin of the Akathistos, see E. Wellesz, *The Akathistos Hymn*, Monumenta musicae Byzantinae, Transcripta 9 (Copenhagen, 1957).

[120]PG 110, col. 893.

[121]A. Papadopulo-Keramevs, "Akafist Bozhiei Materi," *Vizantiiskii Vremennik* (1903): 357.

ascribes to St Germanos of Constantinople and ties it to the liberation of Constantinople in 717.[122]

According to K. Krumbacher and P. Maas, the first kontakion and the first ikos of the Akathist are found in a kontakion of Romanos the Melode (5th–6th century) on the chaste Joseph, while the refrain of the Akathist ("Rejoice, O unwedded bride!") is found in a kontakion by Romanos for Annunciation. Consequently, according to P. Maas, the Akathist hymn is much more ancient than the various occupations of Constantinople we have just mentioned. Additionally, the content of the Akathist makes no allusion to these events, but in fact summarizes the life of Christ, which leads Karabinov to say that the Akathist was written not to glorify the Mother of God, but Christ as the Savior through his incarnation.[123] Indeed, the hymn contains explicit references to the Annunciation and the cycle of the Nativity of Christ. Also, the first kontakion of the current Akathist is also the kontakion for the feast of Annunciation. For this reason, Karabinov, following P. Maas, considers that the origin of the solemnity on the fifth Saturday of Great Lent is linked to a shift in the feast of Annunciation.[124] We know that, in the spirit of Canon 51 of the Council of Laodicea (c. 365), it was not appropriate to celebrate feasts during Great Lent, and such celebrations consequently had to be shifted to the following Saturday or Sunday.[125] It was only the Council in Trullo (692) that decided to celebrate Annunciation on the very day (March 25).[126] From this point, the solemnity of Saturday of the Akathist became a doublet of the feast of Annunciation, and the late Byzantine texts sought to justify the practice by reference to the deliverance of Constantinople from various invaders, as does, for example, Nicephoras Kallistos Xanthopoulos in his Synaxarion.

According to Karabinov, the celebration of the Akathist did in fact coincide with the end of the war between Heraclius and the Persians: peace negotiations began on the eve of Annunciation, on March 24, 628. The

[122]P. De Meester, "L'imno acatisto," *Bessarione* 81 (1904): 213.

[123]Karabinov, *Postnaia Triod'*, 40, 42.

[124]Ibid., 44; Maas, "Recension sur l'article de P. De Meester 'L'imno acatisto,'" *Byzantinische Zeitschrift* 14 (1905): 647.

[125]P.-P. Joannou, *Discipline générale antique* (Fonti, fasc. 9), vol. 1, 1 (Rome, 1962), 151.

[126]Indeed, Canon 52 of Trullo states: "On the days of Great Lent, except on Saturdays and Sundays, *and on the holy day of Annunciation*, no liturgy can be celebrated except the Liturgy of the Presanctified." (P.-P. Joannou, *Discipline générale antique* [Fonti, fasc. 9], vol. 1, 1 [Rome, 1962], 189).

end of the war, in the minds of the Byzantines, was no doubt linked to the intercessions of the Mother of God, the protector of the Byzantine capital, where the feast of Annunciation had been instituted for the first time. After the Council in Trullo authorized the celebration of Annunciation on a fixed date, the celebration of the solemnity of Akathist Saturday was kept in memory of the deliverance of Constantinople. This Saturday, which was originally always the Saturday following March 25, was, after the eleventh century, set on the fifth Saturday of Great Lent, perhaps because of an earthquake the struck Constantinople in 790 (which was also at the origin of Thursday of the fifth week).[127] According to Arranz, the solemnity of the Akathist preceded that of the Great Canon, because it is found in the Typikon of the Great Church.[128] In spite of all these explanations, nothing prevents the commemoration of several liberations of Constantinople through the intercessions of the Mother of God from being solemnized by the use of the ancient hymn from Annunciation, adding to it the kontakion "O victorious leader . . ."

ORDO

On Friday at the Presanctified Liturgy, ten stichera are sung at "Lord, I call": the idiomelon from the Triodion three times, one martyrikon and three stichera in honor of the Mother of God (repeated, to bring the total up to seven). At "Glory . . . now and ever," the theotokion from the Triodion is sung.[129] The Presanctified Liturgy continues as usual. At the refectory, wine is permitted.

According to the Sabaite Typikon, the Akathist is sung in four sections at matins, which is usually celebrated on Friday evening. We should note, however, that according to the modern Typikon of the Great Church, the Akathist is sung at compline on Friday night.

At matins, we sing "God is the Lord," and then the troparion of the Mother of God from the Triodion three times. After the first kathisma and the small synapte, the kathisma troparion from the Triodion is sung. Then we begin the first section of the Akathist (ikos 1–kontakion 4). At the begin-

---

[127]Karabinov, *Postnaia Triod'*, 44–45, 49–50, 34–35.

[128]M. Arranz, "Les fêtes théologiques du calendrier byzantin," in *La Liturgie, expression de la foi. Conférences Saint-Serge. XXVe Semaine d'études liturgiques* (Rome, 1979), 47–48.

[129]Note that these three stichera at "Lord, I call" are the same as those for Annunciation (see the Menaion, March 25), as well as the theotokion, which we also find during the matins lauds on Annunciation.

ning and end of each section, we sing the kontakion: "O victorious leader of triumphant hosts." After the second kathisma and the small synapte follows the second section of the Akathist (ikos 4–kontakion 7). After Psalm 50, the canon of the saint of the church is sung with six troparia, and then the Triodion canon in honor of the Mother of God with six troparia. The acrostic of the latter canon is: "Receptacle of grace, it is fitting only for you to rejoice." (If the church is dedicated to the Mother of God, the canon of the Mother of God is sung with twelve troparia.) After the third ode of the canon and the small synapte follow the third section of the Akathist (ikos 7–kontakion 10) and the kathisma troparion from the Triodion. After the sixth ode and the small synapte, we sing the fourth part of the Akathist (ikos 10–kontakion 13). Then comes the reading from the Synaxarion of Nicephoras Kallistos Xanthopoulos. Following the ninth ode and the small synapte, we sing the exaposteilarion from the Triodion. At the lauds, which are sung ("Let every breath"), four stichera from the Triodion are sung, followed by their theotokion, and then the great doxology (in its Constantinopolitan recension). The litanies follow, and then the dismissal. At the hours, the troparion and kontakion from the Triodion are read. On this day, as on every Saturday during Great Lent, the Liturgy of St John Chrysostom is celebrated. We sing the troparion and kontakion from the Triodion. The prokeimenon, Alleluia, and the koinonikon, all from the Triodion, are in honor of the Mother of God. There are, however, two sets of readings: for the Saturday, and for the Theotokos. In Greek practice, as in the Russian, the office of the Saturday Akathist is very solemn and the melodies highly ornate.

The Feast of Annunciation during Great Lent

As we have already seen, it was the Council in Trullo (692) that decided to celebrate Annunciation on the very day (March 25).[130] This decision led to the redaction of a series of "Chapters of Mark" (see the Menaion or the Typikon for March 25) to resolve this highly complex situation. We will now describe the three most common possibilities. It is nonetheless necessary to study the "Chapters of Mark" in detail to understand the various combinations between the celebration of the feast and the ordo of the Triodion.

---

[130]See Canon 52 of the Council in Trullo: P.-P. Joannou, *Discipline générale antique* (Fonti, fasc. 9), vol. 1, 1 (Rome, 1962), 189.

1) If March 25 falls on a weekday during Great Lent, from Tuesday to Friday, at vespers on the eve, if there is a Presanctified Liturgy, we sing ten stichera at "Lord, I call": the idiomelon (twice) and three stichera from the Triodion, then three festal stichera from the Menaion (singing two of them twice), "Glory . . . now and ever . . . ," followed by the theotokion from the Menaion. If there is no Presanctified Liturgy, then eight stichera are sung at "Lord, I call": three stichera from the Triodion, then three festal stichera from the Menaion (singing two of them twice), followed by the theotokion from the Menaion. After the entrance, we say the two prokeimena from the Triodion and add the three Old-Testament readings from the Menaion to the two from the Triodion. Then the Presanctified Liturgy continues as usual. If there is no Presanctified Liturgy, at the end of vespers we sing the festal troparion, followed by the ektene and the Prayer of St Ephrem only once, with three prostrations.

The vigil of the feast consists of great compline and matins. At compline, after the first trisagion, we sing the troparion of the feast instead of the troparia from the Horologion. After the second trisagion, we sing the kontakion of the feast instead of the troparia from the Horologion. After the doxology come the *lite* and the artoklasia (see the stichera in the Menaion), after which follow the hexapsalmos and matins.

After the first kathisma, the two kathisma troparia from the Triodion are sung immediately, with no small synapte. After the second and third kathismata, we say the small synapte and sing the kathisma troparion from the Menaion. The polyeleos follows. After this come the kathisma troparia from the Menaion, the first antiphon of the anabathmoi in tone 4, the festal prokeimenon (see the Menaion), and then "Let every breath" and the reading of the festal gospel. After Psalm 50 and its troparia, we sing the idiomelon from the Menaion, followed by the festal canon (from the Menaion), to which we add the two three-ode canons from the Triodion. For the odes where only the Menaion is used, the canon is sung with twelve troparia, and the hirmos of the festal canon is sung as the katabasia. For those odes for which there is a Triodion canon, the canon from the Menaion is sung with six troparia, and the two three-ode canons with eight troparia, and the katabasia is taken from the Triodion. After the third ode, the kathisma troparion from the Menaion is sung; after the sixth ode, we sing the kontakion from the Menaion. At the ninth ode, the Magnificat is replaced by the festal refrains (see the Menaion). After the ninth ode, the exaposteilarion of the feast is read (see the Menaion). The lauds are sung ("Let every breath") with the four stichera and the-otokion for the feast (Menaion). The doxology is read. After the synapte with demands, we sing the aposticha from the Triodion and the festal theotokion (from the Menaion). The psalm prayer, "It is good to confess the Lord," is said only once. After the Lord's Prayer, we sing the festal troparion. The ektene follows, then the Prayer of St Ephrem only once, with three prostrations, and the first hour follows immediately.

At the hours, the appointed kathismata are read, but without the usual prostrations. The troparia and kontakia from the Horologion are replaced by the troparion and kontakion of the feast (from the Menaion). At the end of each hour, the Prayer of St Ephrem is only said once, with three prostrations. At the sixth hour, the customary Old-Testament reading is done.

In conformity with Canon 52 of the Council in Trullo, the Liturgy of St John Chrysostom is celebrated on this day. Nevertheless, this liturgy begins with vespers, because, by reason of the fast, it is supposed to be celebrated in the afternoon, following the ninth hour of the day. At "Lord, I call," eleven stichera are sung: the idiomelon (twice), three stichera idi-omela from the Triodion, then three festal stichera from the Menaion (March 25) and the three stichera for the Archangel Gabriel (March 26). Following "Glory . . . now and ever . . . ," we sing the theotokion from the Menaion. After the entrance with the gospel follow the two prokeimena from the Triodion, and two Old-Testament readings from the Menaion are added to the two Triodion readings. The small synapte, and then the trisagion follow. The eucharistic liturgy then proceeds as usual, with the reading of the festal epistle and gospel. The Typika indicated that after the liturgy on Annunciation, fish, wine, and oil are permitted at table.

2) If March 25 falls on a Saturday or Sunday during Great Lent, it is necessary to consult the "Chapters of Mark" to know how the differ-ent services of the Triodion are affected. If the feast falls on a Saturday, the vespers on the eve of the feast are celebrated with the Presanctified Liturgy. To the two Triodion readings are added the five Old-Testament readings from the Menaion. The vigil of the feast consists of great com-pline and matins. If the feast falls on a Sunday, the vigil consists of ves-

pers and matins. At vespers, the five Old-Testament readings from the Menaion are done. If the feast falls on Saturday, the Liturgy of St John Chrysostom is celebrated after the sixth hour; if it falls on Sunday, the Liturgy of St Basil is celebrated after the sixth hour.

3) If March 25 falls on a Monday, the vigil of the feast consists of vespers and matins. At vespers, following the entrance and the great prokeimenon, three Old-Testament readings from the Menaion are done. The ordo of matins is as described above, for a weekday. The Liturgy of St John Chrysostom begins with vespers, and two Old-Testament readings from the Menaion are added to the two from the Triodion.

The fifth Sunday: Commemoration of St Mary of Egypt

ORIGIN

The fifth Sunday of Great Lent commemorates St Mary of Egypt. In the spirit of Canon 51 of Laodicea, the memorial of this saint has shifted from April 1 to a Sunday during Lent in order to be able to celebrate it with greater solemnity, just as in the case of St John Climacus on the fourth Sunday. The life of this saint, who is particularly venerated in Palestine and who lived during the sixth century, is known to us thanks to the account attributed to Patriarch Sophronius of Jerusalem (6th–7th century), who presents her as a model of conversion. Her feast was fixed on the fifth Saturday of Great Lent from the eleventh century, no doubt in connection with the reading of the Great Canon of St Andrew of Crete, which was, at this same period, fixed on the fifth Thursday of Lent. We know as well that a canon in honor of St Mary of Egypt was added to the penitential Canon of St Andrew of Crete, and this confirms the connection between these two elements of the Triodion.[131]

ORDO

As on all Sundays during the period of the Triodion, only the Octoechos and Triodion are used. At "Lord, I call" at vespers, six stichera from the Octoechos and 4 from the Triodion are sung, and a doxastikon from the Triodion. The Triodion also contains a doxastikon and theotokion for the aposticha. At the artoklasia, "Mother of God and Virgin" is sung three times.

[131]Karabinov, *Postnaia Triod'*, 34, 50.

THE TYPIKON DECODED

At "God is the Lord" in matins, the Sunday troparion is sung twice, then the troparion for the saint and the Sunday theotokion. After Psalm 50, the penitential troparia from the Triodion are sung (as during the preparatory period). The canon of the Resurrection from the Octoechos is sung with four troparia, of the Mother of God (from the Octoechos) with two troparia, and then the first Triodion canon (an ancient canon on the theme of the rich man and Lazarus—the theme of the gospel read on this Sunday in Jerusalem in ancient times) with four troparia, and the second Triodion canon (of St Mary of Egypt) with four troparia. The katabasia are taken from the Canon of the Mother of God ("My mouth will open"). After the third ode, we sing the kathisma troparia from the Triodion. After the sixth ode, we sing the kontakion and ikos of the saint from the Triodion. After the ninth ode, after "Holy is the Lord, our God," an exaposteilarion from the Triodion is added to the gospel exaposteilarion. At the lauds, eight stichera from the Octoechos are sung, then an idiomelon sticheron from the Triodion, which is also repeated as the doxastikon.

At the hours, we read the Sunday troparion and the troparion for the saint, alternating the kontakia for Sunday and for the saint.

This Sunday, as on the preceding Sundays, we celebrate the Liturgy of St Basil and prepare and consecrate the additional lambs for the Presanctified Liturgies of the following Wednesday and Friday. After the entrance, we sing the Sunday troparion, [the troparion of the church, if it is dedicated to the Mother of God or to a saint,] the troparion of the saint, the kontakion of the saint, and the Sunday kontakion [if the church is dedicated to the Mother of God, the Sunday kontakion is sung first, then the kontakion for the saint, and finally the kontakion of the church; if it is consecrated to a saint, the kontakia are in the following order: Sunday, of the church, of the saint, and of the Mother of God]. We sing both the prokeimena of the tone and of the saint, and two epistles and two gospels are read: for Sunday and for the saint. The koinonika of both Sunday and the saint are sung.

Particularities of the sixth week

The sixth and final week of Great Lent reaches its climax with Lazarus Saturday and Palm Sunday, although these are not really a part of it, since, at the aposticha of matins on Friday of the sixth week, we sing: "Having completed the forty days which are useful for the soul" (doxastikon). Friday of the sixth week is indeed the fortieth day of Great Lent, while Saturday, which commemorates the raising of Lazarus, and Sunday, which commemorates the Entrance of the Lord into Jerusalem, are already in a way the beginning of Holy Week. Nonetheless, because the sixth week culminates with Palm Sunday, in the Triodion it is called "the week of Palms." It functions in a way as the pre-feast of the Entrance of the Lord into Jerusalem (see the kathisma troparia after the third kathisma at Monday matins). And because the resurrection of Lazarus occurred four days after his death, the second three-ode canon, attributed to St Theodore the Studite, at matins of the sixth week commemorates the agony of Lazarus: his illness (Monday, Tuesday), his death (Wednesday), his burial (Thursday), as well as the preparation for the entrance into Jerusalem through sending the disciples to find a donkey (Friday). The ordo of the services nevertheless follows that of the Great Lent (office with "Alleluia").

Lazarus Saturday

ORIGIN

Lazarus Saturday is a very ancient celebration, tracing its origin to the ancient liturgy of Jerusalem. Egeria speaks of it in chapter 29 of her *Travels*, specifying that everyone went on that day to the Lazarium.[132] As Maraval notes,

> The meaning of this "Lazarus Saturday," which is initially a particular-ity of the Jerusalem liturgy (before being adopted in the liturgy of other churches) is not originally the commemoration of the resurrection of Lazarus, but of the coming of Christ to Bethany "six days before the Passover" (Jn 12.1).

It functions, through this reminder, as an *announcement* of the Feast of Pascha. To this remembrance of this first event, as can be seen from the reading of Jn 11 in the Church, has been added the encounter of Jesus with the sister of Lazarus, "five hundred steps from the tomb of the latter."[133] So also, in the Armenian Lectionary (5th century), the gospel reading does not recount the story of the raising of Lazarus (Jn 11.1–46), but announces the closeness of Pascha: "The Passover of the Jews being close . . ." (Jn 11.55–12.11).[134] Indeed, Renoux notes that "contrary to the ancient Byzantine Evangelia, it

[132]Égérie, *Journal de voyage* 29, 5 (SC 296, pp. 268–70).
[133]Ibid., 270, note 1.
[134]Renoux, II, 255.

is not the resurrection of Lazarus [. . .] but the coming of Jesus to Bethany and his anointing by Mary that form the content of this pericope."[135]

In contrast to Maraval, who believes that "this 'Saturday of Lazarus' is originally a particularity of the Jerusalem liturgy, before being adopted in other churches,"[136] Talley considers that "Lazarus Saturday" is a Constantinopolitan import to Jerusalem, following the imperial building program and the arrival of numerous pilgrims.[137]

Nevertheless, one thing is clear: if the station at the Lazarium and the readings preceding the gospel provide us the resurrection of Lazarus as a background, the foreground is the gospel account which announces the approach of Pascha, by describing the journey of Jesus to Bethany "six days before the Passover." This Saturday in Jerusalem was no doubt originally an announcement about the Feast of Pascha.

ORDO

We note that the services of this Saturday have, in the Byzantine rite, maintained a paschal character, which can be seen most clearly in the office of matins.

At the Presanctified Liturgy on Friday, ten stichera are sung at "Lord, I call": the idiomelon from the Triodion twice, one martyrikon, and five stichera (repeated to reach the number seven) in honor of Lazarus, and attributed to Emperor Leo the Wise. At "Glory . . . now and ever . . . ," the theotokion from the Triodion is sung. The Presanctified Liturgy then continues as usual.

At great compline Friday evening, one canon (consisting of nine odes, including ode 2) is read, in honor of the righteous Lazarus, attributed to St Andrew of Crete.

At matins, we sing "God is the Lord" and the festal troparion from the Triodion three times ("By raising Lazarus from the dead before your passion"). After the first kathisma (kathisma 16) and the small synapte, the kathisma troparion from the Triodion is sung. Then we begin the second kathisma (kathisma 17), which concludes with the Sunday evlogitaria ("Blessed are you, O Lord . . ."; "The angelic assembly"). During these, the priest, preceded by the deacon with a candle, incenses the whole church. After the small synapte, the kathisma troparion from the Triodion is sung,

[135]Ibid., note 4.
[136]Ibid., 270, note 1.
[137]T. Talley, Les origines de l'année liturgique (Paris, 1990), 195, 200.

and then the sticheron: "Having beheld the resurrection of Christ" (in Greek practice, read by the presider), which is customarily sung on Sunday. After Psalm 50, the Triodion canons are done, up to the sixth ode: the first canon, for Theophany, with eight troparia, the second canon, attributed to St John of Damascus, with six troparia, and katabasiai from the Triodion. After the sixth ode and the small synapte, the kathisma troparia from the Triodion are sung. Beginning with the sixth ode, the two four-ode canons from the Triodion are sung with twelve troparia, the first by Cosmas of Maioum, the second by John of Damascus. After the sixth ode and the small synapte, the kontakion and ikos for Lazarus are sung. Then follows the reading from the Synaxarion of Nicephoras Kallistos Xanthopoulos. At the ninth ode, the Magnificat is omitted (it is omitted through St Thomas Sunday). After the ninth ode and the small synapte, the fixed Sunday exaposteilarion is sung ("Holy is the Lord, our God"), followed by the two exaposteilaria from the Triodion. At the lauds, which are sung ("Let every breath"), eight stichera from the Triodion are sung, by adding special verses (see the Triodion), followed by the doxastikon from the Triodion, the theotokion from Sunday lauds ("You are blessed, O Mother of God and Virgin"), and the great doxology (in its Constantinopolitan redaction). The dismissal follows the litanies. At the hours, the troparion and kontakion of the feat are read (from the Triodion). On this day, the Liturgy of St John Chrysostom is celebrated. We sing the troparion and kontakion of the feast (from the Triodion). The trisagion is replaced with "As many as have been baptized into Christ," a vestige of the baptismal liturgy that was once celebrated this day, in connection with Easter. The prokeimenon, Alleluia, and koinonikon are all for the feast (from the Triodion), as are the epistle and gospel readings.

Palm Sunday

ORIGIN

Palm Sunday is considered to be one of the 12 great feasts of the year. Its origin, as that of the preceding Saturday, is from Jerusalem.

In the account of her voyage, Egeria describes the particularities of this Sunday, which she calls "the Sunday on which they enter the paschal week, which here they call the great week."[138] She tells how at the eleventh hour of the day they read the passage describing the children's coming to greet

---

[138]Égérie, *Journal de voyage* 29, 5 (SC 296, pp. 270–72).

the Lord with branches and palms (Mt 21.8; Jn 12.13), saying: "Blessed is he who comes in the name of the Lord" (Mt 21.9; Ps 117.26). Then the people walked in procession before the bishop, holding branches, "in the same way that they then escorted the Lord," from the top of the Mount of Olives, through the city, to the Anastasis, where the evening office was celebrated. We note similarities between Egeria's account and the rubrics in the Armenian Lectionary, which calls this Sunday "the day of palms." In this fifth-century document, the triumphal entry of Christ into Jerusalem is already the object of the morning celebration at the Anastasis.[139] After the evening gathering on the Mount of Olives, this lectionary similarly indicates that the people went back down to the Anastasis, holding palm branches in their hands.

ORDO

Because this is a major feast of the Lord, the Sunday office on Palm Sunday uses only the Triodion, with nothing from the Sunday office. At "Lord, I call" at vespers, ten stichera from the Triodion are sung. After the entrance, we read the three Old-Testament passages for the feast. At the *lite*, the idiomela from the Triodion are sung. The Triodion also contains the stichera for the aposticha, as well as special psalm verses. At the artoklasia, we twice sing the troparion of the eve of the feast ("By raising Lazarus from the dead before your passion"), and then the troparion ("We were buried with you in baptism, O Christ our God") once.

At Matins, following "God is the Lord," we sing the troparion of the eve ("By raising Lazarus from the dead before your passion") twice, "Glory . . . now and ever . . . ," and the troparion ("We were buried with you in baptism, O Christ our God") once. After each kathisma and small synapte, we sing the corresponding kathisma troparia from the Triodion. The rubrics then call for the reading of the festal homily of St Andrew of Crete. Then the first antiphon of the anabathmoi is sung in tone 4 ("From my youth"), followed by the festal prokeimenon and gospel. After the gospel, "Having beheld the resurrection" is not sung. During Psalm 50, the priest incenses the branches, which have been placed on a table in the center of the church, from all four sides, and reads the prayer of blessing (see the Triodion or the Euchologion). We should note that, in Greek practice, there is no incensa-

[139]Renoux, II, 257. See also C. Renoux, *Le Monde grec ancient et la Bible*, C. Montdesert, ed. (Paris, 1984), 417, note 116.

tion, but during the reading of Psalm 50 the sacristans spread many laurel leaves throughout the church. Then the stichera following the gospel are sung (from the Triodion). When the faithful come to venerate the gospel, the superior hands them branches. On Athos, as he does so, he greets them with "Good resurrection!" After the prayer "O Lord, save your people" follows the festal canon, ascribed to Cosmas of Maioum, with the acrostic "Hosanna, Christ who comes, God." The hirmoi of the canon are repeated as the katabasiai. After the third ode and the small synapte, the hypakoe from the Triodion is read. After the sixth ode and the small synapte, the kontakion and ikos for the feast, from the Triodion, are sung, followed by the reading from the Synaxarion of Nicephoras Kallistos Xanthopoulos. As on major feasts, the Magnificat is not sung. After the ninth ode, only "Holy is the Lord, our God" is sung. At the lauds, which are sung ("Let every breath"), four stichera from the Triodion are intercalated (with two of them sung twice), followed by the idiomelon at "Glory . . . now and ever . . . ." The great doxology follows (in its Constantinopolitan version).

At the hours, the two troparia and the kontakion of the feast are read.

On this Sunday, we celebrate the Liturgy of St John Chrysostom. Three additional lambs are prepared and consecrated for the Presanctified Liturgies on the first three days of Holy Week. We sing the festal antiphons (see the Triodion). After the entrance, we sing only the two troparia and the kontakion of the feast, the trisagion, and the festal prokeimenon, The epistle and gospel readings are for the feast. As for all major feasts, the hymn to the Mother of God ("It is truly meet") is replaced by the hirmos of the ninth ode of the canon. The koinonikon is festal. Afterwards, at table, fish, wine, and oil are permitted because of the feast. We should note that, in Greek practice, fish is authorized only once during Great Lent: on the day of Annunciation (if it precedes Palm Sunday), or on Palm Sunday.

Holy Week

The services of the first three days

VESPERS ON THE EVENING OF PALM SUNDAY

As always on Sunday evening, there is no kathisma at vespers. At "Lord, I call," the 3 idiomela from the Triodion are sung, each two times, followed by the vesperal entrance with censer and candle. The usual Sunday evening prokeimenon is sung ("Bless now") (see the Horologion). After the synapte with demands follow the aposticha from the Triodion. Vespers concludes with the troparia from the Horologion prescribed for the office with "Alleluia," and accompanied with prostrations: "O Mother of God, virgin," "O Forerunner of Christ," "Intercede for us, O holy apostles," as well as "Beneath your compassion" (without a prostration). Instead of the ektene, we say *Kyrie eleison* 40 times, Glory to the Father . . . now and ever . . . More honorable than the Cherubim . . . In the name of the Lord, bless father! The priest says the blessing: "Christ our God, He who is, is blessed . . ." Then the prayer "O heavenly King . . ." The priest then recites the Prayer of St Ephrem once, with only three prostrations. The dismissal is particular: "May he who voluntarily accepted to suffer the passion . . ." (see the Hieratikon).

COMPLINE ON THE FIRST THREE DAYS

Except on Sunday night, when small compline is prescribed, great compline is read on these evenings. At these offices, the Triodion calls for the reading of the three-ode canons ascribed to St Andrew of Crete. This custom reflects Sabaite practice. For example, the Typikon of Alexios the Studite indicates that these canons were to be sung at matins with those of Cosmas of Maioum.

MATINS ON THE FIRST THREE DAYS

At matins during the first three days of Holy Week, "Alleluia" is sung, followed by a special troparion from the Triodion: "Behold, the bridegroom comes at midnight." This troparion has give the name "Bridegroom Matins" to these services. We should point out, however, that in Studite practice, the usual triadica troparia were sung at this point, in the tone of the week.

After each kathisma, the kathisma troparion from the Triodion is sung. We should note that the continuous reading of the Psalter is arranged differently in the different traditions. In the Sabaite tradition, this reading concludes on Holy Wednesday. On the first three days of Holy Week, there is no continuous psalmody at prime and none. At vespers, kathisma 18 is read. In the Studite tradition, there is continuous psalmody at all the hours until Holy Thursday. In contrast, there is no continuous psalmody at vespers, except on Holy Wednesday.

Each day, following the third matins kathisma, the priest reads the gospel passage appointed by the Triodion. After the gospel, Psalm 50 is read, followed by the prayer "O Lord, save your people." Then we begin the canon composed of three (or two) odes attributed to Cosmas of Maioum. Each of these canons is accompanied by a kontakion, an ikos, and a reading from the Synaxarion of Nicephoras Kallistos Xanthopoulos. The Magnificat is not sung. After the ninth ode and the small synapte, we sing a special exaposteilarion, contained in the Triodion: "I see your bridal chamber adorned." This exaposteilarion is found only in Sabaite Triodia; the Studite tradition prescribed the photagogikon in the tone of the week, as done throughout Great Lent.

At the lauds, the two stichera from the Triodion are sung, each two times. The doxology is read in its Hagiopolite redaction. After the synapte with demands, the aposticha from the Triodion are sung. The office concludes as during Great Lent: "It is good to confess the Lord" (twice), etc., with the Prayer of St Ephrem. The dismissal is particular: "May he who voluntarily accepted to suffer the passion . . ." (see the Hieratikon).

THE HOURS AND THE TYPIKA

At the hours, the kathisma are read in accordance with the arrangement of the Psalter during Holy Week. The troparia from the Horologion are read, accompanied by prostrations. The Sabaite tradition also calls for the reading of all four gospels in their entirety during the hours (terce, sext, and none) of the first three days of Holy Week. The Studite tradition did not know this practice.[140] Instead of the kontakia from the Horologion, the kontakion of the day is used (see the Triodion, at matins). At the sixth hour, a reading from Ezekiel is done, accompanied by a troparion of the prophecy and two prokeimena. At the end of each hour, the Prayer of St Ephrem is said twice, with 16 prostrations.

After the celebration of the hours on Wednesday, a rite of forgiveness is prescribed, after which full prostrations are terminated.

VESPERS FROM MONDAY TO WEDNESDAY OF HOLY WEEK

The vespers services from Monday through Wednesday of Holy Week conclude with the Presanctified Liturgy. At "Lord, I call," ten stichera from the Triodion are sung. After the small entrance with the gospel, a prokeimenon from the Triodion is sung, and then a reading from Exodus. After the read-

---

[140]*Sinai gr. 1094*, f. 85r. (edited by Lossky, *Le Typikon byzantin*, 262–63); Mansvetov, *Tsekovnyi ustav*, 214.

ing from Exodus follows a second prokeimenon from the Triodion. Then the deacon says "Command," and the priest: "Wisdom. Arise. The light of Christ illumines all." He then blesses the prostrate assembly with a candle and censer. Then follows the second reading (from the Book of Job). After this reading, the reader chants the selected verses from Psalm 140 ("Let my prayer arise"), followed by the Prayer of St Ephrem recited by the priest and accompanied by three prostrations. Then the deacon reads the gospel of the day, and the Presanctified Liturgy continues as usual.

The services of Holy Thursday

COMPLINE ON WEDNESDAY EVENING

Small compline is read on Wednesday evening of Holy Week. Triodia of Sabaite redaction call for the reading of a three-ode canon ascribed to St Andrew of Crete. In Greek practice, the office of holy anointing (*euchelaio*) replaces compline, just as before Christmas. This is not just a service for the sick, but also a penitential rite at which a prayer of absolution is read. Among the Russians, this service is also celebrated, either after the matins of Holy Wednesday or on another day.

The Triodion notes that, from this day until Thomas Sunday, compline is no longer read in the church.

MATINS OF HOLY THURSDAY

The Triodion calls for the celebration of matins of Holy Thursday at the seventh hour of the night. After the great synapte, "Alleluia" is sung, followed by the troparion of Holy Thursday from the Triodion: "When the glorious disciples."

There are no matins kathismata. Thus, immediately following the troparion, the priest reads the gospel pericope prescribed in the Triodion. After the gospel, Psalm 50 is read. The prayer "O Lord, save your people" is not read. Then begins the nine-ode canon attributed to Cosmas of Maioum. After the third ode and the small synapte, the kathisma troparion from the Triodion is sung. After the sixth ode and the small synapte, the kontakion and ikos are sung, followed by the reading from the Synaxarion of Nicephoras Kallistos Xanthopoulos. The Magnificat is not sung. After the ninth ode and the small synapte, we sing the exaposteilarion from the Triodion: "I see your bridal chamber adorned."

At the lauds, we sing the four stichera from the Triodion. The doxology is read in its Palestinian recension. After the synapte with demands, we sing the aposticha from the Triodion. We say: "It is good to confess the Lord" (once), and the trisagion. After the Lord's Prayer, we sing the troparion of Holy Thursday. The deacon says the ektene. After the ekphonesis by the priest, we read the first hour with the troparion and kontakion of Holy Thursday, as well as a reading from Jeremiah, accompanied by a troparion of the prophecy and two prokeimena. The dismissal is particular: "May he who voluntarily accepted to suffer the passion . . ." (see the Hieratikon).

THE HOURS AND THE TYPIKA

The other hours are read without kathismata. The troparion and kontakion of Holy Thursday are read. The Beatitudes at the typika are read, not sung. On Holy Thursday and Holy Friday (as before Christmas and Theophany), the typika are read with Psalms 102 and 145, not beginning with the Beatitudes, as during Great Lent. The kontakion of Holy Thursday is read, and the dismissal follows.

The Typikon of Alexios the Studite prescribed, after the hours and before the liturgy, a rite of foot washing, as in the practice of the Great Church.[141] In the Sabaite tradition, this office is celebrated following the Divine Liturgy. In our day, it is celebrated only in cathedrals (by the bishop) or in monasteries (by the abbot).[142] It is not celebrated on Mt Athos.

VESPERS AND THE LITURGY OF ST BASIL

The Triodion calls for the celebration of vespers with the Liturgy of St Basil at the eighth hour of the day. At vespers, ten stichera from the Triodion are sung at "Lord, I call." After the entrance with the gospel follow the prokeimenon from the Triodion and the first reading (from Exodus). After the reading comes the second prokeimenon from the Triodion, and then the second reading (from the Book of Job). After this reading follows a third reading from Isaiah. The deacon says the small synapte, and then the trisa-

---

[141]Pentkovskii, *Tipikon*, 250; Dmitrievskii, *Opisanie*, vol. 1, Τυπικά, Pt. 1, 129; Matéos, *Typikon*, II, 72.

[142]On this subject, see A. Lossky, "Lavement des pieds et charité fraternelle: l'exemple du rite byzantin," in *Liturgie et charité fraternelle. Conférences Saint-Serge. 45ᵉ semaine d'études liturgiques*, BEL 101 (Rome, 1999), 87–96; A. Lossky, "La cérémonie du lavement des pieds: un essai d'étude comparée," in *Acts of the International Congress. Comparative Liturgy Fifty Years after Anton Baumstark (1872–1948)*, R. Taft and G. Winkler, eds. (Rome, 2001), 809–32.

gion is sung. The epistle and gospel readings are for Holy Thursday, and the Liturgy of St Basil follows immediately. Instead of the Cherubikon, the koinonikon, and the post-communion troparion ("Let our mouths be filled"), we sing the troparion "Of your mystical supper." Oil and wine are permitted at table, because of the feast.

The services of Holy Friday

COMPLINE ON THURSDAY NIGHT

In the Triodia of Sabaite redaction, a three-ode canon ascribed to St Andrew of Crete is to be read at small compline. In the Studite tradition, as attested in the Typikon of Alexios the Studite, compline was not read that day, and the three-ode canon was read at matins.[143]

MATINS OF HOLY FRIDAY

The Sabaite Typikon prescribes that matins of Holy Friday be celebrated at the second hour of the night. This office, which is also called "The Service of the Holy and Saving Passion of Our Lord Jesus Christ," is also commonly referred to as the "Service of Twelve Gospels." It corresponds totally to the Constantinopolitan vigil of Holy Friday, which in the Typikon of Alexios the Studite and in the Typikon of the Great Church is known under the name of "The Pannychis of the Sufferings of the Passion of Our Lord Jesus Christ."[144] The origin of this service, however, is from Jerusalem. Egeria attests to its existence in the fourth century.[145] The Armenian Lectionary supplies the list of readings used in Jerusalem, and it is interesting to see that these were then taken up by the Great Church of Constantinople and, still today, comprise the twelve passion gospels.[146]

After the great synapte, "Alleluia" is sung, followed by the troparion of Holy Thursday ("When the glorious disciples"). During the troparion, in Russian practice, the priest incenses the entire church (the great censing). The deacon then says the small synapte, and the priest reads the first of the twelve passion gospels. It is the custom, at least among the Russians, to read

[143]Pentkovskii, *Tipikon*, 252–53, 255, 376.
[144]Pentkovskii, *Tipikon*, 253; Matéos, *Typikon*, II, 76.
[145]Égérie, *Journal de voyage*, 35, 3—36, 5 (SC 296, pp. 280–85).
[146] Renoux, II, 270–81; Matéos, *Typikon*, II, 76–78; for a comparative table, see my article, J. Getcha, "Le système de lectures bibliques du rite byzantin," in *La Liturgie, interprète de l'Écriture, I. Les lectures bibliques pour les dimanches et fêtes. Conférences Saint-Serge. 48ᵉ semaine d'études liturgiques*, BELS 19 (Rome, 2002), 39.

the gospel from the middle of the church, in front of the Cross. In Greek practice, the superior reads the gospel from the solea, facing the people as usual, and the subsequent gospels are read by the other priests, in order of seniority; only the last gospel is read by the deacon in front of the Cross. Then we begin singing the 15 antiphons.

After the third antiphon, the deacon recites the small synapte. Then the kathisma troparion is sung, during which, in Russian practice, the priest incenses (the small censing). The priest then reads the second gospel.

After the sixth antiphon, the deacon recites the small synapte. Then the kathisma troparion is sung, during which, in Russian practice, the priest incenses (the small censing). The priest then reads the third gospel.

After the ninth antiphon, the deacon recites the small synapte. Then the kathisma troparion is sung, during which, in Russian practice, the priest incenses (the small censing). The priest then reads the fourth gospel.

After the twelfth antiphon, the deacon recites the small synapte. Then the kathisma troparion is sung, during which, in Russian practice, the priest incenses (the small censing). The priest then reads the fifth gospel.

In Greek practice, following the thirteenth antiphon, the sacristans prepare the stand for the Cross in the center of the church. After the fifteenth antiphon, the priest leaves the sanctuary through the north door carrying the Crucified Christ, preceded by a deacon carrying a candle and incensing. The priest hangs the image of the Crucified Christ on the Cross, which he then incenses from all four sides as during the artoklasia, and the relic of the Cross is laid out (if such is the case). Then the abbot and the entire community, in order of seniority, come to venerate the Cross. A vigil light is placed in front of the Cross, and the icon of the "Extreme Humility" is placed there for veneration.

After the fifteenth antiphon, the deacon recites the small synapte. Then the kathisma troparion is sung, during which, in Russian practice, the priest incenses (the small censing). The priest then reads the sixth gospel.

The Beatitudes are then read, accompanied by their troparia. At this time, in Russian practice, the priest incenses. Then the prokeimenon is sung ("They divided my garments among them . . ."), and the priest reads the seventh gospel.

After Psalm 50, the priest reads the eighth gospel.

Then the tree-ode canon by Cosmas of Maioum is sung. After the fifth ode, the deacon recites the small synapte, and we sing the kontakion, fol-

lowed by its ikos. We then read from the Synaxarion of Nicephoras Kallistos
Xanthopoulos. At the ninth ode, the Magnificat is not sung. After the ninth
ode, the deacon says the small synapte, and the exaposteilarion of Holy
Friday is sung three times: "The wise thief . . . ." The priest then reads the
ninth gospel.

The lauds ("Let every breath") are sung with four stichera, and the priest
then reads the tenth gospel.

The doxology is read in its Palestinian redaction.[147] The deacon recites
the small synapte, and the priest then reads the eleventh gospel.

The aposticha from the Triodion are then sung, and the priest reads the
twelfth gospel. Note that, in Greek practice, this last gospel is read by the
deacon.

We then read: "It is good to confess the Lord" (once). After the Lord's
Prayer, we sing the troparion: "You ransomed us . . . ." The deacon says the
ektene, and the priest does the appropriate dismissal, "May he who endured
the spitting, the blows . . ." (see the Hieratikon).

THE ROYAL HOURS

In contemporary practice, the first hour is not read after the matins dismissal. On Holy Friday, prime, terce, sext, and none are all read together,
one after the other, forming, as on the eves of Christmas and Epiphany,
what are called the "Great" or "Royal" Hours. Additionally, Old-Testament,
epistle, and gospel readings are indicated at each hour. The Triodion also
prescribes several specific psalms, different from those in the Horologion,
as well a series of stichera.

The Typikon of Alexios the Studite, however, called for the reading of
the first hour immediately following matins, and the other hours at their
proper time, with gospel readings at the third, sixth, and ninth hours, and
an Old-Testament reading at the sixth hour.[148] The Typikon of the Great
Church only called for the office of ter-sext (τριτοέκτη) with its Old-Testament reading. As Matéos notes, "we note the absence of the Great Hours of
Palestinian origin."[149]

[147]We note in passing that this structure: lauds—("Let every breath"), the doxology
(Palestinian version), and the aposticha,—was common to all the matins on great feasts
in the Studite tradition. The matins office in the Sabaite tradition no doubt derives from
this tradition.
[148]Pentkovskii, *Tipikon*, 253–54.
[149]Matéos, *Typikon*, II, 79, note 3.

The Sabaite tradition prescribes the reading of the Great Hours, or "Royal Hours," on the morning of Good Friday. In current practice, the hours are read one after the other. Some manuscripts, however, witness to an earlier practice according to which prime was read at the first hour of the day, and the other hours at the seventh hour.

The Sabaite tradition ignores the "service of the twelve troparia of the holy sufferings," which in the Studite tradition was celebrated on Holy Tuesday at the tenth hour of the day, between terce and sext.[150] However, if we compare the description of this office in the Typikon of Alexios the Studite with the service of Great Hours on Holy Friday in the Triodia of Hagiopolite provenance,[151] we find the same hymnographic and scriptural material, as is evident in the table below:

Studite tradition	Sabaite tradition
Great and Holy Tuesday	**Great and Holy Friday**
Third hour	Service of the Great Hours
Service of the Twelve Troparia of the	*First hour:*
Holy Sufferings	After the psalms, the troparion, and the theotokion, the following stichera
First antiphon: troparia:	idiomela:
1. Today, the curtain of the temple.	1. Today, the curtain of the temple.
2. As a lamb led to the slaughter.	2. As a lamb led to the slaughter.
3. The impious ones having captured you.	3. The impious ones having captured you.
Prokeimenon, tone 8: For I am ready for the wounds. Verse: O Lord, in your anger (Ps 6. 3, 2).	Prokeimenon, tone 4: His heart has accumulated iniquity. Verse: Blessed is he who understands (Ps 40. 7, 2).
OT reading: Zech 11.10–13.	OT reading: Zech 11.10–13.
Epistle: Gal 6.14–18.	Epistle: Gal 6.14–18.
Gospel: Mt 27. 1–56.	Gospel: Mt 27. 1–56.
	Third hour:
[Second antiphon]: troparia:	After the psalms, the troparion, and the theotokion, the following three troparia out of the twelve:
4. Because of the fear of the Jews.	1. Because of the fear of the Jews.

[150]Mansvetov, *Tserkovnyi ustav*, 82, 145. This office is described in the Typikon of Alexios the Studite: Pentkovskii, *Tipikon*, 248–49.

[151]See, for example, *Triod' postnaia* (reprint: Moscow, 1992), 448–460v.

5. Before your true [Cross].

6. Nailed to the Cross.

Prokeimenon, tone 8: His heart has accumulated iniquity. Verse: Blessed is he who understands (Ps 40. 7, 2).

OT reading: Is 8.4–11.

Epistle: Rom 5.6–11.

Gospel: Mk 15.16–41.

[Third antiphon]: troparia:

7. This is what the Lord said to the Jews.

8. Come, O Christ-bearing people.

9. The lawgivers.

Prokeimenon, tone 6: They gave me gall to drink. Verse. Save me, O God (Ps 68. 22, 2).

OT reading: Is 52.13–15; 53.1–12; 54.1.

Epistle: Heb 2.11–18.

Gospel: Lk 23.32–49.

[Fourth antiphon]: troparia:

10. It was terrifying to see.

11. When on the Cross.

12. Today is suspended upon the Cross.

Prokeimenon, tone 6: They placed me in the depth of the pit. Verse. O Lord, God of my salvation (Ps 87. 7, 2).

OT reading: Jer 12.1–15.

Epistle: Heb 10.19–31.

Gospel: Jn 18.28–19.37.

Sixth hour

2. Before your true [Cross].

3. Nailed to the Cross.

Prokeimenon, tone 4: For I am ready for the wounds. Verse: O Lord, in your anger (Ps 6. 3, 2).

OT reading: Is 8.4–11.

Epistle: Rom 5.6–11.

Gospel: Mk 15.16–41.

Sixth hour:

After the psalms, the troparion, and the theotokion, the following three troparia out of the twelve:

1. This is what the Lord said to the Jews.

2. Come, O Christ-bearing people.

3. The lawgivers.

Prokeimenon, tone 4: O Lord, our Lord, your name is admirable in all the earth. Verse. For your magnificence surpasses the heavens (Ps 8.2).

OT reading: Is 52.13–15; 53.1–12; 54.1.

Epistle: Heb 2.11–18.

Gospel: Lk 23.32–49.

Ninth hour:

After the psalms, the troparion, and the theotokion, the following three troparia out of the twelve:

1. It was terrifying to see.

2. When on the Cross.

3. Today is suspended upon the Cross.

Prokeimenon, tone 6: The fool said in his heart, there is no God. Verse. There is no one who does good (Ps 13.1).

OT reading: Jer 12.1–15.

Epistle: Heb 10.19–31.

Gospel: Jn 18.28–19.37.

In the liturgical manuscripts, the troparia are sometimes attributed to St Cyril of Alexandria, and at other times to St Sophronius of Jerusalem, who is possibly also the author of the troparia in the Royal Hours of Christmas and Theophany.[152] This last detail leads us to think that the service of troparia on Holy Friday is of Hagiopolite origin, just like the troparia of Christmas and Theophany, especially since there is a connection between these idiomelon hymns, from which it appears that the hymnography of Holy Friday is certainly more ancient than that for Christmas and Theophany, and it served as a model for the hymnography of these two feasts.[153]

Egeria, who visited Jerusalem during Holy Week in 384, witnesses to the antiquity of this service when she describes that, on Holy Friday,

> When the sixth hour comes, they go before the Cross, [. . .] from the sixth to the ninth hour, they do not stop doing readings and singing hymns, in order to show everyone that what the prophets had predicted about the passion of the Lord has been fulfilled, as it is described in the gospels and in the writings of the apostles.[154]

In examining various ancient manuscripts, it appears that the service of twelve troparia was originally an independent office inserted between the sixth and ninth hours, but which was eventually distributed among the various hours.[155] According to E. Diakovskii, the shifting of the service of the twelve troparia by the Studites from Holy Friday to Holy Tuesday may have been an attempt to preserve the integrity of the office from a process of fragmentation.[156]

It thus appears once more that the spread of the Sabaite Typikon beginning in the fourteenth century led to revisions in the liturgical books and, in the present case, of the Triodion.

After the ninth hour, Psalms 102 and 145 are read, followed by the Beatitudes and the rest of the typika. As at each of the preceding hours, the kontakion of Holy Friday is used.

In the Triodion, we find the following rubric, explaining that

[152]E. Diakovskii, "Posledovanie chasov velikoi piatnitsy," *TDKA* 3 (1909): 389–90.
[153]E. Diakovskii, "Tsarskie chasy Rozhdestva Khristova i Bogoiavleniia," *TDKA* 12 (1908): 500–01. On the use of idiomela as links between the hymnography of different feasts, see my article: J. Getcha, "L'utilisation des automèles en tant que liens entre les différentes fêtes de l'économie du salut dans le rite byzantin," in *L'Hymnographie. Conférences Saint-Serge. 46ᵉ Semaine d'études liturgiques*, BELS 105 (Rome, 2000), 201–13.
[154]Égérie, *Journal de voyage*, 35, 3—36, 5 (SC 296, pp. 286–89).
[155]E. Diakovskii, "Posledovanie chasov velikoi piatnitsy," *TDKA* 3 (1909): 414.
[156]Ibid., 417.

We have received from Palestine [the tradition] not to celebrate the Pre-sanctified Liturgy on this holy day of the crucifixion, nor to celebrate the liturgy, nor to set the table or to eat. If someone is weak and aged, and cannot endure the fast, let him be given bread and water after sunset. We have also received from the holy apostles [the tradition] not to eat on Good Friday, for such is the word of the Lord, who said to the Phari-sees: "For when the bridegroom will be taken away from them, then they will fast in those days" [Lk 5.35]. This is what the divine apostles have received, and having found [this tradition], the apostolic canons have transmitted it [to us]. And the righteous epistle of the holy archbishop Dionysius of Alexandria orders this with [supporting] evidence.[157]

This rubric refers to the instructions found in the fifth book of the *Apostolic Constitutions*, which commanded abstention from all food on Friday and Saturday of Holy Week.[158] We also find the practice described in the *Apostolic Constitutions* in Canon 1 of Dionysius of Alexandria.[159] This reflects a very ancient church practice, which Tertullian referred to as "the fast in the absence of the bridegroom."[160] Since Holy Friday is a strict fast day, it was inconceivable for the Sabaite tradition, which always showed itself to be rig-orous, to break the fast by allowing a eucharistic celebration. This is why this tradition did not have a Presanctified Liturgy. According to S. Janeras, this

---

[157] *Triod' postnaia* (reprint: Moscow, 1992), 460v.

[158] In Book V, ch. 18, of the *Apostolic Constitutions*, we read: "Fast therefore during the days of Pascha, beginning on Monday until Friday and Saturday, which is six days. Take only bread, salt, and vegetables, and water to drink. Abstain from wine and meat on these days, for they are days of mourning and not feasting. Fast totally on Friday and Saturday, those who have the strength, and taste nothing until the nocturnal cockcrow. If someone cannot extend the fast for two days, then let him at least observe the Saturday; for the Lord himself said somewhere, speaking about himself: 'For when the bridegroom will be taken away from them, then they will fast in those days' [Lk 5:35]." *Apostolic Constitutions* V, 18, French translation by M. Metzger, SC 329 (Paris, 1986), 268–71.

[159] Canon 1 in the canonical letter of St Dionysius of Alexandria says: "Indeed, even dur-ing the six fast days that precede [Pascha], not all keep them in the same way or similarly. Some take no food at all for all six days, while others allow only two days to pass, some three, others four, and some none at all. See P.-P. Joannou, *Discipline générale antique* (Fonti, fasc. 9), vol. 2 (Rome, 1963), 4–11.

[160] Tertullian, *On the Fast* 2, 2 (CCL 2), 1258. On this subject, see R. Taft, "In the Bride-groom's Absence. The Paschal Triduum in the Byzantine Church," in *La celebrazione del Triduo pasquale: anamnesis e mimesis. Atti del III Congresso Internazionale di Liturgia, Roma, Pontificio Instituto Liturgico, 9–13 maggio 1988* (Rome, 1990), 71 (= Studia Ansel-miana 102 = Studia Liturgica 14).

represented not only the Palestinian monastic tradition, but also that of the Anastasis in Jerusalem, in which there was no communion on that day.[161]

The Typikon of Alexis the Studite and the Typikon of the Great Church, on the other hand, called for the celebration of the Presanctified Liturgy after vespers.[162] This celebration followed the normal pattern in Constantinople of celebrating the Presanctified Liturgy daily during Great Lent. It is thought that the suppression of the Presanctified Liturgy on this day in Constantinople dates to the twelfth century and was initiated by the Evergetis Monastery.[163] In Russia, however, it was only with the reform of Metropolitan Cyprian that the Presanctified Liturgy on Holy Friday was eliminated. This explains the amazement of the pilgrim Anthony from Novgorod, who visited Constantinople toward 1200 and saw that the Presanctified Liturgy was not celebrated that day.[164] St Symeon of Thessalonica explains that the Presanctified Liturgy was eliminated in Constantinople under the influence of the Palestinian monastic Typikon, and because of the tradition of complete fasting.[165] As a result, following the reform of the fourteenth century, vespers on the evening of Holy Friday has kept the vesperal portion of the Presanctified Liturgy with the readings of the epistle and the gospel indicated in the Typikon of the Great Church, but without the elements proper to the Presanctified Liturgy, such as "The Light of Christ illumines all" and the great prokeimenon consisting of verses from Psalm 140.[166]

[161]S. Janeras, *Le Vendredi saint dans la tradition liturgique byzantine. Structure et histoire de ses offices* (Rome, 1988) (= Analecta Liturgica 13 = Studia Anselmiana 99), 383–86.

[162]Dmitrievskii, *Opisanie*, vol. 1, Τυπικά, pt. 1, 131; Matéos, *Typikon*, II, 82; Pentkovskii, *Tipikon*, 254.

[163]The Typikon of Evergetis implies that the Presanctified Liturgy is celebrated for the last time on Wednesday of Holy Week: Dmitrievskii, *Opisanie*, vol. 1, Τυπικά, pt. 1, 553. See S. Janeras, *Le Vendredi saint dans la tradition liturgique byzantine. Structure et histoire de ses offices* (Rome, 1988) (= Analecta Liturgica 13 = Studia Anselmiana 99), 356–57.

[164]S. De Khitrowo, *Itinéraires russes en Orient*, traduits pour la Société de l'Orient latin, I, 1 (Geneva, 1889), 105; See S. Janeras, *Le Vendredi saint dans la tradition liturgique byzantine. Structure et histoire de ses offices* (Rome, 1988) (= Analecta Liturgica 13 = Studia Anselmiana 99), 374–75; T. Pott, *La Réforme liturgique byzantine: Étude du phénomène de l'évolution non spontanée de la liturgie byzantine*, BEL 104 (Rome, 2000), 156–57.

[165]Symeon of Thessalonica, *On sacred prayer* (PG 155, cols. 905–07. See T. Pott, *La Réforme liturgique*, 157.

[166]On these elements, see S. Janeras, "La partie vespérale de la liturgie byzantine des Présanctifiés," *OCP* 30 (1964): 215–16.

The services of Holy Saturday

VESPERS

The Triodion indicates that vespers is served at the tenth hour of the day. At "Lord, I call," we sing six stichera from the Triodion. After the entrance with the gospel comes the first prokeimenon from the Triodion, and then the first Old-Testament reading (from Exodus). The second prokeimenon from the Triodion follows, and then the second Old-Testament reading (from the Book of Job). Then a third reading from Isaiah is added. Then a prokeimenon for the epistle, after which the epistle and gospel for Holy Friday are read. These readings were assigned to the Presanctified Liturgy by the Typikon of the Great Church, and have been taken up by the Typikon of Alexios the Studite.[167]

In contemporary Greek practice, at the moment when the passage about the descent from the Cross is read, a priest vested in a phelonion and a deacon exit the sanctuary through the holy doors, the priest removes the image of the crucified Lord from the Cross, and the deacon covers it with a winding sheet. They then present it to the abbot (or the bishop) on the throne, who sprinkles is with perfumed water; and then the priest returns to the sanctuary through the holy doors and places the image of the crucified Lord on the altar table. After the ektene, during which sacristans place a table in front of the Cross (if it has not already been done), follow the prayer "Vouchsafe, O Lord," the synapte with demands, and the aposticha from the Triodion are sung.

During the singing of the doxastikon, the priest incenses the *epitaphion* on the altar table. Following the Canticle of St Symeon, the trisagion prayers, and the Lord's Prayer, the troparia of Holy Saturday are sung: "The noble Joseph" and "To the myrrhbearing women." During these troparia, the clergy remove the epitaphion from the altar table, carry it to the center of the church, and place it on the table that has been prepared. We should note, however, that nothing about the epitaphion is mentioned in the Typika and the Triodia, and that the epitaphion appeared only very late, after the fourteenth century.[168]

---

[167]Dmitrievskii, *Opisanie*, vol. 1, Τυπικά, pt. 1, 131; Matéos, *Typikon*, II, 82; Pentkovskii, *Tipikon*, 254.

[168]The epitaphion is an iconographic representation on a cloth, either embroidered or painted, of the placing of Christ in the tomb. On the epitaphion, see: Lisitsyn, *Pervonachal'nyi Slaviano-Russkii Tipikon*, 149–51, note 171; G. Wagner, "Réalisme et symbolisme dans

In contemporary Greek practice, four priests carry the epitaphion at the beginning of the aposticha. The first holds the gospel book, the second carries a relic of the Cross. After they place the epitaphion on the table, the abbot descends from his throne and places flowers around it. Then the deacon incenses the epitaphion from all four sides, as at the artoklasia, and the abbot venerates it, followed by the entire assembly. The singing of "Glory . . . now and ever . . ." is one of the most ornate chants in the Byzantine repertory.

COMPLINE

The Triodion indicates that compline and the midnight office are read by the monks individually, in their cells. The Typikon of Alexios the Studite did not call for the reading of compline individually. In contemporary Russian practice, however, it is customary to read compline, consisting of the canon by Symeon Logothetes on the weeping of the Mother of God, in church, in front of the epitaphion. This is no longer done in Greek practice.

MATINS

According to the Triodion, matins of Holy Saturday is celebrated at the seventh hour of the night. After the great synapte, we sing "God is the Lord" and the troparia of Holy Saturday: "The noble Joseph . . ."; "Glory . . .": "When you descended . . ."; "Now and ever . . .": "To the myrrhbearing women . . . ." During the troparia, the clergy leave the sanctuary and go in front of the epitaphion, the priests vested in phelonia. The priest incenses the entire church, preceded by a deacon with a candle. Everyone in the assembly holds a candle, as at a funeral service. Then the choir sings Psalm 118 (kathisma 17). After each verse of the psalm, a troparion of praise is inserted. Regrettably, for practical reasons, in modern Greek practice, the psalm is read first, and then the troparia (*egkomia*) are sung afterward, without the psalm verses. Kathisma 7 is divided into three sections. After each section, the deacon says the small synapte. At the beginning of each section, the priest incenses the epitaphion. The third part concludes with the singing of the Resurrection evlogitaria ("Blessed are you, O Lord . . ."; "The angelic choir . . ."). After the small synapte, the kathisma troparia from the Triodion are sung. "Having beheld the resurrection of Christ" is not sung. Psalm 50 is

l'explication de la liturgie," in *La Liturgie, expérience de l'Église. Études liturgiques,* AS 1 (Paris, 2003), 187.

read, and the canon of Holy Saturday follows. Odes one to five are by Mark the Monk; odes six to nine are the ancient four-ode canon by Cosmas of Maioum. After the third ode and the small synapte, the kathisma troparion from the Triodion is sung. After the sixth ode and the small synapte, we sing the kontakion and its ikos, and then read from the Synaxarion of Nicephoras Kallistos Xanthopoulos. The Magnificat is not sung at the ninth ode. Following the ninth ode and the small synapte, we sing the fixed Sunday exaposteilarion in tone 2 three times ("Holy is the Lord, our God"). The lauds ("Let every breath") are sung with four stichera from the Triodion, followed by the great doxology in its Constantinopolitan redaction. During the great doxology, the priest incenses three times around the epitaphion. During the final trisagion, the epitaphion is carried in procession around the church. In contemporary Greek practice, the procession stops four times and petitions are made, and then, as the people return into the church, they pass under the epitaphion, which is held up by the priests at the door of the church, while a sacristan sprinkles them with perfumed water. Once all have entered the church, the epitaphion is carried up to the holy doors, and, following the ekphonesis by the priest: "Wisdom! Stand aright!" ("Let us attend. Peace be unto all. Wisdom" in Greek practice) the epitaphion is, in Russian practice, placed back on the table in the center of the church, and the priest incenses it again while the choir sings the troparion: "The noble Joseph." In Greek practice, the epitaphion is placed on the altar table, where it will remain until the leavetaking of Pascha.

Three readings follow: the prophecy of Ezekiel (preceded by a troparion of the prophecy and a prokeimenon), an epistle (preceded by the epistle prokeimenon), and a gospel (preceded by Alleluia and its verses: "Let God arise . . ."). It is interesting to read the relevant rubric in the Typikon of Alexios the Studite, underlining that:

> *As in the Great Church*, "Glory to God in the highest" is sung after these [stichera] *in asmatic fashion*. When they sing "Glory," the priest does the *entrance* with the deacon holding the gospel, preceded by a candle. Then he ascends to the *synthronon*. After the peace is given, the prokeimenon is said immediately [. . .] "Glory to God in the highest" is sung in *asmatic* fashion, in a way that we are never accustomed to doing it, except, in truth, on this day. The prokeimenon of the day is sung in tone 6. Then the *entrance* of the priest occurs, and another office is indicated because of this exceptional day. After [the prokeimenon], the Epistle to the Cor-

inthians: "Brethren, a little leaven." Alleluia, tone 4: Let God arise. Then the Gospel of Matthew: "On the morning which is after the Friday." It is read by the priest at the altar table. After the gospel comes the ektene by the deacon and the dismissal as usual.[169]

This rubric thus appeals to the Typikon of the Great Church, which indicated the following:

> After orthros, at the trisagion of "Glory to God in the highest," the entrance of the patriarch and the priests takes place with the gospel. The psalmists ascend the ambo and say the troparion [. . .] After this, he [the patriarch] goes to the synthronon and sits on the throne on top. Then the prokeimenon [. . .] a reading [. . .] second prokeimenon [. . .] epistle [. . .] Alleluia [. . .] gospel.[170]

Taking account of such expressions as "entrance," "asmatic," and "synthronon," we can conclude that our contemporary Triodion contains a vestige of the ancient Constantinopolitan tradition, in which matins concluded with scriptural readings.[171] However, the solemn entrance with the gospel book in the Great Church of Constantinople was transformed, after the fourteenth century, into a solemn procession with the epitaphion around the church.[172]

Matins concludes with the ektene and the synapte with demands. After the dismissal, the first hour is read.

THE HOURS AND THE TYPIKA

The other hours are read before the Divine Liturgy. The troparia and kontakion of Holy Saturday are read. The Beatitudes at the typika are read (not sung), preceded by Psalms 102 and 145. The kontakion of Holy Saturday is read, and then the lesser dismissal.

VESPERS AND THE LITURGY OF ST BASIL

The Triodion indicates that vespers with the Liturgy of St Basil should begin at the tenth hour. This liturgy was initially a part of the ancient paschal vigil,

---

[169]Pentkovskii, *Tipikon*, 255.

[170]Matéos, *Typikon*, II, 83. Compare with Dmitrievskii, *Opisanie*, vol. 1, Τυπικά, pt. 1, 132.

[171]See Lisitsyn, *Pervonachal'nyi Slaviano-Russkii Tipikon*, 32, 43.

[172]According to Lisitsyn, this change occurred during the 16th–17th centuries. Lisitsyn, *Pervonachal'nyi Slaviano-Russkii Tipikon*, 149–51, note 171.

which explains why it has such a strong resurrectional character. This is also the reason why all the vestments are changed to white during the service, if not before.

At "Lord, I call," we sing eight stichera from the Triodion. The first four come from the Octoechos, tone 1 (three resurrectional stichera from "Lord, I call," and the first sticheron from the aposticha). The next three are for Holy Saturday ("Today, hell cries out groaning . . ."). It is interesting to note that the Typikon of Alexios the Studite called for the singing of only these three, attributed to St Theodore the Studite, twice each, with their doxastikon.[173] The contemporary redaction of the Triodion adds the dogmatikon theotokion from the Octoechos, tone 1.

After the little entrance with the gospel, there is no prokeimenon, and we immediately begin a long series of 15 Old-Testament readings. Commonly today in Greece, most of these readings are done before or during the hours, leaving only three at vespers. These readings come from the Typikon of the Great Church, in which they were used to occupy the assembly while the patriarch performed baptisms in the baptistery. Indeed, in the Typikon of the Great Church we read the following notice after the seventh reading: "If the patriarch must still baptize for a long time, eighth reading . . ." (and the rest of the readings).[174] In our day, baptisms are no longer performed during these readings, yet they are still all read. The sixth reading concludes with the singing of the Canticle of Moses ("Let us sing to the Lord, for he has been glorified"). The fifteenth reading is concluded with the singing of the Song of the Three Youths ("Sing to the Lord and glorify him through all the ages") with a refrain, as was the custom in Constantinople.

The deacon then says the small synapte. Instead of the trisagion, we sing the baptismal hymn: "As many as have been baptized into Christ." This amply demonstrates that this was originally a baptismal liturgy. The epistle is from Romans (the same reading as at the baptismal service). Instead of the "Alleluia," we sing "Arise, O God, and judge the earth . . ." At this moment, in Russian practice, all the vestments, altar covers, and other decorations are changed from dark to white. In Greek practice, the bells are rung during this chant and the priest goes through the church throwing laurel leaves. Then comes the reading of the resurrectional gospel from Matthew. The Liturgy of St Basil follows. Instead of the Cherubic Hymn, we sing the hymn "Let all

[173]Pentkovskii, Tipikon, 255.
[174]Matéos, Typikon, II, 86–87.

mortal flesh keep silent." Instead of the hymn to the Mother of God, we sing the hirmos of the ninth ode of the canon. The koinonikon for Holy Saturday, which is not a biblical text, comes from the Triodion: "The Lord awoke as one asleep and arose, saving us." In Greek practice, instead of singing after communion the hymn "We have seen the true light," we sing "Remember us, O compassionate one, as you remembered the thief, in your heavenly Kingdom."

We note that the ordo of this vesperal liturgy on Holy Saturday, which in the Sabaite tradition is the paschal vigil, corresponds to the descriptions found both in the Typikon of the Great Church and the Typikon of Alexios the Studite.[175] The Studite Typikon of Alexios, however, called for breaking the fast after this vesperal liturgy by eating fish, cheese, and eggs in the refectory.[176] This custom is typically Studite, as it is also found in the *Hypotyposis* ascribed to St Theodore the Studite.[177] The contemporary Triodion, however, reflects the more rigorous Sabaite tradition. We read the following rubric:

> After the dismissal, the priest distributes the antidoron. The blessing of bread and wine follows the dismissal. The ecclesiarch should watch that the dismissal of the liturgy should take place at the second hour of the night. After the dismissal of the liturgy, we do not leave the church, but all should stay seated in their place. The cellarer comes and gives each brother a piece of bread and six figs or dates and a glass of wine. While we are seated, the great reading of the Book of Acts takes place.[178]

According to T. Pott,

> The different ways in which the time between the paschal vigil (vespers and liturgy) and matins has been filled themselves witness to the evolution that these rites underwent in the Byzantine rite. Two factors played an important role: the extraordinary evolution that turned the matins of Pascha into the real climax of the feast, to the detriment of the ancient

---

[175]Dmitrievskii, *Opisanie*, vol. 1, Τυπικά, pt. 1, 132–35; Matéos, *Typikon*, II, 84–90; Pentkovskii, *Tipikon*, 255.

[176]Pentkovskii, *Tipikon*, 377.

[177]There we read: "On Holy Saturday, at the 11th hour, the lucernarium begins; and after the dismissal, we eat cheese, fish, and eggs, and drink three [glasses]" ("τῷ δὲ ἁγίῳ Σαββάτῳ ὥρᾳ ἑνδεκάτῃ ἄρχεται τὸ λυχνικὸν καὶ ὅπου σώσει ἡ ἀπόλυσις, ἐσθίομεν δὲ τυρὸν καὶ ἰχθῦς καὶ ὠὰ καὶ πίνομεν ἀνὰ γ᾽") PG 99, cols. 1716.

[178]*Triod' postnaia* (reprint: Moscow, 1992), 502v.

and venerable vigil liturgy, and, no doubt linked to this, the lack of clarity as to the precise moment when Lent concludes. Furthermore, we are dealing here with the real symptom of the monasticization of the Byzantine liturgy.[179]

However, in spite of the principle of the "monasticization" of the Byzantine rite suggested by this last author, we should not forget that the time at which the Holy Week fast ends has been an object of discussion throughout history. In his canonical letter to Bishop Basilides, St Dionysius of Alexandria (3rd century) treated this question at length.[180] According to him, the Christians of Rome waited for cockcrow to break the fast, while those in Alexandria did so from the evening of the previous day. Dionysius reviews the resurrection accounts in the gospels: "on the night of Saturday" in Matthew, "in the early dawn while it was still dark" in John, "at the first break of day" in Luke, and "in the early morning, at the rising of the sun" in Mark. Dionysius writes: "At what moment he was resurrected, none of them tells us clearly, but only that, late on Saturday night, at dawn of the first day of the week, those who came to the tomb did not find him there."[181] Unable therefore to establish the precise time at which to break the fast, Dionysius concludes:

> This being the case, we answer those who seek to determine the time, to within an hour, or a half hour, or a quarter hour, when it is fitting to begin celebrating the resurrection from the dead of our Lord. Those who are in too much of a hurry, and who relax [the fast] even before the night has approached its midpoint, these we censure as faint-hearted and intemperate, for they end their race just a little before the goal, whereas a wise man has said: "it is not a small thing in life to miss the goal by little." As for those who delay and wait for the longest possible time, persevering until the fourth watch, when the Lord, walking on the sea, appeared to those who were traveling by boat, we commend them as courageous and devotees of penitence. Those who, between these two extremes, ended the fast according to their internal disposition and their ability, let us not trouble beyond measure; for indeed, not even the six days of fasting

[179]T. Pott, "L'évolution de l'intermezzo entre les vigils et l'orthros de Pâques," in *La Réforme liturgique byzantine*, 162.

[180]Canon 1 of St Dionysius of Alexandria. See P.-P. Joannou, *Discipline générale antique* (Fonti, fasc. 9), vol. 2 (Rome, 1963), 4–11.

[181]Ibid., 6.

that come before are kept equally or similarly—some let all six days go
by without taking any food, while others allow only two days, others
three, others four, others none. For those who have struggled greatly
in spending the days without food, and who are exhausted and almost
faint, we excuse them for taking food a little earlier; while those who not
only did not pass these days without food, but who did not fast at all or
even feasted during the first four days, and abstained from food only on
the last two days, that is, on Friday and Saturday, and think that they are
doing something great and splendid if they keep the fast until dawn on
Sunday, I think that such people did not struggle as hard as those who
exercised themselves for many days.[182]

Later, the Council in Trullo established that:

After having spent the days of the saving passion in fasting, prayer, and
compunction of heart, the faithful should break the fast only at midnight on Holy Saturday, because the evangelists Mathew and Luke, one
through the words "late in the night that follows Saturday" [Mt 28.1], the
other through the expression "at early dawn" [Lk 24.1], specify the late
hour of the night.[183]

MIDNIGHT OFFICE

The Sabaite tradition preserved in the current redaction of the Triodion has
thus shown itself to be more rigorous in observing the canons by breaking
the fast only after the Divine Liturgy celebrated very early Sunday morning, during the night from Saturday to Sunday. On Saturday evening, after
the eucharistic liturgy that concludes the paschal vigil, all are expected to
remain in church, listening to the reading of the Book of Acts. After this,
the parecclesiarch lights all the lamps and goes out to strike the large simandron, after which the midnight office begins, following a particular order.
After the trisagion, Psalm 50 is read, and the canon of Holy Saturday is
sung once more. At the end of the ninth ode, the hirmos of the ninth ode is
repeated as the katabasia. It is during the katabasia that, in Russian practice,
the priest returns the epitaphion to the sanctuary and places it on the altar
table, where it will remain until the leavetaking of Easter. After the ninth
ode, the trisagion is read, and after the Lord's Prayer, the troparion of the

[182]See ibid., 9–11.
[183]Canon 89 of Trullo. See P.-P. Joannou, *Discipline générale antique* (Fonti, fasc. 9), vol.
1, 1 (Rome, 1962), 225.

resurrection in tone 2 is sung: "When you descended." The ektene and dismissal follow. This office is absent from the Typikon of Alexios the Studite for the obvious reasons we mentioned above. In contemporary Greek practice, for practical reasons, the canon is sung first with, after the third ode, the reading of the magnificent sermon about Holy Saturday attributed to St Epiphanius ("Give me this stranger . . ."), which inspired the hymnography, and the reading of the synaxarion of the day after the sixth ode. Then, after the ninth ode, the reading of the Book of Acts begins, which is interrupted at the exact moment of the resurrection (the sixth hour of the night), with all the lights extinguished until the appearance of the holy light.

CHAPTER FIVE

The Services of the Pentecostarion

The Week of Pascha

The services of Pascha

PASCHAL MATINS

Following the midnight office, it is customary nowadays to leave the church for the paschal procession. In Greek practice, the priest leaves the sanctuary and distributes the paschal fire while singing: "Come and receive light from the unfading light, and glorify Christ who rose from the dead." This chant, found in the contemporary *Typikon of the Great Church*, reflects a practice that became common in the nineteenth century, and which is rooted in the tradition of Jerusalem, no doubt in connection with the miraculous paschal fire attested since the twelfth century. For several years on Mt Athos and in Greece, the holy light, which is sent by plane from Jerusalem (via Athens and Thessalonica), is received from the hands of the harbor police, since the office of the holy light was already celebrated in the afternoon at the Basilica of the Resurrection in Jerusalem. This practice is beginning to spread to other Orthodox countries, such as Ukraine. The procession around the church is accompanied by the singing of the troparion, "Your resurrection, O Christ our Savior," which is found at the aposticha for Sunday in tone 6 in the Octoechos. After the procession, either once or three times around the church, we stop in front of the doors of the church, which are closed. The modern *Typikon of the Great Church* calls for the reading of the pericope from Mark 16, a custom that appeared in the nineteenth century.

The ancient Typika say nothing about a procession. They simply indicate that all go out into the narthex. Only a sacristan remains in the church to light all the candles and lamps. He prepares two candles which he places, lit, in the center of the church. He also lights the other candles in front of the holy doors and prepares the censer in the sanctuary. Filling it with a large amount of incense, he incenses the entire church. All the doors of the church remain closed. The priest puts on all his white vestments and goes to the narthex through the north door, incensing and holding the three-branched paschal candle, preceded by the two candles. The abbot or the ecclesiarch distributes candles to all the brothers, which they then light. After the priest has incensed the entire assembly, he stands before the royal doors (which lead from the narthex into the nave) and, tracing the sign of the Cross with the censer, says the initial blessing of paschal matins. He then sings the paschal troparion. We find the same description of this office in the Typikon of Alexios the Studite, which reminds us of the beginning of the sung office in the narthex,[1] except that the latter says that the brothers, who had been sleeping, were then awakened at the third watch of the night.[2]

After the opening blessing of matins ("Gory to the holy, consubstantial . . ."), the priests sings the paschal troparion three times, as does the choir, followed by four psalm verses, each followed by the paschal troparion.[3] The first three verses (Ps 67.2–4) already appear in the ancient Sabaite Typikon, *Sinai gr. 1096*.[4] The Typikon of Alexios the Studite has only two verses,[5] while the contemporary Byzantine rite adds a fourth (Ps 117.24), resulting here in a compromise between two traditions.[6] Then the priest again sings the first half of the troparion. The doors are then opened, and the priest enters the church, preceded by the candles and followed by the abbot and the brothers who sing the end of the troparion. The priest goes into the sanctuary and recites the great synapte. It is customary to leave all the sanctuary doors open throughout the week of Pascha. After the ekphonesis, the superior intones the paschal canon attributed to St John of Damascus.[7] The two choirs alternately sing the troparia of the canon. At each ode, small synaptes are said from inside the sanctuary, with special ekphoneses (see the Pentecostarion). The Typika indicate that the priest incenses at the beginning of the canon. It is, however the custom on this day to incense the entire church

[1]Lisitsyn, *Pervonachal'nyi Slaviano-Russkii Tipikon*, 81, note 87.

[2]Pentkovskii, *Tipikon*, 256.

[3]For example, *Typikon* (Moscow, 1906), 459–459v.

[4]Dmitrievskii, *Opisanie*, vol. 3, Τυπικά, pt. 2, 64. In *Sinai gr. 1094*, we also find three verses, but not the same ones. See f. 46v. (edited by: Lossky, *Le Typikon byzantin*, 206). See also G. Bertonière, *The Historical Development of the Easter Vigil and Related Services in the Greek Church*, OCA 193 (Rome, 1972), 272–73.

[5]Pentkovskii, *Tipikon*, 256.

[6]For example *Typikon* (Moscow, 1906), 459–459v.

[7]On the paschal canon, see A. Lossky, "Le canon des matines pascales byzantines: ses sources bibliques et patristiques," in *L'Hymnographie. Conférences Saint-Serge. 46ᵉ Semaine d'études liturgiques*, BELS 105 (Rome, 2000), 257–84.

at each ode. After the third ode and the hypakoe, there is an indication to read a sermon of St Gregory the Theologian, entitled "I want to remain at my post."[8] Following the sixth ode and the kontakion, it is prescribed to read the first sermon of St Gregory the Theologian, entitled "The Day of the Resurrection: a promising beginning."[9] The printed Pentecostaria include, at this point, the Synaxarion of Nicephoras Kallistos Xanthopoulos. After these readings, we sing three times the sticheron "Having beheld the Resurrection of Christ," followed by "Jesus has risen from the tomb," also three times. After the ninth ode and the exaposteilarion, the choir sings the psalm verses, "Let every breath," intercalating four resurrectional stichera in tone 1 from the Octoechos, followed by the paschal stichera. The Typikon of Alexios the Studite called for a different matins ending. At the lauds, four stichera idiomela were sung, after which the doxology was sung "in a low voice" in its Hagiopolite redaction. Then, instead of the aposticha, the paschal stichera were sung.[10]

At the end of the paschal stichera, the assembly exchanges the paschal kiss. The priest, holding the gospel, stands in front of the holy doors. The superior comes to venerate the holy gospel, then kisses the priest, takes the gospel from him, and goes to stand on his right. The brothers then go up in order to exchange the paschal kiss. In contemporary Greek practice, the priests go out and stand in the choir on the right side during the paschal stichera, and everyone comes to kiss the gospel book which the abbot holds, standing at his throne. After the paschal kiss has been exchanged, the superior reads the paschal homily attributed to St John Chrysostom.[11] During this reading, out of respect for this illustrious Father of the Church, it is specified that all remain standing. When the reading is complete, the priest says the two litanies and gives the paschal dismissal, holding the Cross and the three-branched paschal candlestick. We find the same description in the Typikon of Alexios the Studite, except that matins concludes with only one litany, the one that normally follows the aposticha.[12]

---

[8]Gregory the Theologiam, *Sermon 45* (E. Devolder, *Saint Grégoire de Nazianze* [Namur, 1961], 118–62).

[9]Gregory the Theologian, *Sermon 1* (SC 247 [Paris 1978], 72–83).

[10]Pentkovskii, *Tipikon*, 256.

[11]Catechetical homily attributed to St John Chrysostom, PG 59, cols. 721–724.

[12]Pentkovskii, *Tipikon*, 257.

THE PASCHAL HOURS

The hours on the day of Pascha follow a particular order. The customary hours in the Horologion are replaced by a particular office in the Pentecostarion, entirely sung, each (the hours and compline) repeated three times throughout Bright Week, according to the most ancient Typika (from Easter Sunday until the next Saturday). The paschal troparion is first sung three times, and then "Having beheld the resurrection," also three times. The hypakoe is sung, and then the kontakion and the troparia: "In the tomb according to the flesh," "As the bearer of life," and "Sanctified by the Most-High." Then *Kyrie eleison* (40 times), "More honorable . . . ," and the dismissal, after which the paschal troparion is again sung three times.

The *Typikon* of Alexios Studite had a different ordo for the hours. It called for the singing of the paschal troparion three times, then the resurrectional troparion in tone 3, the paschal kontakion, and the theotokion of the hour. Then the trisagion and the other prayers through the Lord's Prayer, and *Kyrie eleison* twelve times.[13]

THE DIVINE LITURGY

The Typika then prescribe the celebration of the Divine Liturgy of St John Chrysostom. After the initial blessing, the priest, holding the Cross and the three-branched paschal candlestick, incenses the church while singing the paschal troparion three times, which is then sung three times by the choir, and then intones the four psalm verses, each followed by the paschal troparion (sung by the choir). Instead of the usual antiphons, festal antiphons are sung. At the entrance, following the festal entrance verse, the troparion "Christ is risen") is sung, and then the hypakoe and the kontakion. Instead of the trisagion, we sing "As many as have been baptized into Christ." The epistle and gospel are for the feast. Among the Russians, it is customary to read the gospel in several languages, beginning with the ancient tongues. This practice traces its origin to Constantinople where, on the day of Easter, the Prologue of John was read by the patriarch, and then repeated, verse by verse, by the deacon standing on the ambo.[14] Among the Greeks, this practice is observed at vespers of Pascha. Instead of the hymn to the Mother of God, we sing the refrain and hirmos of the ninth ode. At communion, instead of "Blessed is he who comes . . . ," "Let our mouths be filled . . . ,"

[13]Ibid.
[14]Matéos, *Typicon*, II, 94–96.

and "We have seen the true light," we sing the paschal troparion, "Christ is risen." The liturgy concludes with the singing of the paschal troparion and the dismissal of Easter, which the priest says while holding the Cross and the three-branched paschal candlestick. After the dismissal, the priest blesses the *artos*, the paschal bread symbolizing the risen Christ, which will be distributed on the following Saturday. Following the Divine Liturgy, a "great consolation" in the refectory is foreseen for the monks.

VESPERS OF PASCHA

The service of vespers begins much like matins. On Sunday evening, the priest puts on all his vestments. After the opening benediction of vespers ("Blessed is our God . . ."), the paschal troparion is sung three times by the priest and three times by the choir, then the four psalm verses are sung, with the paschal troparion after each. During the verses, the priest, holding the cross and the three-branched candlestick, incenses the entire church. The deacon then says the great synapte. At "Lord, I call," we sing six stichera in tone 2 from the Octoechos, followed by the doxastikon and theotokion. The entrance is done with the gospel. After "O gladsome Light," the great prokeimenon is sung ("Who is so great a God"). Then Jn 20.19–25, is read. In Greek practice, it is customary to read this gospel in several languages. The ektene follows, then we sing the prayer "Vouchsafe, O Lord," followed by the synapte with demands. We sing the first aposticha sticheron from the Octoechos in tone 2, and then the paschal stichera. The service concludes with the dismissal by the priest, who holds the Cross and the three-branched paschal candlestick.

Particularities of the services during the week of Pascha

During the entire week following Pascha (Bright Week or Renewal Week), the services are celebrated just as on Easter, as if this entire week were one and the same day. This is a vestige of the ancient Easter octave, attested to in Jerusalem at the end of the fourth century by Egeria, during which the neophytes baptized on Easter gathered to hear the mystagogical catecheses. These services, do, however, have some particularities. First, except on Easter day, the priest does not wear all his vestments. There is no procession at the beginning of matins. At the beginning of vespers, matins, and the Divine Liturgy, the priest, holding the Cross and the three-branched candlestick, incenses the church while singing the paschal troparion three times. The troparion is then sung three times by the choir, after which the priest chants the four psalm verses, with the choir singing the paschal troparion after each. A procession does occur daily, however, after the eucharistic liturgy, which is celebrated each day. In Greek practice, there is a procession on Monday or Tuesday of Easter week, and the blessing of water takes place to signify the participation of the created world in the mystery of the Resurrection. In ancient times in Constantinople, as we see in the Typikon of the Great Church, a procession took place only on Easter Monday at the tenth hour, as on Palm Sunday. The gospel is read only at vespers on Sunday evening.

Each day, at "Lord, I call" and the aposticha at vespers and at the lauds in matins, different stichera from the Octoechos are sung. This week is considered as the week with seven Sundays, with each day dedicated to one tone from the Octoechos: tone 1 on Sunday; tone 2 on Monday; tone 3 on Tuesday; tone 4 on Wednesday; tone 5 on Thursday; tone 6 on Friday; tone 8 on Saturday. On each evening during the week, a different great prokeimenon is sung.

At matins, beginning on Monday morning, theotokia by Theophanes and Joseph are added to the paschal canon of St John of Damascus at "Glory" and "now and ever." In Greek practice, these theotokia are sung only on the following Sundays, at the paschal canon. Small synaptes are said only after the third, sixth, and ninth odes. An incensation, therefore, is done at the beginning of each of the three sections of the canon (at the first, fourth, and seventh odes), as well as at the ninth ode. In Greek practice, the small synapte is said at each ode, as on Easter Sunday, but the incensation occurs only at the first and ninth odes.

The services of vespers, matins, and the Divine Liturgy all conclude with the paschal dismissal, which the priest pronounces holding the Cross and the three-branched paschal candlestick.

On Friday of Bright Week, we commemorate the life-giving spring in Constantinople. The Pentecostarion contains a special service for this, attributed to Nicephoras Kallistos Xanthopoulos. This office can be combined with the paschal office. Because of this solemnity, it is customary to bless water on this day. In Greek practice, the blessing of water occurs on Monday or Tuesday.

Saturday brings the paschal week to a close. In the Studite tradition, the leavetaking of Pascha took place on Saturday of Bright Week, and not on

Wednesday of the sixth week, as is done today. After the Divine Liturgy, the artos is distributed. After the ninth hour, the doors of the sanctuary are closed. In Greek practice, however, often the doors are closed only when, at vespers, the sticheron beginning with "All the doors being closed" is sung.

The Second Week after Pascha

Thomas Sunday (Antipascha)

ORIGIN

The second Sunday of Pascha, i.e., the Sunday following Easter, is dedicated to the encounter of Thomas with the risen Lord. It is also called "Antipascha" (Ἀντιπάσχα) or "Renewal Sunday." It concludes the paschal octave, whose particular celebration in Jerusalem in the late fourth century is attested to by Egeria in her journal and by the Armenian Lectionary in the fifth century. In chapter 39 of her journal, Egeria tells us that "these feasts of Pascha are celebrated over eight days."[15] She specifies that, on the day of the octave,

> The lucernare [vespers] is celebrated both at the Anastasis and at the Cross, and then all the people, without exception, with hymns escort the bishop to Sion. When they arrive there, they again sing hymns appropriate to the place and the day, and the gospel passage is read again describing how, eight days after Pascha, the Lord entered where the disciples were and reproached Thomas for having been doubtful.[16]

The Armenian Lectionary provides more information about the ordo of the offices. On Sunday, the day of the octave, it prescribes that the Prologue of John (Jn 1.1–17) be read at the liturgy, a passage that in the Byzantine rite today is read on Pascha, in accordance with the Constantinopolitan tradition, attested already in the Typikon of the Great Church. The passage from John (Jn 20.26–31), in which the Lord appears to the apostles on the eighth day and proves to Thomas that he is indeed raised from the dead, was read in Jerusalem on Sunday evening at vespers, which was celebrated on Sion. This pericope, in the Constantinopolitan rite, was read at the liturgy which was to give the name of "Thomas Sunday" to the second Sunday of Pascha.

[15]Égérie, *Journal de voyage* 39, 1 (SC 296, p. 293).
[16]Égérie, *Journal de voyage* 40, 2 (SC 296, p. 295).

Since the fifty-day period following Easter has been a period of rejoicing from early Christian times, the hymnography about the resurrection
of Christ, normally reserved for the Sunday office, is gradually extended
to the other days of the week. This fifty-day paschal period is, just as Great
Lent, marked by several solemnities that we find in the Pentecostarion.
The themes of the different Sundays are taken from the gospels read at the
eucharistic liturgy. Consequently, they follow the Lectionary of the Great
Church.[17] This lectionary prescribed for the paschal period a continuous
reading of the Book of Acts and the Gospel of John, concluding on the
Feast of Pentecost. It must be said that Acts and John were also being read
in Jerusalem during the same period. However, the choice of pericopes in
Constantinople differed from that in Jerusalem.[18] We therefore conclude
that the current redaction of our Pentecostarion is Constantinopolitan, as
it follows the themes of the Sunday gospel readings as prescribed in the
Typikon of the Great Church. We can surmise that this is the work of the
Studites.

The continuous reading of John began in Constantinople with the reading of the Prologue on Easter day (Jn 1.1–17), a passage read on the Sunday
following Easter in Jerusalem. We can note three exceptions to the rule
concerning the gospel readings: on Easter Tuesday, we read the pericope
from Lk 24.12–35, about the disciples in Emmaus, which was the passage
appointed for this day by the Armenian Lectionary,[19] which witnesses to the
liturgy of Jerusalem in the first half of the fifth century; the pericope from
Mk 15.43–16.8 read on the third Sunday of Easter, describing the burial
and the empty tomb, a reading chosen because of the commemoration that
day of the myrrhbearing women, Joseph of Arimathea, and Nicodemus;
and finally, the pericope from Lk 24.36–53, read on Ascension Thursday, a
reading chosen because of this feast.

In the Studite tradition, Thomas Sunday was considered as a major feast
with a one-day after-feast.[20] The contemporary Byzantine rite, influenced
by the Sabaite tradition, does not have a special ordo for Monday of the

[17]See Dmitrievskii, *Opisanie*, vol. 1, Τυπικά, pt. 1, 135–48; Matéos, *Typicon*, II, 92–138.
On this cycle of readings, see J. Getcha, "Le système de lectures bibliques du rite byzantin,"
41–43.
[18]See the comparative table in S. Janeras, "Les lectionnaires de l'ancienne liturgie de
Jérusalem," *CCO* 2 (2005): 84–85.
[19]Renoux, II, 316–17.
[20]See, for example, Pentkovskii, *Tipikon*, 262.

second week. We should note, however, that the entire week following this Sunday has the structure of an after-feast. This will also be the case for the following Sundays.

ORDO

Beginning on Thomas Sunday, the liturgical offices more or less resume their normal ordo. Beginning on this day, the reading of kathismata from the Psalter, which was interrupted on Holy Wednesday, resumes. On each Sunday during the fifty-day period, only the Pentecostarion is used. The office for the saint in the Menaion is shifted to compline (or to another day), except in the case of an office with the polyeleos. Until the leavetaking of Easter, every service begins with the singing of the paschal troparion, "Christ is risen." This troparion is sung three times at the beginning major services (vespers, matins, and the liturgy) and recited three times at the beginning of the other offices.

The office of Thomas Sunday follows the ordo of a major feast. Before the ninth hour, the doors of the iconostasis, which remain open all through the week of Pascha, are closed. On Athos, they are closed during the first sticheron at "Lord, I call." At "Lord, I call" in vespers, ten stichera from the Pentecostarion, ascribed to John the Monk (Damascene), are sung, followed by their doxastikon. The Pentecostarion also contains stichera for the *lite* and the aposticha. During the artoklasia, the troparion of the feast is sung three times: "The tomb being sealed." Between vespers and matins (if vigil is celebrated), it is appointed during the paschal period to read from the beginning the commentaries of St John Chrysostom on the Acts of the Apostles.

Matins begins with the singing of the troparion, "Christ is risen," three times, followed by the hexapsalmos. At "God is the Lord," the troparion of the feast ("The tomb being sealed") is sung three times. After each kathisma from the Psalter, the kathisma troparia from the Pentecostarion are sung. We sing the polyeleos, and the selected psalm verses with the megalynarion of the feast. This exception stems from the fact that the Sunday office is combined with that for a major feast. After the small synapte, the kathisma troparion for the feast is sung, and then the first antiphon of the anabathmoi in tone 4 ("From my youth"), followed by the prokeimenon of the feast (from the Pentecostarion) and the reading of the first matins gospel (of the Resurrection). The sticheron "Having beheld the resurrection" is sung three times. After Psalm 50, the customary Sunday stichera are sung: "Glory . . . ," "Through the prayers of the apostles"; "Now and ever . . . ," "Through the prayers of the Theotokos"; "Have mercy on me"; "Christ having risen from the dead." After the prayer "O Lord, save your people," the canon of the feast (from the Pentecostarion), attributed to John the Monk (Damscene) is sung with fourteen troparia, each ode concluding with the hirmos of the paschal canon as the katabasia. After the third ode, the hypakoe from the Pentecostarion is read. After the sixth ode, the kontakion and ikos from the Pentecostarion are sung, immediately followed by the reading from the Synaxarion of Nicephoras Kallistos Xanthopoulos. At the ninth ode, the Magnificat is omitted. Following the ninth ode, after "Holy is the Lord, our God" in tone 1, we add an exaposteilarion from the Pentecostarion. At the lauds, four stichera from the Pentecostarion are sung with their doxastikon, followed by the great doxology (in its Constantinopolitan redaction) and the troparion of the feast. Between the dismissal and the first hour, we sing the first gospel sticheron, followed, according to the Typikon, by a *lite* for the dead and the reading in the narthex of a catechetical lecture of St Theodore the Studite.

At the Divine Liturgy of St John Chrysostom, after the opening blessing, the paschal troparion is sung three times. At the entrance, only the troparion and kontakion of the feast are sung. The prokeimenon, epistle, Alleluia verses, gospel, and koinonikon are all festal. Instead of the hymn to the Mother of God, we sing the refrain and hirmos of the ninth ode of the paschal canon: "The angel cried," "Shine, shine." The troparion "We have seen the true light" is replaced by "Christ is risen." Before the dismissal and after "Glory to you, O Christ our God," we sing the troparion "Christ is risen" three times.

In the Russian tradition, Tuesday of the second week after Easter is called *Radonitsa* (day of rejoicing). It is customary on this day to go to the cemetery, there to commemorate the dead in order to share the paschal joy with them. However, the ordo of the office is not altered. In the church, only a panikhida is celebrated, either after vespers or following the eucharistic liturgy. This custom is based on the fact that, according to the Typikon, the celebration of memorial services for the dead may resume after the matins service of Thomas Sunday.

Weekday services during the paschal period

During the fifty days after Pascha, the themes of the Sundays (which are labeled "feasts") are carried through the following week, until Saturday, thus constituting the "after-feast." The Pentecostarion and Menaion are employed.

All the daily services begin with the singing or reading of the troparion, "Christ is risen," three times. The prayer to the Holy Spirit, "O heavenly King," is not read until Pentecost. At the end of the office each day, the priest uses the Sunday dismissal ("May he who rose from the dead").

At vespers, we sing 3 festal stichera from the Pentecostarion and three stichera from the Menaion (in the case of an office without a sign). [On the evening of Thomas Sunday, exceptionally, at vespers the great prokeimenon, "Who is so great a God," is sung after the entrance.] At the aposticha, we sing the stichera from the Octoechos appointed by the Pentecostarion (second week, tone 1; third week, tone 2; fourth week, tone 3; fifth week, tone 4; sixth week, tone 5), followed by a festal doxastikon (Pentecostarion). Following the trisagion and the Lord's Prayer, we sing the troparion of the preceding Sunday, "Glory . . . ," the troparion of the saint from the Menaion, "Now and ever . . . ," and the Sunday theotokion in the tone of the troparion of the saint from the Menaion. During the week after Thomas Sunday, we sing only the troparion of the saint from the Menaion, "Glory . . . ," "Now and ever . . . ," and the troparion of the feast.

At compline, the three-ode canons by Joseph of Thessalonica, the brother of St Theodore the Studite, are read. These canons are found in an appendix to the Slavic editions of the Pentecostarion.[21] They are, however, absent from the modern Greek editions. It is interesting to note that, in the Studite tradition, these canons were chanted at matins.[22] Therefore, when the Sabaite Typika spread beginning in the fourteenth century, these canons of Studite origin were incorporated in the Sabaite tradition, but were relegated to compline, as was also the case with the three-ode canons of Andrew of Crete during Holy Week.

At matins, the royal office is suppressed. After "God is the Lord," we sing the troparion of the preceding Sunday, "Glory . . . ," the troparion of the saint from the Menaion, "Now and ever . . . ," and the Sunday theotokion in the tone of the troparion of the saint from the Menaion. During the week

[21]See, for example, *Triod' tsvetnaia* (Moscow, 1992), 289ff.
[22]See, for example, Pentkovskii, *Tipikon*, 263.

following Thomas Sunday, we sing the troparion of the feast, "Glory . . . ,"
the troparion of the saint from the Menaion, "Now and ever . . . ," and the
troparion of the feast. After the first kathisma and the small synapte, we sing
the kathisma troparion from the Octoechos, as appointed by the Pentecostarion (second week, tone 1; third week, tone 2; fourth week, tone 3; fifth
week, tone 4; sixth week, tone 5). After the second kathisma and the small
synapte, we sing the kathisma troparion of the feast (Pentecostarion). We
then sing the sticheron "Having beheld the resurrection of Christ" (once),
and then read Psalm 50. The canon of the feast (from the Pentecostarion)
follows, together with the canon of the saint from the Menaion:

1) If the saint in the Menaion has no sign, the festal canon (from the
   Pentecostarion) is sung with eight troparia, and the canon of the saint
   with 4. After the third ode, we sing the kontakion, the ikos, and the
   kathisma troparion of the Saint, followed by the kathisma troparion
   of the feast. After the sixth ode, we sing the kontakion and ikos of
   the feast.

2) If the saint in the Menaion is "with six stichera," the festal canon (Pentecostarion) is sung with six troparia and the canon of the saint from
   the Menaion with six troparia. After the third ode, we sing the kontakion and ikos of the feast, and then the kathisma troparion of the
   saint followed by the kathisma troparion of the feast. After the sixth
   ode, we sing the kontakion and ikos of the saint from the Menaion.

3) If there are two saints in the Menaion, then we sing the canon of the
   feast (from the Pentecostarion) with six troparia, and the canons of
   the two saints with eight troparia.

4) On Saturday morning, the canon of the feast (from the Pentecostarion) is sung with six troparia, the canon of the patron saint of the
   church (if and only if the church is dedicated to a saint) with four
   troparia, and the canon for the saint from the Menaion with four
   troparia.

At the ninth ode, the Magnificat is sung. After the ninth ode, we sing the exaposteilarion of the feast, "Glory . . . ," the exaposteilarion from the Menaion
(if there is one), "Now and ever . . . ," and the second exaposteilarion for
the feast.

At the lauds, which are read in their Palestinian redaction, resurrectional stichera from the Octoechos are added as indicated in the Pentecostarion (second week, tone 1; third week, tone 2; fourth week, tone 3; fifth week, tone 4; sixth week, tone 5), followed by a festal doxastikon (Pentecostarion). At the aposticha, we sing the festal stichera (Pentecostarion). After "It is good to confess" (read only once) follow the Trisagion and the Lord's Prayer, then the troparion of the saint from the Menaion, "Glory . . . ," "Now and ever . . . ," and the troparion of the feast.

At the hours, we read: the troparion of the feast, "Glory . . . ," the troparion of the saint from the Menaion, "Now and ever . . . ," and the theotokion from the Horologion. However, we read only the festal kontakion (from the Pentecostarion).

At the liturgy, at the little entrance we sing "O come let us worship . . . who rose from the dead," and then: the troparion of the feast (Pentecostarion), the troparion of the church (if it is dedicated to the Mother of God or a saint), the troparion or troparia of the saint(s) from the Menaion, the kontakion of the church (if it is dedicated to the Mother of God or a saint), the kontakion or kontakia of the saint(s) from the Menaion, and the kontakion of the feast (Pentecostarion). The prokeimenon, Alleluia verses, and the koinonikon are all for the feast (of the preceding Sunday, from the Pentecostarion). If the Menaion so indicates, verses from the Menaion are added to those of the Pentecostarion. If the Menaion appoints verses for the saint being commemorated, these are read after those for the day. Instead of the hymn to the Mother of God, we sing the refrain and hirmos of the ninth ode of the paschal canon: "The angel cried . . . ," "Shine, shine . . . ." We should note, however, that on Athos they continue to sing "It is truly meet . . . ," and the hirmos of the paschal canon is sung only on Sundays and feast days. The troparion "We have seen the true light" is replaced by "Christ is risen." Before the dismissal and after "Glory to you, O Christ our God," we sing the troparion "Christ is risen" three times.

Services for a saint with a polyeleos during the paschal season

Generally, the feast with a polyeleos, including those of the great martyr George (April 23), the holy Apostle John the Theologian (May 8), St Nicholas (May 9 in Russian practice, May 20 in Greek practice), and Sts Constantine and Helen (May 21), fall during the paschal period.

At vespers, we sing 3 festal stichera from the Pentecostarion, followed by 5 stichera from the Menaion, the doxastikon from the Menaion, and, at "Now and ever . . . ," the festal idiomelon from the Pentecostarion. After the entrance and the evening prokeimenon follow three Old-Testament readings from the Menaion. At the *lite*, we sing the idiomela of the saint of the church, then those from the Menaion, followed by the festal doxastikon from the Pentecostarion appointed for the matins aposticha. The aposticha stichera are taken from the Menaion, followed by a festal doxastikon (from the Pentecostarion). After the Trisagion and the Lord's Prayer, if there is only one office with the polyeleos, we sing the troparion of the saint from the Menaion, "Glory . . . ," "Now and ever . . . ," and the Sunday theotokion. If there is a vigil, then the troparion of the saint from the Menaion is sung twice, and "Mother of God and Virgin" once.

At matins, after "God is the Lord," we sing the troparion of the feast (Pentecostarion), "Glory . . . ," the troparion of the saint (Menaion), "Now and ever . . . ," and the Sunday theotokion. After the first kathisma and the small synapte, we sing the festal kathisma troparion (Pentecostarion). After the second kathisma and the small synapte, the kathisma troparion of the saint from the Menaion, followed by that for the feast (Pentecostarion). The polyeleos is then sung, followed by the selected psalm verses with the megalynarion. After the small synapte, we sing the kathisma troparion from the Menaion, and then the first antiphon of the anabathmoi in tone 4 ("From my youth"). Following the prokeimenon and gospel appointed by the Menaion, we sing the sticheron "Having beheld the resurrection of Christ" (once), and then read Psalm 50. We sing the customary verses and the idiomelon from the Menaion appointed for after the gospel. Following the prayer "O Lord, save your people," we sing the canon of the feast (from the Pentecostarion) with six troparia, and the canon for the saint (from the Menaion) with eight troparia. The hirmoi of the paschal canon are sung as the katabasiai. After the third ode, we sing the kontakion and ikos for the feast, the kathisma troparion for the saint, and then that for the feast. After the sixth ode, we sing the kontakion and ikos of the saint from the Menaion. At the ninth ode, the Magnificat is sung. After the ninth ode, we sing the exaposteilarion of the saint from the Menaion, "Glory . . . ," "Now and ever . . . ," and the exaposteilarion for the feast. At the lauds (sung in their Constantinopolitan redaction), we sing the four stichera from the Menaion, "Glory . . . ," the doxastikon from the Menaion, "Now and ever . . . ," the sticheron of the feast

(Pentecostarion). After the great doxology (Constantinopolitan redaction), we sing the troparion of the saint from the Menaion, "Glory . . . ," "Now and ever . . . ," and the Sunday theotokion.

At the hours, we read the troparion of the feast (Pentecostarion), "Glory . . . ," the troparion of the saint from the Menaion, "Now and ever . . . ," and the theotokion from the Horologion.

At the liturgy, at the little entrance, we sing "O come let us worship . . . who rose from the dead," and then: the troparion of the feast (Pentecostarion), the troparion of the church (if it is dedicated to the Mother of God), the troparion of the saint from the Menaion, the kontakion of the church (if it is dedicated to the Mother of God), the kontakion of the saint from the Menaion, and the kontakion of the feast (Pentecostarion). The prokeimenon, Alleluia verses, and koinonikon of the feast (of the preceding Sunday, from the Pentecostarion) are sung first, followed by those for the saint from the Menaion. Instead of the hymn to the Mother of God, we sing the refrain and hirmos of the ninth ode of the paschal canon: "The angel cried . . . ," "Shine, shine . . . ." The troparion "We have seen the true light" is replaced by "Christ is risen." Before the dismissal and after "Glory to you, O Christ our God," we sing the troparion "Christ is risen" three times.

The Third Week after Pascha

Sunday of the Myrrhbearing Women

ORIGIN

The third Sunday of Easter commemorates the myrrhbearing women, Joseph of Arimathea, and Nicodemus. The gospel reading appointed for the liturgy by the Typikon of the Great Church on this Sunday is Mk 15.43–16.8, recounting the burial of Christ and the empty tomb. This Sunday that follows the paschal octave represents a kind of "synaxis" of all the witnesses to the burial and the resurrection of Christ, somewhat like the synaxis of the Mother of God on the day after Christmas, or the synaxis of John the Baptist following Theophany.

We should be aware that, in the Jerusalem tradition, Mk 15. 42–16.8 was read at the liturgy on Easter Sunday, while Jn 2.1–11 was read on the third Sunday of Pascha.[23] It is only in Constantinople that this passage was

---

[23]See the appointed readings in the Georgian Lectionary: *Le Grand Lectionnaire de*

read on the third Sunday of Easter, thus constituting an exception to the continuous reading of the Gospel of John. We can therefore deduce that the solemnity of this day is of Constantinopolitan origin.

ORDO

As on all Sundays during the paschal season, the office scrupulously follows the Pentecostarion. The office for the saint in the Menaion is transferred to compline (or to another day), except in the case of an office with the polyeleos.

At "Lord, I call" in vespers, we sing 7 stichera from the Octoechos, tone 2, which are also found in the Pentecostarion (3 resurrectional, and 4 "anato-lika," or "oriental"), followed by three stichera for the myrrhbearing women (also called "anatolika"), a doxastikon attributed to Cosmas of Maioum, and the dogmatikon theotokion in tone 2. At the *lite*, we sing the stichera idi-omela from the Pentecostarion. At the aposticha, we sing the resurrectional sticheron from the Octoechos, tone 2, also found in the Pentecostarion, followed by the paschal stichera, to which is added the doxastikon from the aposticha on Holy Friday: "You who clothe yourself with light as with a garment." At the artoklasia, the troparion "Mother of God and Virgin" is sung three times.

Matins begins with the singing of the paschal troparion, "Christ is risen," three times, and then the hexapsalmos. At "God is the Lord," the follow-ing troparia are sung: "When you descended" (Sunday troparion, tone 2), "Glory . . . ," "The noble Joseph," "Now and ever . . . ," "To the myrrhbearing women" (kathisma troparia after the first kathisma at Sunday matins in the Octoechos, tone 2, also sung as troparia on Holy Friday). After the first kathisma, we sing the kathisma troparia taken by the Pentecostarion from the Octoechos, tone 2. After the second kathisma, we sing the kathisma troparia for the feast, from the Pentecostarion. We then sing the polyeleos and the resurrectional evlogitaria. After the small synapte, we sing the kathisma troparion of the feast (Pentecostarion), and then the anabath-moi from the Octoechos, tone 2 (which also appear in the Pentecostarion), the prokeimenon for Sunday morning from the Octoechos in tone 2 (also appearing in the Pentecostarion), and the third (resurrection) matins gos-pel is read, followed by "Having beheld the resurrection of Christ" (three

l'Église de Jérusalem, M. Tarchnisvili, ed., CSCO 189, pp. 115, 124. See the comparative table in S. Janeras, "Les lectionnaires de l'ancienne liturgie de Jérusalem," *CCO* 2 (2005): 84–85.

times). After Psalm 50, the customary Sunday stichera are sung: "Glory . . . ," "Through the prayers of the apostles," "Now and ever . . . ," "Through the prayers of the Theotokos," "Have mercy on me," and "Jesus having risen from the tomb." After the prayer "O Lord, save your people," the paschal canon is sung with the theotokia of Theophanes with six troparia, followed by the canon of the feast (of the myrrhbearing women), attributed to Andrew of Crete, with eight troparia, with the hirmoi of the paschal canon as katabasiai. Note that the canon of Andrew of Crete has more than eight troparia and begins with resurrectional troparia; the custom is to omit the latter and to count eight from the end, and to sing the omitted troparia during days of the after-feast. After the third ode, the kontakion of Pascha is sung, followed by the kathisma troparia from the Pentecostarion. After the sixth ode, the kontakion and ikos of the feast (of the myrrhbearing women) are sung. Then comes the reading from the synaxarion of Nicephoras Kallistos Xanthopoulos. At the ninth ode, the Magnificat is omitted. The Magnificat is not sung on Sundays until the leavetaking of Pascha because the paschal canon is sung with its own megalynaria. Following the ninth ode and "Holy is the Lord, our God" in tone 2, we sing the exaposteilarion of Pascha and the exaposteilarion of the feast (of the myrrhbearing women). At the lauds, eight stichera from the Octoechos, tone 2, are sung (also appearing in the Pentecostarion) (4 resurrectional, and 4 "anatolika"), to which is added a sticheron for the feast (of the myrrhbearing women), "Glory . . . ," the second idiomelon eothinon of the gospel (tone 2), "Now and ever . . . ," and the theotokion ("You are most blessed, O Mother of God and Virgin"). After the great doxology, the troparion appointed for the end of Sunday matins is sung ("Having risen from the tomb").

At the hours, the following troparia are read: "When you descended," "Glory . . . ," "The noble Joseph," "Now and ever . . . ," and the theotokion from the Horologion. The kontakion for the feast (of the myrrhbearing women) is read.

At the Divine Liturgy of St John Chrysostom, following the opening blessing, the paschal troparion is sung three times. The entrance is followed by the troparia: "When you descended," "The noble Joseph," Glory . . . ," the kontakion from the Pentecostarion, "Now and ever . . . ," the kontakion of Pascha. The prokeimenon, epistle, Alleluia verses, and the gospel are all festal (from the Pentecostarion). Instead of the hymn to the Mother of God, we sing the refrain and hirmos of the ninth ode of the paschal canon: "The angel cried . . . ," "Shine, shine . . . ." The troparion "We have seen the true light" is replaced by "Christ is risen." Before the dismissal and after "Glory to you, O Christ our God," we sing the troparion "Christ is risen" three times.

Services during the third week of Pascha

The services during the third week of Pascha follow the ordo indicated for all the weekday offices during the paschal period (see above). We should point out, however, that the order of the troparia differs:

1) At the end of vespers and of matins: "The noble Joseph," "Glory . . . ," the troparion of the saint from the Menaion, "Now and ever . . . ," "To the myrrhbearing women"; or "When you descended," "Glory . . . ," the troparion of the saint from the Menaion, "Now and ever . . . ," "To the myrrhbearing women."

2) At the beginning of matins, after "God is the Lord": "The noble Joseph," "When you descended," "Glory . . . ," the troparion of the saint from the Menaion, "Now and ever . . . ," "To the myrrhbearing women."

3) At the hours, we read the following troparia: "The noble Joseph" at prime and none, "When you descended" at terce, "To the myrrhbearing women" at sext, and then "Glory . . . ," and the troparion of the saint from the Menaion. The kontakion for the feast (of the myrrhbearing women) is read.

4) At the liturgy, following the entrance: "The noble Joseph," "When you descended," "To the myrrhbearing women," the troparion of the church (if it is dedicated to the Mother of God or a saint), the troparion of the saint from the Menaion (one or two), the kontakion of the saint from the Menaion, and the kontakion of the feast (of the myrrhbearing women).

The Fourth Week after Pascha

Sunday of the Paralytic

ORIGIN

The fourth Sunday of Pascha is called the "Sunday of the Paralytic," because of the gospel pericope appointed for this day by the Typikon of the Great Church (Jn 5.1–15). In the tradition of Jerusalem, the gospel this Sunday was Jn 4.4–23, about the Samaritan woman.[24] This passage was read in Constantinople on the following Sunday. The hymnography about the paralytic, therefore, is of Constantinopolitan origin.

ORDO

As on all Sundays during the paschal season, the office scrupulously follows the Pentecostarion. The office for the saint in the Menaion is transferred to compline (or to another day), except in the case of an office with the polyeleos.

At "Lord, I call" in vespers, we sing 7 stichera from the Octoechos, tone 3, all found as well in the Pentecostarion (3 resurrectional, and 4 "anatolika"), then three stichera idiomela for the paralytic, followed by a doxastikon for the paralytic and the dogmatikon theotokion in tone 3. At the *lite*, we sing the idiomelon of the church, and then the doxastikon and theotokion from the Pentecostarion. At the aposticha, we sing one resurrectional sticheron from the Octoechos, tone 3, also found in the Pentecostarion, followed by the paschal stichera to which is added a doxastikon for the paralytic. At the artoklasia, the troparion "O Mother of God and Virgin" is sung three times.

Matins begins with the singing of the paschal troparion, "Christ is risen," three times, and then the hexapsalmos. At "God is the Lord," the Sunday troparion in tone 3 is sung, as well as its theotokion. After the first and second kathismata, we sing the kathisma troparia from the Octoechos, tone 3, which are also found in the Pentecostarion. After Psalm 118, the evlogitaria of the resurrection are sung. After the small synapte, we sing the hypakoe from the Octoechos, tone 3, also found in the Pentecostarion, and then the

[24]See the readings indicated in the Georgian Lectionary: *Le Grand Lectionnaire de l'Église de Jérusalem*, M. Tarchnisvili, ed., CSCO 189, p. 127). See the comparative table in S. Janeras, "Les lectionnaires de l'ancienne liturgie de Jérusalem," *CCO* 2 (2005): 84–85.

anabathmoi from the Octoechos, tone 3, also found in the Pentecostarion. The Sunday morning prokeimenon from the Octoechos, tone 3, also found in the Pentecostarion follows, and then the fourth matins resurrection gospel is read. "Having beheld the resurrection of Christ" is sung three times. After Psalm 50, the usual Sunday stichera are sung: "Glory . . . ," "Through the prayers of the apostles," "Now and ever . . . ," "Through the prayers of the Theotokos," "Have mercy on me," and "Jesus having risen from the tomb." After the prayer "O Lord, save your people," the paschal canon is sung with the theotokia of Theophanes with eight troparia, followed by the canon of the feast (of the paralytic) with six troparia. The troparion that precedes the doxastikon of this canon is dedicated to the Archangel Michael, who descended to stir the waters of the healing pool. The troparion preceding this is the only one that refers to the paralytic. The hirmoi of the paschal canon are sung as the katabasiai. After the third ode, we sing the kontakion and ikos of Pascha, and then the kathisma troparia of the paralytic (from the Pentecostarion). After the sixth ode, we sing the kontakion and ikos of the feast (of the paralytic). Then follows the reading from the Synaxarion of Nicephoras Kallistos Xanthopoulos. At the ninth ode, the Magnificat is not sung. Following the ninth ode and "Holy is the Lord, our God" in tone 3, the exaposteilarion of Easter and that of the feast (of the paralytic) are sung. At the lauds, we sing eight stichera from the Octoechos, tone 3, also found in the Pentecostarion (4 resurrectional, and 4 anatolika), then the doxastikon for the feast (in honor of the paralytic), "Now and ever . . . ," and the theotokion ("You are most blessed, O Theotokos, Virgin"). Following the great doxology (Constantinopolitan redaction), we sing the resurrectional troparion appointed for the end of Sunday matins ("Today, salvation has come to the world"). After the dismissal, we sing: "Glory . . . now and ever . . . ," and the third gospel sticheron (tone 3). Then the catechesis of St Theodore the Studite is read, followed by the first hour.

At the hours, we read the Sunday troparion (tone 3) and the kontakion from the Pentecostarion.

At the Divine Liturgy of St John Chrysostom, after the opening blessing, the troparion "Christ is risen" is sung three times. Following the entrance, we sing the Sunday troparion in tone 3, "Glory . . . ," the kontakion from the Pentecostarion, "Now and ever . . . ," and the kontakion of Pascha. The prokeimenon, epistle, Alleluia verses, and the gospel are all festal (from the Pentecostarion). Instead of the hymn to the Mother of God, we sing the refrain and hirmos of the ninth ode of the paschal canon: "The angel cried . . . ," "Shine, shine . . . ." Two koinonika are sung: "Receive the body of Christ" and "Praise the Lord from the heavens." The troparion "We have seen the true light" is replaced by "Christ is risen." Before the dismissal and after "Glory to you, O Christ our God," we sing the troparion "Christ is risen" three times.

The Feast of Mid-Pentecost

The services during the third week of Pascha follow the ordo indicated for all the weekday offices during the paschal period (see above). We should note, however, that the office of the Sunday of the Paralytic is sung only on Monday and Tuesday. Indeed, on Wednesday of the fourth week, we have the Feast of Mid-Pentecost, which is celebrated for an entire week.

ORIGIN

The origin of this feast is Constantinopolitan.[25] The first indication is found in a homily of Peter Chrysologos, Bishop of Ravenna during the second quarter of the fifth century. Severus of Antioch witnesses to the existence of this feast in Antioch in the sixth century. The first properly Constantinopolitan reference to this feast also goes back to the sixth century, in the homily of Leontius of Constantinople. In his day, the gospel passage of Jn 9.1–14 was read, but this passage was, before the tenth century, replaced with Jn 7.14–30, the passage we use today, because of the words "About the middle of the feast." The gospel text obviously refers to the Feast of Tabernacles, which the Church transferred to the fifty-day paschal period. We could suppose the solemnization of the middle of the fifty-day paschal period did not come before the development of the feasts on the fiftieth and fortieth days after Pascha. The theme of wisdom which is developed in the Old-Testament readings and the hymnography of this feast may be connected with the tradition on this day, at least during this period, of convening regional synods of bishops, in conformity with the prescriptions of Canon 5 of Nicea. The development of this feast may also have been used

---

[25]On Mid-Pentecost, see S. Garnier, *La Mi-Pentecôte dans la liturgie byzantine des VIᵉ–Xᵉ siècles* (unpublished master's thesis defended at the E.P.H.E.) (Paris, 1998); S. Garnier, "Les leçons scriptuaires de la Mi-Pentecôte," in *La Liturgie, interprète de l'Écriture, I. Les lectures bibliques pour les dimanches et fêtes. Conférences Saint-Serge. 48ᵉ Semaine d'études liturgiques*, BELS 119 (Rome, 2002), 213–20.

to combat the boredom and laxity that set in more than usually with all the merry-making during the fifty-day paschal period, as we can see already in the correspondence between Barsanuphius and John of Gaza in Palestine in the fifth century.[26]

In our day, the feast lasts for an entire octave. The Typikon of Alexios the Studite, however, calls for the office of Mid-Pentecost to be sung only until Saturday.[27]

The pericope selected for this feast by the Typikon of the Great Church is Jn 7.14–30, in which Jesus taught in the Temple "in the middle of the feast" (Jn 7.14). This passage is in fact a prelude to the discourse about the living water (Jn 7.37–52) that follows, but will only be read at Pentecost. Thus the interdependence of these two feasts is concretely underlined. This pericope is surrounded by the account of the healing of the paralytic (Jn 5.1–15), the theme of the fourth Sunday after Easter, and the account of the conversation with the Samaritan woman (Jn 4.5–42), read on the fifth Sunday. These two pericopes, with their allusion to water as a symbol of the Holy Spirit, perfectly frame the feast. In Jerusalem, Jn 7.28–36 was read on the fifth Sunday of Pascha. In his Synaxarion, Nicephoras Kallistos Xanthopoulos already noticed the inversion in the continuous reading of the Gospel of John, and he explained it as follows:

> This is also, I believe, the reason why the feast of the Samaritan woman in celebrated after Mid-Pentecost, for she speaks voluminously about the messiahship of Christ, as well as about water and thirst, just as here [at Mid-Pentecost]. In the Gospel of John, however, the healing of the man born blind follows immediately, and not the Samaritan woman, about whom we spoke earlier.

ORDO

The services of Mid-Pentecost scrupulously follow the Pentecostarion. The office for the saint in the Menaion is shifted to compline (or to another day), unless it is an office with the polyeleos.

At "Lord, I call" in vespers, we sing six stichera for the feast, "Glory . . . now and ever . . . ," and an idiomelon. After the entrance and the evening prokeimenon, we read three Old-Testament passages for the feast. At the

---

[26]Barsanuphe et Jean de Gaza, *Correspondance*, Lettre 452 (Solesmes, 1993), 331.
[27]Pentkovskii, *Tipikon*, 266.

aposticha, we sing the festal stichera attributed to John of Damascus. After the Lord's Prayer, the festal troparion is sung.

Matins begins with the singing of the troparion, "Christ is risen," three times, and then the hexapsalmos. At "God is the Lord," the festal troparion is sung three times. After the first and second kathismata, the festal kathisma troparia are sung. After the second kathisma troparion, we sing "Having beheld the resurrection of Christ" only once. Following Psalm 50, we sing the two canons for the feast, with fourteen troparia. The first canon is attributed to Theophanes, the second to St Andrew of Crete, with the hirmoi of the second canon used as the katabasiai. After the third ode, the kathisma troparia for the feast are sung. After the sixth ode follow the kontakion and ikos of the feast, and then the reading from the Synaxarion of Nicephoras Kallistos Xanthopoulos. At the ninth ode, the Magnificat is not sung. After the ninth ode, the exaposteilarion of the feast is sung three times. At the lauds, four stichera for the feast are intercalated, then "glory . . . now and ever . . . ," and the idiomelon for the feast. After the great doxology follows the festal troparion.

At the hours, the troparion and kontakion of the feast are read.

At the Divine Liturgy of St John Chrysostom, the paschal troparion is sung three times after the opening blessing. The troparion and kontakion of the feast are sung after the entrance. The prokeimenon, epistles, Alleluia verses, and the gospel are all festal. Instead of the hymn to the Mother of God, the hirmos of the ninth ode of the festal canon is sung (as well as on the day of the leavetaking of Mid-Pentecost), while on the other days, the refrain and hirmos of the ninth ode of the paschal canon are sung. The koinonikon is festal: "He who eats my flesh and drinks my blood . . . ." The troparion "We have seen the true light" is replaced by "Christ is risen." Before the dismissal and after "Glory to you, O Christ our God," we sing the troparion "Christ is risen" three times.

Following the Divine Liturgy, it is customary, at least in Russian practice, to celebrate the Lesser Blessing of Water, in connection with the theme of the feast.

During the eight days that follow, the offices follow the ordo of services for weekdays during the paschal period (see above). We should note, however, that the office "of the feast" added to the Menaion is that of Mid-Pentecost, and not of the preceding Sunday. Each day, one of the two canons of Mid-Pentecost is alternated and sung with six troparia together with the canon from the Menaion.

The Fifth Week after Pascha

Sunday of the Samaritan Woman

ORIGIN

The fifth Sunday of Easter is called the "Sunday of the Samaritan Woman," in connection with the gospel reading for this Sunday selected by the Typikon of the Great Church (Jn 4.5–42). In the Jerusalem tradition, on the other hand, Jn 4.4–23 was read on the fourth Sunday of Pascha. On the fifth Sunday, Jn 7.28–36 was read, a text also read partially in Constantinople on Mid-Pentecost.[28] Note that the hymnography about the Samaritan woman is of Studite, Constantinopolitan origin.

ORDO

As on all Sundays during the paschal season, the office scrupulously follows the Pentecostarion. The office for the saint in the Menaion is transferred to compline (or to another day), except in the case of an office with the polyeleos.

At "Lord, I call" in vespers, we sing four stichera from the Octoechos, tone 4, which are also found in the Pentecostarion (three for the resurrection and one "anatolika"), then three stichera for Mid-Pentecost and three stichera idiomela for the Samaritan woman, followed by a doxastikon for the Samaritan woman and the dogmatikon theotokion in tone 4. At the *lite*, we sing the sticheron of the church, "Glory . . . now and ever . . . ," and the idiomelon for the Samaritan woman (from the Pentecostarion). At the aposticha, we sing the first resurrection sticheron from the Octoechos, tone 4, also found in the Pentecostarion, followed by the paschal stichera, to which the doxastikon for the Samaritan is added from the Pentecostarion. At the artoklasia, the troparion "O Mother of God and Virgin" is sung three times.

---

[28]See the readings indicated in the Georgian Lectionary: *Le Grand Lectionnaire de l'Église de Jérusalem*, M. Tarchnisvili, ed., CSCO 189, pp. 127, 129. See the comparative table in S. Janeras, "Les lectionnaires de l'ancienne liturgie de Jérusalem," *CCO* 2 (2005): 84–85.

Matins begins with the singing of the paschal troparion, "Christ is risen," three times, and then the hexapsalmos. At "God is the Lord," the Sunday troparion in tone 4 is sung, and then the troparion of Mid-Pentecost. After the first and second kathismata, the kathisma troparia are taken from the Octoechos, tone 4 (also found in the Pentecostarion). After Psalm 118, we sing the evlogitaria of the resurrection. After the small synapte, we sing the hypakoe from the Octoechos, tone 4, also found in the Pentecostarion. Then follow the anabathmoi from the Octoechos, tone 4, also found in the Pentecostarion, and the Sunday morning prokeimenon from the Octoechos, tone 4, also found in the Pentecostarion. The seventh matins resurrection gospel is read, followed by "Having beheld the resurrection of Christ" three times. After Psalm 50, the usual Sunday stichera are sung: "Glory . . . ," "Through the prayers of the apostles," "Now and ever . . . ," "Through the prayers of the Theotokos," "Have mercy on me," and "Jesus having risen from the tomb." After the prayer "O Lord, save your people," the paschal canon is sung with the theotokia of Theophanes with six troparia, the second canon of Mid-Pentecost (by St Andrew of Crete) with four troparia, and the canon of the feast (of the Samaritan woman), attributed to Joseph the Hymnographer, with four troparia. The hirmoi of the paschal canon are sung as the katabasiai. After the third ode, the kontakion and ikos of Mid-Pentecost are sung, and then the kathisma troparia for the Samaritan woman (from the Pentecostarion). After the sixth ode, we sing the kontakion and ikos of the feast (of the Samaritan woman), and then read from the Synaxarion of Nicephoras Kallistos Xanthopoulos. At the ninth ode, the Magnificat is not sung. After the ninth ode, we sing the exaposteilarion of Pascha, the exaposteilarion of the Samaritan woman, and the exaposteilarion of Mid-Pentecost. At the lauds, we sing six stichera from the Octoechos, tone 4, also found in the Pentecostarion (four for the resurrection, and two "anatolika"), then two idiomela for the Samaritan woman with their doxastikon, "Now and ever . . . ," and the theotokion: "You are most blessed, O Theotokos, Virgin." Following the great doxology (Constantinopolitan redaction), we sing the resurrectional troparion appointed for the end of Sunday matins ("Having risen from the tomb"). After the dismissal, we sing: "Glory . . . now and ever . . . ," and the seventh gospel sticheron (tone 7). Then the catechesis of St Theodore the Studite is read, followed by the first hour.

At the hours, we read the Sunday troparion in tone 4, "Glory . . . now and ever . . . ," and the troparion of Mid-Pentecost. We alternate reading the kontakia of Mid-Pentecost and of the Samaritan woman.

At the Divine Liturgy of St John Chrysostom, after the opening blessing, the troparion "Christ is risen" is sung three times. Following the entrance, we sing the Sunday troparion in tone 4 and the troparion of Mid-Pentecost, "Glory . . . ," the kontakion of the Samaritan woman, "Now and ever . . . ," and the kontakion of Mid-Pentecost. The prokeimenon, epistle, Alleluia verses, and the gospel are all for the Samaritan woman (from the Pentecostarion). Instead of the hymn to the Mother of God, we sing the refrain and hirmos of the ninth ode of the paschal canon: "The angel cried . . . ," "Shine, shine . . . ." Two koinonika are sung: "Receive the body of Christ" and "Praise the Lord from the heavens." The troparion "We have seen the true light" is replaced by "Christ is risen." Before the dismissal and after "Glory to you, O Christ our God," we sing the troparion "Christ is risen" three times.

Services during the fifth week of Pascha

The services during the fifth week of Pascha follow the ordo indicated for all the weekday offices during the paschal period (see above). We should note, however, that the office "for the feast" is that of Mid-Pentecost on Monday, Tuesday, and Wednesday (the leave-taking of Mid-Pentecost). On the day of the leavetaking of Mid-Pentecost, the entire festal office is repeated (suppressing the office in the Menaion), except for the entrance and the Old-Testament readings. On Thursday, Friday, and Saturday, the office "for the feast" is that for the Samaritan woman.

The Sixth Week after Pascha

Sunday of the Man Born Blind

ORIGIN

The sixth Sunday of Pascha, called the "Sunday of the man born blind," takes its name from the gospel reading appointed by the Typikon of the Great Church for this Sunday (Jn 9.1–38). In the Jerusalem tradition, Jn 2.12–25 was read, about the merchants in the Temple and the saying of Christ about his rising on the third day.[29] This passage is read on Wednesday of Bright

[29]See the readings indicated in the Georgian Lectionary: *Le Grand Lectionnaire de*

Week in the Constantinopolitan tradition. Consequently, the hymnography about the man born blind is of Constantinopolitan origin.

ORDO

As on all Sundays during the paschal season, the office scrupulously follows the Pentecostarion. The office for the saint in the Menaion is transferred to compline (or to another day), except in the case of an office with the polyeleos.

At "Lord, I call" in vespers, we sing 7 stichera from the Octoechos, tone 5, also found in the Pentecostarion (3 for the resurrection, and 4 "anatolika"), then the 3 idiomela for the man born blind, followed by a doxastikon for the blind man and the dogmatikon theotokion in tone 5. At the *lite*, the idiomelon for the church is sung first, followed by the doxastikon and the theotokion from the Pentecostarion. At the aposticha, we sing the first resurrectional sticheron from the Octoechos, tone 5, also found in the Pentecostarion, followed by the paschal stichera, to which the doxastikon for the blind man is added from the Pentecostarion. At the artoklasia, the troparion "O Mother of God and Virgin" is sung three times.

Matins begins with the singing of the paschal troparion, "Christ is risen," three times, and then the hexapsalmos. At "God is the Lord," the Sunday troparion in tone 5 is sung, and then its theotokion. After the first and second kathismata, the kathisma troparia from the Octoechos, tone 5, are sung, also found in the Pentecostarion. After the small synapte, we sing the hypakoe from the Octoechos, tone 5, also found in the Pentecostarion. Then follow the anabathmoi from the Octoechos, tone 5, also found in the Pentecostarion, and the Sunday morning prokeimenon from the Octoechos, tone 5, also found in the Pentecostarion. The eighth matins resurrection gospel is read, followed by "Having beheld the resurrection of Christ" three times. After Psalm 50, the usual Sunday stichera are sung: "Glory . . . ," "Through the prayers of the apostles," "Now and ever . . . ," "Through the prayers of the Theotokos," "Have mercy on me," and "Jesus having risen from the tomb." After the prayer "O Lord, save your people," the paschal canon is sung with the theotokia of Theophanes, with eight troparia, and the canon of the feast (of the blind man) with six troparia. Only the troparion before the doxastikon of the canon is in fact dedicated to the blind man—the others focus

---

l'Église de Jérusalem, M. Tarchnisvili, ed., CSCO 189, p. 132. See the comparative table in S. Janeras, "Les lectionnaires de l'ancienne liturgie de Jérusalem," *CCO* 2 (2005): 84–85.

on the crucifixion, the burial, and the resurrection. The hirmoi of the canon of Ascension are sung as the katabasiai. After the third ode, the kontakion and ikos of Pascha are sung, followed by the kathisma troparia for the man born blind (from the Pentecostarion). After the sixth ode, the kontakion and ikos of the feast (of the blind man) are sung, after which comes the reading from the Synaxarion of Nicephoras Kallistos Xanthopoulos. The Magnificat is not sung at the ninth ode. Following the ninth ode and "Holy is the Lord, our God" in tone 5, we sing the exaposteilarion of Pascha and the two festal exaposteilaria (of the blind man). At the lauds, we sing 7 stichera from the Octoechos, tone 5, also found in the Pentecostarion (4 resurrectional and 3 "anatolika"), then an idiomelon and doxastikon for the feast (of the blind man), "Now and ever . . . ," and the theotokion: "You are most blessed, O Theotokos, Virgin." Following the great doxology (Constantinopolitan redaction), we sing the resurrectional troparion appointed for the end of Sunday matins ("Today salvation has come to the world"). After the dismissal, we sing: "Glory . . . now and ever . . . ," and the eighth gospel sticheron (tone 7). Then the catechesis of St Theodore the Studite is read, followed by the first hour.

At the hours, the Sunday troparion, tone 5, is read, and the kontakion of the man born blind.

At the Divine Liturgy of St John Chrysostom, after the opening blessing, the troparion "Christ is risen" is sung three times. Following the entrance, we sing the Sunday troparion in tone 5, "Glory . . . ," the kontakion from the Pentecostarion, "Now and ever . . . ," and the paschal kontakion. The prokeimenon, epistle, Alleluia verses, and the gospel are all for the blind man (from the Pentecostarion). Instead of the hymn to the Mother of God, we sing the refrain and hirmos of the ninth ode of the paschal canon: "The angel cried . . . ," "Shine, shine . . . ." Two koinonika are sung: "Receive the body of Christ" and "Praise the Lord from the heavens." The troparion "We have seen the true light" is replaced by "Christ is risen." Before the dismissal and after "Glory to you, O Christ our God," we sing the troparion "Christ is risen" three times.

The Leavetaking of Pascha

The services on the first two days of the sixth week of Pascha follow the ordo indicated for all the weekday offices during the paschal period (see above). On Wednesday of the sixth week, we move to the leavetaking of the feast of

Pascha, which has a particular ordo, combining three different offices: those of Pascha, of the pre-feast of Ascension, and of the blind man.

ORIGIN

The celebration of the leavetaking of Pascha on Wednesday of the sixth week, the eve of Ascension, became generalized during the fourteenth century with the spread of the Sabaite Typikon. In fact, in the Studite tradition up to that point, the leavetaking of Easter occurred on Saturday of Bright Week. For this reason, on Wednesday of the sixth week, only the pre-feast of Ascension and the saint from the Menaion were celebrated.[30] The Sabaite tradition, however, may have sought to preserve a more ancient tradition, in which Pascha actually lasted through the entire fifty-day paschal season. The fifty days came to be somewhat abbreviated when Ascension came to be celebrated on the fortieth day, out of concern for historicity.

ORDO

The services of the leavetaking of Pascha scrupulously follow the Pentecostarion. The office for the saint in the Menaion is transferred to compline (or to another day), except in the case of an office with the polyeleos.

At vespers, before Psalm 103, the service begins as during Bright Week: the priest, holding the Cross and the three-branched paschal candlestick, incenses the church and sings the paschal troparion and its psalm verses. At "Lord, I call," we sing six stichera for the blind man, followed by a sticheron at "Glory . . . now and ever." At the aposticha, we sing the first sticheron from the Octoechos, tone 5, also found in the Pentecostarion, and then the paschal stichera. After the Lord's Prayer, we sing the Sunday troparion in tone 5 and its theotokion.

Matins begins as during Bright Week: the priest, holding the Cross and the three-branched paschal candlestick, incenses the church and sings the paschal troparion and its psalm verses. The hexapsalmos follows. At "God is the Lord," the Sunday troparion in tone five is sung twice, and then its theotokion. After the first kathisma, we sing the Sunday kathisma troparia from the Octoechos, tone 5, also found in the Pentecostarion. After the second kathisma, we sing the kathisma troparion for the blind man (from the Pentecostarion), and then "Having beheld the resurrection of Christ" (once only). After Psalm 50 follow the paschal canon with six troparia, the

[30]Pentkovskii, *Tipikon*, 261, 268.

canon for the blind man with four troparia, and the canon for the pre-feast of Ascension with four troparia. The hirmoi of the canon of Ascension are sung as the katabasiai. After the third ode, the kontakion, ikos, and kathisma troparia for the blind man are sung; after the sixth ode, the kontakion and ikos of Pascha. Strangely, the Pentecostarion then calls for the reading of the Synaxarion from the Menaion, even if the office for the saint in the Menaion is not celebrated. In Athonite practice, however, it is the custom to read the synaxarion from the Menaion every day after the sixth ode, even if the office for the saint is not celebrated. At the ninth ode, the Magnificat is not sung. After the ninth ode, the exaposteilarion of Pascha is sung twice, and then the exaposteilarion for the blind man (once). At the lauds, after the four stichera for the blind man, the paschal stichera are added. After the great doxology (Constantinopolitan redaction), we sing the Sunday troparion in tone 5 and its theotokion.

At the hours, the Sunday troparion in tone 5 is read, as well as the kontakion for the blind man.

The Divine Liturgy of St John Chrysostom begins as on Easter with the opening blessing, and then the incensation of the entire church by the priest, who holds the Cross and the three-branched paschal candlestick and sings the paschal troparion and its psalm verses. At the entrance, we sing the Sunday troparion in tone 5, "Glory . . . ," the kontakion from the Pentecostarion, "Now and ever . . . ," the paschal kontakion. The epistle reading is preceded by the prokeimenon of Pascha. The Alleluia verses are also paschal. The epistle and gospel readings are specific for the day. The rest of the Divine Liturgy follows the order of Pascha. The refrain and hirmos of the ninth ode of the paschal canon replace the hymn to the Mother of God. The koinonikon is that of Pascha ("Receive the body of Christ"). At communion, instead of "Blessed is he who comes . . . ," "Let our mouths be filled . . . ," and "We have seen the true light . . . ," we sing the paschal troparion: "Christ is risen." The liturgy concludes, as on Easter, with the singing of the paschal troparion and the dismissal of Pascha, which the priest pronounces holding the Cross and the three-branched candlestick. Following the liturgy, the epitaphion, which has been on the altar table since Pascha, is removed and put in its place. On this Wednesday, fish is permitted in the refectory, as well as wine and oil.

We should note that, according to the modern Typikon of the Great Church (19th century), which is observed in this case even on Mt Athos, the leavetaking of the blind man is celebrated on Tuesday of the sixth week. On Wednesday, the leavetaking of Pascha, the full paschal office is performed. At "Lord, I call" in vespers, six stichera from the Sunday Octoechos, tone 1, are sung, followed by the dogmatikon theotokion. At the stichera, the Sunday sticheron from the Octoechos in tone 1 is followed by the paschal stichera. Matins, the hours, and the Divine Liturgy are celebrated exactly as on Easter.

It is necessary to know that, beginning on the leavetaking of Pascha until Pentecost, the prayer to the Holy Spirit ("O heavenly King") is still not said at the beginning of the services, nor the paschal troparion—but we begin directly with the trisagion.

Somewhat paradoxically in the modern, nineteenth-century Typikon of the Great Church, the ninth hour on Tuesday is already paschal, followed by paschal vespers, but the ninth hour on Wednesday is celebrated normally with its customary psalm readings. It concludes with the solemn singing of the paschal troparion, during which the entire assembly venerates the icon of the resurrection that is placed on a stand in the narthex, and the bells are rung. Once the veneration is completed, the priest, vested in his phelonion, takes the icon into the sanctuary through the holy doors, and the small vespers of Ascension begins.

Ascension

ORIGIN

On Thursday of the sixth week, forty days after Pascha, we celebrate the feast of the Ascension of Christ. Even though the Book of Acts clearly states that the resurrected Christ appeared during forty days before ascending to heaven (Acts 1.3), this feast has not always been celebrated on the fortieth day after Easter. Indeed, in the early centuries, the entire fifty-day paschal period was a time of rejoicing in the resurrection of Christ, during which fasting and kneeling were suppressed.[31] The integrity of this period was fractured, out of concern for historicity, by the introduction of the feast of Ascension on the fortieth day.

---

[31]Epiphanius of Salamis, for example, writes: "It is in this way that the fast is observed during the entire year in the holy, catholic Church, I mean on Wednesday and Friday, until the ninth hour, except during the 50-day Pentecost, during which we do not bend the knee or fast . . ." (Epiphanius, *De fide*, 22). Similarly, Egeria says in chapter 41 of her account that there is no fasting during the 50-day paschal period, including on Wednesdays and Fridays.

Some see in Egeria the first indication of the feast of Ascension on the fortieth day following Pascha. It is indeed true that she mentions, in chapter 42 of her *Travels*, a solemnity in Bethlehem on the fortieth day. Some have seen this as evidence for the feast of Ascension.[32] Others, however, suppose that on the year that Egeria visited the Holy Land, there was a coincidence of the fortieth day after Easter with a fixed feast celebrated in Bethlehem, such as, for example, the dedication of the Church of the Nativity, celebrated on May 31,[33] or the feast of the Holy Innocents, celebrated on May 18.[34]

The notion of such a coincidence of a feast with the fortieth day, however, raises the issue of the precedence of a feast of the Lord over the remembrance of a saint.[35] Would not Ascension normally have precedence over the feast of the Holy Innocents? This would support the notion that the fortieth day after Pascha mentioned by Egeria may have nothing to do with Ascension. Cabrol has noted that Egeria did not call the feast "Ascension," and that the celebration took place not on the Mount of Olives, but in Bethlehem—all of which led him to conclude that in Egeria's time the feast of Ascension was still combined with that of Pentecost, as can be seen in Egeria's description of the latter feast.[36] Thus the "fortieth day of Easter" was, in Egeria, an independent solemnity, which Cabrol interprets as being the feast of Annunciation.[37]

We should note that, in chapter 43 of the *Travels*, Egeria tells us that on the fiftieth day, after the assembly at the Anastasis in the morning, the office takes place in the afternoon on Sion (the site of the descent of the Holy Spirit), and then "the gospel passage that recounts the ascension of the Lord" and the passage "from the Acts of the Apostles, which speaks about the ascension of the Lord into the heavens after the resurrection" are read on the Mount of Olives.[38]

---

[32]J.G. Davies, "The Peregrinatio Egeriae and the Ascension," *Vigiliae Christianae* 8 (1954): 96.

[33]Dom E. Dekkers, "De datum der *Peregrination Egeriae* en het feest van Ons Heer hemelvaart," *Sacris Erudiru* I (1948): 181–205. His thesis is summarized in J.G. Davies, "The Peregrinatio Egeriae and the Ascension," *Vigiliae Christianae* 8 (1954): 93–94.

[34]C. Renoux, "Liturgie de Jérusalem et lectionnaires arméniens: Vigiles et année liturgique," in Mgr Cassien-Dom Botte, *La Prière des heures*, LO 35 (Paris, 1963), 197–98.

[35]J. Crehan, "Assumption and the Jerusalem Liturgy," *TS* 30 (1969): 315–16.

[36]Dom Cabrol, *Étude sur la Peregrinatio Silviae: Les églises de Jérusalem, la discipline et la liturgie au IVe siècle* (Paris, 1895), 122–23.

[37]Ibid., 79.

[38]Égérie, *Journal de voyage* 43, 5 (SC 296, p. 300).

The description of Egeria thus reflects the ancient tradition in which the fiftieth day marked the conclusion of the paschal mystery, and in which the Ascension of Christ, the moment at which the Bridegroom left his disciples, was associated with the end of the paschal season, which was marked by the absence of both fasting and kneeling.[39] This is confirmed by other, more ancient, texts. Eusebius of Caesarea, for example, in his treatise *De sollemnitate paschali*, written *c.* 332, writes the following about the 50-day paschal season:

> And the number of the fifty days does not even end with these seven weeks, but, after having gone beyond the seven weeks, he sets the seal to the ultimate unity which follows these [weeks] with the highly festal day of the Ascension of Christ. It is therefore for good reason that, during the holy days of the 50-day season, in image of the future rest, we rejoice in our souls and refresh our bodies, as if henceforth united with the Bridegroom and unable to fast.[40]

Eusebius tells us practically the same thing in another passage drawn from the *Vita* of the Emperor Constantine, composed around 335–340, who died on the day of Pentecost:

> All these events occurred during the great feast, that is, the highly venerable and most holy Pentecost, which is honored during seven weeks and sealed with a unity, during which took place, as the divine books tell us, the ascension into the heavens of our common Savior and the descent of the Holy Spirit on humanity. The emperor was favored to reach this day, the final day of the entire series, which we would not err in calling the feast of feasts. Toward the noon hour, he made his ascent to God.[41]

On the basis of these different texts, S. Salaville concluded early in the twentieth century that the actual celebration of "the fortieth day after Pascha in Egeria" was the feast of the Holy Innocents, and not Ascension.[42] Such was also the view of B. Botte.[43]

---

[39]Égérie, *Journal de voyage* 41 (SC 296, p. 296).

[40]Eusebius of Caesarea, *De sollemnitate paschali* (PG 25, col. 697C).

[41]Eusebius of Caesarea, *De vita Constantini* 1, IV, c. LXIV (PG 20, col. 1220).

[42]S. Sallaville, "La tessarokostê, Ascension et Pentecôte au IVᵉ siècle," *Échos d'Orient* 28 (1929): 267.

[43]B. Botte, *Les Origines de la Noël et de l'Épiphanie* (Louvain, 1932), 17.

In a more recent study, R. Cabié also considers that the fortieth day after Easter in Egeria has nothing to do with Ascension, but is an independent feast, because Ascension was still celebrated on the fiftieth day, with the descent of the Holy Spirit. According to Cabié,

> The liturgy of Jerusalem at the time of Egeria was no doubt at an intermediate state between the earlier practice, which consisted, at the end of the fifty days, of celebrating the global mystery of the glorification of Christ and the effusion of the Spirit, and a later practice, which separates the various elements according to the historical developments of the events of salvation. The Palestinian tradition of Ascension on the fiftieth day, it seems, came up against a topographical conception in the Holy City that was likely born toward the end of the fourth century. It was normal that pilgrims, arriving from throughout the Christian world for feasts, desired to combine their veneration of the holy places with the celebration of the liturgical mystery connected with each place. This would seem all the more legitimate to them, because in their own churches, some celebrated Ascension and Pentecost on different days.[44]

Cabié similarly suggested that the "fortieth day after Easter" in Egeria was the feast of the Holy Innocents.[45]

The Armenian Lectionary, the most ancient manuscript of which cannot date before 417, provides us, in section 167, with an ordo for the Feast of Ascension. This supports the argument that the "historicizing" celebration of Ascension on the fortieth day appeared at some point early in the fifth century, if not during the last years of the fourth century.

C. Renoux explains that

> Ascension, already celebrated in different places at the end of the fourth century (see the second homily of St John Chrysostom on Pentecost delivered in Antioch [PG 50, col. 463]; the sermon *In Ascensione* of Gregory of Nyssa [PG 46, cols. 690–694]), and apparently in Jerusalem, is well-established at the beginning of the fifth century.[46]

---

[44]R. Cabié, *La Pentecôte. L'évolution de la cinquantaine pascale au cours des cinq premiers siècles* (Tournay, 1965), 168.

[45]Ibid., 169.

[46]Renoux, II, 337, note LVII—1.

It is precisely the homily of Gregory of Nyssa for the Feast of Ascension that tells us about the origin of this feast. The patristics scholar Jean Daniélou tells us:

> It is normal that it was after the Council of 381 and in Cappadocia that the transfer took place. Indeed, the main goal of the Council was to define the divinity of the Holy Spirit. From this, we understand that from this moment the primary accent of the feast on the fiftieth day fell on the descent of the Holy Spirit. This is as well the theme of the sermons about Pentecost by Gregory of Nazianzus and Gregory of Nyssa. But from that point the Ascension was no longer solemnized. There were numerous reasons for attaching it to the fortieth day. This day was already important in church life. In addition, the Acts of the Apostles place the Ascension on the fortieth day. [...] The Feast of Ascension on the fortieth day follows the Council of 381. It must even come several years later, if indeed it is a consequence of the concentration on the pouring out of the Holy Spirit on the fiftieth day.[47]

Daniélou sees the confirmation of this thesis in the mention of the Feast of Ascension in the *Apostolic Constitutions*, which originate in the area around Antioch during the last years of the fourth century, as well as in the homily of St John Chrysostom, also delivered in Antioch in 392, according to the dating proposed by Tillemont.[48] Daniélou thus makes St Gregory of Nyssa the initiator of the Feast of Ascension on the fortieth day by dating his homily to the year 388.[49]

This theory of Daniélou thus contradicts Renoux's affirmation that "it is unthinkable that the pilgrim Egeria did not know of Ascension at the end of the fourth century, while the feast existed everywhere in Asia Minor."[50] Indeed, it does appear that the years of her pilgrimage (381–384) corresponded exactly to the gradual spread from Constantinople of the Feast of Ascension on the fortieth day. Thus, we consider that Egeria is the final witness to the Feast of Ascension on the fiftieth day, and that the Armenian

---

[47]J. Daniélou, "Grégoire de Nysse et l'origine de la fête de l'Ascension," in *Kyriakon—Festschrift Johannes Quasten* (eds. P. Granfield and J.A. Jungmann), vol. II (Münster Weste: Verlag Aschendorff, 1970), 664.

[48]Ibid., 664.

[49]Ibid., 666.

[50]Renoux, I, 73, note 32.

Lectionary witnesses to the shift that took place in Jerusalem at the turn of the fourth and fifth centuries.

ORDO

The services of Ascension, one of the twelve great feasts, scrupulously follow the Pentecostarion. The office for the saint in the Menaion is shifted to another day.

At "Lord, I call" in vespers, five stichera from the Pentecostarion are sung, each sung twice, for a total of ten, and then a doxastikon idiomelon at "Glory . . . now and ever." After the entrance, we read three Old-Testament readings for the feast. At the *lite*, the idiomela from the Pentecostarion are sung. The Pentecostarion also contains the aposticha stichera with special verses. At the artoklasia, the festal troparion is sung three times.

At "God is the Lord" in matins, the festal troparion is sung three times. After each kathisma and small synapte, the kathisma troparia are taken from the Pentecostarion. After the polyeleos, the selected verses, and the small synapte, we sing the kathisma troparion from the Pentecostarion. It is then appointed to read the homily of St Andrew of Crete for the feast. Then we sing the first antiphon of the anabathmoi in tone 4 ("From my youth"), followed by the festal prokeimenon and the reading of the festal gospel. After the gospel, "Having beheld the resurrection of Christ" is sung once. Psalm 50 is followed by the post-gospel stichera: "Glory . . . ," "Through the prayers of the apostles," "Now and ever . . . ," "Through the prayers of the Theotokos," "Have mercy on me," and the idiomelon for the feast. After the prayer "O Lord, save your people," two festal canons are sung. The first is attributed to St John of Damascus, the second to Joseph the Hymnographer. At each ode, the hirmoi of the canon of Pentecost are sung as the katabasiai. After the third ode and the small synapte, we sing the kathisma troparion from the Pentecostarion. Following the sixth ode and the small synapte, we sing the kontakion and ikos of the feast from the Pentecostarion, and then read from the Synaxarion of Nicephoras Kallistos Xanthopoulos. As on the other major feasts, the Magnificat is omitted. After the ninth ode, the festal exaposteilarion is sung three times. At the lauds, we sing three stichera idiomela from the Pentecostarion, repeating one of them, "Glory . . . now and ever . . . ," and the festal doxastikon idiomelon. After the singing of the great doxology, the festal troparion is sung. After the matins dismissal, the usual reading of a catechesis of St Theodore the Studite takes place in the narthex.

At the hours, the troparion and kontakion of the feast are read.

At the Divine Liturgy of St John Chrysostom, the festal antiphons are sung (see the Pentecostarion). After the entrance and the festal entrance verse (*eisodikon*), we sing the troparion and kontakion of the feast. After the trisagion come the festal prokeimenon, epistle, Alleluia verses, and gospel. As on all major feasts, the hymn to the Mother of God ("It is truly meet") is replaced by the hirmos of the ninth ode of the canon. The koinonikon is festal. The troparion "We have seen the true light" is replaced by the festal troparion.

The after-feast of Ascension

The after-feast of Ascension continues until Friday of the seventh week. The services combine the offices from the Pentecostarion with those from the Menaion.

At "Lord, I call" in vespers, three stichera from the Menaion (in the case of an office with no sign) are added to 3 from the Pentecostarion. [At vespers on the evening of Ascension, there is an entrance, and, as on the evening of major feasts, the great prokeimenon is sung: "Our God, in heaven and on earth."] At the aposticha, festal stichera are sung (from the Pentecostarion).

At matins, following each kathisma, the kathisma troparion of the feast is used (from the Pentecostarion). After Psalm 50, one of the two festal canons (from the Pentecostarion) is alternated each day, with six troparia, followed by the canon for the saint in the Menaion with four troparia. After the third ode, the kontakion and ikos for the feast are read, and then the kathisma troparion for the saint from the Menaion and the kathisma troparion for the feast (Pentecostarion). After the sixth ode follow the kontakion and ikos of the feast (Pentecostarion). At the ninth ode, the Magnificat is sung. Following the ninth ode, we sing the exaposteilarion of the feast, "Glory . . . ," the exaposteilarion from the Menaion (if there is one), "Now and ever . . . ," and the second festal exaposteilarion. At the aposticha, the festal stichera are sung (from the Pentecostarion).

The Seventh Sunday after Pascha

Sunday of the Holy Fathers of the Council of Nicea

ORIGIN

As S. Salaville has shown, the feasts of the councils in the Byzantine rite originate from the feast of the Fathers of the first six ecumenical councils on the Sunday closest to July 16, which is originally the feast of the Council of Chalcedon. Indeed, after the death of the Monophysite Emperor Anastasius and the ascent to the throne of the Orthodox Emperor Justin I, the populace took advantage of the first appearance of the new sovereign in the Great Church to call for the removal of Severus of Antioch and the restoration of the Council of Chalcedon. When Patriarch John II of Constantinople publicly proclaimed the decisions of the Council of Chalcedon on July 15, 518, the people demanded that he establish a solemn feast, a synaxis of the Council of Chalcedon. Bowing to their demands, on the next day, July 16, 518, the patriarch created a synaxis of the Holy Fathers of Chalcedon, with whom were also associated the Holy Fathers of the earlier Councils of Nicea, Constantinople, and Ephesus. From that time, this decision was included in the liturgical books, which not only mention this feast, but also include the hymnography that was subsequently composed in honor of these Fathers and the theology of these councils. Later, the Sixth Council was added to the list. The Seventh Ecumenical Council was celebrated on the Sunday closest to October 11, a feast found in the eighth century in the Typikon of the Great Church.[51]

The Feast of the 318 Holy God-bearing Fathers of Nicea is also included in this Typikon on the Sunday following Ascension. This date corresponds more or less with the opening of this council, which was held from May 20 to August 25, 325.[52] This feast may well have been instituted in connection with the Feast of Ascension which clearly shows, as Nicephoras

---

[51]S. Salaville, "La fête du concile de Nicée et les fêtes des conciles dans le rite byzantin," *Échos d'Orient* 24 (1924): 445–70; S. Salaville, "La fête du concile de Chalcédoine dans le rite byzantin," in A. Grillmeier and H. Bacht, *Das Konzil von Chalkedon. Geschichte und Gegenwart*, II (Würzburg, 1953), 677–95; A. Grillmeier, *Le Christ dans la tradition chrétienne. Le concile de Chalcédoine (451): reception et opposition*, "Cogitation fidei" 154 (Paris, 1990), 443–47. See also M. Arranz, "Les fêtes théologiques du calendrier byzantin," in *La Liturgie, expression de la foi. Conférences Saint-Serge. XXVᵉ Semaine d'études liturgiques* (Rome, 1979), 48–54.

[52]Héfélé-Leclercq, *Histoire des conciles*, Vol. 1 (Paris, 1907), 417.

Kallistos Xanthopoulos underlines in his Synaxarion, that "the Son of God truly became man, and the perfect man has ascended to heaven as God and sits at the right of his Majesty in the heights." For the fathers of this council "proclaimed him thus, confessing him to be consubstantial with and sharing the same honor as the Father."

ORDO

The services of this Sunday scrupulously follow the Pentecostarion. The office for the saint in the Menaion is transferred to compline (or to another day), except in the case of an office with the polyeleos.

At "Lord, I call" in vespers, we sing 3 resurrectional stichera from the Octoechos, tone 6, also found in the Pentecostarion, three stichera for the Ascension, and four stichera for the Holy Fathers, followed by their doxastikon and the dogmatikon theotokion in tone 6. After the entrance and the evening prokeimenon follow three Old-Testament readings (from the Pentecostarion). At the *lite* we sing the sticheron of Ascension, the doxastikon for the Holy Fathers, and, after "Now and ever . . . ," the idiomelon of Ascension. At the aposticha, we sing the resurrectional stichera from the Octoechos, tone 6, also found in the Pentecostarion, followed by the doxastikon for the Holy Fathers and, after "Now and ever . . . ," the idiomelon of Ascension. At the artoklasia, the troparion "O Mother of God and Virgin" is sung three times.

At "God is the Lord" at matins, we sing the Sunday troparion in tone 6 twice, "Glory . . . ," the troparion of the Holy Fathers, "Now and ever . . . ," the troparion of Ascension. After the first and second kathismata, we sing the kathisma troparia from the Octoechos, tone 6, also found in the Pentecostarion. After Psalm 118, the resurrectional evlogitaria, and the small synapte, we sing the hypakoe and the anabathmoi from the Octoechos, also appearing in the Pentecostarion. After the Sunday morning prokeimenon from the Octoechos, tone 6, also found in the Pentecostarion, the tenth resurrectional matins gospel is read. After "Having beheld the resurrection of Christ" (only one time) and Psalm 50, the usual Sunday stichera are sung. After the prayer "O Lord, save your people," we sing the resurrectional canon from the Octoechos, in tone 6, with four troparia; then the first Ascension canon with four troparia, and the canon for the Holy Fathers (whose acrostic is: "I sing the first synaxis of the pastors") with six troparia. The hirmoi of the canon of Pentecost are sung as the katabasiai. After the third ode, the kontakion and ikos of Ascension are sung, and then the kathisma troparia of the Holy Fathers and the kathisma troparion of Ascension; following the sixth ode, the kontakion and ikos of the Holy Fathers. Then comes the reading from the Synaxarion of Nicephoras Kallistos Xanthopoulos. At the ninth ode, the Magnificat is sung. After the ninth ode, following "Holy is the Lord, our God," tone 6, we sing the exaposteilaria of the tenth resurrection gospel, of the Holy Fathers, and of Ascension. At the lauds, following the four resurrectional stichera from the Octoechos, tone 6, found also in the Pentecostarion, we add three stichera for the Holy Fathers (singing one of them twice) with their doxastikon, then "Now and ever . . . ," and the theotokion: "You are blessed above all, O Mother of God and Virgin." After the great doxology, we sing the resurrectional troparion appointed for the end of Sunday matins: "Having risen from the tomb." After the dismissal, we sing: "Glory . . . now and ever . . . ," and the tenth gospel sticheron, in tone 6. Then the catechesis of St Theodore the Studite is read, followed by the first hour.

At the hours, the Sunday troparion in tone 6 is read, then "Glory . . . ," the troparia of Ascension and of the Holy Fathers alternately, and the kontakia of Ascension and of the Holy Fathers alternately.

At the Divine Liturgy of St John Chrysostom, following the entrance, we sing the Sunday troparion in tone 6, the troparion of Ascension, the troparion of the Holy Fathers, "Glory . . . ," the kontakion of the Holy Fathers, "Now and ever . . . ," and the kontakion of Ascension. The prokeimenon and the Alleluia verses are for the Holy Fathers. The epistle and gospel readings are for the day. Instead of the hymn to the Theotokos, we sing the hirmos of the ninth ode of the canon for Ascension. There are two koinonika: for Sunday ("Praise the Lord from the heavens") and for the Holy Fathers ("Rejoice in the Lord"). The troparion "We have seen the true light" is replaced by the troparion of Ascension.

Services during the Seventh Week of Pascha

Sunday evening at vespers is the closing of the feast of the Holy Fathers. At "Lord, I call," we sing three stichera for the Holy Fathers and three stichera from the Menaion, followed by the doxastikon for the Holy Fathers, "Now and ever . . . ," and an idiomelon for Ascension. At the aposticha, we sing the stichera for the Holy Fathers that were sung at the lauds in Sunday matins, followed by the doxastikon for the Holy Fathers, "Now and ever . . . ," and the idiomelon for Ascension. After the Lord's Prayer, we sing the troparion for the Holy Fathers, "Glory . . . ," the troparion from the Menaion (if one is appointed), "Now and ever . . . ," and the troparion of Ascension.

During the rest of the seventh week until Friday, the services follow the ordo appointed for the after-feast of Ascension (see above).

On Friday, we celebrate the leavetaking of Ascension. The Pentecostarion calls for repeating entirely the office of the feast (shifting the office from the Menaion to compline), except for the entrance, the Old-Testament readings, and the polyeleos.

The Universal Commemoration of All the Dead

On Saturday of the seventh week is appointed the commemoration of "our fathers and brothers, of all deceased, pious Christians who have fallen asleep throughout the ages." The ordo of the services is exactly the same as on Meat-Fare Saturday.

At "Lord, I call" in vespers, we sing three stichera (in honor of the martyrs) from the Octoechos, also found in the Pentecostarion, and three stichera for the dead from the Pentecostarion. The doxastikon is taken from the Pentecostarion, and then, as on all Friday evenings, we sing the dogmatikon theotokion from the Octoechos, tone 6, also found in the Pentecostarion. There is no entrance. Instead of the evening prokeimenon, we sing "Alleluia" in tone 8 with the psalm verses for the dead ("Blessed are those whom you have chosen," "Their souls shall dwell with the righteous"). At the aposticha, we sing the stichera from the Octoechos, tone 6, also appearing in the Pentecostarion, with the psalm verses for the dead. After the Lord's Prayer, the troparion for the dead is sung in tone 8 ("In the depth of wisdom") with its theotokion ("We have a refuge in you").

The Pentecostarion calls the celebration of the panikhida (office for the deceased) after the dismissal of vespers, at which we sing in tone 6 the canon for the dead from the Octoechos (also included in the Pentecostarion). On Athos, vespers and the panikhida are both celebrated at the cemetery.

At matins, we sing "Alleluia" in tone 8 with the psalm verses for the dead ("Blessed are those whom you have chosen," "Their souls shall dwell with the righteous"), then the troparion for the dead in tone 8 ("In the depth of wisdom") twice, followed by its theotokion ("We have a refuge in you"). As on all Saturdays, kathismata 16 and 17 are read. After the first kathisma, we sing the kathisma troparia from the Octoechos, tone 6, also found in the Pentecostarion. As in the office for the dead, kathisma 17 is read with refrains and divided into two stanzas. The priest, accompanied by the deacon, leaves the sanctuary and goes to the memorial table for the dead (on which memorial candles are placed and where many leave the kollyvo or other offerings). The deacon continuously incenses the table. After the first stanza (Ps 118.1–93) follows a litany and a prayer for the dead. The second stanza of the kathisma follows (Ps 118.94–176), after which the evlogitaria troparia for the dead are sung ("The assembly of the saints," etc.). During the evlogitaria, the priest incenses the entire church, preceded by the deacon with a candle. Following the evlogitaria, there is again a litany and a prayer for the dead, and then the kathisma troparion from the Pentecostarion ("Give rest with the righteous"). The priest and deacon then return to the sanctuary.

Psalm 50 is read, and the canon begins: first the canon of the dedication of the church (the feast or the saint after which the church is named) with six troparia; then the canon from the Pentecostarion, attributed to Theodore the Studite, with eight troparia. Note that the canon from the Pentecostarion has a second ode, which is therefore sung with only eight troparia. After the third ode, after the customary small synapte, we sing the kathisma troparion from the Pentecostarion with its theotokion. After the sixth ode, at the singing of the katabasia, the priest and deacon again go out to the memorial table for the dead. The litany and prayer for the dead are repeated, and then the kontakion for the dead is sung ("With the saints give rest"). While the kontakion is sung, the deacon incenses the table from all four sides, and then the iconostasis, the priest, and all the faithful. The celebrants then return to the sanctuary. At the ninth ode, the Magnificat is sung as usual. After the ninth ode, the usual small synapte is said, followed by the exaposteilarion and theotokion from the Pentecostarion.

At the lauds, which are read, we sing four stichera, a doxastikon, and a theotokion, all from the Pentecostarion. The doxology is read. At the aposticha, we sing the stichera for the dead from the Octoechos, tone 6, also in the Pentecostarion, with the psalm verses for the dead ("Blessed are those whom you have chosen," "Their souls shall dwell with the righteous"). After the Lord's Prayer, the troparion for the dead is sung in tone 8 ("In the depth of wisdom") with its theotokion ("We have a refuge in you"). Matins then concludes as on ordinary days.

At the hours and the eucharistic liturgy, the troparion and kontakion for the dead are sung. At the liturgy, a theotokion is added: "We have a refuge in you." The prokeimenon, Alleluia verses, and koinonikon are all for the dead. Two epistles and two gospels are read, for the day and for the dead. Instead of the troparion "We have seen the true light," it is customary among the Russians to sing the troparion for the dead ("In the depth of wisdom"). In Greek practice, as on Holy Saturday, we sing: "Remember us in the Kingdom of Heaven, O compassionate one, as you remembered the thief."

Pentecost

Pentecost Sunday

ORIGIN

As we have already seen, the fiftieth day after Pascha, at least in Jerusalem, originally marked the completion of the paschal season, as Egeria witnesses in her description of the feast of Ascension-Pentecost, which she calls "a very heavy day for the people" in chapter 43 of her account of her journey.[53] After the customary office at the Anastasis in Jerusalem, the community in those days then went to Sion at the third hour of the day, there to commemorate the descent of the Holy Spirit; and then, after taking refreshment and resting, the people went to the Mount of Olives, to the place from which the Lord ascended to heaven, in order to commemorate the Ascension.

By the first half of the fifth century, however, the Armenian Lectionary already indicates two distinct feasts. The office described in section 58[54] commemorates the descent of the Holy Spirit. At the liturgy in the Anastasis, the account of the descent of the Holy Spirit upon the apostles (Acts 2.1–21) was read, as well as the pericope from John (Jn 14.15–24) about the promise of the Lord to send a Paraclete. At the third hour, the people went to Sion to commemorate, at the very place and time, the descent of the Spirit. Then, at the tenth hour, they went to the Mount of Olives where, after the readings, a kneeling prayer, repeated three times, was read. We find here the embryo of the three kneeling prayers at vespers on Pentecost Sunday evening, about which we will speak below.

---

[53]Égérie, *Journal de voyage* 43, 1 (SC 296, p. 298).
[54]Renoux, II, 339.

We should note that the office on the Mount of Olives on the evening of Pentecost described in the Armenian Lectionary is not simply "a kind of conservatism that is rather frequent in liturgical practice," as R. Cabié leads us to believe. Indeed, the words spoken to the apostles at this place on the day of Ascension by "men dressed in white"—"Men of Galilee, why do you stand looking into heaven? This Jesus, who was taken up from you into heaven, will come in the same way as you saw him go into heaven" (Acts 1.11)—give an eschatological character to the Mount of Olives. The Mount of Olives is therefore not simply the place from which the Christ departed, but also the place where he will return. This is what Renoux reminds us about:

> The church on the Mount of Olives, a memorial of the Ascension, was also tied, by the teachings that Jesus pronounced there about himself and on the end time, *to the entire economy of salvation, to his departure for the heavens, to his return in glory, and through these to the expectation of humanity.* [. . .] Facing the destroyed Temple, the church on *Eleona*, to the east of Jerusalem, reminded Christians of the sovereignty of the risen Lord, ascended in glory, and living in a new land from which he will come to draw his people there. It is not from the earthly Jerusalem, but from his Orient, from the heaven to which Jesus went, that salvation will come. Beyond its function as a memorial—to keep the memory of the Ascension—Eleona, to the east of the Holy City, also evoked the entire mystery of Christ and the future of humanity which is tied to him. Eleona, a sign of the *Parousia*, thus reminded the faithful, each time they gathered there, that the Lord, celebrated in this or that particular mystery, was also the one who will come.[55]

The gathering on the Mount of Olives on the afternoon of Pentecost, therefore, shows well that, even after Ascension was split off from this day after the Second Ecumenical Council in order to place greater emphasis on the divinity of the Holy Spirit, the fiftieth day still set the seal on the paschal season and on the entire mystery of salvation. This mystery, in an eschatological perspective, will culminate in the second and glorious coming of Christ, which every Christian of every era confesses and awaits through proper preparation.

[55]C. Renoux, "En tes murs, Jerusalem: Histoire et mystère," in *La Liturgie: son sens, son esprit, sa méthode. Conférences Saint-Serge. XXVIIIᵉ Semaine d'études liturgiques* (Rome, 1982), 259–60.

ORDO

The services of Pentecost scrupulously follow the Pentecostarion.[56] The office for the saint in the Menaion is transferred to another day.

At "Lord, I call" in vespers, we sing eight stichera idiomela from the Pentecostarion (with 2 repeated, for a total of 10), followed by "Glory.. now and ever . . . ," and the doxastikon idiomelon—"Come, O people, let us venerate the tri-hypostatic divinity . . . ," attributed to Emperor Leo the Wise. After the entrance follow three Old-Testament readings. At the *lite*, the stichera idiomela from the Pentecostarion are sung. The Pentecostarion also contains the aposticha stichera, with special verses. The third of these stichera is the hymn "O heavenly King." At the artoklasia, the troparion of the feast is sung three times.

At "God is the Lord" in matins, the festal troparion is sung three times. After each kathisma and small synapte, the kathisma troparia from the Pentecostarion are sung. After the polyeleos and small synapte, the kathisma troparion from the Pentecostarion is sung. Then is prescribed the reading of the sermon of St Gregory the Theologian on Pentecost.[57] This patristic reading, one of the earliest homilies for Pentecost, has inspired the hymnography of the feast, particularly the first sticheron at "Lord, I call" and the canon. The first antiphon of the anabathmoi in tone 4 is then sung ("From my youth"), followed by the festal prokeimenon. Following the reading of the ninth matins resurrectional gospel, which is read, as on feast days, in the middle of the church (in Russian practice) or on the solea (in Greek practice), rather than from the altar table, the sticheron "Having beheld the resurrection of Christ" is not sung, but Psalm 50 is read immediately. We then sing the post-gospel stichera: "Glory . . . ," "Through the prayers of the apostles," "Now and ever . . . ," "Through the prayers of the Theotokos," "Have mercy on me . . . ," and the sticheron "O heavenly King." After the prayer "O Lord, save your people," the two festal canons are sung. The first is attributed to Cosmas of Maioum. Its acrostic repeats the first words of Sermon 41 of St Gregory the Theologian: "We celebrate Pentecost." The second, a canon in iambic verse, is attributed to John of Damascus. Following the third ode and the small synapte, the kathisma troparion from the

[56]On Pentecost in the Orthodox Church, read V. Zander, "La Pentecôte dans l'Église orthodoxe," *Sanctae Ecclesiae* 29 (1948): 83–102; V. Zander, "La Pentecôte dans le rite byzantin," *Irénikon* 5 (1928): 256–61; R. Bornert, "La Pentecôte dans le rite byzantin," *Notes de Pastorale Liturgique* 38 (1962): 9–14.

[57]Grégoire le Théologien, *Discours* 41 (SC 358 [Paris, 1990]), 312–55.

Pentecostarion is sung; after the sixth ode and the small synapte, the kontakion and ikos of the feast from the Pentecostarion, followed by the reading from the Synaxarion of Nicephoras Kallistos Xanthopoulos. The Magnificat is omitted. After the ninth ode, which is sung with its megalynaria, the two exaposteilaria of the feast are sung (the first is sung twice). At the lauds, the three stichera idiomela from the Pentecostarion are each sung twice, then "Glory . . . now and ever . . . ," and the sticheron "O heavenly King." After the great doxology, we sing the festal troparion.

At the hours, the troparion and kontakion of the feast are read.

At the Divine Liturgy of St John Chrysostom, the festal antiphons are sung (see the Pentecostarion). Following the entrance and the special festal entrance verse, we sing the troparion and kontakion of the feast. Instead of the trisagion, "As many as have been baptized into Christ" is sung.[58] The prokeimenon, Alleluia verses, the epistle, the gospel, and the koinonikon are all festal. As on all major feasts, the hirmos of the ninth ode of the canon is sung instead of the hymn to the Theotokos ("It is truly meet").

KNEELING VESPERS

On the afternoon of Pentecost, kneeling vespers is celebrated, a service with several particularities. During this office, seven kneeling prayers are read, arranged in three parts. As we have seen above, the origin of this office is the synaxis that took place in Jerusalem, at the third hour on Pentecost, on Sion. It is common in many places to celebrate this service immediately following the dismissal of the liturgy.

Originally, this service solemnly marked the fact that one could once more pray while kneeling—something that is not done from Pascha to Pentecost. At first, the kneeling service, of Palestinian origin, was adopted in Constantinople as a pious devotion. In the beginning of the eleventh century, these prayers were read after the antiphons of sung vespers. After the fourteenth century, the schema of the cathedral office of the Great Church of Constantinople was incorporated into the monastic vespers of the Palestinian Horologion.[59]

[58]The singing of this chant at the liturgy is explained by the fact that, in Constantinople, baptisms were performed on this day, just as on Pascha. See Matéos, *Typicon*, II, 136–37.

[59]On the evolution of these prayers in Constantinople, see M. Arranz, "Les prières de Gonyklisia ou de la Génuflexion du jour de la Pentecôte dans l'ancien Euchologue byzantin," *OCP* 48 (1982): 92–123. On their Palestinian origin, see especially A. Renoux, "L'office de la génuflexion dans la tradition arménienne," in *Le Saint-Esprit dans la Liturgie. Conférences Saint-Serge 1969*, BELS 8 (Rome, 1977), 149–63.

Special petitions are added to the great synapte at the beginning of vespers, asking that the grace of the Holy Spirit descend on the assembly (see the Euchologion or the Pentecostarion). At "Lord, I call," the three stichera from the lauds of the festal matins are sung, each twice, followed by "O heavenly King." As on the evening of any major feast, there is an entrance, followed by the singing of the great prokeimenon, "Who is so great a God as our God?" After the great prokeimenon, the deacon says: "Again and again, on bended knee, let us pray to the Lord." The assembly kneels for the first time since Easter. The priest (abbot, or bishop), facing the people from the middle of the open holy doors of the iconostasis, then reads the first two kneeling prayers. The deacon then finishes the small synapte and, following the ekphonesis by the priest, continues with the ektene. After the ekphonesis of the priest, the deacon again says: "Again and again, on bended knee, let us pray to the Lord." The assembly kneels once more. The priest, facing the people, then reads the third and fourth kneeling prayers. The deacon then finishes the small synapte. After the ekphonesis by the priest, the prayer "Vouchsafe, O Lord" is read. The deacon again says: "Again and again, on bended knee, let us pray to the Lord." The assembly kneels once more, and the priest reads the fifth, sixth, and seventh kneeling prayers. The deacon finishes the small synapte, the priest says the ekphonesis, and the deacon recites the synapte with demands. At the aposticha, the stichera idiomela from the Pentecostarion are sung. After the Lord's Prayer follows the festal troparion. The dismissal of vespers is particular: "May he who lowered himself . . ." (see the Euchologion, Hieratikon, or Pentecostarion).

That evening at small compline, we read the canon to the Holy Spirit, attributed to Theophanes Graptos, with the acrostic: "I sing the Holy Spirit who fashioned all creation" (this canon is absent from contemporary Greek books). The Monday following Pentecost is indeed called "the day of the Holy Spirit," which is the synaxis of the Feast of Pentecost. As Nicephoras Kallistos Xanthopoulos explains in his Synaxarion, on this day we celebrate "the most holy, life-giving and all-powerful Spirit, God, one of the Holy Trinity, sharing the same honor, consubstantial and glorified together with the Father and the Son." The office of Pentecost is repeated, and the office from the Menaion is transferred to another day. We should note, however, that the ninth-century Typikon of the Great Church indicated for this day "the synaxis of the holy apostles."[60] The only difference is that the polyeleos

[60]Matéos, *Typicon*, II, 140–41.

is not sung. At the Divine Liturgy, we sing the trisagion as usual, and not "As many as have been baptized . . . ." Instead of "It is truly meet," we sing the hirmos of the ninth ode of the second canon, and after communion, we resume singing "We have seen the true light . . . ."

The first week after Pentecost

The after-feast of Pentecost continues until the following Saturday. The services combine the office in the Pentecostarion with that from the Menaion.

At "Lord, I call" in vespers, we sing three stichera for the feast (Pentecostarion), and 3 from the Menaion. All the theotokia are replaced by festal idiomela. The aposticha stichera are taken from the Pentecostarion.

After each kathisma at matins, the festal kathisma troparion is sung (from the Pentecostarion). After Psalm 50, one of the two festal canons (from the Pentecostarion) is sung with eight troparia, followed by the canon for the saint (Menaion) with four troparia. After the third ode, we sing the kontakion, ikos, and kathisma troparion from the Menaion, followed by the kathisma troparion for the feast (Pentecostarion); after the sixth ode, the kontakion and ikos of the feast (Pentecostarion). At the ninth ode, the Magnificat is sung. After the ninth ode, we sing the exaposteilarion from the Menaion and the one for the feast. The aposticha stichera are festal (from the Pentecostarion).

On Saturday, the leavetaking of the feast, the festal office is fully repeated (except for the Old-Testament readings, the *lite*, the polyeleos, and the matins gospel). The office from the Menaion is shifted to another day.

The First Sunday after Pentecost

The Sunday of All Saints

ORIGIN

The Synaxarion of Nicephoras Kallistos Xanthopoulos (fourteenth century) gives us three reasons why the Orthodox Church commemorates all the saints in connection with the descent of the Holy Spirit, on the first Sunday following Pentecost. First, to show that the Holy Spirit is the source of sanctity; second, to commemorate all the saints from the past and from the future, known and unknown; third, to demonstrate that all the saints we celebrate are united in Christ. Further, Nicephoras Kallistos notes that the feast of all the saints, which completes the Triodion-Pentecostarion cycle, shows how the divine economy is accomplished:

> For the Triodion, in summary, includes in detail everything that God has done for us through ineffable words. The first account [of the Triodion] is the fall of the Devil from the heavens, the expulsion of Adam and sin. [Then follows] the entire economy of God the Word on our behalf, and how we have again ascended to heaven thanks to the Holy Spirit, and how we have fulfilled the order that was destroyed, as can be recognized in all the saints. We should know that today we celebrate all those whom the Spirit has sanctified by his grace . . . .[61]

Nicephoras Kallistos, in his Synaxarion, also gives us the historical reason for the institution of this final solemnity in the Pentecostarion. According to him, Leo VI the Wise (886–912) wanted to build a church in honor of his wife, Theophano, who, despite her external appearance as the empress, led a life of asceticism, and who, after her death in 893, accomplished numerous miracles through her relics, which were placed in the Church of the Twelve Apostles. Having built a large and magnificent church very close to the Church of the Twelve Apostles, the emperor said to himself that it would not be fitting to consecrate this church to the one who had only recently, until her death, been the empress.

> The wise emperor then dedicated the church he had just built to all the saints in the universe, in accordance with a conciliar decision of the entire Church, saying to himself: "If Theophano is holy, let her be united with all the saints."[62]

ORDO

The services on this Sunday scrupulously follow the Pentecostarion. The office for the saint in the Menaion is transferred to compline (or to another day), unless it is an office with the polyeleos. This is the final office in the Pentecostarion. The hymns taken from the Octoechos are in tone 8. Thus an

[61]On the Sunday of All Saints, see I. Fundulis, "Prazdnik vsekh sviatykh," *Vechnoe* 333 (1976): 19–24.

[62]On the Church of All Saints in Constantinople, see R. Janin, *La Géographie ecclésiastique de l'empire byzantin*, Part 1, Vol. III (Paris, 1969), 389–90; G. Downey, "The Church of All Saints (Church of St Theophano) near the Church of the Apostles at Constantinople," *DOP* 9–10 (1956): 301–05.

Octoechos cycle is also completed during the 50-day paschal period, with tone 7 omitted. Beginning on the second Sunday after Pentecost, the usual Octoechos cycle resumes, beginning with tone 1, with all the tones succeeding one another, with no omission, until the following Easter.

At "Lord, I call" in vespers, we sing six stichera from the Octoechos, tone 8, also found in the Pentecostarion (3 for the resurrection and 3 "anatolika"), followed by four stichera for all saints, a doxastikon for all saints, and the dogmatikon theotokion in tone 8. After the entrance and the evening prokeimenon follow three Old-Testament readings for the feast. At the *lite*, the stichera of the church are sung and the idiomela for all saints. The aposticha stichera are resurrectional from the Octoechos, tone 8, also found in the Pentecostarion, to which is added the doxastikon for all saints. At the artoklasia, the troparion "O Mother of God and Virgin" is sung twice, followed once by the troparion of all saints.

At "God is the Lord" in matins, we sing the Sunday troparion in tone 8 twice, "Glory . . . ," the troparion of all saints, tone 4, "Now and ever . . . ," the Sunday theotokion, tone 4. After the first and second kathismata, we sing the kathisma troparia from the Octoechos, tone 8, also found in the Pentecostarion. Psalm 118 is sung, followed by the resurrectional evlogitaria. After the small synapte, the hypakoe from the Octoechos, tone 8 (also found in the Pentecostarion) is read, followed by the kathisma troparion for all saints. The anabathmoi and the Sunday matins prokeimenon from the Octoechos, tone 8 (also found in the Pentecostarion), are then sung, followed by the reading of the first resurrection matins gospel (read at the altar table in the sanctuary). Starting on this Sunday, we begin to read the 11 resurrectional matins gospels, one after the other, each Sunday until the following Pascha. After the singing of "Having beheld the resurrection of Christ" (only once), Psalm 50 is read, followed by the usual Sunday stichera. After the prayer "O Lord, save your people," we sing the resurrectional canon with four troparia, the canon of the Cross and the Resurrection with two troparia, and the canon for the Mother of God with two troparia, all taken by the Pentecostarion from the Octoechos, tone 8, to which is added the canon for all saints with six troparia (whose acrostic is: "I sing the orders of all the saints with many names." The hirmoi of the canon for the Mother of God ("My mouth will open") are sung as the katabasiai. After the third ode, we sing the kontakion and ikos of the resurrection, followed by the kathisma troparia of all saints; after the sixth ode, the kontakion and ikos of all saints, and then the reading from the Synaxarion of Nicephoras Kallistos Xantho-poulos. At the ninth ode, the Magnificat is sung. After the ninth ode, we sing "Holy is the Lord, our God" in tone 8, followed by the exaposteilarion of the first resurrectional gospel and the exaposteilarion of all saints with its theotokion. At the lauds, we sing five stichera from the Octoechos, also found in the Pentecostarion (four resurrectional and one "anatolika"), fol-lowed by three stichera for all saints, "Glory . . . ," the eothinon idiomelon of the first resurrectional gospel, "Now and ever . . . ," and the theotokion: "You are most blessed, O Mother of God and Virgin." After the great doxology, we sing the resurrectional troparion appointed for the end of Sunday matins: "Today salvation has come to the world."

At the hours, we read the Sunday troparion in tone 8, "Glory . . . ," the troparion for all saint, and the kontakion for all saints.

At the Divine Liturgy of St John Chrysostom, following the entrance, we sing the Sunday troparion in tone 8, the troparion of all saints, "Glory . . . now and ever . . . ," and the kontakion of all saints. The prokeimena, Alleluia verses, and the koinonika are taken from both the Octoechos, tone 8, and for the feast, from the Pentecostarion. The epistle and gospel readings are for all saints.

The Apostles' Fast

A rubric in the Pentecostarion at the end of the offices of Pentecost speci-fies that, throughout the week after Pentecost, eggs, cheese, fish, wine, and oil are permitted at table. The fast is therefore suppressed during the entire week, and lay persons may even eat meat. This rubric is not found in the Pentecostaria or Typika of Sabaite redaction. It is also absent from the Typ-ikon of Alexios the Studite. This can be explained by the fact that the latter Typikon gave such a dispensation for the entire 50-day paschal period.[63]

Indeed, in conformity with the ancient tradition of the Church, the 50-day paschal period was a time of rejoicing, during which both fasting and kneeling were eliminated. Egeria,[64] St John Cassian,[65] as well as Canon 20 of the Council of Nicea,[66] all testify to this. However, the week immediately

---

[63]Pentkovskii, *Tipikon*, 261, 378.

[64]Égérie, *Journal de voyage* 41 (SC 296, pp. 296–97). She does not mention the elimina-tion of kneeling.

[65]Jean Cassien, *Conférences*, XXI, 11 (SC 64 [Paris, 1959], 85–86).

[66]Canon 20 of Nicea states: "Because there are some who kneel on Sunday and during the time of Pentecost, the holy council has decided that, in order to follow a uniform prac-

after Pentecost,[67] or its octave,[68] marked a return to regular observance with the resumption of fasting.

The fast, which originally lasted one week,[69] later developed into a fast of several days. Around the year 700, three fasting periods were observed in church discipline: Great Lent, the apostles' fast following Pentecost, and the fast before Christmas. Various commentators have seen this as a parallel with the three fasting periods during the year prescribed by the Lord to Moses at the Exodus. According to some sources, the apostles' fast that was prolonged to last 40 days was even extended to the Feast of Dormition (August 15). That is the point at which the Church exercised "economy" and created two separate fasts: the apostles' fast, lasting until the feast of the Apostles Peter and Paul, and the Dormition fast (from August 1 to 14).[70]

Thus, in conformity with ancient Church tradition, fasting resumes on Monday following the Sunday of All Saints and continues until the feast of Peter and Paul on June 29. This is what Patriarch Michael II of Constantinople explains in a letter attributed to him (c. 1143–c. 1146), seeking to justify a genuinely apostolic tradition:

> The apostles' fast is observed as follows: because the apostles fasted for seven days after the descent of the Holy Spirit, this practice was handed down to the church as a model. Later, after the apostles were consumed by martyrdom on June 29, because the fast fell during this time, it was decided to observe it until the day of their feast. This is why the number of days of this fast was not fixed, as it is for the other penitential periods, its length being subordinated to the liturgical cycle, that is, to the date of Easter. Indeed, it often lasts only nine days, which corresponds more or less to the length of the fast observed by the apostles.[71]

Called the "apostles' fast," it is attested by both the Studite[72] and neo-Sabaite traditions.

tice in all dioceses, all should address their prayers to God while remaing standing." See P.-P. Joannou, *Discipline générale antique* (Fonti, fasc. 9), vol. 1, 1 (Rome, 1962), 41.

[67]Égérie, *Journal de voyage* 44, 1 (SC 296, p. 305).

[68]*Apostolic Constitutions*, Book 8, 20, 14 (SC 329 [Paris, 1986], 282–83).

[69]Ibid.

[70]On this question, read the thorough article by V. Grumel, "Le jeûne de l'Assomption dand l'Église grecque," *Échos d'Orient* 32 (1933): 162–94. On fasts in the Orthodox Church, see also I. Mansvetov, *O postakh pravoslavnoi vostochnoi Tserkvi* (Moscow, 1886).

[71]Michel II, "Au sujet de jeûne des saints apôres," I. Oudot, *Patriarchatus Constantinopoli, Acta Selecta I*, Fonti, Series II, fasc. III (Rome, 1941), 28–29.

[72]Pentkovskii, *Tipikon*, 261, 275.

The more rigorous Sabaite tradition, however, reintroduced fasting on Wednesdays and Fridays during the paschal period, except for the week following Easter and the week after Pentecost. To compensate for this, this tradition granted a dispensation from fasting during the week after Pentecost.[73]

Just as the Nativity fast, the apostles' fast is less rigorous than the fast before Dormition. In monasteries, on Tuesdays and Thursdays, oil is permitted, and there are two meals. On Saturdays and Sundays, fish is eaten, and oil and wine are consumed.

[73]We read, for example: "Beginning on Monday after Thomas Sunday, after having read the third and sixth hours according to their ordo, as well as the intermediary hours and the typika, it is appropriate to allow the brethren, on Monday, Wednesday, and Friday of the 50 days, to eat only two biscuits. It is only after the ninth hour that it is permitted to eat fully. The same applies on the eves of Christmas and Theophany when these fall on a Saturday or a Sunday. On the Sunday of the Descent of the Holy Spirit, there is kneeling at vespers and, on the week that follows, it is permitted to eat fish, cheese, eggs, and milk, and for the laity to eat meat, until the Sunday of All Saints." *Typikon*, ch. 32 (Moscow, 1906), 39.

Glossary

Acrostic: [Gk. ἀκροστιχίς; Sl. κρλεϛтро́чїє or κρλεгрλнє́сїє] The initial letters of a series of *troparia* which, when combined, form a sentence.

After-feast: [Gk. μεθεόρτα; Sl. попра́зднϛтво] The period following a major feast during which the festal office continues to be sung until the *leavetaking*. Some after-feasts last for an entire octave (eight days).

Agrypnia: [Gk. ἀγρυπνία; Sl. бдѣнїє] According to the Sabaite Typikon, the office of the *all-night vigil*, consisting of *great vespers*, a reading, and *matins* with the *polyeleos*, celebrated on the eve of Sundays and great feasts.

Akathist: [Gk. ἀκάθιστος; Sl. ἀκάдᲈнϛт᲎] A hymn consisting of thirteen *kontakia* and twelve *ikoi* sung while the people stand, as its name indicates. The best known akathist is the Akathist to the Mother of God, sung on the fifth Saturday of Great Lent, which is the prototype for all akathists.

Akolouthia: [Gk. ἀκολουθία; Sl. посл'ѣдоклнїє] A term signifying the unfolding of a service. It can signify the ordo of an office, or the body of hymnography constituting an office.

Alleluia: [Heb. Hallelujah; Gk. ἀλληλούϊα; Sl. ἀллнл᲎їλ] A term literally meaning "Praise the Lord." 1) It can designate the office called "Alleluia," i.e., the office on fast days when "God is the Lord" is not sung at matins, but instead Alleluia with psalm verses sung by the *canonarch*. 2) It can also refer to the doxology: "Alleluia, alleluia, alleluia, glory to you, O God."

All-night vigil: [Sl. ксено́щноє бдѣнїє] See *Agrypnia*.

Alphabetical, Stichera: [Gk. ἀλφαβήτου; Sl. по ἀлфλкн́т᲎] A series of *stichera* sung at Saturday evening vespers, the first letter of each in alphabetical order.

Ambo: [Gk. ἄμβων; Sl. ἀмко́н᲎] Originally, a raised platform in the center of the church where readings were done. In contemporary usage, the central part of the *solea* in front of the *holy doors*.

Amomoi: [Gk. ἄμομοι; Sl. непорóчны] A term designating *kathisma* 17 (Ps 118).

Anabathmoi: [Gk. ἀναβαθμοί; Sl. стєпéнны] Graduals. *Antiphonal* hymns, distributed in the eight tones of the *Octoechos*, composed on the basis of the gradual psalms (Pss 119-133) and sung at festal matins before the *prokeimenon* and the gospel reading. On Sundays, the anabathmoi are sung in the tone of the Sunday, while on feast days, the first *antiphon* of the anabathmoi in tone 4 is sung.

Antidoron: [Gk. ἀντίδωρον; Sl. антїдѡ́рх] A term literally meaning "instead of the gift." The bread distributed by the priest at the end of the Divine *Liturgy*, consisting of the remains of the *prosphora* used at the *proskomide*.

Antimension: [Gk. ἀντι + Lat. *mensa*; Sl. антїмѝнсх] A term originally designating the cover of a tomb, later the altar erected over the tomb of a martyr, and finally the altar table. A silk or linen cloth, about 40 x 60 cm, on which is represented the burial of Christ, consecrated and signed by the local bishop and containing the parcel of a relic, thus constituting a portable altar.

Antiphon: [Gk. ἀντίφωνον; Sl. антїфѡ́нх] 1) Psalm (or group of hymns) appointed to be sung *antiphonally*. 2) One of the three sections constituting a *kathisma* and concluding with a doxology.

Antiphonally: See "With two *choirs*."

Apodeipnon: [Gk. ἀπόδειπνον; Sl. повечéрїє] See *Compline*.

Apolytikion: [Gk. ἀπολυτίκιον; Sl. тропáрь ѿпУститнтельный] A hymn, generally brief, sung at the end of *vespers*, and at the beginning and end of *matins*.

Aposticha: [Gk. ἀπόστιχα; Sl. на стїхóвнѣ] *Stichera* accompanied by psalm verses [Gk. στίχοι; Sl. стїхѝ] sung at the end of *vespers* during the entire year and at the end of non-festal *matins*.

Artoklasia: [Gk. ἀρτοκλασία; Sl. блгословéнїє хлѣ́бовх or хлѣ́бница] The blessing of bread, wheat, wine, and oil at the end of *vespers* at a *vigil*.

Artophorion: [Gk. ἀρτοφορίον; Sl. дарохранйітельннца] A box, often shaped like a church, used to contain the consecrated gifts reserved for the communion of the sick or for the *Presanctified Liturgy*.

Automelon: [Gk. αὐτόμελον; Sl. (само)подóбенх] A hymn serving as the rhythmic and melodic model for other hymns (called *prosomia*, meaning "based on").

Baptistery: [Gk. λουτῆρ; Sl. крͣтйлнцɪе] The place, generally adjacent to the *narthex*, housing the baptismal fonts, where baptisms and the blessing of water are celebrated.

Beatitudes: [Gk. μακαρισμοί; Sl. блжéнны] Verses taken from the Sermon on the Mount (Mt 5.3-12) beginning with the word "Blessed," sung at the *typika* and at the *liturgy*, which are intercalated with troparia from the *Octoechos* (troparia of the Beatitudes) or troparia taken from the canon of festal *matins*.

Canon: [Gk.κανών; Sl. канώнх] A hymnographic composition consisting of *hirmoi* and *troparia*. The latter were originally intercalated between the verses of the nine *biblical canticles*. This explains why the canons consist of nine *odes*, the second usually absent, because the second biblical canticle is only sung during *Great Lent*. Some canons, however, contain only four odes [tetra-ode], or three odes [tri-ode], or of two odes [di-ode].

Canonarch: [Gk. κανονάρχης; Sl. каноніáрхх] The *chanter* appointed to chant (from the center of the church) certain psalm refrains and to proclaim their verses.

Canticles, biblical or of Moses: [Gk. ᾠδή; Sl. пѣснь] The nine biblical canticles constituting the structure of the *canon* of *matins* and contained in the Palestinian *Psalter*: 1) the canticle of Moses (Ex 15.1-19; 2) the canticle of Moses (Dt 32.1-43); 3) the prayer of Hannah (1 Kgs 2.1-10); 4) the prayer of Habakkuk (Hab 3.1-19); 5) the prayer of Isaiah (Is 26.9-20); 6) the prayer of Jonah (Jonah 2.3-10); 7) the prayer of the three youths (Dan 3.26-56; 8) the canticle of the three youths (Dan 3.57-88); 9) The Magnificat and the Benedictus (Lk 1.46-55, 68-79).

Chanter: [Gk. ὑμνωδός; Sl. пѣвéцх] The person leading the singing of the *choir*, or appointed to perform a reading (see *Reader* and *Canonarch*).

Cheese-Fare Week or Sunday: [Gk. τυροφάγου; Sl. сыропꙋстнаа] The eighth week before Pascha. The last week (or the last Sunday) before the beginning of Great Lent, during which the laity already abstain from meat, but the consumption of eggs and dairy products is permitted, even on Wednesday and Friday.

Cherubikon: [Gk. χερυβικόν; Sl. херꙋвнмскаа пѣснь] The Hymn of the Cherubim, sung during the Great Entrance in the Divine *Liturgy*.

Choir: [Gk. κλῆρος; Sl. клнросъ or лнкъ] A term designating the place, to the left and right of the *iconostasis*, where the *chanters* stand during the *office*. A number of chants are performed "with two choirs," or "antiphonally," indicating that each of the choirs, in turn, sings a verse.

Compline: [Gk. ἀπόδειπνον; Sl. повечеріе] The office following *vespers* and, usually, the evening meal. Great compline is distinguished from small compline.

Diakonika: [Gk. διακονικά; Sl. дїаконествꙗ] See *Ektene*; *Synapte*.

Diataxis: [Gk. διάταξις; Sl. оуставъ] The prescribed order for a service. Ordo.

Dismissal: [Gk. ἀπόλυσις; Sl. ѡтпꙋстъ] The liturgical formula of dismissal at the conclusion of an *office*, consisting of the final blessing by the celebrating priest.

Diptychs: [Gk. δίπτυχα; Sl. днптнхъ] A book in which are inscribed the names of the living and the dead commemorated during the Divine *Liturgy*.

Diskos: [Gk. δισκάριον; Sl. днскосъ] A liturgical vessel, shaped like a plate with a pedestal, used to hold the holy bread (lamb). Paten.

Doors, Holy: [Gk. ἀγίαι θυραί or ἀγίαι πυλάι; Sl. стыа дверн] The central doors of the *iconostasis*, leading to the *altar table*. Not to be confused with the *Royal Doors*.

Doors, Royal: [Gk. βασίλειαι θυραί or βασίλειαι πυλάι; Sl. цѧрскїа вратꙗ] The central doors between the *narthex* and the nave.

Doxastikon: [Gk. δοξαστικόν; Sl. славннкъ] *Sticheron* sung after "Glory to the Father...."

Ecclesiarch: [Gk. ἐκκλησιάρχης; Sl. є̀кклнсїа́рхъ] The person responsible to watch over the good order of the *offices* (see *Typikarist*) and often replacing the *higoumenos* (or the superior) in his absence.

Eisodikon: [Gk. εἰσοδικόν; Sl. входно́є] Psalm verse chanted during the small entrance at the Divine *Liturgy*.

Ekphonesis: [Gr. ἐκφώνησις; Sl. во́зглаⷭъ] A doxological formula, said aloud by the priest, which concludes a *synapte* or an *ektene*.

Ektene: [Gk. ἐκτενής; Sl. є̀ктенїа́ (ѹ̀сѹ́гѹбаⷶ)] A collection of short sentences by which the deacon (or, in his absence, the priest) invites the assembly to pray for various intentions, and to which the assembly (or the *choir*) responds with a triple "Lord, have mercy" (*Kyrie eleison*). See *Diakonika*, *Synapte*.

Eothinon: See *Matins Gospel*.

Evlogitaria: [Gk. εὐλογητάρια; Sl. бл҃гослове́нны] *Troparia* in honor of the resurrection or in memory of the dead sung after Psalm 118, with the refrain "Blessed are you, O Lord, teach me your statutes" (Ps 118.12).

Exaposteilarion: [Gk. ἐξαποστειλάριον; Sl. є̀ѯапостїла́рїй] Literally meaning "hymn of sending out" (from the Greek ἐξαποστέλλω), synonymous with *photagogikon*. This hymn gets its name from its content, not its place in the *office*. It alludes to the sending out of the apostles after the Resurrection (on Sunday) or of the light (during the week), and not to the dismissal of the community. The expression "matins exaposteilarion" (Sl. є̀ѯапостїла́рїй оу́треннїй) designates one of the eleven hymns attributed to Emperor Constantine Porphyrogenitos and sung following the *canon* at Sunday *matins*, accompanying the reading of one of the eleven resurrectional gospels.

Fast: [Gk. νηστεία; Sl. по́стъ] 1) An ascetical practice consisting of abstinence from certain kinds of food (meat, eggs and dairy products, fish, wine, and oil) or from all food. 2) A type of *office* celebrated on fast days and consisting of a large number of *prostrations*, the singing of *Alleluia* at the beginning of *matins*, and the reading of the Prayer of St Ephrem, accompanied by prostrations, at the conclusion of each office, following a particular order. 3) A synonym of *Great Lent*.

Feast of the Lord: [Gk. δεσποτική; Sl. гд҃скїй] The great feasts of the Lord are: the Exaltation of the Cross, the Nativity, Theophany, the Entrance into Jerusalem, Ascension, Pentecost, and Transfiguration.

God is the Lord: [Gk. θεὸς κύριος; Sl. бг҃ъ гд҃ь] A selection of psalm verses from Psalm 117 sung by the *canonarch* at the beginning of *matins*, with Psalm 117.26, 25, as the refrain. Generally speaking, this expression indicates the festal *office*, as distinct from what was once the usual *office*, kept today only on fast days and referred to as the *office* with *Alleluia*.

Gospel sticheron: [Gk. στιχηρά τῶν ἑωθινῶν εὐαγγελίων; Sl. стїхира ҁѵльскаа] One of the eleven hymns attributed to Leo VI, the Wise, each connected to one of the eleven resurrectional *matins* gospels.

Hegoumenos: [Gk. ἡγούμενος; Sl. иг꙼менъ) The superior or abbot of a monastery.

Hexapsalmos: [Gk. ἐξάψαλμος; Sl. шестоѱалмїе] The six psalms (3, 37, 62, 87, 102, and 142) read every day at the beginning of *matins*.

Hirmos: [Gk. εἱρμός; Sl. ірмосъ] A term that in Greek literally means a "link." The hymn opening each *ode* of the *canon*, thus creating the "link" between the biblical *canticle* and the hymnography.

Hour: [Gk. ὥρα; Sl. часъ] An *office* composed of three psalms, hymns, and prayers, read at a particular time during the day. There exist the first hour (prime), the third hour (terce), the sixth hour (sext), and the ninth hour (none).

Hypakoe: [Gk. ὑπακοή; Sl. ѵпакои] From the Greek "ὑπακούω," meaning "to listen attentively." A hymn sung on Sunday after the Trinitarian *canon* during the *mesonyktikon* (midnight office) and following the *evlogitaria* (resurrectional troparia) of *matins*. The *offices* on great feasts also sometimes contain an hypakoe after the third ode of the *canon*.

Iconostasis: [Gk. εἰκονοστάσιον; Sl. іконостасъ] Row(s) of icons separating the sanctuary from the nave. At the center of the iconostasis, the *holy doors* lead to the holy *Table*.

Idiomelon: [Gk. ἰδιόμελον; Sl. самоглаѵенъ] A sticheron with its own rhythmic structure and its own melody, which is not imitated by other stichera.

Ikos: [Gk. οἶκος; Sl. ἴκοϲх] Hymn following the kontakion.

Indiction: [Gk. ἰνδικτιών; Sl. ἰнди́кꞩх] beginning of the ecclesiastical year, September 1. Originally, the indiction corresponded to the fixing of the annual tax in the Roman Empire.

Intermediate Hour: [Gk. μεσώριον; Sl. межд̆очáꙓïе] An *office* read between two of the *hours* on certain days of the year, following one of the *hours*.

Katabasia: [Gk. καταβασία; Sl. катавáꙓïл] The *hirmos* sung at the end of the third, sixth, eighth, and ninth odes of the *canon* at *matins* (and at the end of each ode on feast days) as the conclusion of the ode. The term comes from the Greek "καταβαίνω," meaning "to go down," because, originally, the two *choirs* would go down from their places and come together in the center of the church to execute this chant.

Kathisma: [Gk. κάθισμα; Sl. кад̆íꙓмл] One of the twenty sections of the Palestinian *Psalter*.

Kathisma troparion: [Gk. κάθισμα; Sl. с̓ѣд̆áленх] A *troparion* following the reading of a *kathisma* or a section of the *canon*, during which it is permitted to sit.

Koinonikon: [Gk. κοινωνικόν; Sl. прꙑчáстенх] Communion verse. Psalm verse sung at the Divine *Liturgy* during the communion of the clergy (and the faithful).

Kollyvo: [Gk. κόλλυβα; Sl. коли́ко] A platter of boiled wheat grains with honey, offered in memory of a saint or a dead person.

Kontakion: [Gk. κοντάκιον; Sl. конд̆áкх] Hymn sung after the sixth *ode* of the *canon* at *matins*.

Lauds: [Gk. αἶνοι; Sl. χвали́те] The morning psalms (148, 149, and 150) read or sung daily at the end of *matins*. The name comes from the verb "to praise," which is repeated many times in the psalms. On feast days, *stichera* are intercalated between the verses of these psalms.

Leavetaking: [Gk. ἀπόδοσις; Sl. ѿд̆áнïе] The last day of the *after-feast*, which brings to an end the festal period following a major feast, and on which the festal *office* is repeated almost entirely.

Lent, Great or Holy: [Gk. τεσσαρακοστή; Sl. ЧЕТЫРЕДЕСА́ТНИЦА] The period of fasting beginning on the seventh week before Pascha. Note that Holy Week is not, properly speaking, part of the forty-day Great Lent.

"Let every breath": [Gk. πᾶσα πνοή; Sl. ВСА́КОЕ ДЫХА́НЇЕ] 1) The singing of the *lauds* at festal *matins*, beginning with the singing of the verse "Let every breath praise the Lord" (Ps 150.5). 2) The singing of the verse, "Let every breath praise the Lord" (Ps 150.5) as a fixed *prokeimenon*, with the verse, "Praise him in his saints, praise him in the firmament of his power" (Ps 150.1), after the *matins prokeimenon*. This last practice reminds us that, in the sung office, the gospel was read at the end of *matins,* after the *lauds*.

Lighter of the lamps: [Gr. κανδηλάπτης; Sl. КАНДИЛОВЖИГА́ТЕЛЬ] The person appointed to light the lamps in the church. Generally synonymous with *parecclesiarch*.

Lite: [Gk. λιτή; Sl. ЛИТЇА́] A procession, often including an intercessory *ektene*. There is a *lite* at the end of *vespers* at a *vigil*. The assembly generally processes to the *narthex* while singing the *lite stichera*, after which the deacon recites the long litany of intercession. There can also be a *lite* at the end of *matins*, and this is the time at which prayers are offered for the dead. Because of this, the term *"lite"* is often used to refer to a short *office* of intercession for the dead.

Liturgy: [Gk. λειτουργία; Sl. ЛЇТУ́РГІА] A term generally used to refer to the eucharistic Divine Liturgy.

Liturgy, complete: [Gk. λειτουργία τελεία; Sl. ПО́ЛЬНАА ЛЇТУ́РГІА] An expression referring to the regular eucharistic Divine Liturgy, i.e., with the anaphora and the consecration of the holy gifts, as opposed to the *Presanctified Liturgy*.

Liturgy, vesperal: [Gk. λειτουργία ἑσπερινή; Sl. ЛЇТУ́РГІА ВЕЧЕ́РНА) Divine *Liturgy* that begins with *vespers* because of a strict fast day. For example, on the eves of Christmas and Theophany, Holy Thursday, and Holy Saturday.

Lord, I call: [Gk. κύριε ἐκέκραξα; Sl. ГДИ ВОЗЗВА́ХЪ] An expression containing the first words of the evening psalms (Pss 140, 141, 129, and 116), sung daily at *vespers*. The final verses of these psalms are intercalated with *stichera*.

Martyrikon: [Gk. μαρτυρικόν; Sl. мⷱченⷩичен҇ъ] Hymn in honor of the holy martyrs.

Matins: [Gk. ὄρθρος; Sl. оу҇трена] Morning *office*, celebrated after the midnight office, before the rising of the sun.

Matins Gospel: [Gk. ἑωθινὸν εὐαγγέλιον; Sl. ꙅ҇лїе восⷦрⷩно] One of the eleven resurrectional gospels read at Sunday *matins*.

Meat-Fare Week or Sunday: [Gk. ἀποκρέω; Sl. мⷶсопꙋ҇стная] The ninth week before Easter, concluding with the eighth Sunday before Pascha. The last week during which meat is permitted.

Megalynarion: [Gk. μεγαλυνάριον; Sl. велⷩичⷶнїе] 1) Refrain accompanying the singing of the ninth *ode* of the *canon* of certain feasts. 2) Refrain accompanying the singing of selected psalm verses following the *polyeleos*.

Menaion: [Gk. μηναῖον; Sl. мⷩнеⷶ] The liturgical book for the fixed annual cycle. From the Greek word "μήν," meaning "month," the book containing the hymnography for each day of the month. There are twelve such volumes, one for each month of the year.

Menologion: [Gk. μηνολόγιον; Sl. мⷱсⷶцесло́въ] See *Synaxarion*.

Mesonyktikon: [Gk. μεσονυκτικόν; Sl. полꙋ҇нощⷩница] Midnight office.

Metania: [Gk. μετάνοια; Sl. поклонъ or метⷶнїе] Prostration. A small metania is a prostration made by touching the floor with one's hand. A full prostration is one in which one's head touches the floor, implying a bending of the knees. We should note that, in this book, the expression "three full prostrations" sometimes implies that they accompany the Prayer of St Ephrem.

Narthex: [Gk. νάρθηξ; Sl. прⷩитво́ръ] The vestibule at the western end of the church, separated from the central nave by the *royal doors*. It is customarily here that the *midnight office, the hours,* and *compline* are read, and where the *lite* at *vigil* is celebrated.

Nekrotikon: [Gk. νεκρώσιμον; Sl. покойⷩн or мⷡртвенъ] Hymn in honor of the dead.

Octoechos: [Gk. ὀκτώηχος; Sl. Ѻктоⷩихъ] Book of eight *tones* or modes. This book contains the hymnography for each day of the week, in a cycle of eight weeks, each corresponding to a tone.

Ode: [Gk. ᾠδή; Sl. пѣснь] One of the divisions of the canon, consisting of an *hirmos* and *troparia*, originally accompanying the verses of a *biblical canticle*. NB: We use the term "ode" for the hymnographic material, and the term "canticle" for the biblical material, even though this distinction does not exist in either Greek or Slavonic.

Office: [Sl. слꙋжба] See *Akolouthia*.

Orthros: [Gk. ὄρθρος] See *Matins*.

Paramone: [Gk. παραμονή; Sl. навечеріе] A Greek term literally meaning eve, vigil, urgent expectation. Used for the eves of the Nativity of Christ and Theophany, during which everyone fasts strictly while awaiting the feast.

Paraecclesiarch: [Gk. παραεκκλησιάρχης; Sl. параекклисіар́хъ] The person responsible for the functions in the sanctuary. Sacristan. See the *Lighter of the lamps*.

Paremia: [Gk. παρειμία; Sl. паремі́а] A term generally used to designate an Old Testament reading at *vespers*. On occasion, this reading can be taken from the New Testament. See *Prophecies*.

Paschal period: [Gk. πεντηκοστή; Sl. пѧтьдесѧ́тница] The festal period of fifty festal days, from Pascha to Pentecost.

People: [Gk. λαός; Sl. лю́діе] A term referring to the liturgical assembly.

Permission: [Gk. κατάλυσις; Sl. разрѣше́ніе] A term designating a moderation of a fasting rule, thus allowing, generally because of a feast, the consumption of certain foods which are normally not permitted, such as wine, oil, and fish. Dispensation.

Photagogikon: [Gk. φωταγωγικόν; Sl. свѣтиленъ] A hymn chanted after the conclusion of the *canon*, near the end of *matins*, at the moment when the morning light should begin to appear. Often, the theme of Christ as the light of the world is developed. This is why this hymn is called the "hymn of light." See *Exaposteilarion*.

Polychronion: [Gk. πολυχρόνιον; Sl. многолѣ́тіе] A chant of acclamation asking the Lord to grant someone many years. Originally, the polychronion was used for the emperor, and later for the patriarch and the bishop.

Polyeleos: [Gk. πολυέλεος; Sl. полѷєлéй] The singing of Pss 134 and 135, with the refrain "Alleluia" intercalated between the verses. Sung at *matins* on feast days and certain Sundays, thus constituting a third section of *psalmody*.

Prayer of the Ambo: [Gk. ὀπισθάμβονος εὐχή; Sl. заамвóнниаѧ мл́тка] The final prayer of the Divine *Liturgy* recited by the priest standing behind the *ambo*, which consists of a final intercession before the *dismissal*.

Pre-feast: [Gk. προεόρτια; Sl. прєдпрáзднєтко] The day(s) preceding a major feast, with festal hymnography preparing the faithful to celebrate the mystery of the feast.

Presanctified Liturgy: [Gk. προηγιασμένων; Sl. прєждєоскаціéнниаѧ] An evening *office* with eucharistic communion, celebrated following vespers on days of strict fasting, when the *complete Liturgy* is not permitted. Communion is distributed from the holy gifts which have been consecrated at the preceding Divine *Liturgy*, usually on the previous Sunday, hence the expression "presanctified."

Prokeimenon: [Gk. προκείμενον; Sl: прокíмєнѫ] Psalm refrain accompanied by psalm verses read by the *canonarch* or the *reader*, generally preceding a biblical reading.

Prophecy: [Gk. προφητεία; Sl. проро́чєєткѧ] See *Paremia*.

Proskynitarion: [Gk. προσκυνητήριον; Sl. ѧналóгїй or ѧналóй] A stand, pulpit, or angled table generally used to hold an icon for veneration.

Proskomide: [Gk. προσκομιδή or πρόθεσις; Sl. проєкомíдїѧ] Prothesis. The first part of the Divine *Liturgy*, at which the priest prepares the eucharistic bread and wine and commemorates all the members of the Church, alive and dead.

Prosomion: [Gk. προσόμιον; Sl. подóбєнѫ] A hymn whose rhythm and melody are copied from an *automelon*.

Prosphora: [Gk. προσφορά; Sl. проєфорá] A liturgical bread used for the Eucharist during the *proskomide*.

Prothesis: See *Proskomide*.

Psalmody: [Gk. στιχολογία; Sl. єтїхоєлóкїє] The reading of a *kathisma* from the *Psalter*.

Psalter: [Gk. ψαλτήριον; Sl. ѱалтирь] The liturgical book containing the 150 psalms of the Septuagint, divided into twenty *kathismata* in the Palestinian Psalter, as well as the nine *biblical canticles.*

Reader: [Gk. ἀναγνώστος; Sl. чтецъ] The person appointed to carry out a *reading.*

Readings: [Gk. ἀνάγνωσμα or ἀνάγνωσις; Sl. чтенїе] See *Paremia.* This term, in the singular, can also designate biblical, patristic, or hagiographic readings at the *vigil,* at the end of great *vespers* ("Great reading") after the *polyeleos,* after the third and sixth odes of the *canon,* or at the end of *matins.*

Sanctuary: [Gk. βῆμα or θυσιαστήριον; Sl. ѻлтарь] The eastern part of the church, separated from the *nave* by the *iconostasis,* where the *altar table* is found.

Skeuophylakion: [Gk. σκευοφυλάκιον; Sl. сосудохранильница] Sacristy. The place, usually close to the *sanctuary,* where the sacred vessels and precious relics are kept.

Sluzhebnik: [Gk. ἱερατικόν; Sl. служебникъ] The liturgical book containing the prayers and litanies said by the priest (or deacon) at *vespers, matins,* and the three liturgies.

Solea: [Gk. σωλέας; Sl. солеа] The raised area in front of the *iconostasis.*

Stasis: [Gk. στάσις; Sl. статїа or слава] One of the three sections of a *kathisma.*

Sticheron: [Gk. στιχήρον; Sl. стїхира] A hymn intercalated between psalm verses.

Superior: [Gk. προεστώς; Sl. настоѧтель] A term used for the *hegumenos,* or the rector of the church.

Synapte: [Gk. συναπτή; Sl. ѥктенїа] A collection of short sentences by which the deacon (or, in his absence, the priest) invites the assembly to pray for various intentions, and to which the assembly (or the *choir*) responds with "Lord, have mercy" (*Kyrie eleison*). The *great synapte* (or "litany of peace") is found at the beginning of services and consists of at least twelve petitions. It is distinguished from the *small synapte,* which has only three petitions and is found throughout the services.

Synapte with demands: [Gk. αἴτησις; Sl. є҆ктенїа̀ (проси́тельнаѧ)] A collection of short sentences by which the deacon (or, in his absence, the priest) invites the assembly to pray for various intentions, and to which the assembly (or the *choir*) responds with "Lord, have mercy" (*Kyrie eleison*) or "Grant this, O Lord" (for the demands).

Synaxarion: [Gk. συναξάριον; Sl. сѷнаѯа́рїй] Menologion. A list of saints, feasts, and solemnities celebrated on each day of the year. It covers the twelve months of the liturgical year, from September to August.

Synaxis: [Gk. σύναξις; Sl. собо́рх] Assembly. 1) This term is generally used for the eucharistic assembly. Within anchorite monasticism, it is used to designate the moment when all the monks gather in the *katholikon* of the monastery on the occasion of an important feast to celebrate a vigil and the Divine Liturgy. 2) This term is also used in reference to the day after a major feast, honoring the person whom God chose to serve in the accomplishment of his plan. For example, on the day after Christmas, the Church celebrates the Synaxis of the Most Holy Theotokos. 3) This term can also designate the feast of a group of saints, such as the synaxis of the twelve apostles, the synaxis of the seventy apostles, etc.

Synodikon: [Gk. συνοδικόν; Sl. сѷноді́кх] The text read on the Sunday of Orthodoxy (the first Sunday of Great Lent) containing the anathemas against heretics, particularly against the iconoclasts.

Table, holy: [Gk. ἁγία τράπεζα; Sl. ст҃а́ѧ трапе́за or престо́лх] Altar table in the *sanctuary* on which the Divine Liturgy is celebrated.

Tetraode: [Gk. τετραῴδιον; Sl. четвероп҃ѣ́снецх] A *canon* consisting of four *odes*, found generally at the Saturday *office* during period of the *Triodion*.

Theotokion: [Gk. θεοτόκιον; Sl. бг҃оро́днчень] Hymn in honor of the Mother of God, concluding a series of *troparia* or *stichera*.

Theotokos: [Gk. θεοτόκος; Sl. бг҃оро́дица] The ancient patristic title accorded to the Virgin Mary, approved at the Third Ecumenical Council (Ephesus, 431). It is often translated by the expression "Mother of God," though this term more accurately translates the expression "μήτηρ τοῦ θεοῦ" [Sl. мт҃и бж҃їа].

Thomas Sunday (Renewal Sunday): [Gk. ἡ κυριακὴ τῆς διακαινήσιμου; Sl. нóваѧ недѣ́лѧ] The first Sunday after Easter.

Tone: [Gk. ἦχος; Sl. глас] One of the eight types of melody (voice or mode) of Byzantine chant, forming the base for the *Octoechos*.

Trebnik: [Gk. εὐχολόγιον; Sl. трéбникъ] From the Slavonic word "трéба," meaning "need." The liturgical book containing the services of various sacraments and blessings.

Triadicon: [Gk. τριαδικόν; Sl. трóиченъ] A *troparion* in honor of the Holy Trinity.

Triodion: [Gk. τριῴδιον; Sl. трїώдь] 1) The liturgical book for the annual moveable cycle, containing hymnography for the preparatory period before Great Lent, starting on the Sunday of the Publican and the Pharisee (tenth Sunday before Easter) to Cheese-Fare Sunday (seventh Sunday before Easter, as well as all of Great Lent and Holy Week. 2) A *canon* consisting of three odes (three-ode, Sl. трипѣ́снецъ], which gave its name to the period preceding Pascha, during which this type of canon is commonly used.

Trisagion: [Gk. τρισάγιον; Sl. трисгóе] A term designating the prayer "Holy God, Holy Mighty, Holy Immortal, have mercy on us."

Troparion: [Gk. τροπάριον; Sl. тропáрь] A hymn, generally brief.

Typika: [Gk. τυπικά; Sl. обѣ́дница or изобрази́тельны] This term generally designates the *office* which, originally in Palestine, accompanied individual communion in monastic cells. Later, it became a service substituting for the Divine Liturgy when the latter could not be celebrated. The term is also used for Pss 102 and 145, which are chanted at the beginning of this *office*.

Typikarist: [Gk. τυπικάρις; Sl. оуставникъ] Person responsible for the ordo of the *office* and its proper execution.

Verse: [Gk. στίχος; Sl. стіхъ] A term generally used to designate a psalm verse.

Vespers: [Gk. ἑσπερινός; Sl. вечéрнѧ] Evening *office*, celebrated at sunset.

Bibliography

LITURGICAL SOURCES

Brightman, F. E., *Liturgies Eastern and Western* (Oxford, 1896).

Christ, W. and Paranikas, M., *Anthologia graeca carminum christianorum* (Leipzig, 1871).

Cummins, D., *The Rudder (Pedalion)* (Chicago, 1957).

Delehaye, H., *Propylaeum ad Acta Sanctorum Novembris. Synaxarium Ecclesiae Constantinopolitanae e codice Sirmondiano, nunc Berolinensi, adjunctis synaxariis selectis* (Brussels, 1902).

Dmitrievskii, A.A., *Opisanie liturgicheskikh rukopisei, khraniashchikhsia v bibliotekakh Pravoslavnogo Vostoka*, Vol. 1, Τυπικά, Pt. 1, *Pamiatniki patriarshikh ustavov i ktitorskie monastyrskie tipikony* (Kiev, 1901); vol. 3, Τυπικά, Pt. 2 (Petrograd, 1917).

Égérie, *Journal de Voyage* (SC 296), ed, and trans. P. Maraval (Paris, 2002).

Garitte, G., *Le Calendrier palestino-géorgien du Sinaïticus 34* (Subsidia Hagiographica 30) (Brussels, 1958).

Goar, J., Ἐυχολόγιον *sive Rituale Graecorum Complectens* (Paris, 1647).

Janin, R., *La Géographie ecclésiastique de l'empire byzantin* (Paris, 1969).

Joannou, P.-P., *Discipline générale antique* (Fonti, fasc. 9), vols. I–II (Rome, 1962–1963).

Jordan, R.H., *The Synaxarion of the Monastery of the Theotokos Evergetis* (Belfast Byzantine Texts and Translations 6.5) (Belfast, 2000).

Haberti, Ἀρχιερατικόν *sive Liber ponrificalis ecclesiae graecae* (Paris, 1643).

Longo, A., "Il testo integrale della 'Narrazione degli Abati Giovanni e Sofronio' attraverso le 'ΕΡΜΗΝΕΙΑΙ' di Nicone," *Revista di study bizantini e neoellenici* 12–13 (1965–1966): 223–267.

Macaire de Simonos Petras, Hiéromoine, *Le Synaxaire*, vols. 1–5 (Thessalonica, 1988–1996).

Matéos, J., *Le typikon de la Grande Église*, I and II (OCA 165 and 166) (Rome, 1962–1963).

_____, "Un Horologion inédit de Saint-Sabas," *Studi e testi* 233 (Vatican, 1964), 47–76.

Παπαδόπουλος-Κεραμευς, Α. Ἀνάλεκτα ἱεροσολυμιτικῆς σταχυολογίας (St Petersburg, 1894).

Parenti, S., and Velkovska, E., *Eucologio Barberini gr. 336* (BELS 80) (Rome, 2000²).

Πηδάλιον (Athens, 1886).

Pentkovskii, A., *Tipikon Aleksiia Studita* (Moscow, 2001).

Petit, L., *Bibkiographie des acolouthies grecques* (Analecta Bollandiana 16) (Brussels, 1926).

Pitra, I.B., *Juris ecclesistici graecorum historia et monumenta* (Rome, 1868).

Pseudo-Kodinos, *Traités des offices* (introduction, text, and translation by J. Verpeaux) (Le Monde byzantin 1) (Paris, 1966).

Rahlfs, A., *Die alttestamentlichen Lektionen der griechischen Kirche* (Nachrichten von der Kgl. Gesellschaft der Wiss. zu Göttingen, Phil.-hist. Kl.) (Göttingen, 1915).

Renoux, A., *Le Codex arménien Jérusalem 121*. I, PO XXXV, 1, No. 163 (Turnhout, 1969); II, PO XXXVI, 2, No. 168 (Turnhout, 1971).

_____, *Le Lectionnaire de Jérusalem en Arménie. Le Casoce*, II (PO 48, fasc. 2, No. 214) (Turnhout, 1999).

_____, *Les Hymnes de la Réurrection, I. Hymnographie liturgique géorgienne* (Sources liturgique 3) (Paris, 2000).

Schiro, I., *Analecta hymnica graeca e codicibus eruta Italiae inferioris,* vols. I–XII (Rome, 1966–1980).

Tarchnisvili, M., *Le Grand Lectionnaire de l'Église de Jérusalem* (CSCO 188–189, 204–205) (Scriptores Iberici 9–10, 13–14) (Louvain, 1959–1960).

Thomas, J., and Hero, A.C., *Byzantine Monastic Foundation Documents*, Vol. 3 (Dumbarton Oaks Studies 35) (Washington, DC, 2000).

Ὡρολόγιον (Grottaferrata, 1950).

STUDIES IN WESTERN LANGUAGES

Arranz, M., "Les prières sacerdotales des vêpres byzantines," *OCP* 37 (1971): 85–124.

_____, "Le sacerdoce ministeriel dans les prières secrètes des vêpres et des matines byzantines," *Euntes docete* 24 (1971): 186–219.

_____, "Les prières presbytérales des matines byzantines," *OCP* 37 (1971): 406–36; 38 (1972): 64–115.

_____, "Les prières presbytérales des Petites Heures dans l'ancien Eucologue byzantin," *OCP* 39 (1973): 29–82.

_____, "Les prières presbytérales de la 'Pannychis' de l'ancien Eucologue byzantin et la 'Pannikhida' des défunts," *OCP* 40 (1974) 314–43; 41 (1975): 119–39.

_____, "Les grandes étapes de la liturgy byzantine: Palestine-Byzance-Russie. Essai d'aperçu historique," in *Liturgie de l'Église particulière et liturgie de l'Église universelle* (BELS 7) (Rome, 1976), 43–72.

_____, "L'office de veillée nocturne dans l'Église grecque et l'Église russe," *OCP* 42 (1976): 117–55, 402–25.

_____, "Les prières presbytérales de la Tritoektî de l'ancien Euchologue byzantin," *OCP* 43 (1977): 70–93, 335–54.

_____, "L'office de l'Asmatikos Hesperinos ('Vêpres chantées') de l'ancien Euchologue byzantin," *OCP* 44 (1978): 107–30, 391–412.

_____, "La liturgie des Heures selon l'ancien Euchologue byzantin," in *Eucholigia: Miscellanea liturgica in onore di P. Burkhard Neunheuser* (Studia Anselmiana 68, Analecta Liturgica I) (Rome, 1979), 1–19.

_____, "Les fêtes théologiques du calendrier byzantin," in *La Liturgie, expression de la foi. Conférences Saint-Serge. XXVᵉ Semaine d'études liturgiques* (BELS 16) (Rome, 1979), 29–55.

_____, "L'office de l'Asmatikos Orthros ('Matines chantées') de l'ancien Euchologue byzantin," *OCP* 47 (1981): 122–57.

_____, "La liturgie des Présanctifiés de l'ancien Euchologue byzantin," *OCP* 47 (1981): 331–88.

_____, "Les prières de Gonyklisia ou de la Génuflexion du jour de la Pentecôte dans l'ancien Euchologue byzantin," *OCP* 48 (1982): 92–123.

_____, "L'office divin," *DS* 11 (Paris, 1982), cols. 707–720.

Balfour, D., "La réforme de l'Horologion," *Irénikon* 7 (1930): 167–80.

Bardy, G., "André de Crète," *DS* 1 (Paris, 1937), cols. 554–555.

Baumstark, A., *Festbrevier und Kirkenjahr der syrischen Jakobiten* (Paderborn, 1910).

Bertonière, G., *The Historical Development of the Easter Vigil and Related Services in the Greek Church* (OCA 193) (Rome, 1972).

_____, *The Sundays of Lent in the Triodion: The Sundays Without a Commemoration* (OCA 253) (Rome, 1997).

Bornert, R., "La Pentecôte dans le rite byzantin," *Notes de pastorale liturgique* 38 (1962): 9–14.

Botte, B., *Les Origines de la Noêl et de l'Épiphanie* (Louvain, 1932).

Cabié, R., *La Pentecôte. L'évolution de la cinquantaine paschale au cours des cinq premiers siècles* (Tournai, 1965).

Cabrol, Dom, *Étude sur la Peregrinatio Silviae: Les églises de Jérusalem, la discipline et la liturgie au IVe siècle* (Paris, 1895).

Cassien, Mgr., and Botte, B., *La Prière des Heures* (LO 35) (Paris, 1963).

Cody, A., "The Early History of the Octoechos in Syria," in N. Garsoian, T. Mathews, and R. Thomson, eds., *East of Byzantium: Syria and Armenia in the Formative Period* (Washington, DC, 1982), 89–113.

Coquin, R.-G., "Une réforme liturgique du Concile de Nicée?," *Comptes rendus de l'Académie des Inscriptions et Belles-Lettres* (April–June 1967), 178–93.

Crehan, J., "Assumption and the Jerusalem Liturgy," *TS* 30 (1969): 312–25.

Daniélou, J., *Bible et liturgie. La thèologie biblique des sacrements et des fêtes d'après les Pères de l'Église* (LO 11) (Paris, 1951).

_____, "Le dimanche comme huitième jour," in B. Botte, ed., *Le Dimanche* (LO 39) (Paris, 1965), 61–89.

_____, "Grégoire de Nysse et l'origine de la fête de l'Ascension," in *Kyriakon—Festschrift Johannes Quasten* (P. Granfield and J.A. Jungmann, eds.), vol. 2 (Münster Weste: Verlag Aschendorff, 1970), 663–66.

Davies, J.G., "The *Peregrinatio Egeriae* and the Ascension," *Vigiliae Christianae* 8 (1954): 93–100.

De Meester, P., "L'imno acatisto," *Bessarione* 81 (1904): 213.

Deseille, P., *Les Psaumes, prières de l'Église* (Paris, 1979).

Downey, G., "The Church of All Saints (Church of St. Theophano) near the Church of the Apostles at Constantinople," *DOP* 9–10 (1956): 301–05.

Egender, N., *La Prière des Heures—Ὡρολόγιον* (Chevetogne, 1975).

_____, "La formation et l'influence du Typikon liturgique de Saint-Sabas," in J. Patrich, ed., *The Sabaite Heritage in the Orthodox Church from the 5th Century to the Present* (Orientalia Lovaniensa Analecta 98) (Louvain, 2001), 209–16.

Émereau, C., "Hymnographi byzantini," *Échos d'Orient* 21 (1922): 258–79; 22 (1923): 12–25, 420–39; 23 (1924): 196–200, 276–85, 403–14; 24 (1925): 164–79; 25 (1926); 178–84.

Fischer, B., "Les Psaumes, prière chrétienne. Témoignage du IIᵉ siècle," in *La Prière des Heures* (LO 35) (Paris, 1963), 85–99.

Fountoulis, J.M., *Λογικὴ Λατρεία* (Thessalonica, 1970).

Frøyshov, S., "The Early Development of the Liturgical Eight-mode System in Jerusalem," *SVTQ* 51 (2007) 139–78.

Garnier, S., *La Mi-Pentecôte dans la liturgie byzantine des VIe–Xe siècles* (unpublished master's thesis defended at the E.P.H.E.) (Paris, 1998).

_____, "Les leçons scripturaires de la Mi-Pentecôte," in *La Liturgie, interprète de l'Écriture, I. Les lectures bibliques pour les dimanches et fêtes. Conférences Saint-Serge. 48ᵉ semaine d'études liturgiques* (BELS 119) (Rome, 2002), 213–20.

Garrite, G., "Analyse d'un Lectionnaire byzantino-géorgien des évangiles—*Sin. Géorg. 74*," *Le Muséon* 91 (1978), fasc. 1–2, p. 211.

Gastoué, A., "La grande doxologie. Étude critique," *Revue de l'Orient chrétien* 4 (1899): 280–90.

_____, "Le canon des matines pascales byzantines: ses sources bibliques et patristiques," in *L'Hymnographie. Conférences Saint-Serge. 46ᵉ Semaine d'études liturgiques* (BELS 105) (Rome, 2000), 257–84.

_____, "Le système des lectures patristiques prescrites au cours de l'année liturgique par les Typica byzantins: une forme de predication integrée dans l'office divin," in *La Prédication liturgique et les commentaries de la liturgie. Conférences Saint-Serge. 38ᵉ Semaine d'études liturgiques* (BELS 65) (Rome, 1992), 131–51.

_____, *Le Typikon byzantin: edition d'une version grecque partiellement ineditée; analyse de la partie liturgique*, 2 vols. (unpublished doctoral dissertation) (Paris: Institut Saint Serge, 1987).

Maas, P., "Recension sur l'article de P. De Meester 'L'imno acatisto'," *Byzantinische Zeitschrift* 14 (1905): 645.

Macaire, Hiéromoine de Simonos Petras (G. Bonnet), *La Mystagogie du temps liturgique dans le Triodion* (Unpublished thesis, Sorbonne, E.P.H.E., Ve Section) (Paris, 1977).

_____, "Le mystère de la croix dans le Carême orthodoxe," *Irénikon* 52 (1979): 34–53 and 200–13.

Marin, E., "André de Crète," *Dictionnaire de théologie catholique* 1 (1909), cols. 1182–1184.

Matéos, J., *La Célébration de la parole dans la liturgie byzantine* (OCA 191) (Rome, 1971).

_____, "La psalmodie variable dans l'office byzantin," in *Societas Academica Dacoromana, Acta philosophica et theologica*, vol. 2 (Rome, 1964), 327–39.

_____, "La synaxe monastique des vêpres byzantines," *OCP* 36 (1970): 248–72.

_____, "La vigile cathédrale chez Égérie," *OCP* 27 (1961): 281–312.

_____, "Quelques problèmes de l'orthros byzantin," *POC* 11 (1961): 17–35, 201–20.

Mercenier, E., "À propos d'André de Crète," in *Tome commemorative du Millenium de la Bibliothèque d'Alexandrie* (Alexandria, 1953), 70–78.

Mossey, J., *Les Fêtes do Noël et d'Épiphanie d'après les sources littéraires cappadociennes du IVᵉ siècle* (Louvain, 1965).

Noret, J., "Ménologes, Synaxaires, Menées. Essai de clarification d'une termonologie," *Analecta Bollandiana* 86 (1968): 21–24.

Ouspenskii, N., "Le schisme dans l'Église russe au XVIIᵉ siècle comme suite d'une collision de deux theologies," in *La Liturgie, expression de la foi. Conférences Saint-Serge. XXVᵉ Semaine d'études liturgiques* (BELS 16) (Rome, 1979), 229–53.

Parenti, S., "Vino e olio nelle liturgie byzantine," in *Olio e vino nell'alto medioevo* (Settimana di Studio della Fundazione Centro italiano di studi sull'alto medioevo LIV) (Rome, 2007), 1283–85.

Parenti, S., and Velkovska, E., "A Thirteenth Century Manuscript of the Constantinopolitan Euchology: *Grottaferrata Γ.β.I.*, alias of Cardinal Bessarion," *Bolletino della badia greca di Grottaferrata* III, s. 4 (2007): 175–96.

Pargoire, J., "Apodeipnon," *DACL* 1, 2 (Paris, 1907), cols. 2579–2582.

Petit, L., "André de Crète," *DACL* 1 (Paris, 1907), cols. 2034–2041.

Pétridès, S., "Anatolika," *DACL* 1 (Paris, 1907), cols. 2582–2589.

Pott, T., *La Réforme liturgique byzantine: Étude du phenomena de l'évolution non spontanée de la liturgie byzantine* (BEL 104) (Rome, 2000).

Raes, A., "La Communion au Calice dans l'Office byzantin des Présanctifiés," *OCP* 20 (1954): 166–74.

_____, "Les complies dans les rites orientaux," *OCP* 17 (1951): 131–45.

Rahner, H., "Andreas von Kreta," *Lexikon für Theologie und Kirche* 1 (1957), cols. 516–517.

Renoux, C., "En tes murs, Jérusalem: Histoire et mystère," in *La Liturgie: son sens, son esprit, sa methode. Conférences Saint-Serge. XLVIᵉ Semaine d'études liturgiques* (BELS 25) (Rome, 1982), 169–218.

_____, "La lecture biblique dans la liturgie de Jérusalem," in *Le Monde grec ancien et la Bible*, Ed. C. Mondésert (Paris, 1984), 399–420.

_____, "Liturgie de Jérusalem et lectionnaires arméniens: Vigiles et année liturgique," in *La Prière des Heures* (LO 35) (Paris, 1963), 167–99.

_____, "L'office de la génuflexion dans la tradition arménienne," in *Le Saint-Esprit dans la Liturgie. Conférences Saint-Serge 1969* (BELS 8) (Rome, 1977), 149–63.

_____, "Samuel Kamrjajerec'i: le Traité sur l'arajawor," in *From Byzantium to Iran: In Honor of Nina Garsoian* (Atlanta, 1997), 469–72.

_____, "Une hymnographie ancienne conservée en géorgien," in *L'Hymnographie. Conférences Saint-Serge. XLVIᵉ Semaine d'études liturgiques* (BELS 105) (Rome, 2000), 137–51.

Salaville, S., "La fête du concile de Nicée et les fêtes des conciles dans le rite byzantin," *Échos d'Orient* 24 (1924): 445–70.

_____, "La fête du concile de Chalcédoine dans le rite byzantin," in A. Grillmeier and H. Bacht, *Das Konzil von Chalkedon. Geschichte und Gegenwart*, II (Würzburg, 1953), 677–95.

_____, "La tessarokostê, Ascension et Pentecôte au IVᵉ siècle," *Échos d'Orient* 28 (1929): 257–71.

Smothers, E.R., "Φῶς ἱλαρόν," *Recherches de sciences religieuses* 19 (1929): 266–83.

Spassky, T., "La Pâques de Noël," *Irénikon* 30 (1957): 289–306.

Strunk, O., "The Antiphons of the Oktoechos," *Journal of the American Musicologist Society* 13 (1960): 50–67.

_____, "Byzantine Office at Hagia Sophia," *DOP* 9–10 (1955–1956): 175–202.

Taft, R., "Historicisme: Une conception à revoir," *La Maison-Dieu* 147 (1981): 61–83.

_____, "In the Bridegroom's Absence. The Paschal Triduum in the Byzantine Church," in *La celebrazione del Triduo pasquale: anamnesis e mimesis. Atti del III Congresso Internazionale di Liturgia, Roma, Pontificio Instituto Liturgico, 9–13 maggio 1988* (=Studia Anselmiana 102 = Studia Liturgica 14) (Rome, 1990), 71–97.

_____, *La Liturgie des Heures en Orient et en Occident. Origine et sens de l'Office divin* (Turnhout, 1991).

_____, *Le Rite byzantin* (Paris, 1996).

_____, "The Synaxarion of Evergetis in the History of Byzantine Liturgy," in M. Mullet and A. Kirby, eds., *The Theotokos Evergetis and Eleventh Century Monasticism* (Belfast Byzantine Texts and Translations 6.2) (Belfast, 1997), 274–93.

Talley, T., *Les Origines de l'année liturgique* (Paris, 1990).

Tillyard, H.J.W., "*Eothina Anastasima*. The Morning Hymns of the Emperor Leo," *Annual. Brit. School Athens* 30 (1928–1930): 86–108; 31 (1931): 115–47.

Tripolitis, A., "Φῶς ἱλαρόν—Ancient Hymn and Modern Enigma," *Vigiliae Christianae* 24 (1970): 189–90.

Uspensky, N., *Evening Worship in the Orthodox Church* (Crestwood, NY: SVS Press, 1985).

Vailhé, S., "Saint André de Crète," *Échos d'Orient* V (1902): 378–87.

Van Esbroeck, M., "Encore la lettre de Justinien," *Analecta Bollandiana* 87 (1969): 442–44.

_____, "La lettre de l'empereur Justinien sur l'Annonciation et la Noël," *Analecta Bollandiana* 86 (1968): 351–52.

_____, "Le plus ancien Hymnaire," *Bedi Kartlisa* 39 (1981): 54–62.

Van Rossum, J., "Romanos le Mélode et le 'Kontakion'," in *L'Hymnographie. Conférences Saint-Serge. 46ᵉ Semaine d'études liturgiques* (BELS 105) (Rome, 2000), 93–104.

Velkovska, E., "Byzantine Liturgical Books," in A.J. Chupungco, ed., *Handbook for Liturgical Stiudies*, vol. 1: *Introduction to the Liturgy* (Collegeville, MN, 1997), 225–40.

_____, "Lo studio dei lezionari bizantini," *Ecclesia Orans* 13 (1996): 253–71.

Verhelst, S., "Histoire ancienne de la durée du carême à Jérusalem," *Questions liturgiques* 84 (2003): 23–50.

Vidalis, M., "La bénédiction des eaux de la fête de l'Épiphanie selon le rite grec de l'Église orthodoxe," in *La Prière liturgique. Conférences Saint-Serge. 47ᵉ semaine d'études liturgiques* (BELS 115) (Rome 2001), 237–57.

Wade, A., "La prière ἄνες, ἄφες, συγχώρησον. La pratique palestinienne de demander l'absolution pour la communion solitaire et quotidienne. *Lex orandi* pour une orthopraxis perdue?," Θυσία αἰνέσεως. *Mélanges liturgiques offerts àla mémoire de l'archevêque Georges Wagner*, eds. J. Getcha and A. Lossky (Analecta Sergiana 2) (Paris, 2005), 431–35.

_____, "The Oldest Iadgari, The Jerusalem Tropologion, V–VIIIc.," *OCP* 50 (1984): 451–56.

Wagner, G., "Réalisme et symbolisme dans l'explication de la liturgie," in *La Liturgie, expérience de l'Église. Études liturgiques* (Analecta Sergiana 1) (Paris, 2003), 181–90 (= *Mystagogie: Pensée liturgique d'aujourd'hui et liturgie ancienne. Conférences Saint-Serge. 39ᵉ Semaine d'études liturgiques* [BELS 70] [Rome, 1993], 351–59).

Wellecz, E., *A History of Byzantine Music and Hymnography* (Oxford, 1961).

_____, *The Akathistos Hymn* (Monumenta musicae Byzantinae, Transcripta 9) (Copenhagen, 1957).

Zander, V., "La Pentecôte dans l'Église orthodoxe," *Sanctae Ecclesiae* 29 (1948): 83–102.

_____, "La Pentecôte dans le rite byzantin," *Irénikon* 5 (1928): 256–61.

Zuntz, G., "Das byzantinische Septuaginta-Lektionar," *Classica et Mediaevalias* 17 (1956): 183–98.

STUDIES IN SLAVIC LANGUAGES

Afanasii (Sakharov), Episkop, *O pominovenii usopshikh po ustavu Pravoslavnoi Tserkvi* (St Petersburg, 1995).

Alekseev, A., *Bibliia v bogosluzhenii. Vizantiisko-slavianskii lektsionarii* (St Petersburg, 2008).

Arrants, M., *Kak molilis' Bogu drevnie vizantiitsy* (Leningrad, 1979).

_____, *Oko Tserkovnoe—Istoriia Tipikona* (Rome, 1998).

Diakovskii, E., "Posledovanie chasov velikoi piatnitsy," *TDKA* 3 (1909): 389–420.

_____, "Posledovanie nochnykh chasov," *TDKA* 7–8 (1909): 546–95.

_____, "Tsarskie chasy Rozhdestva Khristova i Bogoiavleniia," *TDKA* 12 (1908): 483–501.

Dmitrievskii, A., "Bogosluzhenie v Russkoi Tserkvi v pervye piat' vekov," *PS* 2 (1882): February, pp. 138–66; March, pp. 252–96; July–August, pp. 346–72; September, pp. 372–94; October, pp. 149–67.

_____, "Chto takoe κανὼν τῆς ψαλμῳδίας, tak neredko upominaemyi v zhizneopisanii prepod. Savvy Osviashchennago?," *RukSP* 38 (1889): 69–73.

_____, *Drevneishie patriarshie tipikony. Sviatogrobskii, Ierusalimskii i Velikoi Konstantinopol'skoi Tserkvi* (Kiev, 1907).

_____, "Utrenniia molitvy," *RukSP* 42 (1886): 180–92.

_____, "Vecherniia molitvy," *RukSP* 33 (1888): 494–505; 36 (1888): 20–32.

Dobroklonskii, A.P., *Prepodobnyi Feodor Studit, ispovednik i igumen Studiiskii* (Odessa, 1913).

Filaret (Gumilevskii), Arkhiepiskop, *Istoricheskii obzor pesnopevtsev i pesnopeniia Grecheskoi Tserkvi* (St Petersburg, 1902).

Fundulis, I., "Chasy," *Vechnoe* 331 (1976): 6–12.

_____, "Liturgiia Prezhdeosviashchennykh Darov," *Vechnoe* 332 (1976): 2–8.

_____, "Polunoshchnitsa," *Vechnoe* 325 (1975): 9–12.

_____, "Prazdnik vsekh sviatykh," *Vechnoe* 333 (1976): 19–24.

_____, "Vechernia," *Vechnoe* 334 (1976): 3–13; 335 (1976): 2–9.

_____, "Utrenia," *Vechnoe* 326 (1975): 14–19; 327 (1975): 13–18; 328 (1975): 11–14; 329 (1975): 9–21; 330 (1975): 10–16.

Karabinov, I., "Otzyv o trude M. Lisitsina 'Pervonachal'nyi Slaviano-Russkii Tipikon. Istoriko-arkheologicheskoe issledovanie. Spb., 1911," *Sbornik otchetov o premiiakh i nagradakh, prisuzhdaemykh Rossiiskoi Akademiei Nauk, VII*, otchety za 1912 g. (Petrograd, 1918), 339–47.

_____, *Postnaia Triod'. Istoricheskii obzor* (St Petersburg, 1910).

_____. "Sviataia chasha na liturgii Prezhdeosviashchennykh Darov," *Khristianskoe Chtenie* 1 (1915): 737–53.

Kekelidze, K., *Ierusalimskii kanonar' VII veka* (Tbilisi, 1912).

_____, *Liturgicheskie gruzinskie pamiatniki* (Tbilisi, 1908).

Kern, K., *Liturgika. Gimnografiia i eortologiia* (Paris, 1964) [rep: Moscow, 2000].

Kravetskii, A.G., "Kalendarno-bogosluzhebnaia komissiia," *Uchenye zapiski Rossiiskogo Pravoslavnogo Universiteta ap. Ioanna Bogoslova* 2 (1996): 171–209.

Lisitsyn, M., *Pervonachal'nyi Slaviano-Russkii Tipikon* (St Petersburg, 1911).

Lukashevich, A.A., "Vselenskie subboty," *Pravoslavnaia Entsiklopedia* IX (Moscow, 2005), 565–66.

Mansvetov, I., *Mitropolit Kiprian v ego liturgicheskoi deiatel'nosti* (Moscow, 1882) [= O trudakh mitropolita Kipriana po chaste bogosluzheniia," *PTSO* 29 (1882), vol. 1, 152–204; vol. 2, 413–95; vol. 3, 71–175].

_____, "O pesnennom posledovanii (ᾀσματικὴ ἀκολουθία), ego drevneishaia osnova i obshchii stroi," *PTSO* 3 (1880): 752–97; 4 (1880): 972–1028.

_____, *O postakh pravoslavnoi vostochnoi Tserkvi* (Moscow, 1886).

_____, *Tserkovnyi ustav (Tipik), ego obrazovanie i sud'ba v grecheskoi i russkoi Tserkvi* (Moscow, 1885).

Mironositskii, P.M., "O poriadke tserkovnykh chtenii Evangeliia," in *Bogosluzheb-nye ukazaniia na 1999 god* (Moscow, 1998), 579–96. [Originally published in *Tsekovnye vedomosti* 7 and 9 (1916), and reprinted in *ZhMP* 12 (1956): 16–25.]

Papadopulo-Keramevs, A., "Akafist Bozhiei Materi," *Vizantiiskii Vremennik* 3/4 (1903): 357–401.

Pentkovskii, A., "Konstantinopol'skii i ierusalimskii bogosluzhebnye ustavy," *ZhMP* 4 (2001): 69–80.

_____, "Lektsionarii i chetveroevangeliia v vizantiiskoi i slavianskoi litur-gicheskikh traditsiiakh," in *Evangelie ot Ioanna v slavianskoi traditsii* (Novum Testamentum palaeoslovanice 1) (St Petersburg, 1998), 4–14.

_____, "Studiiskii ustav i ustavy studiiskoi traditsii," *ZhMP* 5 (2001): 69–80.

Prilutskii, V., *Chastnoe bogosluzhenie v Russkoi Tserkvi* (Kazan, 1912) [reprint: Moscow, 2000].

Prokhorov, M., "K istorii liturgicheskoi poezii: gimny i molitvy patriarkha Folo-feia Kokkina," *TODRL* 27 (1972): 140–48.

Sergii (Soaskii), Arkhiepiskop, *Polnyi mesiatseslov vostoka* (Vladimir, 1901).

Skaballanovich, M., *Tolkovyi Tipikon*, vols. 1–2 (Kiev, 1910–1913).

Sliva, E.E., "O nekotorykh tserkovnoslavianskikh Chasoslovakh XIII–XIV vv. (Osobennosti sostava)," in *Rus' i iuzhnye slaviane*, ed. V.M. Zagrebin (St Petersburg, 1998): 185–97.

Talin, V., "O penii na utrene nedeli krestopoklonnoi irmosov paskhal'nogo kanona," *ZhMP* 3 (1968): 74–76.

Uspenskii, N.D., "Bogosluzhebnye otpusty," *ZhMP* 12 (1963): 52–69.

_____, "Chin vsenoshchnogo bdeniia na Pravoslavnom Vostoke i v Russkoi Tserkvi," *BT* 18 (1978): 5–117; 19 (1978): 3–69.

_____, "Eshche neskol'ko slov o penii na utrene nedeli krestopoklonnoi irmosov paskhal'nogo kanona," *ZhMP* 2 (1969): 75–79.

_____, "Istoriia i znachenie prazdnika Rozhdestva Khristova v drevnei Tserkvi," *ZhMP* 12 (1956): 38–47.

_____, "Kolliziia dvukh bogoslovii v ispravlenii russkikh bogosluzhebnykh knig v XVII veke," *BT* 13 (1975): 148–71.

_____, "Liturgiia Prezhdeosviashchennykh Darov. Istoriko-liturgicheskii ocherk," *BT* 15 (1975): 146–84.

_____, "O sentiabr'skoi prestupke evangel'skikh chtenii," in *Pravoslavnyi Tserkovnyi Kalendar' na 1971 god* (Moscow, 1970), 48. [Reprinted in *Bogoslu-zhebmye ukazaniia na 2001 god* (Moscow, 2000), 641–42.]

_____, "Pravoslavnaia Vechernia," *BT* 1 (1960): 7–52.

_____, Sviataia Chetyredesiatnitsa. Istoriko-liturgicheskii ocherk," *ZhMP* 3 (1945): 33–38.

Velkovska, E., "Sistema na vizantiiskite i slavianskite bogosluzhebni knigi v perioda na v"znikvaneto im," in V. Gjuzelev and A. Miltenova, eds., *Medieval Christian Europe: East and West. Tradition, Values, Communications* (Sofia, 2002), 220–36.

Zheltov, M., "Vodoosviashchenie," *Pravoslavnaia Entsiklopedia* IX (Moscow, 2005), 142–44.

Zheltov, M.S., and Pravdoliubov, S., "Bogosluzhenie RPTs X–XX vv.," *Pravoslavnaia Entsiklopedia,*Vol. RPTs (Moscow, 2000), 485–517.